BLACK&DECKER®

THE COMPLETE PHOTO GUIDE TO

HOME
IMPROVEMENT

Creative Publishing
international

MINNEAPOLIS, MINNESOTA
www.creativepub.com

Creative Publishing
international

Copyright © 2009
Creative Publishing international, Inc.
400 First Avenue North, Suite 300
Minneapolis, Minnesota 55401
1-800-328-0590
www.creativepub.com
All rights reserved

Printed in Singapore
10 9 8 7 6 5 4 3 2

Library of Congress Cataloging-in-Publication Data

The complete photo guide to home improvement.
    p. cm.
    "Black & Decker."
    Includes index.
    Summary: "Features more than 200 common do-it-yourself
remodeling projects"--Provided by publisher.
    ISBN-13: 978-1-58923-452-9 (hard cover)
    ISBN-10: 1-58923-452-9 (hard cover)
    1. Dwellings--Maintenance and repair--Amateurs' manuals.
2. Dwellings--Remodeling--Amateurs' manuals. I. Black & Decker
Corporation (Towson, Md.) II. Title.

    TH4817.3.C654 2008
    643'.7--dc22

2008045755
Softcover ISBN 13: 978-1-58923-538-0
Softcover ISBN 10: 1-58923-538-X

President/CEO: Ken Fund

Home Improvement Group

Publisher: Bryan Trandem
Managing Editor: Tracy Stanley
Senior Editor: Mark Johanson
Editor: Jennifer Gehlhar

Creative Director: Michele Lanci-Altomare
Senior Design Managers: Jon Simpson, Brad Springer
Design Managers: James Kegley

Lead Photographer: Joel Schrell
Photo Coordinator: Joanne Wawra
Shop Manager: Bryan McLain
Shop Assistant: Cesar Fernandez Rodriguez

Production Managers: Linda Halls, Laura Hokkanen

Page Layout Artist: Danielle Smith

The Complete Photo Guide to Home Improvement
Created by: The Editors of Creative Publishing international, Inc., in cooperation with Black & Decker.
Black & Decker® is a trademark of The Black & Decker Corporation and is used under license.

Contributing Editors, Art Directors, Set Builders, and Photographers

Phil Aarrestad
Dan Anderson
Glenn Austin
Randy Austin
Kim Bailey
Mark Biscan
Stewart Block
Charlie Boldt
Scott Boyd
Rose Brandt
Gary Branson
Greg Breining
Timothy Bro
Dave Brus
Keith Bruzelius
Ron Bygness
Peter Caley
Jennifer Caliandro
Rudy Calin
Tom Carpenter
Julie Caruso
Dan Cary
Janice Cauley
Marcia Chambers
Scott Christiansen
Tom Cooper
Paul Currie
Cy DeCosse
Jim Destiche
Doug Deutsche
Diane Dreon
Arthur Durkee
Barbara Falk
Jerri Farris
Lyle Ferguson
Mary Firestone
Steve Galvin
Kim Gerber
Abby Gnagey
Patricia Goar
Paul Gorton
John Haglof
Lynne Hanauer
Mark Hardy
David Hartley
Carol Harvatin

Rebecca Hawthorne
Tom Heck
Jon Hegge
Mike Hehner
Tami Helmer
Paul Herda
John Hermansen
Tim Himsel
Jonathan Hinz
Sara Holle
Lori Holmberg
Jim Huntley
Rex Irmen
Troy Johnson
Kari Johnston
Rob Johnstone
William B. Jones
Phil Juntti
Andrew Karre
Patrick Kartes
Geoffrey Kinsey
Tony Kubat
Karl Larson
John Lauenstein
Tom Lemmer
Bill Lindner
Earl Lindquist
Daniel London
Barbara Lund
Curtis Lund
Sarah Lynch
Mark Macemon
Bernice Maehren
Dave Mahoney
Paul Markert
Chris Marshall
Brett Martin
Jamey Mauk
Jeanette Moss McCurdy
John Nadeau
Paul Najlis
Bill Nelson
Charles Nields
Mette Nielsen
Kristen Olson
Carol Osterhus

Brad Parker
Mike Parker
Christian Paschke
Matthew Paymar
Mike Peterson
Greg Pluth
Anne Price-Gordon
John Riha
Joe Robillard
Mary Rohl
Tom Rosch
Susan Roth
Andrea Rugg
Gary Sandin
Joel Schmarje
Philip Schmidt
Mark Scholtes
Ned Scubic
Gina Seeling
Cathleen Shannon
Mike Shaw
Hugh Sherwood
Dane Smith
Danielle Smith
Steve Smith
Angela Spann
Dick Sternberg
Ruth Strother
Lori Swanson
Andrew Sweet
Dianne Talmage
Glenn Terry
Keith Thompson
Adrianne Truthe
Gregory Wallace
Kevin Walton
Robert Weaver
John Webb
Brad Webster
Wayne Wendland
John Whitman
Dan Widerski
Steve Willson
Christopher Wilson
Mike Woodside

Contents

The Complete
Photo Guide to
Home Improvement

Introduction

Home improvement is a huge subject that demands a big book. *The Complete Photo Guide to Home Improvement* fits the bill. With over 200 projects and more than 2,000 color photos, all of the most popular home remodeling subjects and projects are included in this single resource. Here's one way to look at it: If a picture is indeed worth a thousand words, it would require an 8,000-page volume to convey in written form the information packed into the photos in this book. And unlike the tiny pictures found in other home improvement books, the photos within these pages are large and clear and very easy to follow.

Doing your own home remodeling work takes a combination of skills, planning, and specific information. For example, if you decide to remodel your kitchen (the most frequently remodeled room), you should start the process by defining the scale of the project and identifying the tasks within the larger job that you will perform yourself. This phase corresponds to the first section of this book, "Home Improvement Basics." If you love getting your hands dirty this won't be your favorite part, but it is quite important.

Once you have some background information under your belt and a rough plan in your head, it's time to tackle the skillbuilding most of us need. In "Techniques" you will find clear how-to information for just about every task, from demolition to stripping cable. Thorough information on home wiring and home plumbing fill out a large part of the section, followed by step-by-step instructions for installing flooring, finishing walls and ceilings, working with windows and doors, and—finally—upgrading ventilation and lighting.

In the final section of the book you will move from the general to the more specific. Individual chapters on kitchen remodeling and bathroom remodeling deal with projects, planning and information that are specific to each subject. Here you'll find a host of options for installing cabinets and countertops, for example, to supplement the information you've encountered in the Techniques portion of the book. Converting attics and basements also gets its own section of targeted information. And for a strong finish, we offer extended how-to sequences for the two most common exterior improvements—roofing and installing siding.

Whether you are simply freshening up the appearance of your house or embarking on a down-to-the studs remodel of your bathroom, you'll find the information you need. Even if you have special remodeling needs, such as creating accessible kitchens and baths, you'll see that the subjects are covered. More than a quarter of a million homeowners have relied on *The Complete Photo Guide to Home Improvement* as their principal guidebook through the remodeling process. And now, with this new 3rd edition, you'll be pleased that you chose to join them.

HOME IMPROVEMENT SKILLS

Anatomy of a House

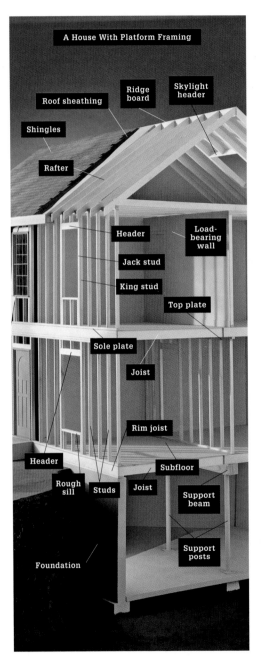

A House With Platform Framing

- Roof sheathing
- Ridge board
- Skylight header
- Shingles
- Rafter
- Header
- Load-bearing wall
- Jack stud
- King stud
- Top plate
- Sole plate
- Joist
- Rim joist
- Header
- Subfloor
- Rough sill
- Studs
- Joist
- Support beam
- Support posts
- Foundation

Before you start a do-it-yourself home improvement project, you should familiarize yourself with a few basic elements of home construction and remodeling. Take some time to get comfortable with the terminology of the models shown on the next few pages. The understanding you will gain in this section will make it easier to plan your project, buy the right materials, and clear up any confusion you might have about the internal design of your home.

If your project includes modifying exterior or load-bearing walls, you must determine if your house was built using platform- or balloon-style framing. The framing style of your home determines what kind of temporary supports you will need to install while the work is in progress. If you have trouble determining what type of framing was used in your

ANATOMY OF A HOUSE WITH PLATFORM FRAMING

Platform framing (photos, left and above) is identified by the floor-level sole plates and ceiling-level top plates to which the wall studs are attached. Most houses built after 1930 use platform framing. If you do not have access to unfinished areas, you can remove the wall surface at the bottom of a wall to determine what kind of framing was used in your home.

home, refer to the original blueprints, if you have them, or consult a building contractor or licensed home inspector.

Framing in a new door or window on an exterior wall normally requires installing a header. Make sure that the header you install meets the requirements of your local building code, and always install cripple studs where necessary.

Floors and ceilings consist of sheet materials, joists, and support beams. All floors used as living areas must have joists with at least 2×8 construction. For modification of smaller joists see page 14.

There are two types of walls: load-bearing and partition. Load-bearing walls require temporary supports during wall removal or framing of a door or window. Partition walls carry no structural load and do not require temporary supports.

ANATOMY OF A HOUSE WITH BALLOON FRAMING

A House With Balloon Framing

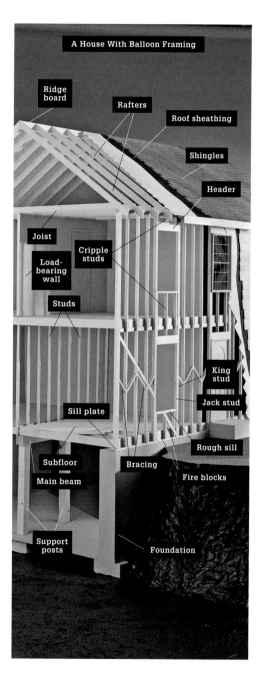

Ridge board · Rafters · Roof sheathing · Shingles · Header · Joist · Cripple studs · Load-bearing wall · Studs · King stud · Jack stud · Sill plate · Rough sill · Subfloor · Bracing · Fire blocks · Main beam · Support posts · Foundation

Balloon framing (photos, right and above) is identified by wall studs that run uninterrupted from the roof to a sill plate on the foundation, without the sole plates and top plates found in platform-framed walls (page opposite). Balloon framing was used in houses built before 1930, and it is still used in some new home styles, especially those with high vaulted ceilings.

Anatomy Details

Many remodeling projects, like adding new doors or windows, require that you remove one or more studs in a load-bearing wall to create an opening. When planning your project, remember that new openings require a permanent support beam called a header, above the removed studs, to carry the structural load directly.

The required size for the header is set by local building codes and varies according to the width of the rough opening. For a window or door opening, a header can be built from two pieces of 2" dimensional lumber sandwiched around ⅜" plywood (chart, right). When a large portion of a load-bearing wall (or an entire wall) is removed, a laminated beam product can be used to make the new header.

If you will be removing more than one wall stud, make temporary supports to carry the structural load until the header is installed.

Recommended Header Sizes

Rough Opening Width	Recommended Header Construction
Up to 3 ft.	⅜" plywood between two 2 × 4s
3 ft. to 5 ft.	⅜" plywood between two 2 × 6s
5 ft. to 7 ft.	⅜" plywood between two 2 × 8s
7 ft. to 8 ft.	⅜" plywood between two 2 × 10s

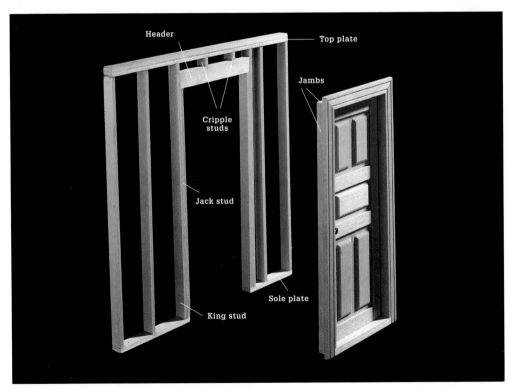

Header — Top plate — Jambs — Cripple studs — Jack stud — King stud — Sole plate

Door opening: The structural load above the door is carried by cripple studs that rest on a header. The ends of the header are supported by jack studs (also known as trimmer studs) and king studs that transfer the load to the sole plate and the foundation of the house. The rough opening for a door should be 1" wider and ½" taller than the dimensions of the door unit, including the jambs. This extra space lets you adjust the door unit during installation.

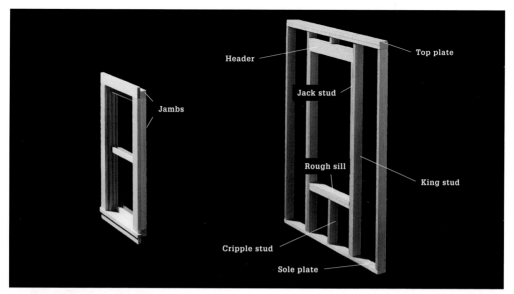

Window opening: The structural load above the window is carried by cripple studs resting on a header. The ends of the header are supported by jack studs and king studs, which transfer the load to the sole plate and the foundation of the house. The rough sill, which helps anchor the window unit but carries no structural weight, is supported by cripple studs. To provide room for adjustments during installation, the rough opening for a window should be 1" wider and ½" taller than the window unit, including the jambs.

Framing Options for Window & Door Openings (new lumber shown in yellow)

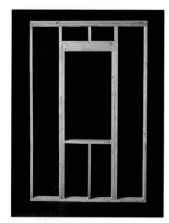
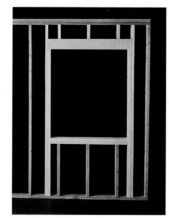

Using an existing opening avoids the need for new framing. This is a good option in homes with masonry exteriors, which are difficult to alter. Order a replacement unit that is 1" narrower and ½" shorter than the rough opening.

Framing a new opening is the only solution when you're installing a window or door where none existed or when you're replacing a unit with one that is much larger.

Enlarging an existing opening simplifies the framing. In many cases, you can use an existing king stud and jack stud to form one side of the new opening.

Floor & Ceiling Anatomy

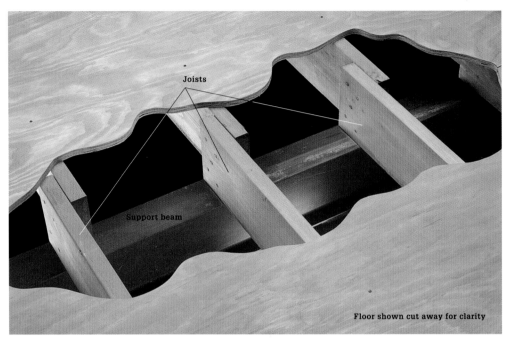

Joists

Support beam

Floor shown cut away for clarity

Joists carry the structural load of floors and ceilings. The ends of the joists rest on support beams, foundations, or load-bearing walls. Rooms used as living areas must be supported by floor joists that are at least 2 × 8" in size. Floors with smaller joists can be reinforced with sister joists (photos, below).

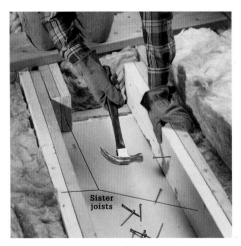

Sister joists

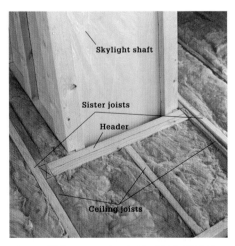

Skylight shaft

Sister joists

Header

Ceiling joists

Floors with 2 × 6 joists, like those sometimes found in attics, cannot support living areas unless a sister joist is attached alongside each original joist to strengthen it (above, left). This often is necessary when an attic is converted to a living area. Sister joists also are used to help support a header when ceiling joists must be cut, such as when framing a skylight shaft (above, right).

Roof Anatomy

Rafters made from 2 × 4s or 2 × 6s spaced every 16" or 24" are used to support roofs in most houses built before 1950. If necessary, rafters can be cut to make room for a large skylight. Check in your attic to determine if your roof is framed with rafters or roof trusses (right).

Trusses are prefabricated "webs" made from 2" dimensional lumber. They are found in many houses built after 1950. Never cut through or alter roof trusses. If you want to install a skylight in a house with roof trusses, buy a unit that fits in the space between the trusses.

Wall Anatomy

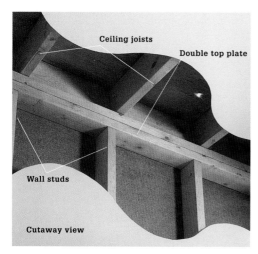

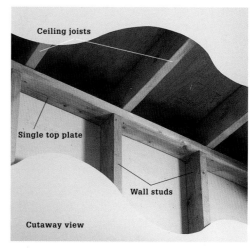

Load-bearing walls carry the structural weight of your home. In platform-framed houses, load-bearing walls can be identified by double top plates made from two layers of framing lumber. Load-bearing walls include all exterior walls and any interior walls that are aligned above support beams.

Partition walls are interior walls that do not carry the structural weight of the house. They have a single top plate and can be perpendicular to the floor and ceiling joists but are not aligned above support beams. Any interior wall that is parallel to floor and ceiling joists is a partition wall.

Building Codes & Permits

Building permits are required for any remodeling project that involves a change or addition to your home's structure or mechanical systems. Building permits are issued to ensure your remodeling project meets local building codes, which establish material standards, structural requirements, and installation guidelines for your project. In short, they ensure that your (or your contractor's) work is done properly.

The areas outlined on pages 17 and 18— room dimensions, exits and openings, light and ventilation, and fire protection—are usually covered by general building permits. If your project involves major changes to your plumbing, electrical, or HVAC systems, you may be required to obtain separate permits from the respective administration departments.

Building permits are required by law, and getting caught without them can result in fines from the city and possible trouble with your insurance company. Also, work done without permits can cause problems if you try to sell your house.

Most local building codes follow the national codes, such as the National Electrical Code, but are adapted to meet the demands of local conditions and legislation. Keep in mind that local codes always supersede national codes. Always check with your local building department before finalizing your plans.

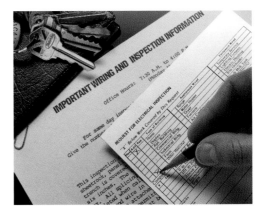

Before issuing permits, your local building department will require plans and cost estimates for your project. After your plans have been approved, you must pay permit fees, which are based on the cost of the project. You'll also learn what inspections are required and when you should call for inspections.

Once issued, a building permit typically is good for 180 days. You can apply for an extension by submitting a written request showing justifiable cause for the delay.

Tip ▶

Here are some tips to help you prepare for the permit process:

- To obtain a building permit, you must fill out a form from your local building department that includes a description of the project; your home's address, legal description, and occupancy; and an estimate of the project cost.
- The building department may require two to four sets of construction documents or drawings of your project— including floor and elevation plans—to be submitted for inspection and approval.
- A building inspector will examine all construction plans and stamp or send written notification of approval and acceptance.
- One set of approved documents is kept by the building official, one set is sent to the applicant, and one set is displayed at the site until the project is completed.
- Some permits are granted by phase of construction. After the work for one phase is completed and inspected, a permit for the next phase is issued. However, building officials will not guarantee issuance of subsequent permits.
- All work is inspected by a building official to ensure compliance with codes and permits.
- Your project is complete only after the local building inspector makes a final inspection and gives approval of your site.

Room Dimensions

- Habitable rooms must be at least 7 ft. wide and 7 ft. deep.
- Ceilings in all habitable rooms, hallways, corridors, bathrooms, toilet rooms, laundry rooms, and basements must be at least 7 ft., 6" high, measured from the finished floor to the lowest part of the ceiling.
- Beams, girders, and other obstructions that are spaced more than 4 ft. apart can extend 6" below the required ceiling height.
- In nonhabitable rooms, such as unfinished basements, ceilings may be 6 ft., 8" from the floor, and beams, girders, and ducts may be within 6 ft., 4" of the floor.
- Habitable rooms cannot have more than 50% of their floor area under sloped ceilings less than 7 ft., 6" high, and no portion of a floor area can be under a ceiling less than 5 ft. high.
- Finished floor is not considered measurable floor area when it is below sloped ceilings less than 5 ft. high or beneath furred ceilings less than 7 ft., 6" high.
- One habitable room in a home must have at least 120 square feet of gross floor area. Other habitable rooms can have gross floor space of 70 sq. ft. minimum.

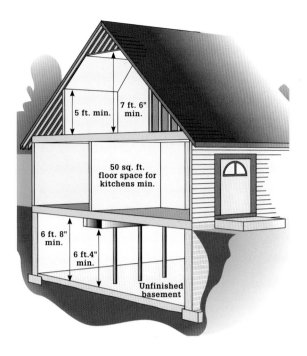

- Kitchens cannot have less than 50 sq. ft. of gross floor area.
- Hallways must be at least 3 ft. wide.

Exits & Openings

- Sleeping rooms and habitable basements must have at least one egress window or exterior door for emergency escape. Occupants must be able to open the exit from inside the home, without a key or tool.
- An egress window must have a net clear opening of at least 5.7 sq. ft., with a minimum height of 24" and a minimum width of 20".
- Window sills on egress windows cannot be more than 44" above the floor.
- Egress windows below ground level must have window wells. If the wells are deeper than 44", they must have permanent ladders or steps. The steps can project up to 6" into the well but must be usable when the window is fully opened. Steps

must be at least 12" wide and project at least 3" from the wall. Ladder rungs must be less than 18" apart.
- Screens, bars, grills, and covers on emergency exits must open easily and be removable from inside the home, without tools or keys.
- Exit doors must be at least 3 ft. wide and 6 ft., 8" high. They must provide direct outside access and operate without special knowledge or tools.
- Bulkhead enclosures may serve as emergency exits in habitable basements if they provide direct access to the basement and meet the dimension requirements for emergency exits.

Natural Light & Ventilation

- Ventilation includes windows, doors, louvers, and other approved openings or mechanical systems.
- Windows must equal at least 8% of the floor area in habitable rooms. The minimum openable area of a window must equal at least 4% of the room's floor area.
- In bathrooms, windows must be at least 3 sq. ft., and at least half of the window must open.
- Windows must open and operate from inside the room, and they must exit to a street, alley, yard, court, or porch.
- Window light can be replaced by an artificial light if it produces 6.46 lux from 30" above the floor.
- Mechanical ventilation can replace operable windows. In bedrooms, ventilation must supply outside air at a rate of 15 cubic ft. per minute (cfm) for each occupant. In primary bedrooms, the rate is based on two occupants. In additional bedrooms, the rate is based on one occupant per room.
- In bathrooms, intermittent mechanical ventilation rates must be 50 cfm, and continuous rates must be 20 cfm. Bathroom ventilation must exhaust to the outside.

Fire Protection

- All concealed and interconnected spaces, such as soffits, drop and cove ceilings, stair stringers, and areas around vents, pipes, ducts, chimneys, and fireplaces must be fireblocked to prevent fire spread.
- Exterior walls must be constructed to resist fire for at least one hour, with exposure from both sides.
- Batts or blankets of fiberglass, mineral wool, or other approved material must be secured between wall studs and partitions, at the ceiling and floor level, and at 10-ft. intervals both vertically and horizontally.
- Foam insulation installed in interior walls covered with ½" wallboard or other approved material must have a flame-spread rating of 75 or less and a smoke-developing index of 450 or less.
- Other insulation, including facings, vapor barriers, and breather papers, must have a flame-spread index of 25 or less and a smoke-developing index of 450 or less.
- Loose-fill insulation mounted with screens or supports must have a flame-spread rating of 25 or less and a smoke-developing index of 450 or less.

- Wall and ceiling finishes must have a flame-classification rating of 200 or less and a smoke-developing index of 450 or less.
- Smoke alarms must be installed in bedrooms, in hallways near bedrooms, and on each full story of a home. Multiple alarms must be wired together so one activation triggers all alarms.

Universal Design ▶

Universal design is intended for all people. While standard home and product designs are based on the "average" person—that is, the average adult male—not everyone fits into that category. Some people are short, some tall; some have difficulty walking, while others walk ably but find bending difficult. And physical abilities change constantly, as do family situations. By incorporating universal design into your remodeling plans, you can create spaces that work better for everyone who lives in or visits your home, regardless of their size, age, or ability.

Universal design is simply good design that improves everyday situations. For example, wide doorways make passage easier for a person carrying a load of laundry as well as for someone in a wheelchair; a lowered countertop enables a child to help prepare dinner and allows a person who tires easily to sit while cooking. More a way of thinking than a set of rules, universal design can be applied to any area of your home—from room layouts to light fixtures to door hardware. In all cases, universal design encourages independence by creating a safe, comfortable environment.

Many people take on remodeling projects to accommodate changes in their households. Perhaps you are remodeling because your aging parents are coming to live with you or your grown children or grandchildren

are coming for an extended visit. Or you may be preparing your home for your own retirement years. Considering both your current and future needs is an essential part of a fundamental universal design concept: creating a lifespan home—one that accommodates its residents throughout their lives. A lifespan home enables your aging parents to live comfortably with you now and will allow you to stay in your home as you grow older. And, while universal design makes your everyday life easier, it will also make your home more appealing to a wide range of potential buyers if you choose to sell.

Much of the universal design information in this book comes from universal design specialists, kitchen and bath designers, physical therapists, specialty builders and manufacturers, and organizations such as the National Kitchen and Bath Association (NKBA). Some suggestions are ADA (Americans with Disabilities Act) requirements; while these generally apply to public spaces, they often are used as guidelines for residential design. As always, be sure that all aspects of your project meet local code requirements.

For more help with planning with universal design, contact a qualified professional. Many kitchen and bath designers, home builders, and product manufacturers specialize in universal design.

Working with Drawings

Drawings are necessary for any remodeling project that involves construction, enlargement, alteration, repair, demolition, or change to any major system within your home. There are two basic types of construction drawings: floor plans and elevation drawings.

Floor plans show a room as seen from above. These are useful for showing overall room dimensions, layouts, and the relationships between neighboring rooms. Elevation drawings show a side view of a room, showing one wall per drawing. Elevations are made for both the interior and exterior of a house and generally show more architectural detail than floor plans.

Both floor plans and elevation drawings provide you with a method for planning and recording structural and mechanical systems for your project. They also help the local building department to ensure your project meets code requirements.

Use existing blueprints of your home, if available, to trace original floor plans and elevation drawings onto white paper. Copy the measurement scale of the original blueprints onto the traced drawings. Make photocopies of the traced drawings, then use the photocopies to experiment with remodeling ideas.

Before you draw up new plans, check with your home's architect, builder, or your local building department. These places often have copies of your home's floor plans on file. If your home is a historic building, your plans may be on file at a state or local historic office or university library.

If you are unable to obtain a copy of your home's floor plans, you can draw your own. This process provides you with a wealth of information about your home. Drawings let you see how changes will affect your home's overall layout and feel. They also help you plot your ideas, list materials, and solve design problems.

Follow the steps on page 21 to create floor plans and elevation drawings. Keep in mind that your plans may change as your ideas develop; until you have worked out all the elements of your design, consider your plans to be drafts. When you have arrived at a plan that meets your needs, draw up final floor and elevation plans to submit to your local building department.

To create floor plans, draw one story at a time. First, measure each room on the story from wall to wall. Transfer the rooms' dimensions to ¼" grid paper, using a scale of ¼" = 1 ft. Label each room for its use and note its overall dimensions. Include wall thicknesses, which you can determine by measuring the widths of door and window jambs—do not include the trim.

Next, add these elements to your drawings:

- Windows and doors; note which way the doors swing.
- Stairs and their direction as it relates to each story.
- Permanent features, such as plumbing fixtures, major appliances, countertops, built-in furniture, and fireplaces.
- Overhead features, such as exposed beams, or wall cabinets—use dashed lines.
- Plumbing, electrical, and HVAC elements. You may want a separate set of drawings for these mechanical elements and service lines.
- Overall dimensions measured from outside the house. Use these to check the accuracy of your interior dimensions.

To create elevation drawings, use the same ¼" = 1 ft. scale, and draw everything you see on one wall (each room has four elevations). Include:

- Ceiling heights and the heights of significant features such as soffits and exposed beams.
- Doors, including the heights (from the floor to the top of the opening) and widths.
- Windows, including the height of the sills and tops of the openings, and widths.
- Trim and other decorative elements.

When your initial floor plans and elevations are done, use them to sketch your remodeling layout options. Use overlays to show hidden elements or proposed changes to a plan. Photographs of your home's interior and exterior may also be helpful. Think creatively, and draw many different sketches; the more design options you consider, the better your final plans will be.

When you have completed your remodeling plans, draft your final drawings and create a materials list for the project.

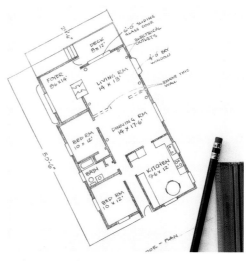

Draft a detailed floor plan showing the layout of the area that will be remodeled, including accurate measurements. Show the location of new and existing doors and windows, wiring, and plumbing fixtures.

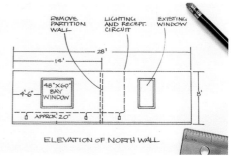

Create elevation drawings showing a side-view layout of windows and doors, as viewed from both inside and outside the home. Indicate the size of windows and doors, ceiling heights, and the location of wiring and plumbing fixtures.

Making Construction Plans

The best way to prepare for a remodel project is to create a construction plan. Having a complete construction plan enables you to view your entire project at a glance. It helps you identify potential problems, provides sense of the time involved, and establishes a logical order of steps. Without a construction plan, it's easy to make costly mistakes, such as closing up a wall with wallboard before the rough-ins have been inspected.

The general steps shown here follow a typical construction sequence. Your plan may differ at several points, but thinking through each of these steps will help you create a complete schedule.

1. CONTACT THE BUILDING DEPARTMENT

To avoid any unpleasant—and expensive—surprises, discuss you project with a building official. Find out about the building codes in your area and what you'll need to obtain the applicable permits. Explain how much of the work you plan to do yourself. In some states, plumbing, electrical, and HVAC work must be done by licensed professionals. Also determine what types of drawings you'll need to get permits and whether you'll need engineer's drawings and calculations.

2. CREATE YOUR DRAWINGS

Make your floor plans and elevation drawings (see pages 20 to 21). This step also involves most of the design work for your project; you may want to get help from a professional for this phase.

3. GET THE PERMITS

Have your final plans reviewed by the building inspector, and make any necessary adjustments required to obtain all of the permits for your project. This is also the time to schedule inspections. Find out what work must be inspected and when to call for inspections.

4. HIRE CONTRACTORS

If you're getting help with your project, it's best to find and hire the contractors early in the process, as their schedules will affect yours. It may be necessary for some contractors to obtain their own work permits from the building department. To avoid problems, make sure all of the contractors know exactly what work they are being hired to do and what work you will be doing yourself. Always check contractors' references and make sure any contractors are licensed and insured before hiring them. This is also the time to order materials and arrange for delivery.

5. COMPLETE THE FRAMING AND MAJOR MECHANICAL CHANGES

Begin the construction work with any major structural or mechanical changes. Move mechanical elements and reroute major service lines. Complete any rough-ins that must happen before the framing goes up, such as adding ducts, installing under-floor drains, or replacing old plumbing. Complete the new framing. Build the rough openings for windows and doors, and install the windows.

6. COMPLETE THE ROUGH-INS

Run drain, waste, and vent (DWV), water, and gas supply lines. Install electrical boxes, and run the wiring. Complete the HVAC rough-ins. Jot down measurements of pipes and locations of wiring, for future reference. Have the building inspector approve your work before you close up the walls. Install any fixtures that go in during the rough-in stage (others will come after the wall surfaces are installed).

7. FINISH THE WALLS AND CEILINGS

After your work has passed inspection, insulate the walls, ceilings, and pipes. Install fiberglass insulation used as fireblocking. Make sure protector plates for pipes and wires running through framing are in place. Add vapor barriers as required by local code.

Make sure everything is in place before you cover up the framing, then finish the walls and ceilings. If you're installing wallboard, do the ceilings first, then the walls. Tape and finish the wallboard. Install other finish treatments. Texture, prime, and paint the wallboard when it's convenient. If you are installing a suspended ceiling, do so after you finish the walls.

8. ADD THE FINISHING TOUCHES

Install doors, moldings, woodwork, cabinets, and built-in shelving, and lay the floor coverings. The best order for these tasks will depend on the materials you're using and the desired decorative effects.

Install any new plumbing fixtures you have chosen for bathrooms, and complete the drain and supply hookups. Make electrical connections, and install all fixtures, devices, and appliances. Get a final inspection from the building inspector.

Working Safely

Your personal safety when working on carpentry projects depends greatly on what safety measures you take. The power tools sold today offer many safety features, such as blade guards, locks to prevent accidental starts, and double insulation to reduce the risk of shock in the event of a short circuit. It's up to you to take advantage of these safety features. For example, never operate a saw with the blade guard removed. You risk injury from flying debris as well as from being cut by the blade.

Follow all precautions outlined in the owner's manuals for your tools and make sure you protect yourself with safety glasses, earplugs, and a dust mask or respirator to filter out dust and debris.

Keep your work environment clean. A cluttered work area is more likely to result in accidents. Clean your tools and put them away at the end of every work period, and sweep up dust and debris.

Some materials emit dangerous fumes or particles. Keep such materials stored away from heat sources and out of the reach of children; always use these products in a well-ventilated area.

Maintaining safety is an ongoing project. Take the time to update your first-aid kit and evaluate your workspace, tools, and safety equipment on a regular basis. To avoid accidents, repair and replace old and worn-out parts before they break.

Read the owner's manual before operating any power tool. Your tools may differ in many ways from those described in this book, so it's best to familiarize yourself with the features and capabilities of the tools you own. Always wear eye and ear protection when operating a power tool. Wear a dust mask when the project will produce dust.

Some walls may contain asbestos. Many homes built or remodeled between 1930 and 1950 have older varieties of insulation that included asbestos. Consult a professional for removal of hazardous pollutants like asbestos, and if you find asbestos or materials that may contain asbestos, do not attempt to remove them on your own. Even if you determine that no asbestos is present, it is a good idea to wear a particle mask and other safety gear when doing demolition.

First-Aid Kits

Assemble a first-aid kit. Cuts from hand or power tools can be serious and require prompt and thoughtful attention. Be prepared for such situations with a well-equipped first-aid kit that is easy to find. Record any emergency telephone numbers on the first-aid kit or by the nearest phone so they are available in an emergency.

Equip your kit with a variety of items (photo right), including bandages, needles, tweezers, antiseptic ointment, cotton swabs, cotton balls, eye drops, a first-aid handbook, a chemical-filled cold pack, elastic bandages, first-aid tape, and sterile gauze.

For puncture wounds, cuts, burns, and other serious injuries, always seek medical attention as soon as first aid—such as washing and wrapping of cuts—has been provided.

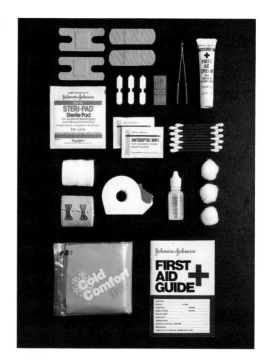

Safe Practices

Keep your tools sharp and clean. Accidents are more likely when blades are dull and tools are filled with sawdust and dirt.

Use a GFCI receptacle, adapter, or extension cord to reduce the risk of shock while operating a power tool outdoors or in wet conditions.

Check with a neon circuit tester to make sure the power is off before removing cover plates, exposing wires, or drilling or cutting into walls that contain wiring.

Techniques

While every home improvement project is different from the others in some way, the basic skills you need come from a common set of DIY techniques. Building walls, running plumbing lines, and adding electrical circuits are some of the chief techniques you'll need to call upon. In this chapter you'll find a condensed version of the essential information you need to put these valuable techniques into practice and become an accomplished do-it-yourselfer.

Once the new walls are up (but before they're covered) you need to fill them with pipes and wires. In the plumbing section that follows you'll learn how to plan new lines and hookups as well as how to work with basic plumbing materials. In the wiring section you'll find useful instructions on working with electrical cables and devices. A handy series of circuit maps shows you exactly how your remodeled room should be wired.

In this chapter:

- Demolition
- Building Walls
- Installing Wallboard
- Understanding Plumbing
- Working with Copper Pipe
- Working with Plastic Pipe
- Working with PEX Pipe
- Planning New Plumbing
- Understanding Wiring
- Working with Wire & Cable
- Working with Conduit
- Working with Boxes
- Working with Switches
- Working with Receptacles
- Planning New Wiring
- Using Circuit Maps

Demolition

Many home remodeling projects actually begin with demolition. When you're remodeling, it's often necessary to cut or enlarge openings for new doors or windows or even to remove entire walls. The basic procedures for this type of demolition are the same whether you're working with doors and windows on exterior walls or altering interior walls.

Your first step will be to determine how your house was framed. House framing variations will dictate the proper procedures for creating openings in walls or removing walls altogether. Then, you'll need to inspect the walls for hidden mechanicals—wiring, plumbing, and HVAC lines.

After you've rerouted any utility lines, you're ready to remove the interior wall surfaces. If you're replacing old windows and doors, now is the time to remove them as well. Where necessary, you can now remove exterior wall surfaces, but don't remove any framing members yet.

The next step will depend on the nature of your project. If you are removing a load-bearing wall or creating a new or enlarged opening in one, you'll need to build temporary supports to brace the ceiling while the work is being done. This step won't be necessary if you are removing a non-loadbearing wall. Then you can remove any wall framing members, following the applicable procedures for load-bearing or non-loadbearing walls.

With the removal steps of the project completed, you'll be ready to install your new windows and doors.

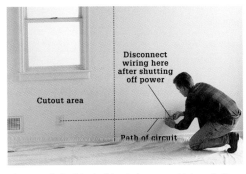

Disconnect electrical wiring before you cut into walls. Trace the wiring back to a fixture outside the cutout area, then shut off the power and disconnect the wires leading into the cutout area. Turn the power back on and check for current with a circuit tester before cutting into the walls.

Demolition is the starting point of most projects where a window or door opening is enlarged.

How to Install Temporary Support (perpendicular joists)

Build a 2 × 4 stud wall that is 4 ft. wider than the planned wall opening and 1¾" shorter than the distance from floor to ceiling.

Raise the stud wall up and position it 3 ft. from the wall, centered on the planned rough opening.

Slide a 2 × 4 top plate between the temporary wall and the ceiling. Check to make sure the wall is plumb, and drive shims under the top plate at 12" intervals until the wall is wedged tightly in place.

How to Install Temporary Support (parallel joists)

Build two 4-ft.-long cross braces, using pairs of 2 × 4s nailed together. Attach the cross braces to the double top plate, 1 ft. from the ends, using countersunk lag screws.

Place a 2 × 4 sole plate directly over a floor joist, then set hydraulic jacks on the sole plate. For each jack, build a post 8" shorter than the jack-to-ceiling distance. Nail the posts to the top plate, 2 ft. from the ends. Cover the braces with the cloth, and set the support structure on the jacks.

Adjust the support structure so the posts are exactly plumb, and pump the hydraulic jacks until the cross braces just begin to lift the ceiling. Do not lift too far or you may damage the ceiling or floor.

How to Remove Wallboard

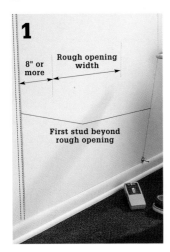

1

8" or more

Rough opening width

First stud beyond rough opening

Mark the width of the rough opening on the wall and locate the first stud on either side of the planned rough opening. If the rough opening is more than 8" from the next stud, use a chalk line to mark a cutting line on the inside edge of the stud.

2

Remove the baseboards and other trim, and prepare the work area. Make a ¾"-deep cut from floor to ceiling along both cutting lines, using a circular saw. Use a utility knife to finish the cuts at the top and bottom and to cut through the taped horizontal seam where the wall meets the ceiling surface.

3

Insert the end of a pry bar into the cut near a corner of the opening. Pull the pry bar until the wallboard breaks, then tear away the broken pieces. Take care to avoid damaging the wallboard outside the project area.

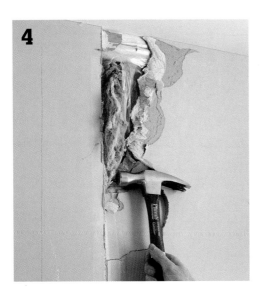

4

Continue removing the wallboard by striking the surface with the side of a hammer and pulling the wallboard away from the wall with the pry bar or your hands.

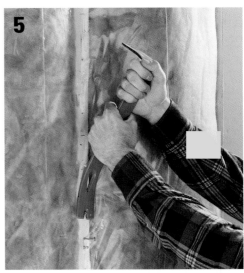

5

Remove nails, screws, and any remaining wallboard from the framing members, using a pry bar. Remove any vapor barrier and insulation.

How to Remove Plaster Walls

1

Shut off the power and inspect the wall for wiring and plumbing. Mark the wall area to be removed by following the directions on page 30. Apply a double layer of masking tape along the outside edge of each cutting line.

2

Score each line several times with a utility knife, using a straightedge as a guide. Scored lines should be at least ⅛" deep.

3

Beginning at the top of the wall in the center of the planned opening, break up the plaster by striking the wall lightly with the side of a hammer. Clear away all plaster from floor to ceiling to within 3" of the marked lines.

4

Break the plaster along the edges by holding a scrap piece of 2 × 4 on edge just inside the scored line and rapping it with a hammer. Use a pry bar to remove the remaining plaster.

5

Cut through the lath along the edges of the plaster, using a reciprocating saw or jigsaw.

6

Remove the lath from the studs, using a pry bar. Pry away any remaining nails, and remove any vapor barrier and insulation.

How to Make an Opening in an Exterior Wall

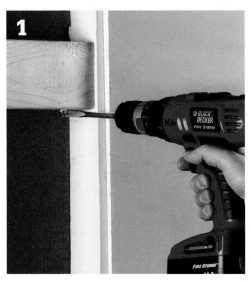

A **cross-section view** of a typical exterior wall with lap siding.

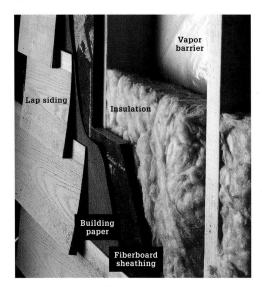

From inside the house, drill through the wall at the corners of the framed opening. Push casing nails through the holes to mark their location. For round-top windows, drill holes around the curved outline (see variation, page 195).

Measure the distance between the nails on the outside of the house to make sure the dimensions are accurate. Mark the cutting lines with a chalk line stretched between the nails. Push the nails back through the wall.

Nail a straight 1 × 4 flush with the inside edge of the right cutting line. Sink the nail heads with a nail set to prevent scratches to the foot of the saw. Set the circular saw to its maximum blade depth.

Rest the saw on the 1 × 4, and cut along the marked line, using the edge of the board as a guide. Stop the cuts about 1" short of the corners to keep from damaging the framing members.

Reposition the 1 × 4, and make the remaining straight cuts. Drive nails within 1½" of the inside edge of the board, because the siding under this area will be removed to make room for door or window brick moldings.

Variation: For round-top windows, make curved cuts using a reciprocating saw or jigsaw. Move the saw slowly to ensure smooth, straight cuts. To draw an outline for round-top windows, use a cardboard template.

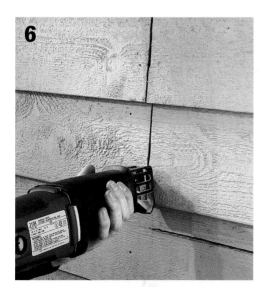

Complete the cuts at the corner with a reciprocating saw or jigsaw.

Remove the cut wall section. If you are working with metal siding, wear work gloves. If you wish, remove the siding pieces from the sheathing and save them for future use.

How to Make an Opening in a Stucco Wall

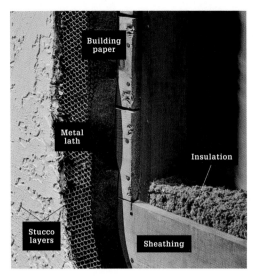

Stucco is a multiple-layer cement product applied to metal lath. Building paper is sandwiched between the metal lath and the sheathing to create a waterproof barrier. Stucco is extremely durable due to its cement base. But if you don't do the removal carefully, it's easy to crack the stucco past the outline for the new window or door.

From inside the house, drill through the wall at the corners of the framed opening. Use a twist bit to drill through the sheathing, then use a masonry bit to finish the holes. Push casing nails through the holes to mark their locations.

On the outside wall, measure the distance between the nails to make sure the rough opening dimensions are accurate. Mark cutting lines between the nails, using a chalk line.

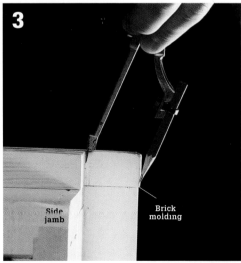

Match the distance between the side jambs and the edge of the brick molding on a window or door with the legs of a compass.

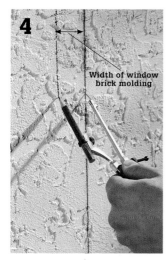

Scribe a cutting line on the stucco by moving the compass along the outline, with the compass point held on the marked line. This added margin will allow the brick molding to fit tight against the wall sheathing.

Width of window brick molding

Score the stucco surface around the outside edge of the scribed line, using a masonry chisel and masonry hammer. The scored grooves should be at least ⅛" deep to serve as a guide for the circular saw blade.

Make straight cuts using a circular saw and masonry-cutting blade. Make several passes with the saw, gradually deepening the cuts until the blade just cuts through the metal lath, causing sparks to fly. Stop cuts just ahead of the corners to avoid damaging the stucco past the cutting line; complete the cuts with a masonry chisel.

Variation: For round-top windows, mark the outline on the stucco, using a cardboard template, and drill a series of holes around the outline, using a masonry bit. Complete the cut with a masonry chisel.

Break up the stucco with a masonry hammer or sledgehammer, exposing the underlying metal lath. Use aviation snips to cut through the lath around the opening. Use a pry bar to pull away the lath and attached stucco.

Outline the rough opening on the sheathing, using a straightedge as a guide. Cut the rough opening along the inside edge of the framing members, using a circular saw or reciprocating saw. Remove the cut section of sheathing.

How to Remove a Partition Wall

Use a utility knife to score the intersections where the wall you're removing meets the ceiling to keep from damaging it during wall removal. Pry away baseboard trim and remove receptacle plates and switch covers to prepare for demolition.

Use the side of a hammer to punch a starter hole in the wallboard, then carefully remove the wallboard with a pry bar. Try to pull off large sections at a time to minimize dust. Remove any remaining wallboard nails or screws from the wall studs.

Reroute outlets, switches, plumbing, or ductwork. Have professionals do this for you if you are not experienced with these systems or confident in your skills. This work should be inspected after it is completed.

Locate the closest permanent studs on the adjacent wall or walls with a stud finder, and carefully remove the wallboard up to these studs. Score the wallboard first with a utility knife, then cut through it with a circular saw.

Remove the wall studs by cutting through them in the middle with a reciprocating saw and prying out the upper and lower sections. Remove the endmost studs where the wall meets an adjacent wall or walls.

Cut through the wall's top plate with a circular saw or reciprocating saw. Pry out the top plate sections carefully to avoid damaging the ceiling.

Remove the sole plate just as you did the top plate by cutting through it and prying up the long pieces.

Patch the walls and ceiling with strips of wallboard, and repair the floor as needed with new floor coverings.

Removing Trim

Remove trim moldings at the edges and tops of the cabinets with a flat pry bar or putty knife.

Remove base shoe from cabinet base if the molding is attached to the floor.

Remove baseboards and other trim moldings with a pry bar. Protect wall surfaces with scraps of wood.Label the trim boards on the back side so you can replace them correctly.

Remove valances above cabinets. Some valances are attached to the cabinets or soffits with screws. Others are nailed and must be pried loose.

How to Remove Cabinets

Remove doors and drawers to make it easier to get at interior spaces. You may need to scrape away old paint to expose hinge screws.

At the backs of cabinets, remove any screws holding the cabinet to the wall. Cabinets can be removed as a group, or can be disassembled.

Detach individual cabinets by removing screws that hold face frames together.

Countertops are usually not salvageable. Cut them into manageable pieces with a reciprocating saw, or take them apart piece by piece with a hammer and pry bar.

Building Walls

Partition walls are constructed between load-bearing walls to divide space. They should be strong and well made, but their main job is to house doors and to support wall coverings. The sole plate at the bottom of the wall should be fastened securely to the subfloor and joists with panel adhesive and 16d common nails. Use masonry fasteners on concrete basement floors.

Anchoring New Partition Walls

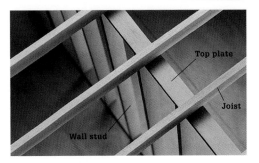

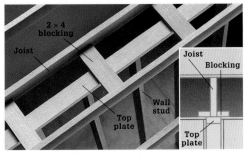

When a new wall is perpendicular to the ceiling or floor joists above, attach the top plate directly to the joists, using 16d nails.

When a new wall falls between parallel joists, install 2 × 4 blocking between the joists every 24". If the new wall is aligned with a parallel joist, install blocks on both sides of the wall, and attach the top plate to the joist (inset).

How to Build a Partition Wall

1

Mark the location of the new wall on the ceiling, then snap two chalk lines or use a scrap piece of 2× lumber as a template to mark layout lines for the top plate. Use a stud finder to locate floor joists or roof framing above the ceiling, and mark these locations with tick marks or tape outside the layout lines.

2

Cut the top and sole plates to length and lay them side by side. Use a combination or framing square to draw pairs of lines across both plates to mark the stud locations. Space the studs at 16" intervals, on center.

3

Mark the location of any door framing on the top and sole plates. Refer to the door's rough opening specifications when marking the layout. Draw lines for both the king and jack studs.

4

Fasten the top plate to the ceiling using 3" deck screws or 10d nails. Be sure to orient the plate so the stud layout faces down.

5

Hang a plumb bob from the edge of the top plate at several points along its length to find the sole plate location on the floor. The tip of the plumb bob should almost touch the floor. Wait until it stops moving before marking the sole plate reference point. Connect the points with a line to establish one edge of the sole plate. Use a piece of scrap 2× material as a template for marking the other edge.

6

Cut away the portion of the sole plate where the new door will be, and nail or screw the two sections to the floor between the sole plate layout lines. Use the cutaway door section as a spacer for the door when fastening the plates. Drive the fasteners into the floor framing. For concrete floors, attach the sole plate with a powder-actuated nail gun or with hardened masonry screws.

7

Measure the distance between the top and sole plates at several places along the wall to determine the stud lengths. The stud length distance may vary, depending on structural settling or an out-of-flat floor. Add 1/8" to the stud length(s), and cut them to size. The extra length will ensure a snug fit between the wall plates.

8

Install the framing members. Use a hammer to tap each stud into position, then toenail the studs to the top and sole plates. Fit, trim, and nail the studs, one at a time. *Tip: If the studs tend to shift during nailing, drive pilot holes for the nails first, or use 3" deck screws instead of nails. (Inset) An option for attaching wall studs to plates is to use metal connectors and 4d nails.*

9

Nail the king studs, jack studs, a header and a cripple stud in place to complete the rough door framing. See page 12 for more information on framing a door opening.

(continued)

If building codes in your area require fire blocking, install 2× cutoff scraps between the studs, 4 ft. from the floor, to serve this purpose. Stagger the blocks so you can endnail each piece.

Drill holes through the studs to create raceways for wiring and plumbing. When this work is completed, fasten metal protector plates over these areas to prevent drilling or nailing through wiring and pipes later. Have your work inspected before proceeding with wallboard.

Cover the wall with wallboard. Plan the layout wisely to minimize waste and to avoid butted joints with untapered seams. If you are installing wallboard on a ceiling as well, do that first. For more on installing wallboard, see pages 44 to 51.

Tools & Materials for Framing with Steel

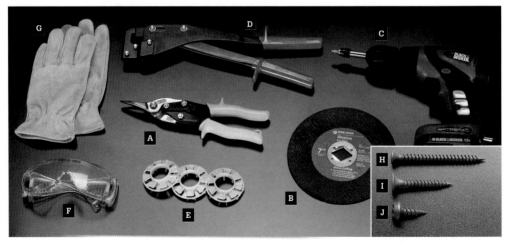

Steel framing requires a few specialty tools and materials. Aviation snips (A) are needed to cut tracks and studs, though a miter saw outfitted with a steel-cutting abrasive blade (B) can speed up the process. A drill or screw gun (C) is required for fastening framing. Handy for large projects, a stud crimper (D) creates mechanical joints between tracks and studs. Plastic grommets (E) are placed in knockouts to help protect utility lines. Protective eyewear and heavy work gloves (F, G) are necessities when working with the sharp edges of hand-cut steel framing. Use self-tapping screws (inset) to fasten steel components. To install wood trim, use type S trim-head screws (H); to fasten wallboard, type S wallboard screws (I); and to fasten studs and tracks together, 7/16" type S panhead screws (J).

Joining Sections Using Steel Studs ▶

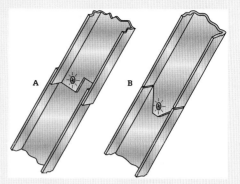

Steel studs and tracks have the same basic structure—a web that spans two flanged sides—however, studs also contain a ¼" lip to improve their rigidity.

Join sections with a spliced joint (A) or notched joint (B). Make a spliced joint by cutting a 2" slit in the web of one track. Slip the other track into the slit and secure with a screw. For a notched joint, cut back the flanges of one track and taper the web so it fits into the other track; secure with a screw.

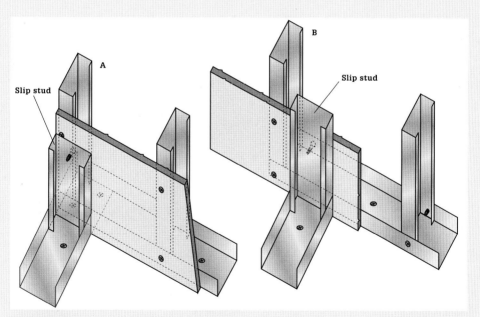

Build corners using a slip stud: A slip stud is not fastened until the adjacent drywall is in place. Form L-shaped corners (A) by overlapping the tracks. Cut off the flange on one side of one track, removing enough to allow room for the overlapping track and drywall. Form a T-shaped corner (B) by leaving a gap between the tracks for the drywall. Secure each slip stud by screwing through the stud into the tracks of the adjacent wall. Also screw through the back side of the drywall into the slip stud, if possible. Where there's no backing behind the slip stud, drive screws at a 45° angle through the back corners of the slip stud and into the drywall.

Installing Wallboard

Hanging wallboard is a project that can be completed quickly and easily with a little preplanning and a helping hand.

Planning the layout of panels will help you reduce waste and deal with problem areas. Where possible, install full panels perpendicular to the framing to add strength and rigidity to walls and ceilings. To save yourself time and trouble during the finishing process, avoid joints where two untapered panel ends are butted together. These are difficult to finish because there's no recess for the compound and tape. In small areas, install long sheets horizontally that run the full length of the walls. Or hang the panels vertically, which produces more seams that need taping but eliminates butted end joints. If butted joints are unavoidable, stagger the seams and locate them away from the center of the wall, or install back blocking to help mask unflattering effects.

Professionals install drywall panels horizontally because a single horizontal seam at chest level (48") and butted seams every 8 ft. are much easier to tape and mud than a series of vertical seams that run every 4 ft. from floor to ceiling. A drywall lifter operated by foot gets panels up off the floor and lets you hang them at a consistent height without using spacers.

Tools & Prep Work

Tools for installing wallboard include: chalkline (A), surform plane (B), compass (C), wallboard compass (D), protective masks (E), drill with hole saw (F), trim router (G), drywall gun (H), utility knife (I), eye protection (J), tape measure (K), wallboard lifter (L), caulk gun (M), pry bar (N), wallboard saw (O), keyhole saw (P), framing square (Q), level (R), wallboard T-square (S).

Preparing for Wallboard Installation

Use protector plates where wires or pipes pass through framing members less than 1¼" from the face. The plates prevent wallboard screws from puncturing wires or pipes.

Nail furring strips to the framing to extend the wall surface beyond any obstructions such as water pipes or heating ducts.

Mark the locations of the studs on the floor with a carpenter's pencil or masking tape. After wallboard covers the studs, the marks indicate the stud locations.

How to Cut Wallboard

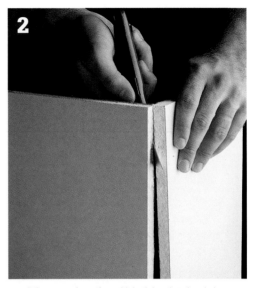

Position the wallboard T-square with the short arm flush against the edge. Use a utility knife to score the wallboard face paper along the arm of the square at the cutting point.

Bend the scored section with both hands to break the plaster core of the wallboard. Fold back the unwanted piece and cut through the back paper to separate the pieces.

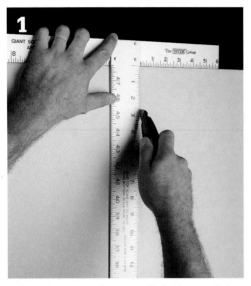

Smooth rough edges with a drywall rasp. One or two passes with the rasp should be sufficient. To help fit a piece into a tight space, bevel the edge slightly toward the back of the panel.

Where untapered panel ends will be butted together, bevel-cut the outside edges of each panel at 45°, removing about ⅛" of material. This helps prevent the paper from creating a ridge along the seam. Peel off any loose paper from the edge.

How to Install Wallboard on Flat Ceilings

1

2

Snap a chalk line perpendicular to the joists, 48⅛" from the starting wall.

Measure to make sure the first panel will break on the center of a joist. If necessary, cut the panel on the end that abuts the side wall so the panel breaks on the next farthest joist. Load the panel onto a rented drywall lift, or use a helper, and lift the panel flat against the joists.

3

4

Position the panel with the leading edge on the chalk line and the end centered on a joist. Fasten the panel with appropriately sized screws driven every 12" along the joists.

After the first row of panels is installed, begin the next row with a half panel. This ensures that the butted end joints will be staggered between rows.

Tip ▶

Drywall stilts bring you within reach of ceilings, so you can fasten and finish the drywall without a ladder. Stilts are commonly available at rental centers and are surprisingly easy to use.

How to Install Wallboard on Walls

1

Plan wallboard placement so joints do not fall at the corners of doors or windows. Wallboard joints at corners often crack and cause bulges that interfere with miter joints in window or door trim.

2

With a helper or a wallboard lift, hoist the first panel tight against the ceiling, making sure the side edge is centered on a stud. Push the panel flat against the framing and drive the starter screws to secure the panel. Make any cutouts, then fasten the field of the panel with drywall screws driven every 12".

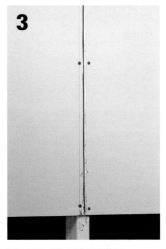

3

Measure, cut, and install the remaining panels along the upper wall. Bevel panel ends slightly, leaving a ⅛" gap between them at the joint. Butt joints can also be installed using back blocking to create a recess.

4

Measure, cut, and install the bottom row, butting the panels tight to the upper row and leaving a ½" gap at the floor. Secure to the framing along the top edge using the starter screws, then make all cutouts before fastening the rest of the panel.

Variation: When installing wallboard vertically, cut each panel so it's ½" shorter than the ceiling height to allow for expansion. (The gap will be covered by base molding.) Avoid placing tapered edges at outside corners; they are difficult to finish.

How to Install Wallboard at Inside Corners

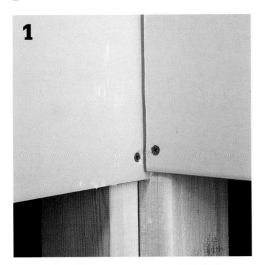

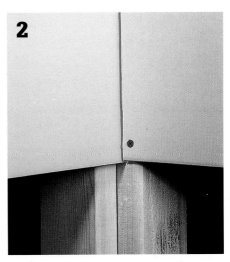

Standard 90° inside corners are installed with the first panel butted against the framing and the adjacent panel butted against the first. The screw spacing remains the same as on a flat wall (see page 48).

Use a "floating corner" to reduce the chances of popped fasteners and cracks. Install the first panel, fastening only to within one stud bay of the corner. Push the leading edge of the adjacent panel against the first to support the unfastened edge. Fasten the second panel normally, including the corner.

How to Install Wallboard at Outside Corners

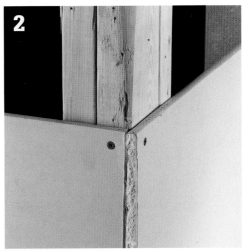

Cut the first panel so it is longer than the opening and extends past the corner framing. Fasten the panel in place, then score the backside and snap cut to remove the waste piece.

Install the second panel on the adjacent wall so it overlaps the end of the first panel slightly. Score and snap-cut so end is flush with first panel wall surface.

How to Tape Wallboard Joints

1

Apply a thin layer of wallboard compound over the joint with a 4" or 6" wallboard knife. To load the knife, dip it into a pan filled with wallboard compound.

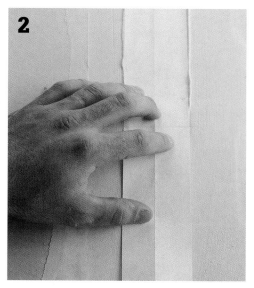

2

Press the wallboard tape into the compound immediately, centering the tape on the joint. Wipe away the excess compound and smooth the joint with a 6" knife. Let dry overnight.

3

Apply a thin finish coat of compound with a 10" wallboard knife. Allow the second coat to dry and shrink overnight. Apply the last coat and let it harden slightly before wet-sanding.

Tip ▸

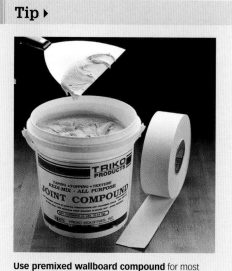

Use premixed wallboard compound for most taping and finishing jobs to eliminate mixing. Use paper wallboard tape when using premixed wallboard compound.

How to Finish Inside Corners

1

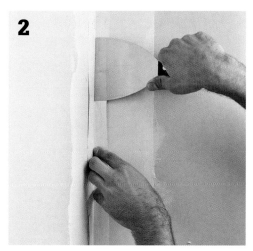

2

Fold a strip of paper wallboard tape in half by pinching the strip and pulling it between thumb and forefinger. Apply a thin layer of wallboard compound to both sides of the inside corner, using a 4" wallboard knife.

Position the end of the folded tape strip at the top of the joint and press the tape into the wet compound with the knife. Smooth both sides of the corner. Finish as described in step 3, preceding page.

How to Finish Outside Corners

1

2

Tip ▶

Position corner bead on outside corners. Using a level, adjust the bead so corner is plumb. Attach with 1¼" wallboard nails or screws spaced at 8" intervals. (Some corner beads are fastened with wallboard compound.)

Cover the corner bead with three coats of wallboard compound, using a 6" or 10" wallboard knife. Let each coat dry and shrink overnight before applying the next coat. Smooth the final coat with a wet sander.

Sand joints lightly after wallboard compound dries. Use a pole sander to reach high areas without a ladder. Wear a dust mask when dry-sanding.

Understanding Plumbing

Because most of a plumbing system is hidden inside walls and floors, it may seem to be a complex maze of pipes and fittings. In fact, home plumbing is simple and straightforward. Understanding how home plumbing works is an important first step toward doing routine maintenance and money-saving repairs.

A typical home plumbing system includes three basic parts: a water supply system, a fixture and appliance set, and a drain system. These three parts can be seen clearly in the photograph of the cut-away house on the opposite page.

Fresh water enters a home through a main supply line (1). This fresh water source is provided by either a municipal water company or a private underground well. If the source is a municipal supplier, the water passes through a meter (2) that registers the amount of water used. A family of four uses about 400 gallons of water each day.

Immediately after the main supply enters the house, a branch line splits off (3) and is joined to a water heater (4). From the water heater, a hot water line runs parallel to the cold water line to bring the water supply to fixtures and appliances throughout the house. Fixtures include sinks, bathtubs, showers, and laundry tubs. Appliances include water heaters,

dishwashers, clothes washers, and water softeners. Toilets and exterior sillcocks are examples of fixtures that require only a cold water line.

The water supply to fixtures and appliances is controlled with faucets and valves. Faucets and valves have moving parts and seals that eventually may wear out or break, but they are easily repaired or replaced.

Waste water then enters the drain system. It first must flow past a drain trap (5), a U-shaped piece of pipe that holds standing water and prevents sewer gases from entering the home. Every fixture must have a drain trap.

The drain system works entirely by gravity, allowing waste water to flow downhill through a series of large-diameter pipes. These drain pipes are attached to a system of vent pipes. Vent pipes (6) bring fresh air to the drain system, preventing suction that would slow or stop drain water from flowing freely. Vent pipes usually exit the house at a roof vent (7).

All waste water eventually reaches a main waste and vent stack (8). The main stack curves to become a sewer line (9) that exits the house near the foundation. In a municipal system, this sewer line joins a main sewer line located near the street. Where sewer service is not available, waste water empties into a septic system.

Water meters and main shutoff valves are located where the main water supply pipe enters the house. The water meter is the property of your local municipal water company. If the water meter leaks, or if you suspect it is not functioning properly, call your water company for repairs.

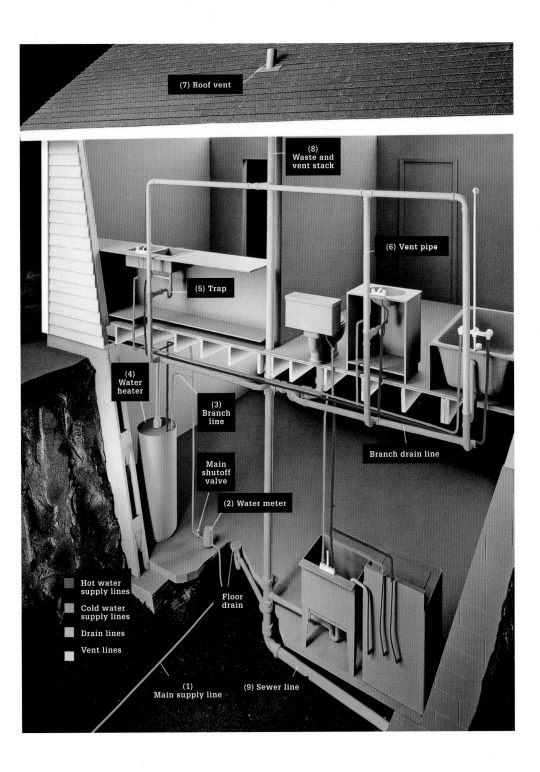

(7) Roof vent

(8) Waste and vent stack

(6) Vent pipe

(5) Trap

(4) Water heater

(3) Branch line

Main shutoff valve

(2) Water meter

Branch drain line

Hot water supply lines

Cold water supply lines

Drain lines

Vent lines

Floor drain

(1) Main supply line

(9) Sewer line

Water Supply System

Water supply pipes carry hot and cold water throughout a house. In homes built before 1960, the original supply pipes were usually made of galvanized iron. Newer homes have supply pipes made of copper. In most areas of the country, supply pipes made of rigid plastic or PEX are accepted by local plumbing codes.

Water supply pipes are made to withstand the high pressures of the water supply system. They have small diameters, usually ½" to 1", and are joined with strong, watertight fittings. The hot and cold lines run in tandem to all parts of the house. Usually, the supply pipes run inside wall cavities or are strapped to the undersides of floor joists.

Hot and cold water supply pipes are connected to fixtures or appliances. Fixtures include sinks, tubs, and showers. Some fixtures, such as toilets or hose bibs, are supplied only by cold water. Appliances include dishwashers and clothes washers. A refrigerator icemaker uses only cold water. Tradition says that hot water supply pipes and faucet handles are found on the left-hand side of a fixture, with cold water on the right.

Because it is pressurized, the water supply system is prone to leaks. This is especially true of galvanized iron pipe, which has limited resistance to corrosion.

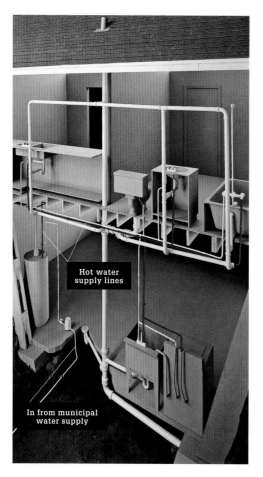

Hot water supply lines

In from municipal water supply

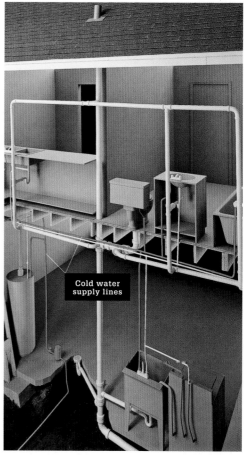

Cold water supply lines

Drain-Waste-Vent System

Drain pipes use gravity to carry waste water away from fixtures, appliances, and other drains. This waste water is carried out of the house to a municipal sewer system or septic tank.

Drain pipes are usually plastic or cast iron. In some older homes, drain pipes may be made of copper or lead. Because they are not part of the supply system, lead drain pipes pose no health hazard. However, lead pipes are no longer manufactured for home plumbing systems.

Drain pipes have diameters ranging from 1¼" to 4". These large diameters allow waste to pass through easily.

Traps are an important part of the drain system. These curved sections of drain pipe hold standing water, and they are usually found near any drain opening. The standing water of a trap prevents sewer gases from backing up into the home. Each time a drain is used, the standing trap water is flushed away and is replaced by new water.

In order to work properly, the drain system requires air. Air allows waste water to flow freely down drain pipes.

To allow air into the drain system, drain pipes are connected to vent pipes. All drain systems must include vents, and the entire system is called the drain-waste-vent (DWV) system. One or more vent stacks, located on the roof, provide the air needed for the DWV system to work.

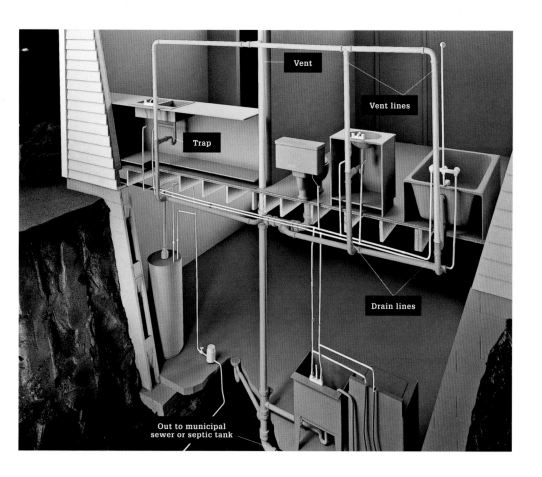

Vent

Vent lines

Trap

Drain lines

Out to municipal sewer or septic tank

Working with Copper Pipe

Copper is the ideal material for water supply pipes. It resists corrosion and has smooth surfaces that provide good water flow. Copper pipes are available in several diameters (page 314), but most home water supply systems use ½" or ¾" pipe. Copper pipe is manufactured in rigid and flexible forms.

Rigid copper, sometimes called hard copper, is approved for home water supply systems by all local codes. It comes in three wall-thickness grades: Types M, L, and K. Type M is the thinnest, the least expensive, and a good choice for do-it-yourself home plumbing.

Rigid Type L usually is required by code for commercial plumbing systems. Because it is strong and solders easily, Type L may be preferred by some professional plumbers and do-it-yourselfers for home use. Type K has the heaviest wall thickness and is used most often for underground water service lines.

Flexible copper, also called soft copper, comes in two wall-thickness grades: Types L and K. Both are approved for most home water supply systems, although flexible Type L copper is used primarily for gas service lines. Because it is bendable and will resist a mild frost, Type L may be installed as part of a water supply system in unheated indoor areas, like crawl spaces. Type K is used for underground water service lines.

A third form of copper, called DWV, is used for drain systems. Because most codes now allow low-cost plastic pipes for drain systems, DWV copper is seldom used.

Copper pipes are connected with soldered, compression, or flare fittings (see chart below). Always follow your local code for the correct types of pipes and fittings allowed in your area.

Soldered fittings, also called sweat fittings, often are used to join copper pipes. Correctly soldered fittings (pages 278 to 280) are strong and trouble-free. Copper pipe can also be joined with compression fittings or flare fittings. See chart below.

Copper Pipe & Fitting Chart ▸

| Fitting Method | Rigid Copper | | | Flexible Copper | | General Comments |
	Type M	Type L	Type K	Type L	Type K	
Soldered	yes	yes	yes	yes	yes	Inexpensive, strong, and trouble-free fitting method. Requires some skill.
Compression	yes	no	no	no	no	Makes repairs and replacement easy. More expensive than solder. Best used on flexible copper.
Flare	no	no	yes	yes	yes	Use only with flexible copper pipes. Usually used as a gas-line fitting. Requires some skill.

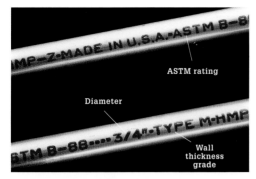

ASTM rating

Diameter

Wall
thickness
grade

Grade stamp information includes the pipe diameter, the wall-thickness grade, and a stamp of approval from the ASTM (American Society for Testing and Materials). Type M pipe (shown) is identified by red lettering, Type L by blue lettering.

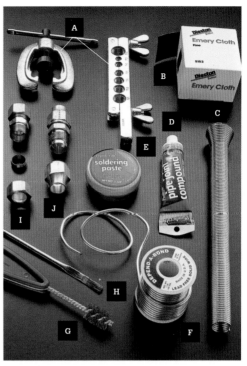

Bend flexible copper pipe with a coil-spring tubing bender to avoid kinks. Select a bender that matches the outside diameter of the pipe. Slip bender over pipe using a twisting motion. Bend pipe slowly until it reaches the correct angle, but not more than 90°.

Specialty tools and materials for working with copper include: flaring tools (A), emery cloth (B), coil-spring tubing bender (C), pipe joint compound (D), soldering paste (flux) (E), lead-free solder (F), wire brush (G), flux brush (H), compression fitting (I), flare fitting (J).

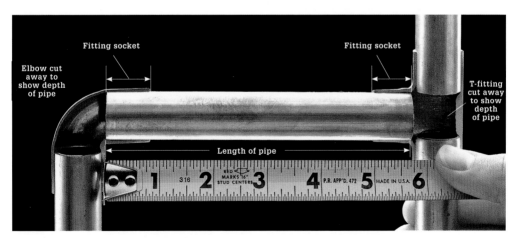

Find the length of copper pipe needed by measuring between the bottom of the copper fitting sockets (fittings shown in cutaway). Mark the length on the pipe with a felt-tipped pen.

Cutting & Soldering Copper

The best way to cut rigid and flexible copper pipe is with a tubing cutter. A tubing cutter makes a smooth, straight cut, an important first step toward making a watertight joint. Remove any metal burrs on the cut edges with a reaming tool or round file.

Copper can be cut with a hacksaw. A hacksaw is useful in tight areas where a tubing cutter will not fit. Take care to make a smooth, straight cut when cutting with a hacksaw.

A soldered pipe joint, also called a sweated joint, is made by heating a copper or brass fitting with a propane torch until the fitting is just hot enough to melt metal solder. The heat draws the solder into the gap between the fitting and pipe to form a watertight seal. A fitting that is overheated or unevenly heated will not draw in solder. Copper pipes and fittings must be clean and dry to form a watertight seal.

Tools & Materials ▸

Tubing cutter with
  reaming tip
  (or hacksaw
  and round file)
Wire brush
Flux brush
Propane torch
Spark lighter
  (or matches)
Round file

Cloth
Adjustable wrench
Channel-type pliers
Copper pipe
Copper fittings
Emery cloth
Soldering paste (flux)
Sheet metal
Lead-free solder
Rag

Protect wood from the heat of the torch flame while soldering, using a double layer (two 18" × 18" pieces) of 26-gauge sheet metal. Buy sheet metal at hardware stores or building supply centers and keep it to use with all soldering projects.

Soldering Tips ▸

Use caution when soldering copper. Pipes and fittings become very hot and must be allowed to cool before handling.

Torch valve

Prevent accidents by shutting off propane torch immediately after use. Make sure valve is closed completely.

How to Cut Rigid & Flexible Copper Pipe

Place the tubing cutter over the pipe and tighten the handle so that the pipe rests on both rollers, and the cutting wheel is on the marked line.

Turn the tubing cutter one rotation so that the cutting wheel scores a continuous straight line around the pipe.

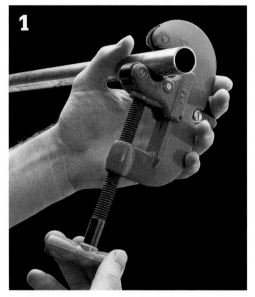

Rotate the cutter in the opposite direction, tightening the handle slightly after every two rotations, until the cut is complete.

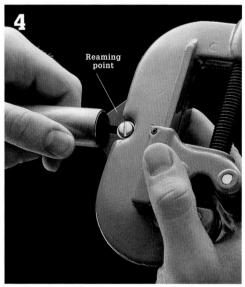

Remove sharp metal burrs from the inside edge of the cut pipe, using the reaming point on the tubing cutter, or a round file.

How to Solder Copper Pipes & Fittings

Clean the end of each pipe by sanding with emery cloth. Ends must be free of dirt and grease to ensure that the solder forms a good seal.

Clean the inside of each fitting by scouring with a wire brush or emery cloth.

Apply a thin layer of soldering paste (flux) to end of each pipe, using a flux brush. Soldering paste should cover about 1" of pipe end.

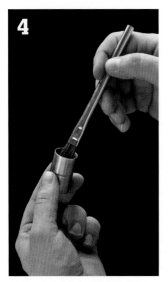

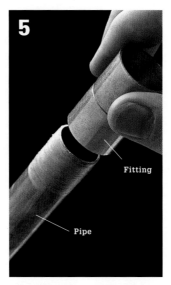

Apply a thin layer of flux to the inside of the fitting.

Assemble each joint by inserting the pipe into the fitting so it is tight against the bottom of the fitting sockets. Twist each fitting slightly to spread soldering paste.

Use a clean dry cloth to remove excess flux before soldering the assembled fitting.

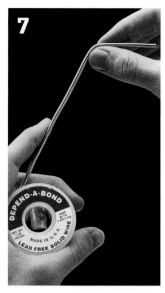

Prepare the wire solder by unwinding 8" to 10" of wire from spool. Bend the first 2" of the wire to a 90° angle.

Open the gas valve and trigger the spark lighter to ignite the torch.

Adjust the torch valve until the inner portion of the flame is 1" to 2" long.

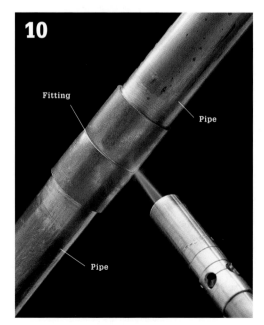

Fitting

Pipe

Pipe

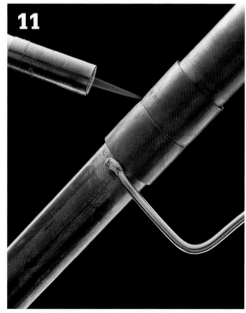

Move the torch flame back and forth and around the pipe and the fitting to heat the area evenly.

Heat the other side of the copper fitting to ensure that heat is distributed evenly. Touch solder to pipe. Solder will melt when the pipe is at the right temperature.

(continued)

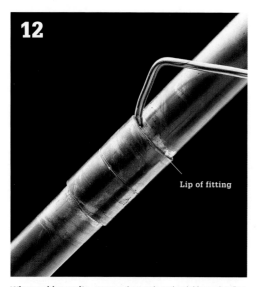

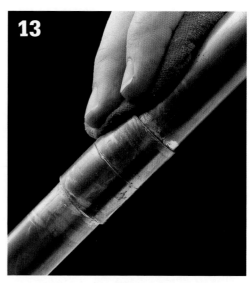

Lip of fitting

When solder melts, remove the torch and quickly push ½" to ¾" of solder into each joint. Capillary action fills the joint with liquid solder. A correctly soldered joint should show a thin bead of solder around the lips of the fitting.

Allow the joint to cool briefly, then wipe away excess solder with a dry rag. *Caution: Pipes will be hot.* If joints leak after water is turned on, disassemble and resolder.

How to Solder Brass Valves

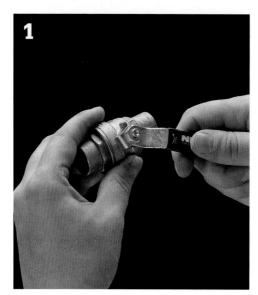

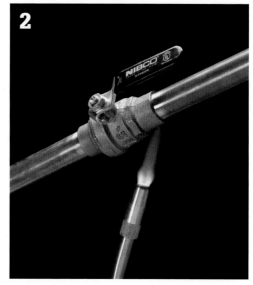

Valves should be fully open during all stages of the soldering process.

To prevent valve damage, quickly heat the pipe and the flanges of the valve, not the valve body. After soldering, cool the valve by spraying with water.

How to Take Apart Soldered Joints

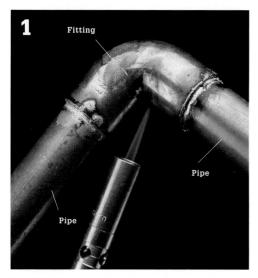

1

Fitting

Pipe

Pipe

Turn off the water and drain the pipes by opening the highest and lowest faucets in the house. Light your torch. Hold the flame tip to the fitting until the solder becomes shiny and begins to melt.

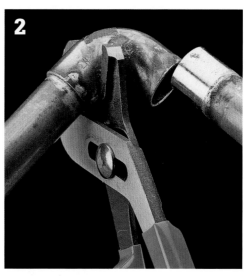

2

Use channel-type pliers to separate the pipes from the fitting.

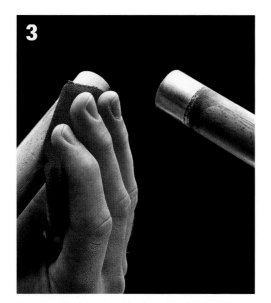

3

Remove old solder by heating the ends of the pipe with your torch. Use a dry rag to wipe away melted solder quickly. *Caution: Pipes will be hot.*

4

Use emery cloth to polish the ends of the pipe down to bare metal. Never reuse fittings.

Working with Plastic Pipe

Cut rigid ABS, PVC, or CPVC plastic pipes with a tubing cutter or with any saw. Cuts must be straight to ensure watertight joints.

Rigid plastics are joined with plastic fittings and solvent glue. Use a solvent glue that is made for the type of plastic pipe you are installing. For example, use ABS solvent on ABS pipe. Some solvent glues, called "all-purpose" or "universal" solvents, may be used on all types of plastic pipe, but create an inferior bond.

Solvent glue hardens in about 30 seconds, so test-fit all plastic pipes and fittings before gluing the first joint. For best results, the surfaces of plastic pipes and fittings should be dulled with emery cloth and liquid primer before they are joined.

Liquid solvent glues and primers are toxic and flammable. Provide adequate ventilation when fitting plastics, and store the products away from any source of heat.

Plastic grip fittings can be used to join rigid or flexible plastic pipes to copper plumbing pipes.

Tools & Materials ▸

Tape measure	Plastic pipe
Felt-tipped pen	Fittings
Tubing cutter	Emery cloth
(or miter box	Plastic pipe primer
or hacksaw)	Solvent glue
Utility knife	Rag
Channel-type pliers	Petroleum jelly
Gloves	

Solvent welding is a chemical bonding process used to permanently join PVC pipes and fittings.

Primer and solvent glue are specific to the plumbing material being used. Do not use all-purpose or multi-purpose products. Light to medium body glues are appropriate for DIYers as they allow the longest working time and are easiest to use. The products work best when fresh, so buy small containers and dispose of any unused product after a few months.

How to Cut Rigid Plastic Pipe

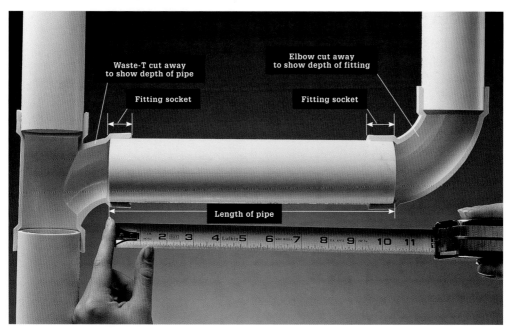

Find the length of plastic pipe needed by measuring between the bottoms of the fitting sockets (fittings shown in cutaway). Mark the length on the pipe with a felt-tipped pen.

The best cutting tool for plastic pipe is a power miter saw with a fine tooth woodworking blade or a plastic-specific blade.

A ratcheting plastic-pipe cutter can cut smaller diameter PVC and CPVC pipe in a real hurry. If you are plumbing a whole house you may want to consider investing in one. They also are sold only at plumbing supply stores.

How to Solvent-Glue Rigid Plastic Pipe

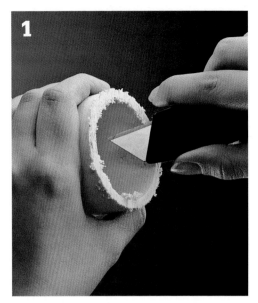

Remove rough burrs on cut ends of plastic pipe, using a utility knife.

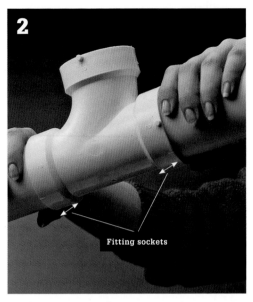

Fitting sockets

Test-fit all pipes and fittings. Pipes should fit tightly against the bottom of the fitting sockets.

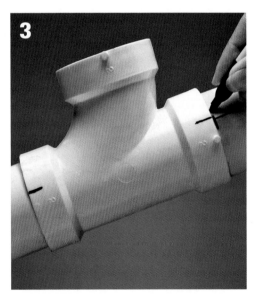

Mark the depth of the fitting sockets on the pipes. Take pipes apart. Clean the ends of the pipes and fitting sockets with emery cloth.

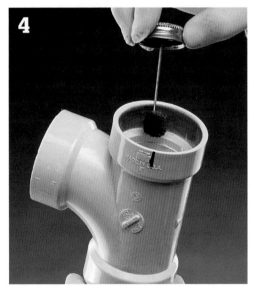

Apply a light coat of plastic pipe primer to the ends of the pipes and to the insides of the fitting sockets. Primer dulls glossy surfaces and ensures a good seal.

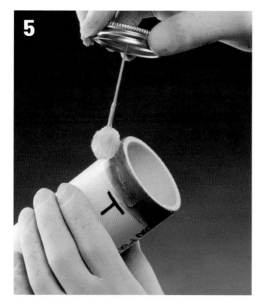

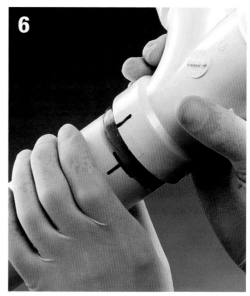

Solvent-glue each joint by applying a thick coat of solvent glue to the end of the pipe. Apply a thin coat of solvent glue to the inside surface of the fitting socket. Work quickly: solvent glue hardens in about 30 seconds.

Quickly position the pipe and fitting so that the alignment marks are offset by about 2". Force the pipe into the fitting until the end fits flush against the bottom of the socket.

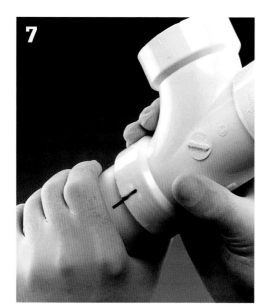

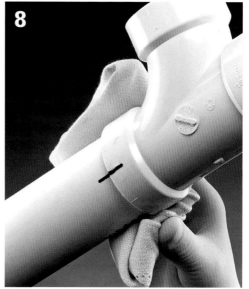

Spread solvent by twisting the pipe until the marks are aligned. Hold the pipe in place for about 20 seconds to prevent the joint from slipping.

Wipe away excess solvent glue with a rag. Do not disturb the joint for 30 minutes after gluing.

Working with PEX Pipe

Cross-linked polyethylene (PEX) is growing quickly in acceptance as a supply pipe for residential plumbing. It's not hard to understand why. Developed in the 1960s but relatively new to the United States, this supply pipe combines the ease of use of flexible tubing with the durability of rigid pipe. It can withstand a wide temperature range (from subfreezing to 180° F); it is inexpensive; and it's quieter than rigid supply pipe.

PEX is flexible plastic (polyethylene, or PE) tubing that's reinforced by a chemical reaction that creates long fibers to increase the strength of the material. It has been allowed by code in Europe and the southern United States for many years, but has won approval for residential supply use in most major plumbing codes only recently. It's frequently used in manufactured housing and recreational vehicles and in radiant heating systems. Because it is so flexible, PEX can easily be bent to follow corners and make other changes in direction. From the water main and heater, it is connected into manifold fittings that redistribute the water in much the same manner as a lawn irrigation system.

For standard residential installations, PEX can be joined with very simple fittings and tools. Unions are generally made with a crimping tool and a crimping ring. You simply insert the ends of the pipe you're joining into the ring, then clamp down on the ring with the crimping tool. PEX pipe, tools, and fittings can be purchased from most wholesale plumbing suppliers and at many home centers. Coils of PEX are sold in several diameters from ¼" to 1". PEX tubing and fittings from different manufacturers are not interchangeable. Any warranty coverage will be voided if products are mixed.

Tools & Materials ▸

Tape measure	Manifolds
Felt-tipped pen	Protector plates
Full-circle crimping tool	PEX fittings
Go/no-go gauge	Utility knife
Tubing cutter	Plastic hangers
PEX pipe	Crimp ring

PEX pipe is a relatively new water supply material that's growing in popularity, in part because it can be installed with simple mechanical connections. In this example, we see a standard 4-outlet copper manifold, with branch water lines being attached with a crimping tool. To ensure leak-free joints, each joint is carefully measured with a go/no-go tool before the water is turned on.

PEX Tools & Materials

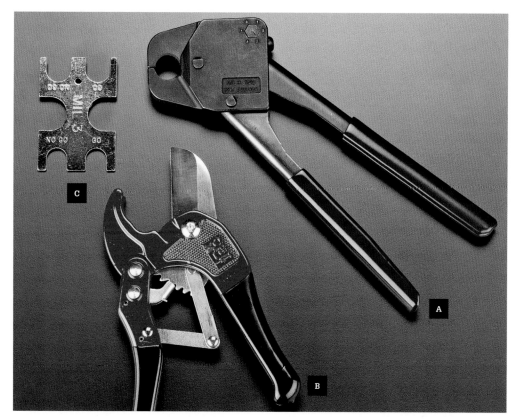

Specialty tools for installing PEX are available wherever PEX is sold. The basic set includes a full-circle crimping tool (A), a tubing cutter (B), and a go/no-go gauge (C) to test connections after they've been crimped.

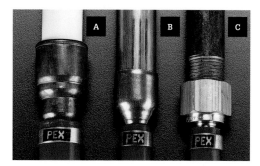

PEX is connected to other water supply materials with transition fittings, including CPVC-to-PEX (A), copper-to-PEX (B), and iron-to-PEX (C).

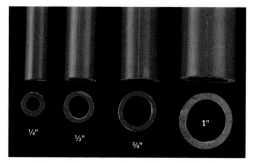

Generally, you should use the same diameter PEX as is specified for rigid supply tubing, but in some "home run" installations (see page 72) you can use ⅜" PEX where ½" rigid copper would normally be used.

PEX Installation

Check with your local plumbing inspector to verify that PEX is allowed in your municipality. PEX has been endorsed by all major plumbing codes in North America, but your municipality may still be using an older set of codes. Follow the guidelines below when installing PEX:

- Do not install PEX in above-ground exterior applications because it degrades quickly from UV exposure.
- Do not use PEX for gas lines.
- Do not use plastic solvents or petroleum-based products with PEX (they can dissolve the plastic).
- Keep PEX at least 12" away from recessed light fixtures and other potential sources of high heat.

- Do not attach PEX directly to a water heater. Make connections at the heater with metallic tubing (either flexible water-heater connector tubing or rigid copper) at least 18" long; then join it to PEX with a transition fitting.
- Do not install PEX in areas where there is a possibility of mechanical damage or puncture. Always fasten protective plates to wall studs that house PEX.
- Always leave some slack in installed PEX lines to allow for contraction and in case you need to cut off a bad crimp.
- Use the same minimum branch and distribution supply-pipe dimensions for PEX that you'd use for copper or CPVC, according to your local plumbing codes.

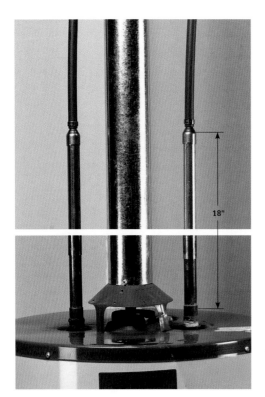

Do not connect PEX directly to a water heater. Use metal connector tubes. Solder the connector tubes to the water heater before attaching PEX. Never solder metal tubing that is already connected to PEX lines.

Bundle PEX together with plastic ties when running pipe through wall cavities. PEX can contract slightly, so leave some slack in the lines.

Buying PEX

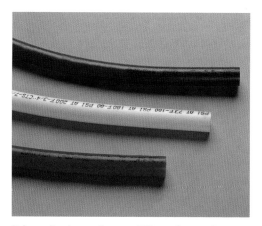

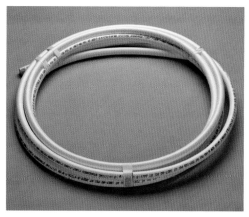

Color coding is a practice many PEX manufacturers have embraced to make identification easier. Because the material is identical except for the color, you can buy only one color (red is more common) and use it for both hot and cold supply lines.

PEX combines the flexibility of plastic tubing with the durability of rigid supply pipe. It is sold in coils of common supply-pipe diameters.

The PEX Advantage ▶

PEX supply tubing offers a number of advantages over traditional rigid supply tubing:

- Easy to install. PEX does not require coupling joints for long runs or elbows and sweeps for turns. The mechanical connections do not require solvents or soldering.
- Easy to transport. Large coils are lightweight and much easier to move around than 10-ft. lengths of pipe.
- Good insulation. The PEX material has better thermal properties than copper for lessened heat loss.

- Quiet. PEX will not rattle or clang from trapped air or kinetic energy.
- Good for retrofit jobs. PEX is easier to snake through walls than rigid supply tubing and is compatible with copper, PVC, or iron supply systems if the correct transition fittings are used. If your metal supply tubes are used to ground your electrical system, you'll need to provide a jumper if PEX is installed in midrun. Check with a plumber or electrician.
- Freeze resistance. PEX retains some flexibility in sub-freezing conditions and is less likely to be damaged than rigid pipe, but it is not frostproof.

General Codes for PEX ▶

PEX has been endorsed for residential use by all major building codes, although some municipal codes may be more restrictive. The specific design standards may also vary, but here are some general rules:

- For PEX, maximum horizontal support spacing is 32" and maximum vertical support spacing is 10 ft.

- Maximum length of individual distribution lines is 60 ft.
- PEX is designed to withstand 210° F water for up to 48 hours. For ongoing use, most PEX is rated for 180 degree water up to 100 pounds per square inch of pressure.
- Directional changes of more than 90 degrees require a guide fitting (see page 75).

System Designs

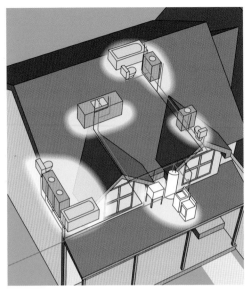

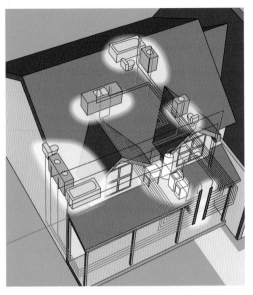

Trunk-and-branch systems are configured in much the same way as a traditional rigid copper or PVC supply systems. A main supply line (the trunk line) carries water to all of the outlets via smaller branch lines that tie into the trunk and serve a few outlets in a common location.

Home run systems rely on one or two central manifolds to distribute the hot and cold water very efficiently. Eliminating the branch fittings allows you to use thinner supply pipe in some situations.

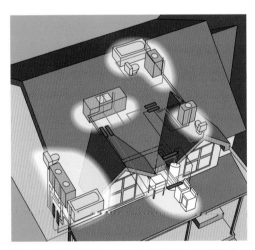

Remote manifold systems are a hybrid between traditional trunk-and-branch systems and home run systems. Instead of relying on just one or two manifolds, they employ several smaller manifolds downline from a larger manifold. Each smaller manifold services a group of fixtures, as in a bathroom or kitchen.

Choosing a PEX system ▸

- For maximum single-fixture water pressure: Trunk and branch
- For economy of materials: Trunk and branch or remote manifold
- For minimal wait times for hot water (single fixture): Home run
- For minimal wait times for hot water (multiple fixtures used at same approximate time): Trunk and branch or remote manifold
- For ease of shutoff control: Home run
- For lowest number of fittings and joints: Home run

How to Make PEX Connections

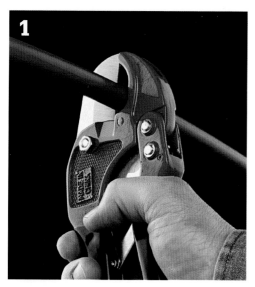

1

Cut the pipe to length, making sure to leave enough extra material so the line will have a small amount of slack once the connections are made. A straight, clean cut is very important. For best results, use a tubing cutter.

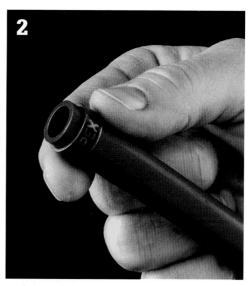

2

Inspect the cut end to make sure it is clean and smooth. If necessary, deburr the end of the pipe with a sharp utility knife. Slip a crimp ring over the end.

3

Insert the barbed end of the fitting into the pipe until it is snug against the cut edges. Position the crimp ring so it is ⅛" to ¼" from the end of the pipe, covering the barbed end of the fitting. Pinch the fitting to hold it in place.

4

Align the jaws of a full-circle crimping tool over the crimp ring and squeeze the handles together to apply strong, even pressure to the ring.

5

Test the connection to make sure it is mechanically acceptable, using a go/no-go gauge. If the ring does not fit into the gauge properly, cut the pipe near the connection and try again.

How to Plumb a PEX Water-Supply System

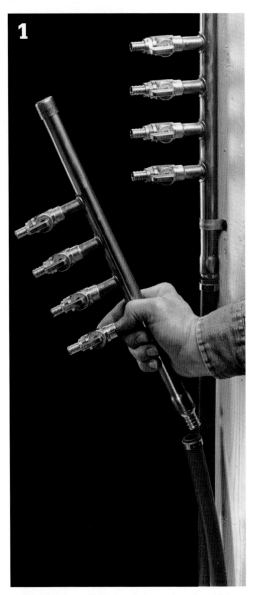

Install copper manifolds (one for hot and one for cold) in an accessible location central to the fixtures. The manifold should have one outlet for each supply line it will support (fixtures that require hot and cold supply will need a separate outlet for each). Run supply lines from the water heater and water main to the copper manifolds. Connect the supply pipes to the manifolds with crimp fittings.

A manifold may be attached vertically or horizontally, but it must be anchored with correctly sized hangers screwed to the framing members.

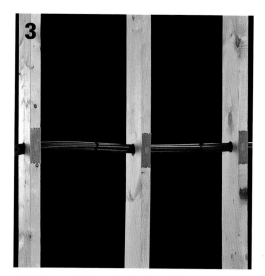

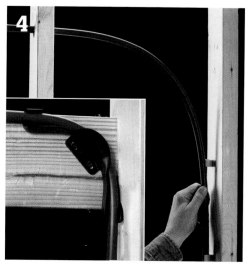

Starting at each fixture (and leaving at least 12" of extra pipe exposed), run appropriately sized PEX through holes in the framing to the manifolds. Pipes may be bundled together loosely with plastic ties. Protect the line with a nailing plate at each stud location. Be sure to leave some slack in the supply lines.

Support the pipe with a plastic hanger near every floor or ceiling and midway up vertical runs. Also use hangers to guide pipe near the beginnings and ends of curves and near fittings. Use a plastic guide for sharp curves (inset). Do not bend PEX so sharply that it kinks.

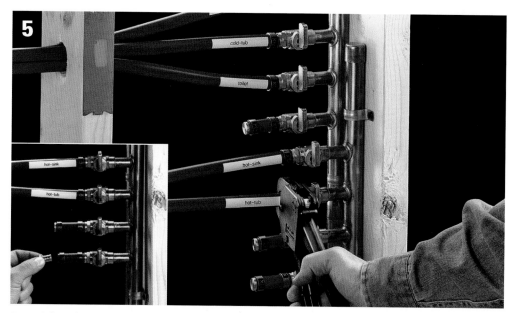

Cut each branch supply line to length (leave some extra in case you need to recrimp). Install shutoff valves for each outlet (most manifolds come with preattached valves). Connect the PEX branch supply lines to the shutoff valves. Label each pipe. Use a short length of PEX and a plug to seal any unused outlets (inset).

Planning New Plumbing

Start planning by drawing maps. Mapping your home's plumbing system is a good way to familiarize yourself with the plumbing layout and can help you when planning plumbing renovation projects. With a good map, you can envision the best spots for new fixtures and plan new pipe routes more efficiently. Maps also help in emergencies, when you need to locate burst or leaking pipes quickly.

Draw a plumbing map for each floor on tracing paper, so you can overlay floors and still read the information below. Make your drawings to scale and have all plumbing fixtures marked. Fixture templates and tracing paper are available at drafting supply stores.

Snoop around your basement for clues about the locations of supply, drain, vent, and gas pipes in your walls.

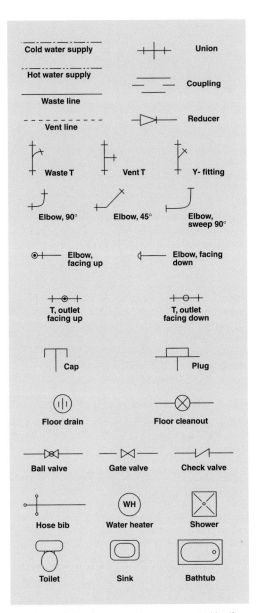

Use standard plumbing symbols on your map to identify the components of your plumbing system. These symbols will help you and your building inspector follow connections and transitions more easily.

Understanding Plumbing Codes

The plumbing code is the set of regulations that building officials and inspectors use to evaluate your project plans and the quality of your work. Codes vary from region to region, but most are based on the National Uniform Plumbing Code, the authority we used in the development of this book.

Code books are available for reference at bookstores and government offices. However, they are highly technical, difficult-to-read manuals. More user-friendly for do-it-yourselfers are the variety of code handbooks available at bookstores and libraries. These handbooks are based on the National Uniform Plumbing Code but are easier to read and include many helpful diagrams and photos.

Plumbing code handbooks sometimes discuss three different plumbing "zones" in an effort to accommodate variations in regulations from state to state. The states included in each zone are listed below.

Zone 1: Washington, Oregon, California, Nevada, Idaho, Montana, Wyoming, North Dakota, South Dakota, Minnesota, Iowa, Wisconsin, Nebraska, Kansas, Utah, Arizona, Colorado, New Mexico, Indiana, parts of Texas.

Zone 2: Alabama, Arkansas, Louisiana, Tennessee, North Carolina, Mississippi, Georgia, Florida, South Carolina, parts of Texas, parts of Maryland, parts of Delaware, parts of Oklahoma, parts of West Virginia.

Zone 3: Virginia, Kentucky, Missouri, Illinois, Michigan, Ohio, Pennsylvania, New York, Connecticut, Massachusetts, Vermont, New Hampshire, Rhode Island, New Jersey, parts of Delaware, parts of West Virginia, parts of Maine, parts of Maryland, parts of Oklahoma.

Remember that your local plumbing code always supersedes the national code. Local codes may be more restrictive than the national code. Your local building inspector is a valuable source of information and may provide you with a convenient summary sheet of the regulations that apply to your project.

The plumbing inspector is the final authority when it comes to evaluating your work. By visually examining and testing your new plumbing, the inspector ensures that your work is safe and functional.

GETTING A PERMIT

To ensure public safety, your community requires that you obtain a permit for most plumbing projects, including most of the projects demonstrated in this book.

When you visit your city building inspection office to apply for a permit, the building official will want to review three drawings of your plumbing project: a site plan, a water supply diagram, and a drain-waste-vent diagram. These drawings are described on this page. If the official is satisfied that your project meets code requirements, he or she will issue you a plumbing permit, which is your legal permission to begin work. The building official also will specify an inspection schedule for your project. As your project nears completion, you will be asked to arrange for an inspector to visit your home while the pipes are exposed to review the installation and ensure its safety.

Although do-it-yourselfers often complete complex plumbing projects without obtaining a permit or having the work inspected, we strongly urge you to comply with the legal requirements in your area. A flawed plumbing system can be dangerous, and it can potentially threaten the value of your home.

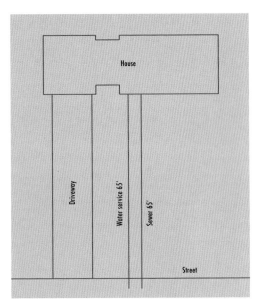

The site plan shows the location of the water main and sewer main with respect to your yard and home. The distances from your foundation to the water main and from the foundation to the main sewer should be indicated on the site plan.

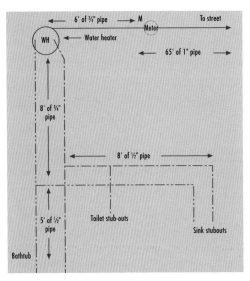

The supply riser diagram shows the length of the hot and cold water pipes and the relation of the fixtures to one another. The inspector will use this diagram to determine the proper size for the new water supply pipes in your system.

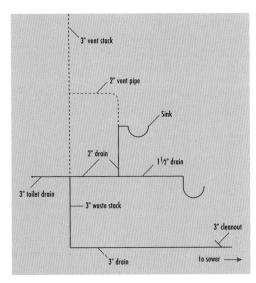

A DWV diagram shows the routing of drain and vent pipes in your system. Make sure to indicate the lengths of drain pipes and the distances between fixtures. The inspector will use this diagram to determine if you have properly sized the drain traps, drain pipes, and vent pipes in your project.

Sizing for Water Distribution Pipes

Fixture	Unit rating	Size of service pipe from street	Size of distribution pipe from water meter	Maximum length (ft.)— total fixture units					
				40	60	80	100	150	200
Toilet	3	¾"	½"	9	8	7	6	5	4
Vanity sink	1	¾"	¾"	27	23	19	17	14	11
Shower	2	¾"	1"	44	40	36	33	28	23
Bathtub	2	1"	1"	60	47	41	36	30	25
Dishwasher	2	1"	1¼"	102	87	76	67	52	44
Kitchen sink	2								
Clothes washer	2								
Utility sink	2								
Sillcock	3								

Water distribution pipes are the main pipes extending from the water meter throughout the house, supplying water to the branch pipes leading to individual fixtures. To determine the size of the distribution pipes, you must first calculate the total demand in "fixture units" (above, left) and the overall length of the water supply lines, from the street hookup through the water meter and to the most distant fixture in the house. Then, use the second table (above, middle) to find the minimum size for the water distribution pipes. Note that the fixture unit capacity depends partly on the size of the street-side pipe that delivers water to your meter.

Sizes for Branch Pipes & Supply Tubes

Fixture	Min. branch pipe size	Min. supply tube size
Toilet	½"	⅜"
Vanity sink	½"	⅜"
Shower	½"	½"
Bathtub	½"	½"
Dishwasher	½"	½"
Kitchen sink	½"	½"
Clothes washer	½"	½"
Utility sink	½"	½"
Sillcock	¾"	N.A.
Water heater	¾"	N.A.

Branch pipes are the water supply lines that run from the distribution pipes toward the individual fixtures. Supply tubes are the vinyl, chromed copper, or braided tubes that carry water from the branch pipes to the fixtures. Use the chart above as a guide when sizing branch pipes and supply tubes.

Valve Requirements

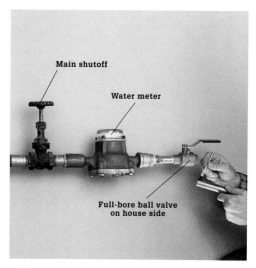

Main shutoff

Water meter

Full-bore ball valve on house side

Full-bore gate valves or ball valves are required in the following locations: on both the street side and house side of the water meter; on the inlet pipes for water heaters and heating system boilers. Individual fixtures should have accessible shutoff valves, but these need not be full-bore valves. All sillcocks must have individual control valves located inside the house.

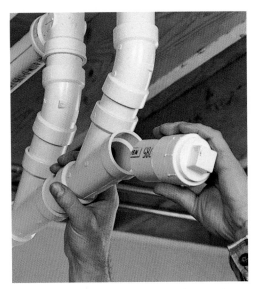

Pipe Support Intervals		
Type of pipe	Vertical-run support interval	Horizontal-run support interval
Copper	10 ft.	6 ft.
PEX	5 ft.	3 ft.
CPVC	10 ft.	3 ft.
PVC	10 ft.	4 ft.
Steel	12 ft.	10 ft.
Iron	15 ft.	5 ft.

Drain cleanouts make your DWV system easier to service. In most areas, the plumbing code requires that you place cleanouts at the end of every horizontal drain run. Where horizontal runs are not accessible, removable drain traps will suffice as cleanouts.

Minimum intervals for supporting pipes are determined by the type of pipe and its orientation in the system. Remember that the measurements shown above are minimum requirements; local code may require supports at closer intervals.

▌Fixture Units & Minimum Trap Size

Fixture	Fixture units	Min. trap size
Shower	2	2"
Vanity sink	1	1¼"
Bathtub	2	1½"
Dishwasher	2	1½"
Kitchen sink	2	1½"
Kitchen sink*	3	1½"
Clothes washer	2	1½"
Utility sink	2	1½"
Floor drain	1	2"

*Kitchen sink with attached food disposer

Minimum trap size for fixtures is determined by the drain fixture unit rating, a unit of measure assigned by the plumbing code. *Note: Kitchen sinks rate 3 units if they include an attached food disposer, 2 units otherwise.*

▌Sizes for Horizontal & Vertical Drain Pipes

Pipe size	Maximum fixture units for horizontal branch drain	Maximum fixture units for vertical drain stacks
1¼"	1	2
1½"	3	4
2"	6	10
2½"	12	20
3"	20	30
4"	160	240

Drain pipe sizes are determined by the load on the pipes, as measured by the total fixture units. Horizontal drain pipes less than 3" in diameter should slope ¼" per foot toward the main drain. Pipes 3" or more in diameter should slope ⅛" per foot. *Note: Horizontal or vertical drain pipes for a toilet must be 3" or larger.*

Vent Pipe Sizes, Critical Distances

Size of fixture drain	Minimum vent pipe size	Maximum critical distance
1¼"	1¼"	2½ ft.
1½"	1¼"	3½ ft.
2"	1½"	5 ft.
3"	2"	6 ft.
4"	3"	10 ft.

Vent pipes are usually one pipe size smaller than the drain pipes they serve. Code requires that the distance between the drain trap and the vent pipe fall within a maximum "critical distance," a measurement that is determined by the size of the fixture drain. Use this chart to determine both the minimum size for the vent pipe and the maximum critical distance.

Vent Pipe Orientation to Drain Pipe

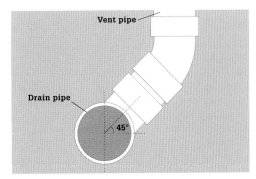

Vent pipes must extend in an upward direction from drains, no less than 45° from horizontal. This ensures that waste water cannot flow into the vent pipe and block it. At the opposite end, a new vent pipe should connect to an existing vent pipe or main waste-vent stack at a point at least 6" above the highest fixture draining into the system.

Wet Venting

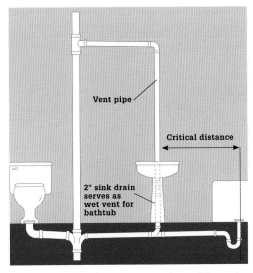

Wet vents are pipes that serve as a vent for one fixture and a drain for another. The sizing of a wet vent is based on the total fixture units it supports (opposite page): a 3" wet vent can serve up to 12 fixture units; a 2" wet vent is rated for 4 fixture units; a 1½" wet vent, for only 1 fixture unit. *Note: The distance between the wet-vented fixture and the wet vent itself must be no more than the maximum critical distance (chart above).*

Auxiliary Venting

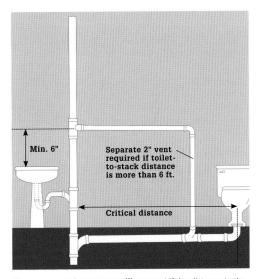

Fixtures must have an auxiliary vent if the distance to the main waste-vent stack exceeds the critical distance (illustration above). A toilet, for example, should have a separate vent pipe if it is located more than 6 ft. from the main waste-vent stack. This secondary vent pipe should connect to the stack or an existing vent pipe at a point at least 6" above the highest fixture on the system.

Understanding Wiring

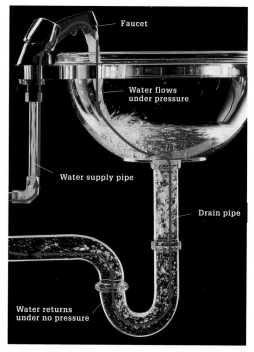

Faucet

Water flows under pressure

Water supply pipe

Drain pipe

Water returns under no pressure

A household electrical system can be compared with a home's plumbing system. Electrical current flows in wires in much the same way that water flows inside pipes. Both electricity and water enter the home, are distributed throughout the house, do their "work," and exit.

In plumbing, water first flows through the pressurized water supply system. In electricity, current first flows along hot wires. Current flowing along hot wires also is pressurized. The pressure of electrical current is called *voltage*.

Large supply pipes can carry a greater volume of water than small pipes. Likewise, large electrical wires carry more current than small wires. This current-carrying capacity of wires is called *amperage*.

Water is made available for use through the faucets, spigots, and showerheads in a home. Electricity is made available through receptacles, switches, and fixtures.

Water finally leaves the home through a drain system, which is not pressurized. Similarly, electrical current flows back through neutral wires. The current in neutral wires is not pressurized and is said to be at zero voltage.

Water and electricity both flow. The main difference is that you can see water (and touching water isn't likely to kill you). Like electricity, water enters a fixture under high pressure and exits under low pressure.

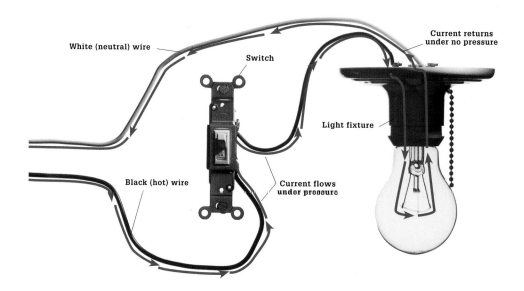

Current returns under no pressure

White (neutral) wire

Switch

Light fixture

Black (hot) wire

Current flows under pressure

The Delivery System

Electrical power that enters the home is produced by large power plants. Power plants are located in all parts of the country and generate electricity with turbines that are turned by water, wind, or steam. From these plants electricity enters large "step-up" transformers that increase voltage to half a million volts or more.

Electricity flows easily at these large voltages and travels through high-voltage transmission lines to communities that can be hundreds of miles from the power plants. "Step-down" transformers located at substations then reduce the voltage for distribution along street lines. On utility power poles, smaller transformers further reduce the voltage to ordinary 120-volt current for household use.

Lines carrying current to the house either run underground or strung overhead and attached to a post called a service mast. Most homes built after 1950 have three wires running to the service head: two power lines, each carrying 120 volts of current, and a grounded neutral wire. Power from the two 120-volt lines may be combined at the service panel to supply current to large 240-volt appliances like clothes dryers or electric water heaters.

Incoming power passes through an electric meter that measures power consumption. Power then enters the service panel, where it is distributed to circuits that run throughout the house. The service panel also contains fuses or circuit breakers that shut off power to the individual circuits in the event of a short circuit or an overload. Certain high-wattage appliances, like microwave ovens, are usually plugged into their own individual circuits to prevent overloads.

Voltage ratings determined by power companies and manufacturers have changed over the years. Current rated at 110 volts changed to 115 volts, then 120 volts. Current rated at 220 volts changed to 230 volts, then 240 volts. Similarly, ratings for receptacles, tools, light fixtures, and appliances have changed from 115 volts to 125 volts. These changes do not affect the performance of new devices connected to older wiring. For making electrical calculations, use a rating of 120 volts or 240 volts for your circuits.

Power plants supply electricity to thousands of homes and businesses. Step-up transformers increase the voltage produced at the plant, making the power flow more easily along high-voltage transmission lines.

Substations are located near the communities they serve. A typical substation takes current from high-voltage transmission lines and reduces it for distribution along street lines.

Utility pole transformers reduce the high-voltage current that flows through power lines along neighborhood streets. A utility pole transformer reduces voltage from 10,000 volts to the normal 120-volt current used in households.

Parts of the Electrical System

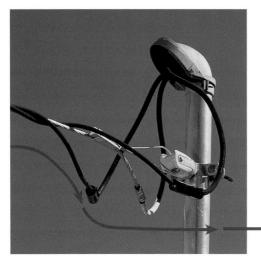

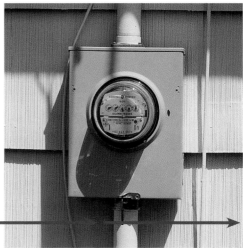

The service mast is the metal pole and weatherhead that create the entry point for electricity into your home. The mast is supplied with two wires carrying 120 volts and a third grounded neutral wire. The current runs to the service mast from the nearest transformer.

The electric meter measures the amount of electrical power consumed. It is usually attached to the side of the house, and connects to the service mast. A thin metal disc inside the meter rotates when power is used. The electric meter belongs to your local power utility company. If you suspect the meter is not functioning properly, contact the power company.

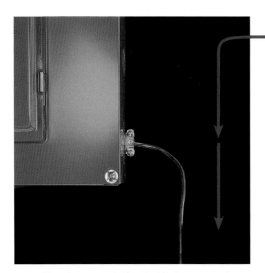

Grounding wire connects the electrical system to the earth through grounding rods or, in older systems, through a cold water pipe. In the event of an overload or short circuit, the grounding wire allows excess electrical power to find its way harmlessly to the earth.

Light fixtures attach directly to a household electrical system. They are usually controlled with wall switches. The two most common types of light fixtures are incandescent and fluorescent.

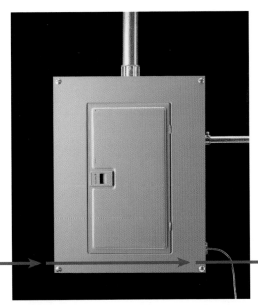

The main service panel, in the form of a fuse box or breaker box, distributes power to individual circuits. Fuses or circuit breakers protect each circuit from short circuits and overloads. Fuses and circuit breakers also are used to shut off power to individual circuits while repairs are made.

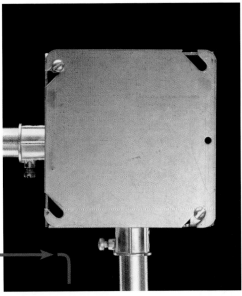

Electrical boxes enclose wire connections. According to the National Electrical Code, all wire splices or connections must be contained entirely in a covered plastic or metal electrical box.

Switches control electrical current passing through hot circuit wires. Switches can be wired to control light fixtures, ceiling fans, appliances, and receptacles.

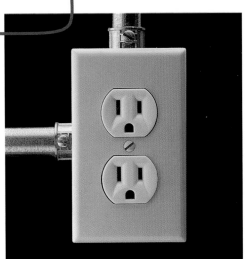

Receptacles, sometimes called outlets, provide plug-in access to electrical power. A 120-volt, 15-amp receptacle with a grounding hole is the most typical receptacle in wiring systems installed after 1965. Most receptacles have two plug-in locations and are called *duplex receptacles.*

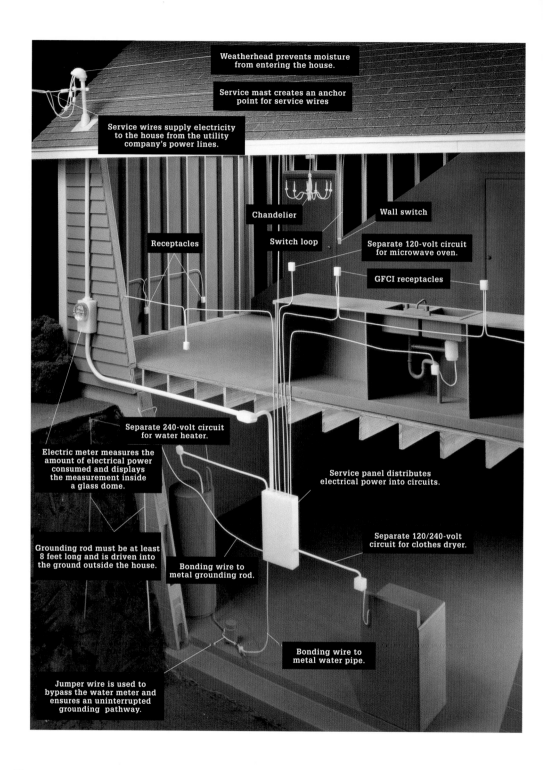

Weatherhead prevents moisture from entering the house.

Service mast creates an anchor point for service wires

Service wires supply electricity to the house from the utility company's power lines.

Chandelier

Wall switch

Receptacles

Switch loop

Separate 120-volt circuit for microwave oven.

GFCI receptacles

Separate 240-volt circuit for water heater.

Electric meter measures the amount of electrical power consumed and displays the measurement inside a glass dome.

Service panel distributes electrical power into circuits.

Separate 120/240-volt circuit for clothes dryer.

Grounding rod must be at least 8 feet long and is driven into the ground outside the house.

Bonding wire to metal grounding rod.

Bonding wire to metal water pipe.

Jumper wire is used to bypass the water meter and ensures an uninterrupted grounding pathway.

Glossary of Electrical Terms ▸

Ampere (or amp): Refers to the rate at which electrical power flows to a light, tool, or appliance.

Armored cable: Two or more wires that are grouped together and protected by a flexible metal covering.

Box: A device used to contain wiring connections.

BX: See armored cable (Bx is the older term).

Cable: Two or more wires that are grouped together and protected by a covering or sheath.

Circuit: A continuous loop of electrical current flowing along wires or cables.

Circuit breaker: A safety device that interrupts an electrical circuit in the event of an overload or short circuit.

Conductor: Any material that allows electrical current to flow through it. Copper wire is an especially good conductor.

Conduit: A metal or plastic pipe used to protect wires.

Continuity: An uninterrupted electrical pathway through a circuit or electrical fixture.

Current: The movement of electrons along a conductor.

Duplex receptacle: A receptacle that provides connections for two plugs.

Feed wire: A conductor that carries 120-volt current uninterrupted from the service panel.

Fuse: A safety device, usually found in older homes, that interrupts electrical circuits during an overload or short circuit.

Greenfield: Materials used in flexible metal conduit. See armored cable.

Grounded wire: See neutral wire.

Grounding wire: A wire used in an electrical circuit to conduct current to the earth in the event of a short circuit. The grounding wire often is a bare copper wire.

Hot wire: Any wire that carries voltage. In an electrical circuit, the hot wire usually is covered with black or red insulation.

Insulator: Any material, such as plastic or rubber, that resists the flow of electrical current. Insulating materials protect wires and cables.

Junction box: See box.

Meter: A device used to measure the amount of electrical power being used.

Neutral wire: A wire that returns current at zero voltage to the source of electrical power. Usually covered with white or light gray insulation. Also called the grounded wire.

Outlet: See receptacle.

Overload: A demand for more current than the circuit wires or electrical device was designed to carry. Usually causes a fuse to blow or a circuit breaker to trip.

Pigtail: A short wire used to connect two or more circuit wires to a single screw terminal.

Polarized receptacle: A receptacle designed to keep hot current flowing along black or red wires, and neutral current flowing along white or gray wires.

Power: The result of hot current flowing for a period of time. Use of power makes heat, motion, or light.

Receptacle: A device that provides plug-in access to electrical power.

Romex: A brand name of plastic-sheathed electrical cable that is commonly used for indoor wiring. Commonly known as NM cable.

Screw terminal: A place where a wire connects to a receptacle, switch, or fixture.

Service panel: A metal box usually near the site where electrical power enters the house. In the service panel, electrical current is split into individual circuits. The service panel has circuit breakers or fuses to protect each circuit.

Short circuit: An accidental and improper contact between two current-carrying wires, or between a current-carrying wire and a grounding conductor.

Switch: A device that controls electrical current passing through hot circuit wires. Used to turn lights and appliances on and off.

UL: An abbreviation for Underwriters Laboratories, an organization that tests electrical devices and manufactured products for safety.

Voltage (or volts): A measurement of electricity in terms of pressure.

Wattage (or watt): A measurement of electrical power in terms of total energy consumed. Watts can be calculated by multiplying the voltage times the amps.

Wire connector: A device used to connect two or more wires together. Also called a *wire nut*.

Wiring Safety

Safety should be the primary concern of anyone working with electricity. Although most household electrical repairs are simple and straightforward, always use caution and good judgment when working with electrical wiring or devices. Common sense can prevent accidents.

The basic rule of electrical safety is: Always turn off power to the area or device you are working on. At the main service panel, remove the fuse or shut off the circuit breaker that controls the circuit you are servicing.

Then check to make sure the power is off by testing for power with a current tester. Restore power only when the repair or replacement project is complete.

Follow the safety tips shown on these pages. Never attempt an electrical project beyond your skill or confidence level. Never attempt to repair or replace your main service panel or service entrance head. These are jobs for a qualified electrician and require that the power company shuts off power to your house.

Shut power OFF at the main service panel or the main fuse box before beginning any work.

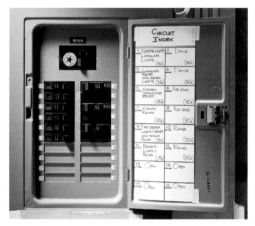

Create a circuit index and affix it to the inside of the door to your main service panel. Update it as needed.

Confirm power is OFF by testing at the outlet, switch, or fixture with a current tester.

Use only UL-approved electrical parts or devices. These devices have been tested for safety by Underwriters Laboratories.

Wear rubber-soled shoes while working on electrical projects. On damp floors, stand on a rubber mat or dry wooden boards.

Use fiberglass or wood ladders when making routine household repairs near the service mast.

Extension cords are for temporary use only. Cords must be rated for the intended usage.

Breakers and fuses must be compatible with the panel manufacturer and match the circuit capacity.

Never alter the prongs of a plug to fit a receptacle. If possible, install a new grounded receptacle.

Do not penetrate walls or ceilings without first shutting off electrical power to the circuits that may be hidden.

Working with Wire & Cable

Wires are made of copper, aluminum, or aluminum covered with a thin layer of copper. Solid copper wires are the best conductors of electricity and are the most widely used. Aluminum and copper-covered aluminum wires require special installation techniques and are rarely used in new installation, due to safety concerns.

A group of two or more wires enclosed in a metal, rubber, or plastic sheath is called a *cable* (photo, opposite page). The sheath protects the wires from damage. Metal conduit also protects wires, but it is not considered a cable.

Individual wires are covered with rubber or plastic vinyl insulation. An exception is a bare copper grounding wire, which does not need an insulation cover. The insulation is color coded (chart, below left) to identify the wire as a hot wire, a neutral wire, or a grounding wire.

In most wiring systems installed after 1965, the wires and cables are insulated with plastic vinyl. This type of insulation is very durable and can last as long as the house itself.

Before 1965, wires and cables were insulated with rubber. Rubber insulation has a life expectancy of about 25 years. Old insulation that is cracked or damaged can be reinforced temporarily by wrapping the wire with plastic electrical tape. However, old wiring with cracked or damaged insulation should be inspected by a qualified electrician to make sure it is safe.

Wires must be large enough for the amperage rating of the circuit (chart, below right). A wire that is too small can become dangerously hot. Wire sizes are categorized according to the American Wire Gauge (AWG) system. To check the size of a wire, use the wire stripper openings of a combination tool (page 30) as a guide.

Wire Color Chart ▸

Wire color		Function
	White	Neutral wire carrying current at zero voltage.
	Black	Hot wire carrying current at full voltage.
	Red	Hot wire carrying current at full voltage.
	White, black markings	Hot wire carrying current at full voltage.
	Green	Serves as a grounding pathway.
	Bare copper	Serves as a grounding pathway.

Individual wires are color-coded to identify their function. In some circuit installations, the white wire serves as a hot wire that carries voltage. If so, this white wire may be labeled with black tape or paint to identify it as a hot wire.

Wire Size Chart ▸

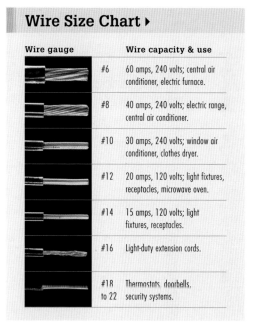

Wire gauge		Wire capacity & use
	#6	60 amps, 240 volts; central air conditioner, electric furnace.
	#8	40 amps, 240 volts; electric range, central air conditioner.
	#10	30 amps, 240 volts; window air conditioner, clothes dryer.
	#12	20 amps, 120 volts; light fixtures, receptacles, microwave oven.
	#14	15 amps, 120 volts; light fixtures, receptacles.
	#16	Light-duty extension cords.
	#18 to 22	Thermostats, doorbells, security systems.

Wire sizes (shown actual size) are categorized by the American Wire Gauge system. The larger the wire size, the smaller the AWG number.

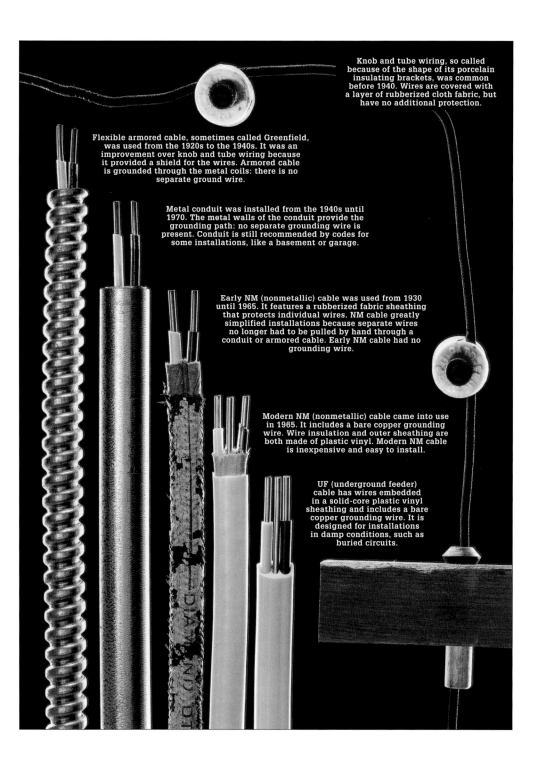

Knob and tube wiring, so called because of the shape of its porcelain insulating brackets, was common before 1940. Wires are covered with a layer of rubberized cloth fabric, but have no additional protection.

Flexible armored cable, sometimes called Greenfield, was used from the 1920s to the 1940s. It was an improvement over knob and tube wiring because it provided a shield for the wires. Armored cable is grounded through the metal coils: there is no separate ground wire.

Metal conduit was installed from the 1940s until 1970. The metal walls of the conduit provide the grounding path: no separate grounding wire is present. Conduit is still recommended by codes for some installations, like a basement or garage.

Early NM (nonmetallic) cable was used from 1930 until 1965. It features a rubberized fabric sheathing that protects individual wires. NM cable greatly simplified installations because separate wires no longer had to be pulled by hand through a conduit or armored cable. Early NM cable had no grounding wire.

Modern NM (nonmetallic) cable came into use in 1965. It includes a bare copper grounding wire. Wire insulation and outer sheathing are both made of plastic vinyl. Modern NM cable is inexpensive and easy to install.

UF (underground feeder) cable has wires embedded in a solid-core plastic vinyl sheathing and includes a bare copper grounding wire. It is designed for installations in damp conditions, such as buried circuits.

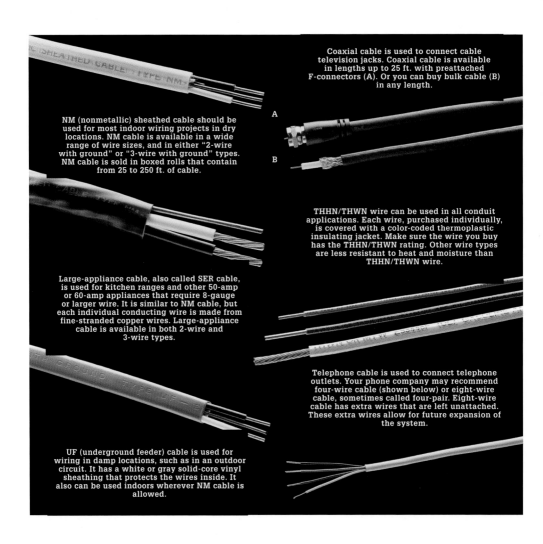

Coaxial cable is used to connect cable television jacks. Coaxial cable is available in lengths up to 25 ft. with preattached F-connectors (A). Or you can buy bulk cable (B) in any length.

A

B

NM (nonmetallic) sheathed cable should be used for most indoor wiring projects in dry locations. NM cable is available in a wide range of wire sizes, and in either "2-wire with ground" or "3-wire with ground" types. NM cable is sold in boxed rolls that contain from 25 to 250 ft. of cable.

THHN/THWN wire can be used in all conduit applications. Each wire, purchased individually, is covered with a color-coded thermoplastic insulating jacket. Make sure the wire you buy has the THHN/THWN rating. Other wire types are less resistant to heat and moisture than THHN/THWN wire.

Large-appliance cable, also called SER cable, is used for kitchen ranges and other 50-amp or 60-amp appliances that require 8-gauge or larger wire. It is similar to NM cable, but each individual conducting wire is made from fine-stranded copper wires. Large-appliance cable is available in both 2-wire and 3-wire types.

Telephone cable is used to connect telephone outlets. Your phone company may recommend four-wire cable (shown below) or eight-wire cable, sometimes called four-pair. Eight-wire cable has extra wires that are left unattached. These extra wires allow for future expansion of the system.

UF (underground feeder) cable is used for wiring in damp locations, such as in an outdoor circuit. It has a white or gray solid-core vinyl sheathing that protects the wires inside. It also can be used indoors wherever NM cable is allowed.

Tips for Working With Wire ▶

Wire gauge		Ampacity	Maximum wattage load
	14-gauge	15 amps	1440 watts (120 volts)
	12-gauge	20 amps	1920 watts (120 volts) 3840 watts (240 volts)
	10-gauge	30 amps	2880 watts (120 volts) 5760 watts (240 volts)
	8-gauge	40 amps	7680 watts (240 volts)
	6-gauge	50 amps	9600 watts (240 volts)

Wire "ampacity" is a measurement of how much current a wire can carry safely. Ampacity varies according to the size of the wires, as shown at left. When installing a new circuit, choose wire with an ampacity rating matching the circuit size. For dedicated appliance circuits, check the wattage rating of the appliance and make sure it does not exceed the maximum wattage load of the circuit.

Reading NM (Nonmetallic) Cable

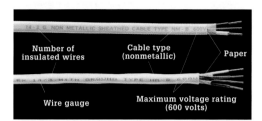

Number of insulated wires

Cable type (nonmetallic)

Paper

Wire gauge

Maximum voltage rating (600 volts)

Reading Unsheathed, Individual Wire

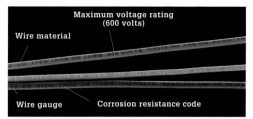

Maximum voltage rating (600 volts)

Wire material

Wire gauge

Corrosion resistance code

NM (nonmetallic) cable is labeled with the number of insulated wires it contains. The bare grounding wire is not counted. For example, a cable marked 14/2 G (or 14/2 WITH GROUND) contains two insulated 14-gauge wires, plus a bare copper grounding wire. Cable marked 14/3 WITH GROUND has three 14-gauge wires plus a grounding wire. NM cable also is stamped with a maximum voltage rating, as determined by Underwriters Laboratories (UL).

Unsheathed, individual wires are used for conduit and raceway installations. Wire insulation is coded with letters to indicate resistance to moisture, heat, and gas or oil. Code requires certain letter combinations for certain applications. T indicates thermoplastic insulation. H stands for heat resistance and two Hs indicate high resistance (up to 194° F). W denotes wire suitable for wet locations. Wire coded with an N is impervious to damage from oil or gas.

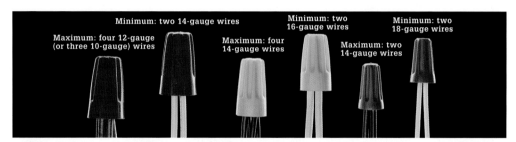

Minimum: two 14-gauge wires

Maximum: four 12-gauge (or three 10-gauge) wires

Maximum: four 14-gauge wires

Minimum: two 16-gauge wires

Maximum: two 14-gauge wires

Minimum: two 18-gauge wires

Use wire connectors rated for the wires you are connecting. Wire connectors are color-coded by size, but the coding scheme varies according to manufacturer. The wire connectors shown above come from one major manufacturer. To ensure safe connections, each connector is rated for both minimum and maximum wire capacity. These connectors can be used to connect both conducting wires and grounding wires. Green wire connectors are used only for grounding wires.

Use plastic cable staples to fasten cables. Choose staples sized to match the cables. Stack-It® staples (A) hold up to four 2-wire cables; ¾" staples (B) for 12/2, 12/3, and all 10-gauge cables; ½" staples (C) for 14/2, 14/3, or 12/2 cables; coaxial staples (D) for anchoring television cables; bell wire staples (E) for attaching telephone cables.

Push-in connectors are a relatively new product for joining wires. Instead of twisting the bare wire ends together, you strip off about ¾" of insulation and insert them into a hole in the connector. The connectors come with two to four holes sized for various gauge wires. These connectors are perfect for inexperienced DIYers because they do not pull apart like a poorly twisted connection can.

How to Strip NM Sheathing & Insulation

1

Cutting point

Measure and mark the cable 8 to 10" from end. Slide the cable ripper onto the cable, and squeeze tool firmly to force cutting point through plastic sheathing.

2

Grip the cable tightly with one hand, and pull the cable ripper toward the end of the cable to cut open the plastic sheathing.

3

Peel back the plastic sheathing and the paper wrapping from the individual wires.

4

Cutting jaws

Cut away the excess plastic sheathing and paper wrapping, using the cutting jaws of a combination tool.

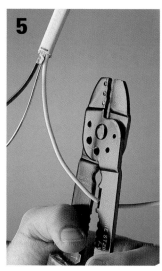

5

Cut individual wires as needed using the cutting jaws of the combination tool.

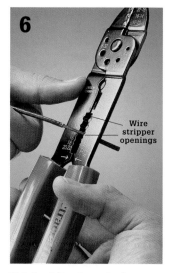

6

Wire stripper openings

Strip insulation for each wire, using the stripper openings. Choose the opening that matches the gauge of the wire, and take care not to nick or scratch the ends of the wires.

How to Connect Wires to Screw Terminals

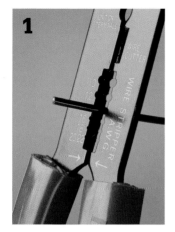

1

2

3

Strip about ¾" of insulation from each wire using a combination tool. Choose the stripper opening that matches the gauge of the wire, then clamp the wire in the tool. Pull the wire firmly to remove plastic insulation.

Form a C-shaped loop in the end of each wire using a needlenose pliers. The wire should have no scratches or nicks.

Hook each wire around the screw terminal so it forms a clockwise loop. Tighten screw firmly. Insulation should just touch head of screw. Never place the ends of two wires under a single screw terminal. Instead, use a pigtail wire (page 97).

How to Connect Wires with Push-ins

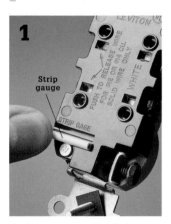

1

Strip gauge

2

3

Release opening

Mark the amount of insulation to be stripped from each wire using the strip gauge on the back of the switch or receptacle. Strip the wires using a combination tool (step 1, above). Never use push-in fittings with aluminum wiring.

Insert the bare copper wires firmly into the push-in fittings on the back of the switch or receptacle. When inserted, wires should have no bare copper exposed. *Note: Although push-in fittings are convenient, most experts believe screw terminal connections (above) are more dependable.*

Remove a wire from a push-in fitting by inserting a small nail or screwdriver in the release opening next to the wire. Wire will pull out easily.

How to Join Wires with a Wire Connector

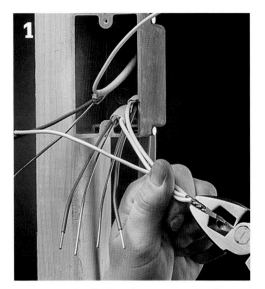

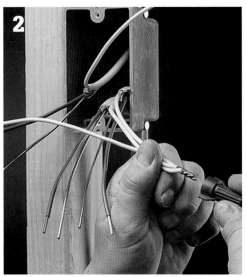

Ensure power is off and test for power. Grasp the wires to be joined in the jaws of a pair of linesman's pliers. The ends of the wires should be flush and they should be parallel and touching. Rotate the pliers clockwise two or three turns to twist the wire ends together.

Twist a wire connector over the ends of the wires. Make sure the connector is the right size (see page 29). Hand-twist the connector as far onto the wires as you can. There should be no bare wire exposed beneath the collar of the connector. Do not overtighten the connector.

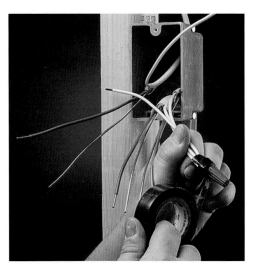

Option: Reinforce the joint by wrapping it with electrician's tape. By code, you cannot bind the wire joint with tape only, but it can be used as insurance. Few professional electricians use tape for purposes other than tagging wires for identification.

Option: Strip ¾" of insulation off the ends of the wires to be joined, and insert each wire into a push-in connector. Gently tug on each wire to make sure it is secure.

How to Pigtail Wires

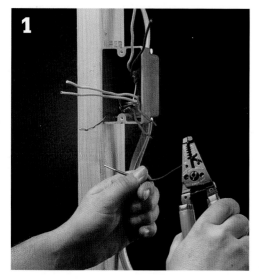

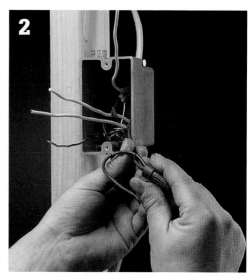

Cut a 6" length from a piece of insulated wire the same gauge and color as the wires it will be joining. Strip ¾" of insulation from each end of the insulated wire. *Note: Pigtailing is done mainly to avoid connecting multiple wires to one terminal, which is a code violation.*

Join one end of the pigtail to the wires that will share the connection using a wire nut (see previous page).

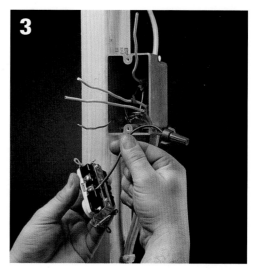

Alternative: If you are pigtailing to a grounding screw or grounding clip in a metal box, you may find it easier to attach one end of the wire to the grounding screw before you attach the other end to the other wires.

Connect the pigtail to the appropriate terminal on the receptacle or switch. Fold the wires neatly and press the fitting into the box.

How to Install NM Cable

Drill ⅝" holes in framing members for the cable runs. This is done easily with a right-angle drill, available at rental centers. Holes should be set back at least 1¼" from the front face of the framing members.

Where cables will turn corners (step 6, page 99), drill intersecting holes in adjoining faces of studs. Measure and cut all cables, allowing 2 ft. extra at ends entering the breaker panel and 1 foot for ends entering the electrical box.

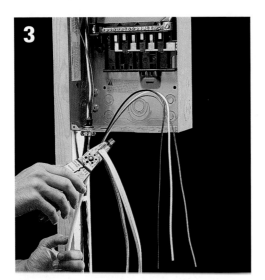

Shut off power to circuit breaker panel. Use a cable ripper to strip cable, leaving at least ¼" of sheathing to enter the circuit breaker panel. Clip away the excess sheathing.

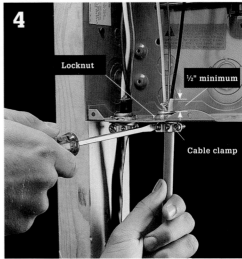

Locknut

½" minimum

Cable clamp

Open a knockout in the circuit breaker panel using a hammer and screwdriver. Insert a cable clamp into the knockout, and secure it with a locknut. Insert the cable through the clamp so that at least ½" of sheathing extends inside the circuit breaker panel. Tighten the mounting screws on the clamp so the cable is gripped securely but not so tightly that the sheathing is crushed.

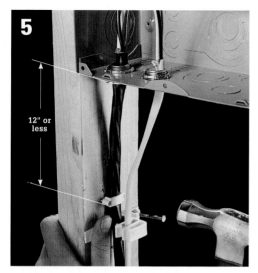

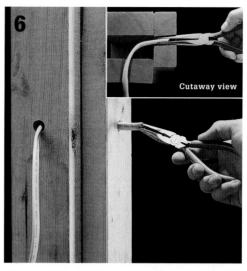

Cutaway view

Anchor the cable to the center of a framing member within 12" of the circuit breaker panel using a cable staple. Stack-It® staples work well where two or more cables must be anchored to the same side of a stud. Run the cable to the first electrical box. Where the cable runs along the sides of framing members, anchor it with cable staples no more than 4 ft. apart.

At corners, form a slight L-shaped bend in the end of the cable and insert it into one hole. Retrieve the cable through the other hole using needlenose pliers (inset).

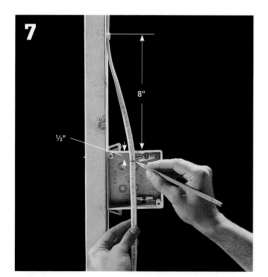

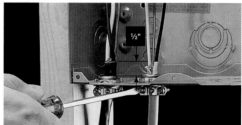

Staple the cable to a framing member 8" from the box. Hold the cable taut against the front of the box, and mark a point on the sheathing ½" past the box edge. Remove sheathing from the marked line to the end using a cable ripper, and clip away excess sheathing with a combination tool. Insert the cable through the knockout in the box.

Variation: Different types of boxes have different clamping devices. Make sure cable sheathing extends ½" past the edge of the clamp to ensure that the cable is secure and that the wire won't be damaged by the edges of the clamp.

(continued)

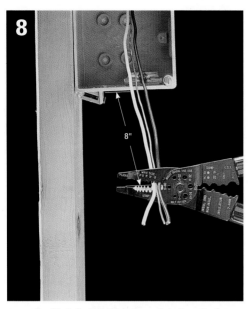

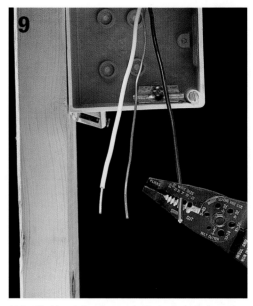

As each cable is installed in a box, clip back each wire so that 8" of workable wire extends past the front edge of the box.

Strip ¾" of insulation from each circuit wire in the box using a combination tool. Take care not to nick the copper.

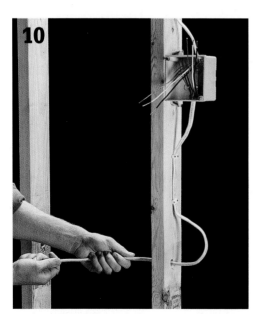

Continue the circuit by running cable between each pair of electrical boxes, leaving an extra 1 ft. of cable at each end.

At metal boxes and recessed fixtures, open knockouts, and attach cables with cable clamps. From inside fixture, strip away all but ¼" of sheathing. Clip back wires so there is 8" of workable length, then strip ¾" of insulation from each wire.

12

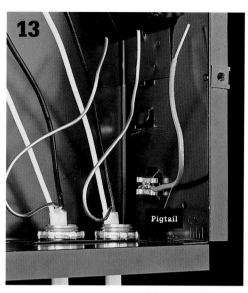

13

Pigtail

For a surface-mounted fixture like a baseboard heater or fluorescent light fixture, staple the cable to a stud near the fixture location, leaving plenty of excess cable. Mark the floor so the cable will be easy to find after the walls are finished.

At each recessed fixture and metal electrical box, connect one end of a grounding pigtail to the metal frame using a grounding clip attached to the frame (shown above) or a green grounding screw.

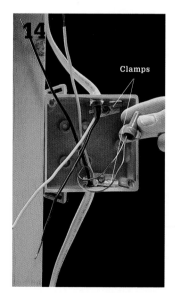

14

Clamps

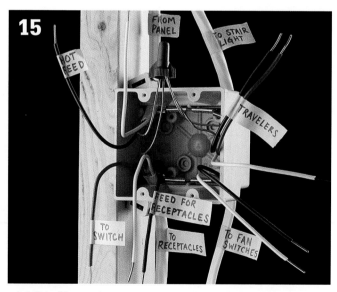

15

FROM PANEL

TO STAIR LIGHT

HOT FEED

TRAVELERS

FEED FOR RECEPTACLES

TO SWITCH

TO RECEPTACLES

TO FAN SWITCHES

At each electrical box and recessed fixture, join grounding wires together with a wire connector. If the box has internal clamps, tighten the clamps over the cables.

Label the cables entering each box to indicate their destinations. In boxes with complex wiring configurations, also tag the individual wires to make final hookups easier. After all cables are installed, your rough-in work is ready to be reviewed by the electrical inspector.

Working with Conduit

Electrical wiring that runs in exposed locations must be protected by rigid tubing called conduit. For example, conduit is used for wiring that runs across masonry walls in a basement laundry and for exposed outdoor wiring. THHN/THWN wire (page 92) normally is installed inside conduit, although UF or NM cable can also be installed in conduit.

There are several types of conduit available, so check with your electrical inspector to find out which type meets code requirements in your area. Conduit installed outdoors must be rated for exterior use. Metal conduit should be used only with metal boxes, never with plastic boxes.

At one time, conduit could only be fitted by using elaborate bending techniques and special tools. Now, however, a variety of shaped fittings are available to let a homeowner join conduit easily.

Electrical Grounding in Metal Conduit

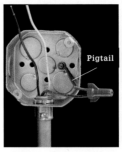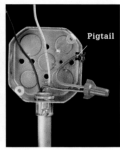

Install a green insulated grounding wire for any circuit that runs through metal conduit. Although code allows the metal conduit to serve as the grounding conductor, most electricians install a green insulated wire as a more dependable means of grounding the system. The grounding wires must be connected to metal boxes with a pigtail and grounding screw (left) or grounding clip (right).

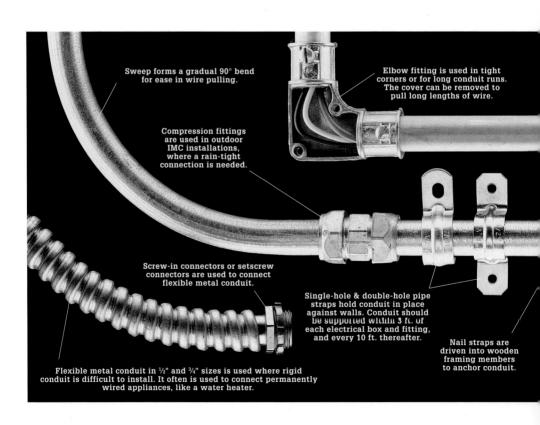

Sweep forms a gradual 90° bend for ease in wire pulling.

Elbow fitting is used in tight corners or for long conduit runs. The cover can be removed to pull long lengths of wire.

Compression fittings are used in outdoor IMC installations, where a rain-tight connection is needed.

Screw-in connectors or setscrew connectors are used to connect flexible metal conduit.

Single-hole & double-hole pipe straps hold conduit in place against walls. Conduit should be supported within 3 ft. of each electrical box and fitting, and every 10 ft. thereafter.

Nail straps are driven into wooden framing members to anchor conduit.

Flexible metal conduit in ½" and ¾" sizes is used where rigid conduit is difficult to install. It often is used to connect permanently wired appliances, like a water heater.

Fill Capacity

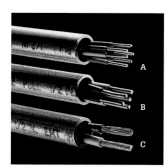

Conduit ½" in diameter can hold up to six 14-gauge or 12-gauge THHN/THWN wires (A), five 10-gauge wires (B), or two 8-gauge wires (C). Use ¾" conduit for greater capacity.

Metal Conduit

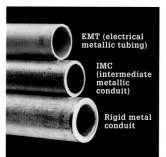

EMT (electrical metallic tubing)

IMC (intermediate metallic conduit)

Rigid metal conduit

EMT is lightweight and easy to install but should not be used where it can be damaged. IMC has thicker galvanized walls and is a good choice for exposed outdoor use. Rigid metal conduit provides the greatest protection for wires, but it is more expensive and requires threaded fittings.

Plastic Conduit

Plastic PVC conduit is allowed by many local codes. It is assembled with solvent glue and PVC fittings that resemble those for metal conduit. When wiring with PVC conduit, always run a green grounding wire.

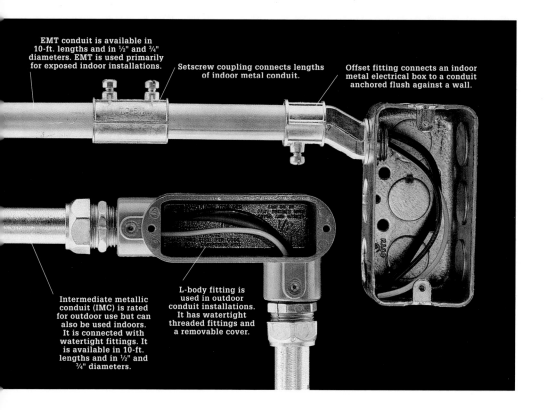

EMT conduit is available in 10-ft. lengths and in ½" and ¾" diameters. EMT is used primarily for exposed indoor installations.

Setscrew coupling connects lengths of indoor metal conduit.

Offset fitting connects an indoor metal electrical box to a conduit anchored flush against a wall.

Intermediate metallic conduit (IMC) is rated for outdoor use but can also be used indoors. It is connected with watertight fittings. It is available in 10-ft. lengths and in ½" and ¾" diameters.

L-body fitting is used in outdoor conduit installations. It has watertight threaded fittings and a removable cover.

Conduit Materials & Tools

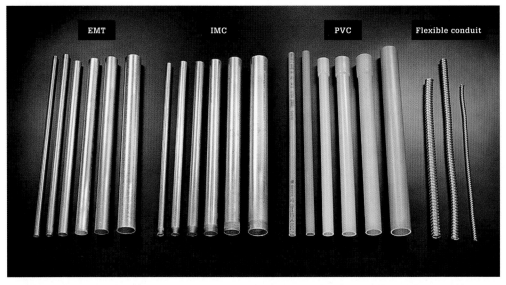

EMT **IMC** **PVC** **Flexible conduit**

Conduit types used most in homes are EMT (electrical metallic tubing), IMC (intermediate metallic conduit), RNC (rigid nonmetallic conduit), and flexible metal conduit. The most common diameters by far are ½" and ¾", but larger sizes are stocked at most building centers.

RNC (PVC) fitting

LB

LB

PVC offset

T

Access pull elbow

Nonmetallic conduit fittings typically are solvent welded to nonmetallic conduit, as opposed to metal conduit, which can be threaded and screwed into threaded fittings or attached with setscrews or compression fittings.

A thin-wall conduit bender is used to bend sweeps into EMT or IMC conduit.

How to Make Nonmetallic Conduit Connections

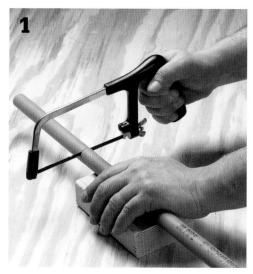

Cut the rigid nonmetallic conduit (RNC) to length with a fine-tooth saw, such as a hacksaw. For larger diameter (1½" and above), use a power miter box with a fine-tooth or plastic cutting blade.

Deburr the cut edges with a utility knife or fine sandpaper such as emery paper. Wipe the cut ends with a dry rag. Also wipe the coupling or fitting to clean it.

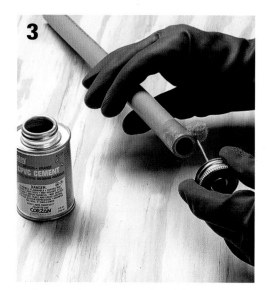

Apply a coat of PVC cement to the end of the conduit. Wear latex gloves to protect your hands. The cement should be applied past the point on the conduit where it enters the fitting or coupling.

Insert the conduit into the fitting or coupling and spin it a quarter turn to help spread the cement. Allow the joint to set undisturbed for 10 minutes.

How to Install Conduit & Wires on a Concrete Wall

1

2

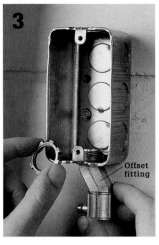

3

Measure from the floor to position electrical boxes on the wall, and mark location for mounting screws. Boxes for receptacles in an unfinished basement or other damp area are mounted at least 2 ft. from the floor. Laundry receptacles usually are mounted at 48".

Drill pilot holes with a masonry bit, then mount the box against a masonry wall with masonry anchors. Or use masonry anchors and panhead screws.

Open one knockout for each length of conduit that will be attached to the box. Attach an offset fitting to each knockout using a locknut.

4

5

6

Measure the first length of conduit and cut it with a hacksaw. Remove any rough inside edges with a pipe reamer or a round file. Attach the conduit to the offset fitting on the box, and tighten the setscrew.

Anchor the conduit against the wall with pipe straps and masonry anchors. Conduit should be anchored within 3 ft. of each box and fitting, and every 10 ft. thereafter.

Make conduit bends by attaching a sweep fitting using a setscrew fitting or compression fitting. Continue conduit run by attaching additional lengths using setscrew or compression fittings.

Use an elbow fitting in conduit runs that have many bends, or in runs that require very long wires. The cover on the elbow fitting can be removed to make it easier to extend a fish tape and pull wires.

At the service breaker panel, turn the power off, then remove the cover and test for power. Open a knockout in the panel, then attach a setscrew fitting, and install the last length of conduit.

Unwind the fish tape and extend it through the conduit from the circuit breaker panel outward. Remove the cover on an elbow fitting when extending the fish tape around tight corners.

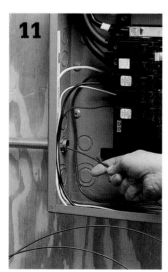

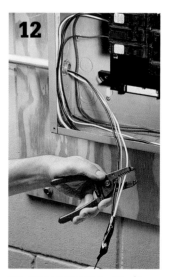

Trim back 2" of outer insulation from the end of the wires, then insert the wires through the loop at the tip of the fish tape.

Retrieve the wires through the conduit by pulling on the fish tape with steady pressure. *Note: Use extreme care when using a metal fish tape inside a circuit breaker panel, even when the power is turned off.*

Clip off the taped ends of the wires. Leave at least 2 ft. of wire at the service panel and 8" at each electrical box.

Working with Boxes

The National Electrical Code requires that wire connections and cable splices be contained inside an approved metal or plastic box. This shields framing members and other flammable materials from electrical sparks.

Electrical boxes come in several shapes. Rectangular and square boxes are used for switches and receptacles. Rectangular (2 × 3") boxes are used for single switches or duplex receptacles. Square (4 × 4") boxes are used any time it is convenient for two switches or receptacles to be wired, or "ganged," in one box, an arrangement common in kitchens or entry hallways. Octagonal electrical boxes contain wire connections for ceiling fixtures.

All electrical boxes are available in different depths. A box must be deep enough so a switch or receptacle can be removed or installed easily without crimping and damaging the circuit wires. Replace an undersized box with a larger box using the Electrical Box Chart (right) as a guide. The NEC also says that all electrical boxes must remain accessible. Never cover an electrical box with drywall, paneling, or wallcoverings.

Electrical Box Fill Chart ▸

Box size and shape	Maximum number of conductors permitted (see Notes below)			
	18 AWG	16 AWG	14 AWG	12 AWG
Junction boxes				
4 × 1¼" R or O	8	7	6	5
4 × 1½" R or O	10	8	7	6
4 × 2⅛" R or O	14	12	10	9
4 × 1¼" S	12	10	9	8
4 × 1½" S	14	12	10	9
4 × 2⅛" S	20	17	15	13
4¹¹⁄₁₆ × 1¼" S	17	14	12	11
4¹¹⁄₁₆ × 1½" S	19	16	14	13
4¹¹⁄₁₆ × 2⅛" S	28	24	21	18
Device boxes				
3 × 2 × 1½"	5	4	3	3
3 × 2 × 2"	6	5	5	4
3 × 2 × 2¼"	7	6	5	4
3 × 2 × 2½"	8	7	6	5
3 × 2 × 2¾"	9	8	7	6
3 × 2 × 3½"	12	10	9	8
4 × 2⅛ × 1½"	6	5	5	4
4 × 2⅛ × 1⅞"	8	7	6	5
4 × 2⅛ × 2⅛"	9	8	7	6

Notes:
- R = Round; O = Octagonal; S = Square or rectangular
- Each hot or neutral wire entering the box is counted as one conductor.
- Grounding wires are counted as one conductor in total—do not count each one individually.
- Raceway fittings and external cable clamps do not count. Internal cable connectors and straps count as either half or one conductor, depending on type.
- Devices (switches and receptacles mainly) each count as two conductors.
- Straps (yokes) from mounting devices each count as two conductors.
- When calculating total conductors, any nonwire components should be assigned the gauge of the largest wire in the box.
- For wire gauges not shown here, contact your local electrical inspections office.

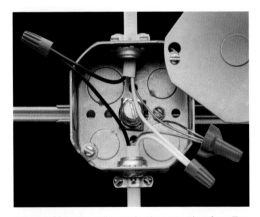

Octagonal boxes usually contain wire connections for ceiling fixtures. Cables are inserted into the box through knockout openings and are held with cable clamps. Because the ceiling fixture attaches directly to the box, the box should be anchored firmly to a framing member. Often, it is nailed directly to a ceiling joist. However, metal braces are available that allow a box to be mounted between joists or studs. A properly installed octagonal box can support a ceiling fixture weighing up to 35 pounds. Any box must be covered with a tightly fitting cover plate, and the box must not have open knockouts.

Common Electrical Boxes

Detachable side

Rectangular boxes are used with wall switches and duplex receptacles. Single-size rectangular boxes (shown above) may have detachable sides that allow them to be ganged together to form double-size boxes.

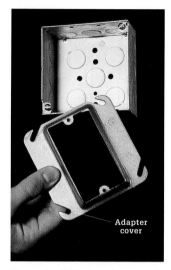

Adapter cover

Square 4 × 4" boxes are large enough for most wiring applications. They are used for cable splices and ganged receptacles or switches. To install one switch or receptacle in a square box, use an adapter cover.

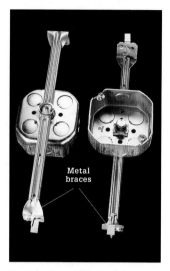

Metal braces

Braced octagonal boxes fit between ceiling joists. The metal braces extend to fit any joist spacing and are nailed or screwed to framing members.

Foam gasket

Outdoor boxes have sealed seams and foam gaskets to guard a switch or receptacle against moisture. Corrosion-resistant coatings protect all metal parts. Code-compliant models include a watertight hood.

Retrofit boxes upgrade older boxes to larger sizes. One type (above) has built-in clamps that tighten against the inside of a wall and hold the box in place.

Plastic boxes are common in new construction. They can be used only with NM (nonmetallic) cable. The box may include preattached nails for anchoring it to framing members. Wall switches must have grounding screws if installed in plastic boxes.

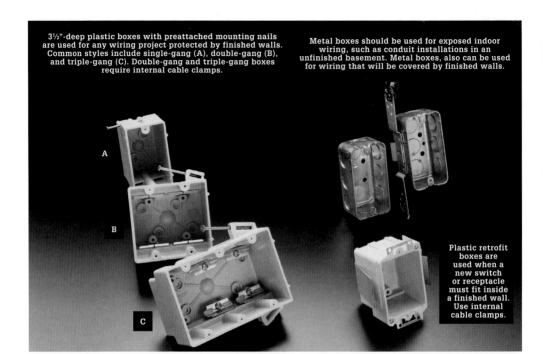

3½"-deep plastic boxes with preattached mounting nails are used for any wiring project protected by finished walls. Common styles include single-gang (A), double-gang (B), and triple-gang (C). Double-gang and triple-gang boxes require internal cable clamps.

Metal boxes should be used for exposed indoor wiring, such as conduit installations in an unfinished basement. Metal boxes, also can be used for wiring that will be covered by finished walls.

A

B

C

Plastic retrofit boxes are used when a new switch or receptacle must fit inside a finished wall. Use internal cable clamps.

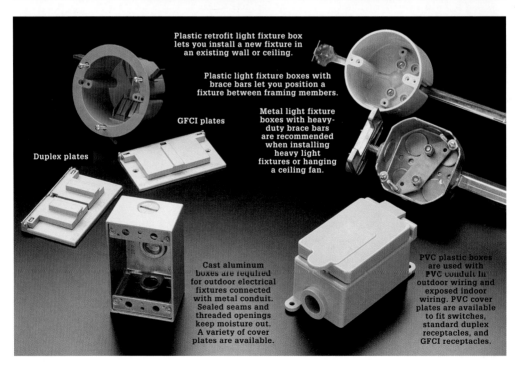

Plastic retrofit light fixture box lets you install a new fixture in an existing wall or ceiling.

Plastic light fixture boxes with brace bars let you position a fixture between framing members.

GFCI plates

Metal light fixture boxes with heavy-duty brace bars are recommended when installing heavy light fixtures or hanging a ceiling fan.

Duplex plates

Cast aluminum boxes are required for outdoor electrical fixtures connected with metal conduit. Sealed seams and threaded openings keep moisture out. A variety of cover plates are available.

PVC plastic boxes are used with PVC conduit in outdoor wiring and exposed indoor wiring. PVC cover plates are available to fit switches, standard duplex receptacles, and GFCI receptacles.

How to Locate Electrical Boxes

Heights of electrical boxes vary depending on use. In the kitchen shown here, boxes above the countertop are 45" above the floor, in the center of 18" backsplashes that extend from the countertop to the cabinets. All boxes for wall switches also are installed at this height. The center of the box for the microwave receptacle is 72" off the floor. The centers of the boxes for the range and food disposer receptacles are 12" off the floor, but the center of the box for the dishwasher receptacle is 6" off the floor.

Typical Wallcovering Thickness

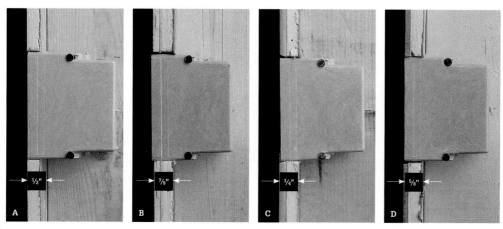

Consider the thickness of finished walls when mounting electrical boxes against framing members. Code requires that the front face of boxes be flush with the finished wall surface, so how you install boxes will vary depending on the type of wall finish that will be used. For example, if the walls will be finished with ½" wallboard (A), attach the boxes so the front faces extend ½" past the front of the framing members. With ceramic tile and wall board (B), extend the boxes ⅞" past the framing members. With ¼" Corian® over wallboard (C), boxes should extend ¾"; and with wallboard and laminate (D), boxes extend ⅝".

How to Install Electrical Boxes for Receptacles

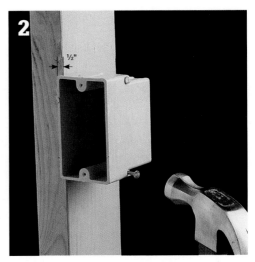

Mark the location of each box on studs. Standard receptacle boxes should be centered 12" above floor level. GFCI receptacle boxes in a bathroom should be mounted so they will be about 10" above the finished countertop.

Position each box against a stud so the front face will be flush with the finished wall. For example, if you will be installing ½" wallboard, position the box so it extends ½" past the face of the stud. Anchor the box by driving the mounting nails into the stud.

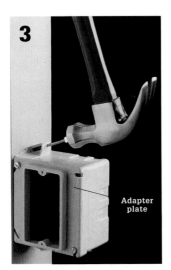

Adapter plate

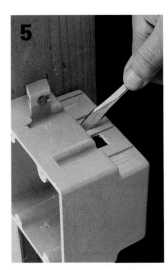

If installing square boxes, attach the adapter plates before positioning the boxes. Use adapter plates that match the thickness of the finished wall. Anchor the box by driving the mounting nails into the stud.

Open one knockout for each cable that will enter the box using a hammer and screwdriver.

Break off any sharp edges that might damage vinyl cable sheathing by rotating a screwdriver in the knockout.

How to Install Electrical Boxes for Light Fixtures

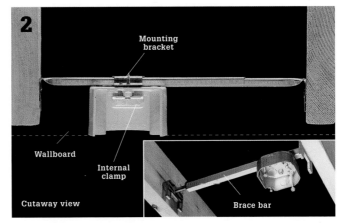

Mounting bracket

Wallboard

Internal clamp

Cutaway view

Brace bar

Position the light fixture box for a vanity light above the frame opening for a mirror or medicine cabinet. Place the box for a ceiling light fixture in the center of the room. Position each box against a framing member so the front face will be flush with the finished wall or ceiling, then anchor the box by driving the mounting nails into the framing.

To position a light fixture between joists, attach an electrical box to an adjustable brace bar. Nail the ends of the brace bar to joists so the face of the box will be flush with the finished ceiling surface. Slide the box along the brace bar to the desired position, then tighten the mounting screws. Use internal cable clamps when using a box with a brace bar. *Note: For ceiling fans and heavy fixtures, use a metal box and a heavy-duty brace bar rated for heavy loads (inset photo).*

How to Install Electrical Boxes for Switches

48"

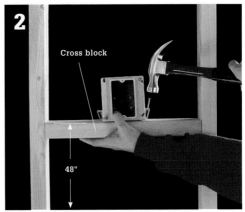

Cross block

48"

Install switch boxes at accessible locations, usually on the latch side of a door, with the center of the box 48" from the floor. The box for a thermostat is mounted at 48 to 60". Position each box against the side of a stud so the front face will be flush with the finished wall, and drive the mounting nails into the stud.

To install a switch box between studs, first install a cross block between studs, with the top edge 46" above the floor. Position the box on the cross block so the front face will be flush with the finished wall, and drive the mounting nails into the cross block.

Ceiling Boxes

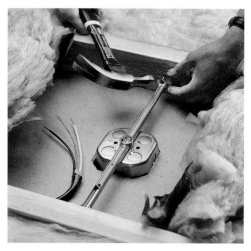

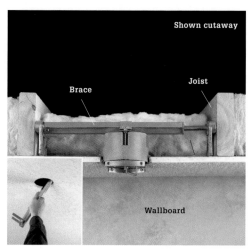

Ceiling boxes for lights are generally round or octagonal in shape to fit typical lamp mounting plates. The easiest way to install one is by nailing the brace to open ceiling joists from above. If the ceiling is insulated, pull the insulation away from the box if the fixture you're installing is not rated IC for insulation contact.

A heavy-duty brace is required for anchoring boxes that will support heavy chandeliers and ceiling fans. A remodeling brace like the one seen here is designed to install through a small cutout in the ceiling (inset photo).

How to Install a Junction Box

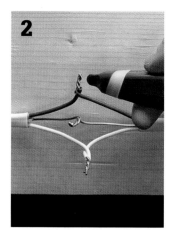

Turn off power to circuit wires at the main service panel. Carefully remove any tape or wire connectors from the exposed splice. Avoid contact with the bare wire ends until the wires have been tested for power.

Test for power. The tester should not glow. If it does, the wires are still hot. Shut off power to correct circuit at the main service panel. Disconnect the illegally spliced wires.

Open one knockout for each cable that will enter the box using a hammer and screwdriver. Any unopened knockouts should remain sealed.

4

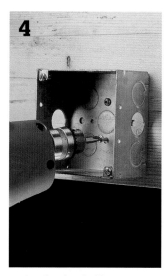

Anchor the electrical box to a wooden framing member using screws or nails.

5

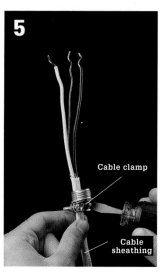

Cable clamp

Cable sheathing

Thread each cable end through a cable clamp. Tighten the clamp with a screwdriver. See if there is any slack in the cables so you can gain a little extra cable to work with.

6

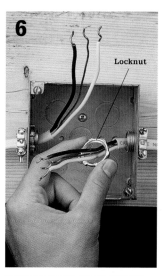

Locknut

Insert the cables into the electrical box, and screw a locknut onto each cable clamp.

7

Locknut

Lugs

Tighten the locknuts by pushing against the lugs with the blade of a screwdriver.

8

Grounding screw

Use wire connectors to reconnect the wires. Pigtail the copper grounding wires to the green grounding screw in the back of the box.

9

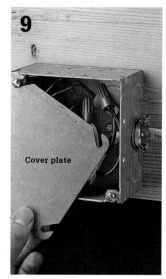

Cover plate

Carefully tuck the wires into the box, and attach the cover plate. Turn on the power to the circuit at the main service panel. Make sure the box remains accessible and is not concealed by finished walls or ceilings.

Working with Switches

Wall switches are available in three general types. To repair or replace a switch, it is important to identify its type.

Single-pole switches are used to control a set of lights from one location. Three-way switches are used to control a set of lights from two different locations and are always installed in pairs. Four-way switches are used in combination with a pair of three-way switches to control a set of lights from three or more locations.

Identify switch types by counting the screw terminals. Single-pole switches have two screw terminals, three-way switches have three screw terminals, and four-way switches have four. Most switches include a grounding screw terminal, which is identified by its green color.

When replacing a switch, choose a new switch that has the same number of screw terminals as the old one. The location of the screws on the switch body varies depending on the manufacturer, but these differences will not affect the switch operation.

Whenever possible, connect switches using the screw terminals rather than push-in fittings. Some specialty switches have wire leads instead of screw terminals. They are connected to circuit wires with wire connectors.

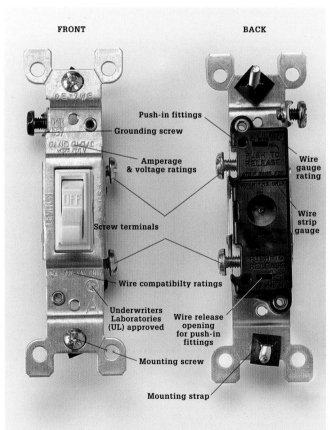

FRONT

BACK

Push-in fittings

Grounding screw

Amperage & voltage ratings

Wire gauge rating

Screw terminals

Wire strip gauge

Wire compatibilty ratings

Underwriters Laboratories (UL) approved

Wire release opening for push-in fittings

Mounting screw

Mounting strap

A wall switch is connected to circuit wires with screw terminals or with push-in fittings on the back of the switch. A switch may have a stamped strip gauge that indicates how much insulation must be stripped from the circuit wires to make the connections.

The switch body is attached to a metal mounting strap that allows it to be mounted in an electrical box. Several rating stamps are found on the strap and on the back of the switch. The abbreviation UL or UND. LAB. INC. LIST means that the switch meets the safety standards of the Underwriters Laboratories. Switches also are stamped with maximum voltage and amperage ratings. Standard wall switches are rated 15A or 125V. Voltage ratings of 110, 120, and 125 are considered to be identical for purposes of identification.

For standard wall switch installations, choose a switch that has a wire gauge rating of #12 or #14. For wire systems with solid-core copper wiring, use only switches marked COPPER or CU. For aluminum wiring, use only switches marked CO/ALR. Switches marked AL/CU can no longer be used with aluminum wiring, according to the National Electrical Code.

Single-pole Wall Switches

A single-pole switch is the most common type of wall switch. It has ON-OFF markings on the switch lever and is used to control a set of lights, an appliance, or a receptacle from a single location. A single-pole switch has two screw terminals and a grounding screw. When installing a single-pole switch, check to make sure the ON marking shows when the switch lever is in the up position.

In a correctly wired single-pole switch, a hot circuit wire is attached to each screw terminal. However, the color and number of wires inside the switch box will vary, depending on the location of the switch along the electrical circuit.

If two cables enter the box, then the switch lies in the middle of the circuit. In this installation, both of the hot wires attached to the switch are black.

If only one cable enters the box, then the switch lies at the end of the circuit. In this installation (sometimes called a switch loop), one of the hot wires is black, but the other hot wire usually is white. A white hot wire sometimes is coded with black tape or paint.

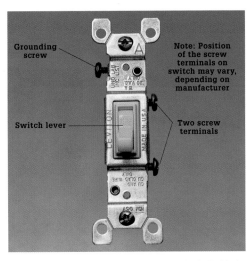

A single-pole switch is essentially an interruption in the black power supply wire that is opened or closed with the toggle. Single-pole switches are the simplest of all home wiring switches.

Typical Single-pole Switch Installations

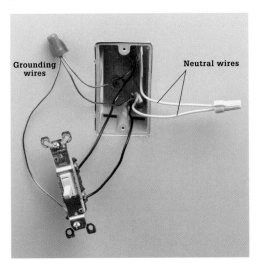

Two cables enter the box when a switch is located in the middle of a circuit. Each cable has a white and a black insulated wire, plus a bare copper grounding wire. The black wires are hot and are connected to the screw terminals on the switch. The white wires are neutral and are joined together with a wire connector. Grounding wires are pigtailed to the switch.

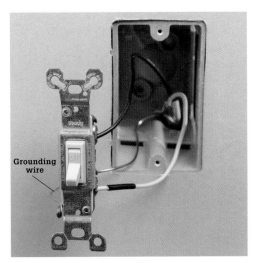

One cable enters the box when a switch is located at the end of a circuit. The cable has a white and a black insulated wire, plus a bare copper grounding wire. In this installation, both of the insulated wires are hot. The white wire may be labeled with black tape or paint to identify it as a hot wire. The grounding wire is connected to the switch grounding screw.

Three-way Wall Switches

Three-way switches have three screw terminals and do not have ON-OFF markings. Three-way switches are always installed in pairs and are used to control a set of lights from two locations.

One of the screw terminals on a three-way switch is darker than the others. This screw is the common screw terminal. The position of the common screw terminal on the switch body may vary, depending on the manufacturer. Before disconnecting a three-way switch, always label the wire that is connected to the common screw terminal. It must be reconnected to the common screw terminal on the new switch.

The two lighter-colored screw terminals on a three-way switch are called the traveler screw terminals. The traveler terminals are interchangeable, so there is no need to label the wires attached to them.

Because three-way switches are installed in pairs, it sometimes is difficult to determine which of the switches is causing a problem. The switch that receives greater use is more likely to fail, but you may need to inspect both switches to find the source of the problem.

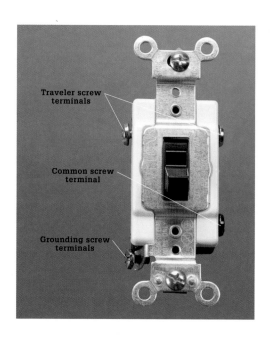

Traveler screw terminals

Common screw terminal

Grounding screw terminals

Typical Three-way Switch Installations

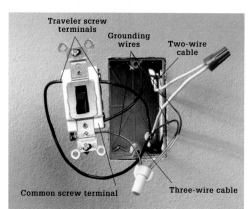

Traveler screw terminals

Grounding wires

Two-wire cable

Common screw terminal

Three-wire cable

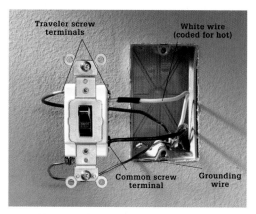

Traveler screw terminals

White wire (coded for hot)

Common screw terminal

Grounding wire

Two cables enter the box if the switch lies in the middle of a circuit. One cable has two wires, plus a bare copper grounding wire; the other cable has three wires, plus a ground. The black wire from the two-wire cable is connected to the dark common screw terminal. The red and black wires from the three-wire cable are connected to the traveler screw terminals. The white neutral wires are joined together with a wire connector, and the grounding wires are pigtailed to the grounded metal box.

One cable enters the box if the switch lies at the end of the circuit. The cable has a black wire, red wire, and white wire, plus a bare copper grounding wire. The black wire must be connected to the common screw terminal, which is darker than the other two screw terminals. The white and red wires are connected to the two traveler screw terminals. The white wire is taped to indicate that it is hot. The bare copper grounding wire is connected to the grounded metal box.

Four-way Wall Switches

Four-way switches have four screw terminals and do not have ON-OFF markings. Four-way switches are always installed between a pair of three-way switches. This switch combination makes it possible to control a set of lights from three or more locations. Four-way switches are common in homes where large rooms contain multiple living areas, such as a kitchen opening into a dining room. Switch problems in a four-way installation can be caused by loose connections or worn parts in a four-way switch or in one of the three-way switches (facing page).

In a typical installation, there will be a pair of three-way cables that enter the box for the four-way switch. With most switches, the white and red wires from one cable should be attached to the bottom or top pair of screw terminals, and the white and red wires from the other cable should be attached to the remaining pair of screw terminals. However, not all switches are configured the same way, and wiring configurations in the box may vary, so always study the wiring diagram that comes with the switch.

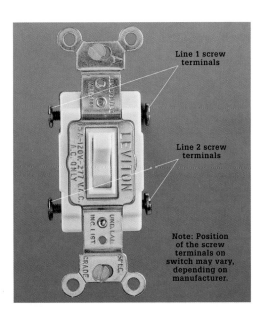

Line 1 screw terminals

Line 2 screw terminals

Note: Position of the screw terminals on switch may vary, depending on manufacturer.

Typical Four-way Switch Installation

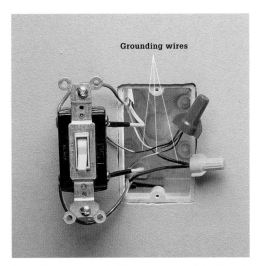

Grounding wires

Four wires are connected to a four-way switch. The red and white wires from one cable are attached to the top pair of screw terminals, while the red and white wires from the other cable are attached to the bottom screw terminals.

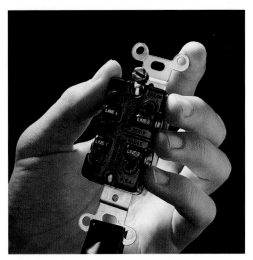

Switch variation: Some four-way switches have a wiring guide stamped on the back to help simplify installation. For the switch shown above, one pair of color-matched circuit wires will be connected to the screw terminals marked LINE 1, while the other pair of wires will be attached to the screw terminals marked LINE 2.

Testing Switches

A switch that does not work properly may have worn or broken internal parts. Test switches with a battery-operated continuity tester. The continuity tester detects any break in the metal pathway inside the switch. Replace the switch if the continuity tester shows the switch to be faulty.

Never use a continuity tester on wires that might carry live current. Always shut off the power and disconnect the switch before testing for continuity.

Some specialty switches, like dimmers, cannot be tested for continuity. Electronic switches can be tested for manual operation using a continuity tester, but the automatic operation of these switches cannot be tested.

How to Test a Single-pole Wall Switch

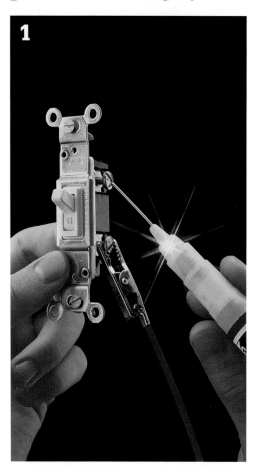

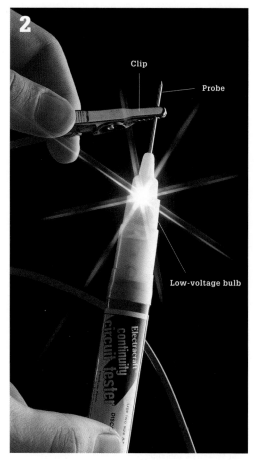

Attach clip of tester to one of the screw terminals. Touch the tester probe to the other screw terminal. Flip switch lever from ON to OFF. If switch is good, tester glows when lever is ON, but not when OFF.

Continuity tester uses battery-generated current to test the metal pathways running through switches and other electrical fixtures. Always "test" the tester before use. Touch the tester clip to the metal probe. The tester should glow. If not, then the battery or lightbulb is dead and must be replaced.

How to Test a Three-way Wall Switch

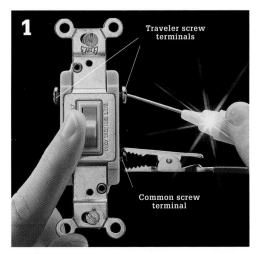

1 Traveler screw terminals

Common screw terminal

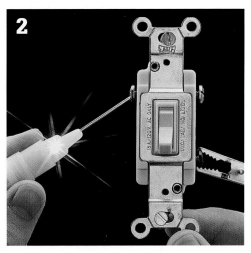

2

Attach tester clip to the dark common screw terminal. Touch the tester probe to one of the traveler screw terminals, and flip switch lever back and forth. If switch is good, the tester should glow when the lever is in one position, but not both.

Touch probe to the other traveler screw terminal, and flip the switch lever back and forth. If switch is good, the tester will glow only when the switch lever is in the position opposite from the positive test in step 1.

How to Test a Four-way Wall Switch

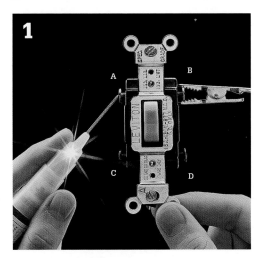

1
A   B

C   D

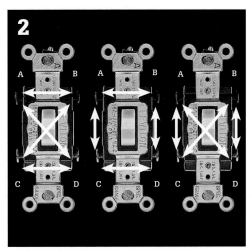

2
A   B   A   B   A   B

C   D   C   D   C   D

Test switch by touching probe and clip of continuity tester to each pair of screw terminals (A-B, C-D, A-D, B-C, A-C, B-D). The test should show continuous pathways between two different pairs of screw terminals. Flip lever to opposite position, and repeat test. Test should show continuous pathways between two different pairs of screw terminals.

If switch is good, test will show a total of four continuous pathways between screw terminals—two pathways for each lever position. If not, then switch is faulty and must be replaced. (The arrangement of the pathways may differ, depending on the switch manufacturer. The photo above shows the three possible pathway arrangements.)

Working with Receptacles

A 120-volt duplex receptacle can be wired to the electrical system in a number of ways. The most common are shown on these pages.

Wiring configurations may vary slightly from these photographs, depending on the kind of receptacles used, the type of cable, or the technique of the electrician who installed the wiring. To make dependable repairs or replacements, use masking tape and label each wire according to its location on the terminals of the existing receptacle.

Receptacles are wired as either end-of-run or middle-of-run. These two basic configurations are easily identified by counting the number of cables entering the receptacle box. End-of-run wiring has only one cable, indicating that the circuit ends. Middle-of-run wiring has two cables, indicating that the circuit continues on to other receptacles, switches, or fixtures.

A split-circuit receptacle is shown on the next page. Each half of a split-circuit receptacle is wired to a separate circuit. This allows two appliances of high wattage to be plugged into the same receptacle without blowing a fuse or tripping a breaker. This wiring configuration is similar to a receptacle that is controlled by a wall switch. Code requires a switch-controlled receptacle in any room that does not have a built-in light fixture operated by a wall switch.

Split-circuit and switch-controlled receptacles are connected to two hot wires, so use caution during repairs or replacements. Make sure the connecting tab between the hot screw terminals is removed.

Two-slot receptacles are common in older homes. There is no grounding wire attached to the receptacle, but the box may be grounded with armored cable or conduit.

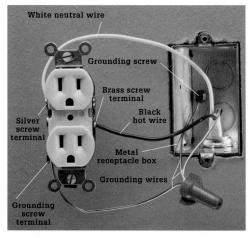

Single cable entering the box indicates end-of-run wiring. The black hot wire is attached to a brass screw terminal, and the white neutral wire is connected to a silver screw terminal. If the box is metal, the grounding wire is pigtailed to the grounding screws of the receptacle and the box. In a plastic box, the grounding wire is attached directly to the grounding screw terminal of the receptacle.

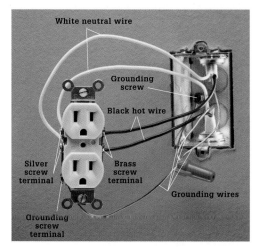

Two cables entering the box indicate middle-of-run wiring. Black hot wires are connected to brass screw terminals, and white neutral wires to silver screw terminals. The grounding wire is pigtailed to the grounding screws of the receptacle and the box.

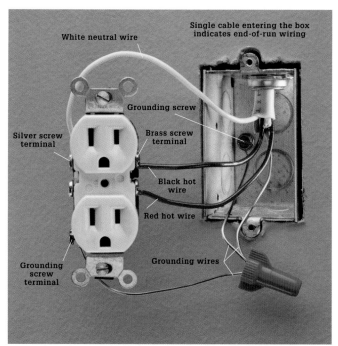

Single cable entering the box indicates end-of-run wiring

White neutral wire

Grounding screw

Silver screw terminal

Brass screw terminal

Black hot wire

Red hot wire

Grounding screw terminal

Grounding wires

A split-circuit receptacle is attached to a black hot wire, a red hot wire, a white neutral wire, and a bare grounding wire. The wiring is similar to a switch-controlled receptacle. The hot wires are attached to the brass screw terminals, and the connecting tab or fin between the brass terminals is removed. The white wire is attached to a silver screw terminal, and the connecting tab on the neutral side remains intact. The grounding wire is pigtailed to the grounding screw terminal of the receptacle and to the grounding screw attached to the box.

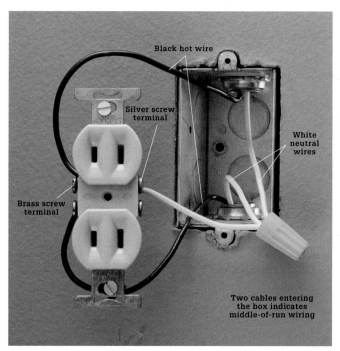

Black hot wire

Silver screw terminal

White neutral wires

Brass screw terminal

Two cables entering the box indicates middle-of-run wiring

A two-slot receptacle is often found in older homes. The black hot wires are connected to the brass screw terminals, and the white neutral wires are pigtailed to a silver screw terminal. Two-slot receptacles may be replaced with three-slot types, but only if a means of grounding exists at the receptacle box. In some municipalities, you may replace a two-slot receptacle with a GFCI receptacle as long as the receptacle has a sticker that reads "No equipment ground."

How to Install a New Receptacle

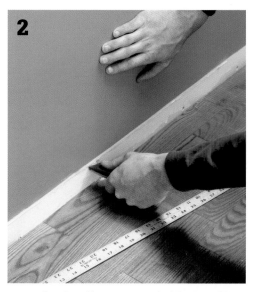

Position the new pop-in box on the wall and trace around it. Consider the location of hidden utilities within the wall before you cut.

Remove baseboard between new and existing receptacle. Cut away the drywall about 1" below the baseboard with a jigsaw, wallboard saw, or utility knife.

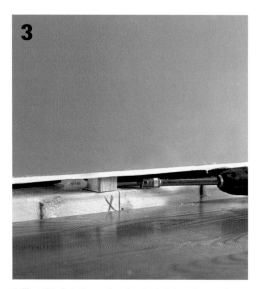

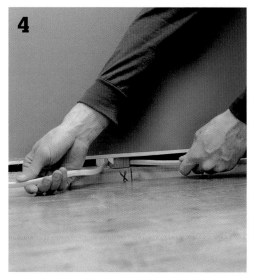

Drill a ⅝" hole in the center of each stud along the opening between the two receptacles. A drill bit extender or a flexible drill bit will allow you a better angle and make drilling the holes easier.

Run the branch cable through the holes from the new location to the existing receptacle. Staple the cable to the stud below the box. Install a metal nail plate on the front edge of each stud that the cable routes through.

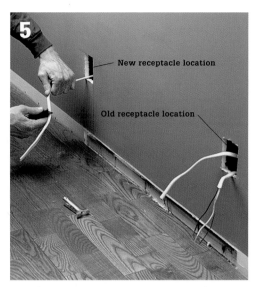

5

New receptacle location

Old receptacle location

Turn off the power at the main panel and test for power.
Remove the old receptacle and its box, and pull the new
branch cable up through the hole. Remove sheathing and
insulation from both ends of the new cable.

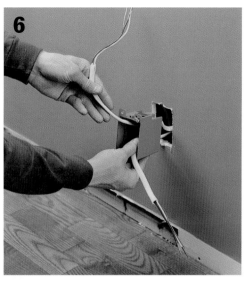

6

Thread the new and old cables into a pop-in box large
enough to contain the added wires and clamp the cables. Fit
the box into the old hole and attach it.

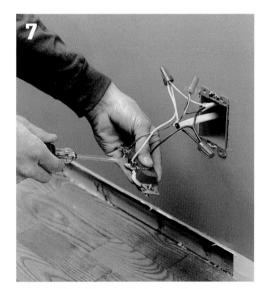

7

Reconnect the old receptacle by connecting its neutral,
hot, and grounding screws to the new branch cable and the
old cable from the panel with pigtails.

8

Pull the cable through another pop-in box for the new
receptacle. Secure the cable and install the box. Connect the
new receptacle to the new branch cable. Insert the receptacle
into the box and attach the receptacle and cover plate with
screws. Patch the opening with ½"-thick wood strips or drywall.
Reattach the baseboard to the studs.

GFCI Receptacles

The ground-fault circuit-interrupter (GFCI) receptacle protects against electrical shock caused by a faulty appliance, or a worn cord or plug. It senses small changes in current flow and can shut off power in as little as ¹⁄₄₀ of a second.

GFCIs are now required in bathrooms, kitchens, garages, crawl spaces, unfinished basements, and outdoor receptacle locations. Consult your local codes for any requirements regarding the installation of GFCI receptacles. Most GFCIs use standard screw terminal connections, but some have wire leads and are attached with wire connectors. Because the body of a GFCI receptacle is larger than a standard receptacle, small crowded electrical boxes may need to be replaced with more spacious boxes.

The GFCI receptacle may be wired to protect only itself (single location), or it can be wired to protect all receptacles, switches, and light fixtures from the GFCI "forward" to the end of the circuit (multiple locations).

Because the GFCI is so sensitive, it is most effective when wired to protect a single location. The more receptacles any one GFCI protects, the more susceptible it is to "phantom tripping," shutting off power because of tiny, normal fluctuations in current flow.

Tools & Materials ▸

Circuit tester
Screwdriver

Wire connectors
Masking tape

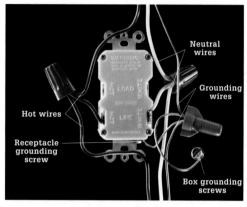

A GFCI wired for single-location protection (shown from the back) has hot and neutral wires connected only to the screw terminals marked LINE. A GFCI connected for single-location protection may be wired as either an end-of-run or middle-of-run configuration (page 110).

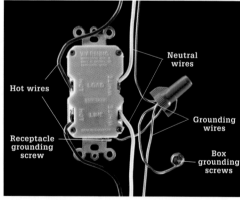

A GFCI wired for multiple-location protection (shown from the back) has one set of hot and neutral wires connected to the LINE pair of screw terminals, and the other set connected to the LOAD pair of screw terminals. A GFCI receptacle connected for multiple-location protection may be wired only as a middle-of-run configuration.

How to Install a Single-location GFCI

1

Pigtail all the white neutral wires together, and connect the pigtail to the terminal marked WHITE LINE on the GFCI (see photo on opposite page).

2

Disconnect all black hot wires from the brass screw terminals of the old receptacle. Pigtail these wires together, and connect them to the terminal marked HOT LINE on the GFCI.

3

If a grounding wire is available, connect it to the green grounding screw terminal of the GFCI. Mount the GFCI in the receptacle box, and reattach the cover plate. Restore power, and test the GFCI according to the manufacturer's instructions.

How to Install Multiple-location GFCIs

1

Connect the white feed wire to the terminal marked WHITE LINE on the GFCI. Connect the black feed wire to the terminal marked HOT LINE on the GFCI.

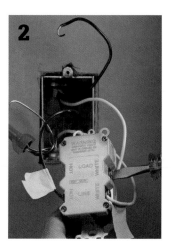

2

Connect the other white neutral wire to the terminal marked WHITE LOAD on the GFCI.

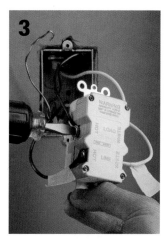

3

Connect the other black hot wire to the terminal marked HOT LOAD on the GFCI.

Planning New Wiring

Careful planning of a wiring project ensures you will have plenty of power for present and future needs. Whether you are adding circuits in a room addition, wiring a remodeled kitchen, or adding an outdoor circuit, consider all possible ways the space might be used, and plan for enough electrical service to meet peak needs.

For example, when wiring a room addition, remember that the way a room is used can change. In a room used as a spare bedroom, a single 15-amp circuit provides plenty of power, but if you ever choose to convert the same room to a family recreation space, you will need additional circuits.

When wiring a remodeled kitchen, it is a good idea to install circuits for an electric oven and countertop range, even if you do not have these electric appliances. Installing these circuits now makes it easy to convert from gas to electric appliances at a later date.

A large wiring project adds a considerable load to your main electrical service. In about 25 percent of all homes, some type of service upgrade is needed before new wiring can be installed. For example, many homeowners will need to replace an older 60-amp electrical service with a new service rated for 100 amps or more. This is a job for a licensed electrician but is well worth the investment. In other cases, the existing main service provides adequate power, but the main circuit breaker panel is too full to hold any new circuit breakers. In this case it is necessary to install a circuit breaker subpanel to provide room for hooking up added circuits.

This chapter gives an easy five-step method for determining your electrical needs and planning new circuits.

Five Steps for Planning a Wiring Project

1

Examine your main service panel (page 130). The amp rating of the electrical service and the size of the circuit breaker panel will help you determine if a service upgrade is needed.

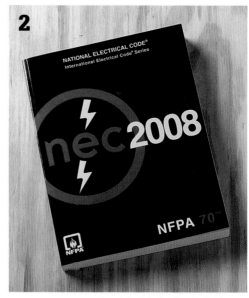

2

Learn about codes (pages 131 to 135). The National Electrical Code (NEC), and local electrical codes and building codes, provide guidelines for determining how much power and how many circuits your home needs. Your local electrical inspector can tell you which regulations apply to your job.

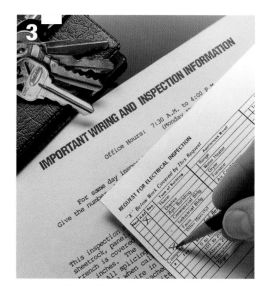

Prepare for inspection. Remember that your work must be reviewed by your local electrical inspector. When planning your wiring project, always follow the inspector's guidelines for quality workmanship.

Evaluate electrical loads. New circuits put an added load on your electrical service. Make sure that total load of the existing wiring and the planned new circuits does not exceed the main service capacity.

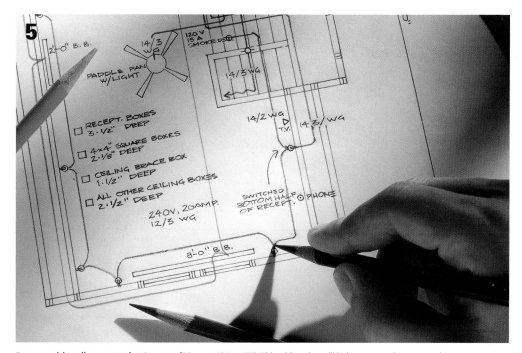

Draw a wiring diagram and get a permit (pages 136 to 137). This wiring plan will help you organize your work.

Examine Your Main Service Panel

The first step in planning a new wiring project is to look in your main circuit breaker panel and find the size of the service by reading the amperage rating on the main circuit breaker. As you plan new circuits and evaluate electrical loads, knowing the size of the main service helps you determine if you need a service upgrade.

Also look for open circuit breaker slots in the panel. The number of open slots will determine if you need to add a circuit breaker subpanel.

Find the service size by opening the main service panel and reading the amp rating printed on the main circuit breaker. In most cases, 100-amp service provides enough power to handle the added loads of projects like the ones shown in this book. A service rated for 60 amps or less may need to be upgraded.

Older service panels use fuses instead of circuit breakers. Have an electrician replace this type of panel with a circuit breaker panel that provides enough power and enough open breaker slots for the new circuits you are planning.

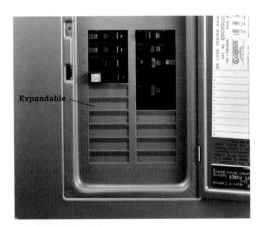

Look for open circuit breaker slots in the main circuit breaker panel or in a circuit breaker subpanel, if your home already has one. You will need one open slot for each 120-volt circuit you plan to install and two slots for each 240-volt circuit. If your main circuit breaker panel has no open breaker slots, install a subpanel to provide room for connecting new circuits.

Learn About Codes

To ensure public safety, your community requires that you get a permit to install new wiring and have the completed work reviewed by an appointed inspector. Electrical inspectors use the National Electrical Code (NEC) as the primary authority for evaluating wiring, but they also follow the local Building Code and Electrical Code standards.

As you begin planning new circuits, call or visit your local electrical inspector and discuss the project with him. The inspector can tell you which of the national and local code requirements apply to your job, and may give you a packet of information summarizing these regulations. Later, when you apply to the inspector for a work permit, he will expect you to understand the local guidelines as well as a few basic National Electrical Code requirements.

The National Electrical Code is a set of standards that provides minimum safety requirements for wiring installations. It is revised every three years. The national code requirements for the projects shown in this book are thoroughly explained on the following pages. For more information, you can find copies of the current NEC, as well as a number of excellent handbooks based on the NEC, at libraries and bookstores.

In addition to being the final authority of code requirements, inspectors are electrical professionals with years of experience. Although they have busy schedules, most inspectors are happy to answer questions and help you design well-planned circuits.

Basic Electrical Code Requirements

Electrical Code requirements for living areas: Living areas need at least one 15-amp or 20-amp basic lighting/receptacle circuit for each 600 sq. ft. of living space and should have a dedicated circuit for each type of permanent appliance, like an air conditioner, computer, or a group of baseboard heaters and within 6 ft. of any door opening. Receptacles on basic lighting/ receptacle circuits should be spaced no more than 12 ft. apart. Many electricians and electrical inspectors recommend even closer spacing. Any wall more than 24" wide also needs a receptacle. Every room should have a wall switch at the point of entry to control either a ceiling light or plug-in lamp. Kitchens and bathrooms must have a ceiling-mounted light fixture.

Selected NEC Standards & Tips

Three-way switches

Measure the living areas of your home, excluding closets and unfinished spaces. A sonic measuring tool gives room dimensions quickly and contains a built-in calculator for figuring floor area. You will need a minimum of one basic lighting/receptacle circuit for every 600 sq. ft. of living space. The total square footage also helps you determine heating and cooling needs for new room additions.

Stairways with six steps or more must have lighting that illuminates each step. The light fixture must be controlled by three-way switches at the top and bottom landings.

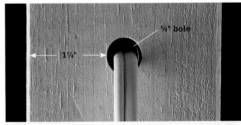

⅝" hole

1¼"

Nail guard

Furring strip

Cutaway view

Kitchen and bathroom receptacles must be protected by a ground-fault circuit-interrupter (GFCI). Also, all outdoor receptacles and general-use receptacles in an unfinished basement or crawl space and garages must be protected by a GFCI.

Cables must be protected against damage by nails and screws by at least 1¼" of wood (top). When cables pass through 2 × 2 furring strips (bottom), protect the cables with metal nail guards.

Closets and other storage spaces need at least one light fixture that is controlled by a wall switch near the entrance. Prevent fire hazards by positioning the light fixtures so the outer globes are at least 12" away from all shelf areas.

Hallways more than 10 ft. long need at least one receptacle. All hallways should have a switch-controlled light fixture.

Amp ratings of receptacles must match the size of the circuit. A common mistake is to use 20-amp receptacles (top) on 15-amp circuits—a potential cause of dangerous circuit overloads because it allows you to plug in appliances that draw over 15 amps.

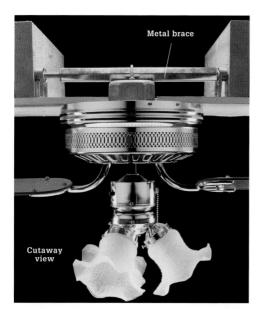

A metal brace attached to framing members is required for ceiling fans and large light fixtures that are too heavy to be supported by an electrical box.

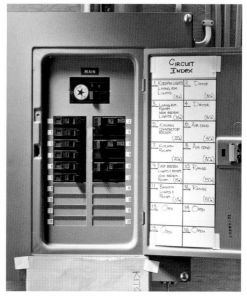

Label new circuits on an index attached to the circuit breaker panel. List the rooms and appliances controlled by each circuit. Make sure the area around the panel is clean, well lit, and accessible.

Highlights of the National Electrical Code ▸

BY MATERIAL

Service Panel (page 130)

- Maintain a minimum 30 × 36" of clearance in front of the service panel.
- Ground all 120-volt and 240-volt circuits.
- Match the amperage rating of the circuit when replacing fuses.
- Locate service panels and subpanels a maximum of 79" above floor level.
- Use handle-tie breakers for 240-volt loads (line to line).
- Close all unused service panel openings.
- Label each fuse and breaker clearly on the panel.

Electrical Boxes (page 108)

- Use boxes that are large enough to accommodate the number of wires entering the box.
- Locate all receptacle boxes 12" above the finished floor (standard).
- Locate all switch boxes 48" above the finished floor (standard). For special circumstances, inspectors will allow switch and location measurements to be altered, such as a switch at 36" above the floor in a child's bedroom or receptacles at 24" above the floor to make them more accessible for someone in a wheelchair.
- Install all boxes so they remain accessible.
- Leave no gaps greater than ⅛" between wallboard and front of electrical boxes.
- Place receptacle boxes flush with combustible surfaces.
- Leave a minimum of 8" of usable cable or wire extending past the front of the electrical box.

Wires & Cables (page 90)

- Use wires that are large enough for the amperage rating of the circuit (see Wire Size Chart, page 90).
- Drill holes at least 2" back from the exposed edge of joists to run cables through. Do not attach cables to the bottom edge of joists.
- Do not run cables diagonally between framing members.
- Run cable between receptacles 20" above the floor.
- Use nail plates to protect cable that is run through holes drilled or cut into studs less than 1¼" from front edge of stud.
- Do not crimp cables sharply.
- Contain spliced wires or connections entirely in a plastic or metal electrical box.
- Use wire connectors to join wires.
- Use staples to fasten cables within 8" of an electrical box and every 48" along its run.

- Leave a minimum ¼" (maximum 1") of sheathing where cables enter an electrical box.
- Clamp cables and wires to electrical boxes with approved NM clamp. No clamp is necessary for one-gang plastic boxes if cables are stapled within 8".
- Label all cables and wires at each electrical box to show which circuits they serve for the rough-in inspection.
- Connect only a single wire to a single screw terminal. Use pigtails to join more than one wire to a screw terminal.

Switches (page 116)

- Use a switch-controlled receptacle in rooms without a built-in light fixture operated by a wall switch.
- Use three-way switches at the top and bottom on stairways with six steps or more.
- Use switches with grounding screw with plastic electrical boxes.
- Locate all wall switches within easy reach of the room entrance.

Receptacles (page 122)

- Match the amp rating of a receptacle with the size of the circuit.
- Include receptacles on all walls 24" wide or greater.
- Include receptacles so a 6-ft. cord can be plugged in from any point along a wall or every 12-ft. along a wall.
- Include receptacles in any hallway that is 10-ft. long or more.
- Use three-prong, grounded receptacles for all 15- or 20-amp, 120-volt branch circuits.
- Include a switch-controlled receptacle in rooms without a built-in light fixture operated by a wall switch.
- Install GFCI-protected receptacles in bathrooms, kitchens, garages, crawl spaces, unfinished basements, and outdoor receptacle locations.
- Install an isolated-ground circuit to protect sensitive equipment, like a computer, against tiny power fluctuations. Computers should also be protected by a standard surge protector.

Light Fixtures

- Use mounting straps that are anchored to the electrical boxes to mount ceiling fixtures.
- Keep non-IC-rated recessed light fixtures 3" from insulation and ½" from combustibles.
- Include at least one switch-operated lighting fixture in every room.

Grounding

- Ground all receptacles by connecting receptacle grounding screws to the circuit grounding wires.
- Use switches with grounding screws whenever possible. Always ground switches installed in plastic electrical boxes and all switches in kitchens, bathrooms, and basements.

BY ROOM
Kitchens/Dining Rooms

- Install a dedicated 40- or 50-amp, 120/240-volt circuit for a range (or two circuits for separate oven and countertop units).
- Install two 20-amp small appliance circuits.
- Install dedicated 15-amp, 120-volt circuits for dish-washers and food disposals (required by many local codes).
- Use GFCI receptacles for all accessible countertop receptacles; receptacles behind fixed appliances do not need to be GFCIs.
- Position receptacles for appliances that will be installed within cabinets, such as microwaves or food disposals, according to the manufacturer's instructions.
- Include receptacles on all counters wider than 12".
- Space receptacles a maximum of 48" apart above countertops and closer together in areas where many appliances will be used.
- Locate receptacles 18" above countertop. If backsplash is more than the standard 4" or the bottom of cabinet is less than 18" from countertop, center the box in space between countertop and bottom of wall cabinet.
- Mount one receptacle within 12" of the countertop on islands and peninsulas that are 12 × 24" or greater.
- Do not put lights on small appliance circuits.
- Install additional lighting in work areas at a sink or range for convenience and safety.

Bathrooms

- Install a separate 20-amp circuit.
- Ground switches in bathrooms.
- Use GFCI-protected receptacles.
- Install at least one ceiling-mounted light fixture.
- Place blower heaters in bathrooms well away from the sink and tub.

Utility/Laundry Rooms

- Install a separate 20-amp circuit for a washing machine.
- Install a minimum feed 30-amp #10 THHN wire for the dryer powered by a separate 120/240-volt major appliance circuit.
- Install metal conduit for cable runs in unfinished rooms.
- Use GFCI-protected receptacles, except for fixed appliances, such as freezers or dryers.

Living, Entertainment, Bedrooms

- Install a minimum of two 15-amp circuits in living rooms.
- Install a minimum of one 15- or 20-amp basic lighting/receptacle circuit for each 600 sq. ft. of living space.
- Install a dedicated circuit for each permanent appliance, like an air conditioner, computer, or group of electric baseboard heaters.
- Do not use standard electrical boxes to support ceiling fans.
- Include receptacles on walls 24" wide or more.
- Space receptacles on basic lighting/receptacle circuits a maximum of 12 ft. apart. For convenience you can space them as close as 6 ft.
- Position permanent light fixtures in the center of the room's ceiling.
- Install permanently wired smoke alarms in room additions that include sleeping areas.

Outdoors

- Check for underground utilities before digging.
- Use UF cable for outdoor wiring needs.
- Run cable in schedule 80 PVC plastic, as required by local code.
- Bury cables housed in conduit at least 18" deep; cable not in conduit must be buried at least 24" deep.
- Use weatherproof electrical boxes with watertight covers.
- Use GFCI-protected receptacles.
- Install receptacles a minimum of 12" above ground level.
- Anchor freestanding receptacles not attached to a structure by embedding the schedule 80 PVC plastic conduit in a concrete footing, so that it is at least 12" but no more than 18" above ground level.
- Plan on installing a 20-amp, 120-volt circuit if the circuit contains more than one light fixture rated for 300 watts, or more than four receptacles.

Stairs/Hallways

- Use three-way switches at the top and bottom on stairways with six steps or more.
- Include receptacles in any hallway that is 10 ft. long or more.
- Position stairway lights so each step is illuminated.

Draw a Diagram & Obtain a Permit

Drawing a wiring diagram is the last step in planning a circuit installation. A detailed wiring diagram helps you get a work permit, makes it easy to create a list of materials, and serves as a guide for laying out circuits and installing cables and fixtures. Use the circuit maps on pages 138 to 145 as a guide for planning wiring configurations and cable runs. Bring the diagram and materials list when you visit electrical inspectors to apply for a work permit.

Never install new wiring without following your community's permit and inspection procedure. A work permit is not expensive, and it ensures that your work will be reviewed by a qualified inspector to guarantee its safety. If you install new wiring without the proper permit, an accident or fire traced to faulty wiring could cause your insurance company to discontinue your policy and can hurt the resale value of your home.

When electrical inspectors look over your wiring diagram, they will ask questions to see if you have a basic understanding of the electrical code and fundamental wiring skills. Some inspectors ask these questions informally, while others give a short written test. Inspectors may allow you to do some, but not all, of the work. For example, they may ask that all final circuit connections at the circuit breaker panel be made by a licensed electrician, while allowing you to do all other work.

A few communities allow you to install wiring only when supervised by an electrician. This means you can still install your own wiring but must hire an electrician to apply for the work permit and to check your work before inspectors review it. The electrician is held responsible for the quality of the job.

Remember that it is the inspectors' responsibility to help you do a safe and professional job. Feel free to call them with questions about wiring techniques or materials.

A detailed wiring diagram and a list of materials is required before electrical inspectors will issue a work permit. If blueprints exist for the space you are remodeling, start your electrical diagram by tracing the wall outlines from the blueprint. Use standard electrical symbols (next page) to clearly show all the receptacles, switches, light fixtures, and permanent appliances. Make a copy of the symbol key, and attach it to the wiring diagram for the inspectors' convenience. Show each cable run, and label its wire size and circuit amperage.

How to Draw a Wiring Plan

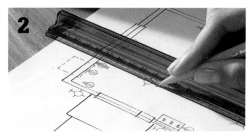

Draw a scaled diagram of the space you will be wiring, showing walls, doors, windows, plumbing pipes and fixtures, and heating and cooling ducts. Find the floor space by multiplying room length by width, and indicate this on the diagram. Do not include closets or storage areas when figuring space.

Mark the location of all switches, receptacles, light fixtures, and permanent appliances using the electrical symbols shown below. Where you locate these devices along the cable run determines how they are wired. Use the circuit maps on pages 138 to 145 as a guide for drawing wiring diagrams.

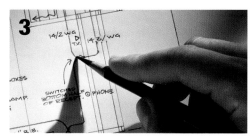

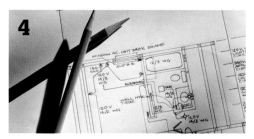

Draw in cable runs between devices. Indicate cable size and type, and the amperage of the circuits. Use a different-colored pencil for each circuit.

Identify the wattages for light fixtures and permanent appliances, and the type and size of each electrical box. On another sheet of paper, make a detailed list of all materials you will use.

Electrical Symbol Key ▶

(copy this key and attach it to your wiring plan)

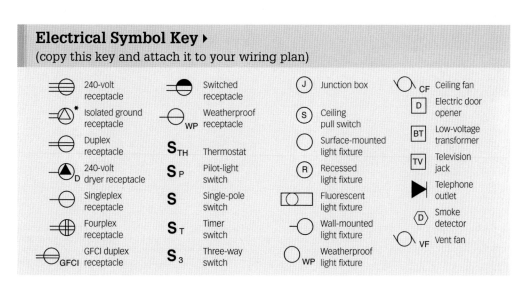

	240-volt receptacle
	Isolated ground receptacle
	Duplex receptacle
	240-volt dryer receptacle
	Singleplex receptacle
	Fourplex receptacle
	GFCI duplex receptacle
	Switched receptacle
	Weatherproof receptacle
S_TH	Thermostat
S_P	Pilot-light switch
S	Single-pole switch
S_T	Timer switch
S_3	Three-way switch
J	Junction box
S	Ceiling pull switch
	Surface-mounted light fixture
R	Recessed light fixture
	Fluorescent light fixture
	Wall-mounted light fixture
	Weatherproof light fixture
CF	Ceiling fan
D	Electric door opener
BT	Low-voltage transformer
TV	Television jack
	Telephone outlet
D	Smoke detector
VF	Vent fan

Using Circuit Maps

The arrangement of switches and appliances along an electrical circuit differs for every project. This means that the configuration of wires inside an electrical box can vary greatly, even when fixtures are identical.

The circuit maps on the following pages show the most common wiring variations for typical electrical devices. Most new wiring you install will match one or more of the maps shown. Find the maps that match your situation and use them to plan your circuit layouts.

The 120-volt circuits shown on the following pages are wired for 15 amps using 14-gauge wire and receptacles rated at 15 amps. If you are installing a 20-amp circuit, substitute 12-gauge cables and use receptacles rated for 20 amps.

In configurations where a white wire serves as a hot wire instead of a neutral, both ends of the wire are coded with black tape to identify it as hot. In addition, each of the circuit maps shows a box grounding screw. This grounding screw is required in all metal boxes, but plastic electrical boxes do not need to be grounded.

Note: For clarity, all grounding conductors in the circuit maps are colored green. In practice, the grounding wires inside sheathed cables usually are bare copper.

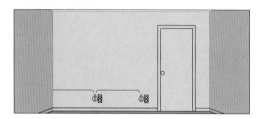

1. 120-VOLT DUPLEX RECEPTACLES WIRED IN SEQUENCE

Use this layout to link any number of duplex receptacles in a basic lighting/receptacle circuit. The last receptacle in the cable run is connected like the receptacle shown at the right side of the circuit map below. All other receptacles are wired like the receptacle shown on the left side. Requires two-wire cables.

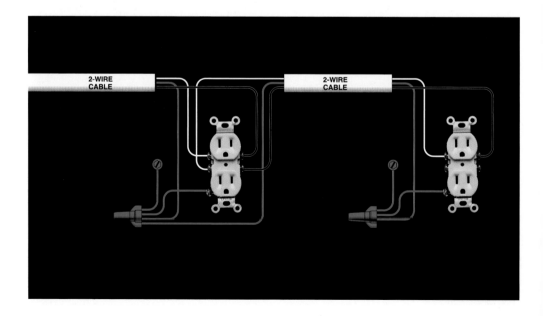

2-WIRE CABLE

2-WIRE CABLE

2. GFCI RECEPTACLES
(Single-location Protection)

Use this layout when receptacles are within 6 ft. of a water source, like those in kitchens and bathrooms. To prevent nuisance tripping caused by normal power surges, GFCIs should be connected only at the line screw terminal so they protect a single location, not the fixtures on the load side of the circuit. Requires two-wire cables. Where a GFCI must protect other fixtures, use circuit map 3.

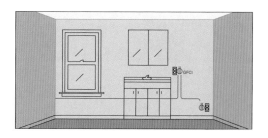

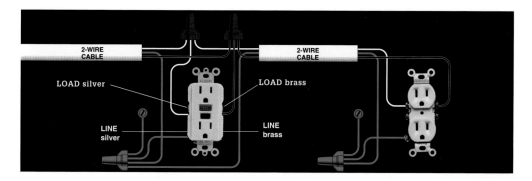

3. GFCI RECEPTACLE, SWITCH
& LIGHT FIXTURE (Wired for
Multiple-location Protection)

In some locations, such as an outdoor circuit, it is a good idea to connect a GFCI receptacle so it also provides shock protection to the wires and fixtures that continue to the end of the circuit. Wires from the power source are connected to the line screw terminals; outgoing wires are connected to load screws. Requires two-wire cables.

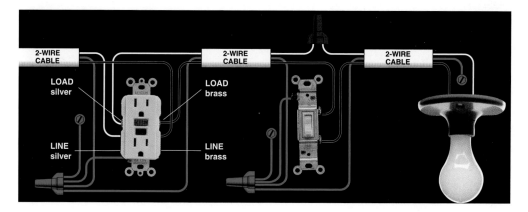

4. SINGLE-POLE SWITCH & LIGHT FIXTURE (Light Fixture at End of Cable Run)

Use this layout for light fixtures in basic lighting/receptacle circuits throughout the home. It is often used as an extension to a series of receptacles (circuit map 1). Requires two-wire cables.

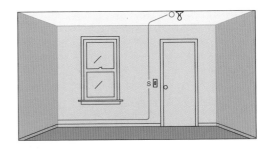

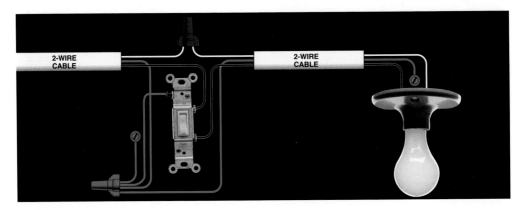

5. SINGLE-POLE SWITCH & LIGHT FIXTURE (Switch at End of Cable Run)

Use this layout, sometimes called a switch loop, where it is more practical to locate a switch at the end of the cable run. In the last length of cable, both insulated wires are hot; the white wire is tagged with black tape at both ends to indicate it is hot. Requires two-wire cables.

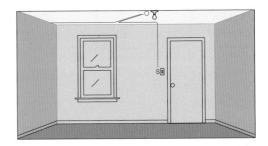

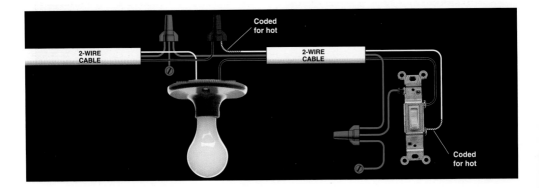

6. SINGLE-POLE SWITCH & TWO LIGHT FIXTURES (Switch Between Light Fixtures, Light at Start of Cable Run)

Use this layout when you need to control two fixtures from one single-pole switch and the switch is between the two lights in the cable run. Power feeds to one of the lights. Requires two-wire and three-wire cables.

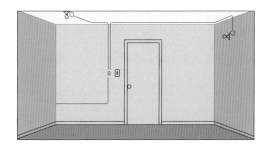

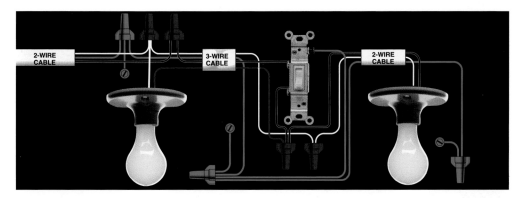

7. SINGLE-POLE SWITCH & LIGHT FIXTURE, DUPLEX RECEPTACLE (Switch at Start of Cable Run)

Use this layout to continue a circuit past a switched light fixture to one or more duplex receptacles. To add multiple receptacles to the circuit, see circuit map 1. Requires two-wire and three-wire cables.

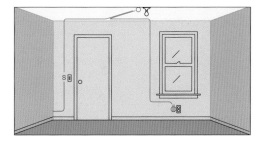

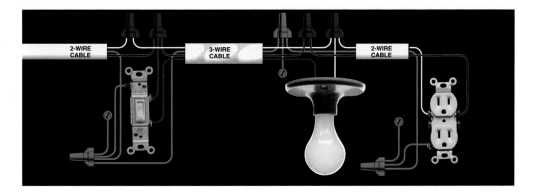

8. DOUBLE RECEPTACLE SMALL-APPLIANCE CIRCUIT WITH GFCIs & SHARED NEUTRAL WIRE

Use this layout to wire a double receptacle circuit when code requires that some of the receptacles be GFCIs. The GFCIs should be wired for single-location protection (see circuit map 2). Requires three-wire and two-wire cables.

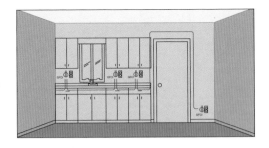

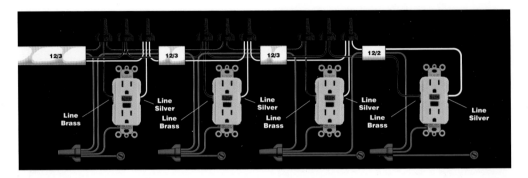

9. DOUBLE RECEPTACLE SMALL APPLIANCE CIRCUIT WITH GFCIs & SEPARATE NEUTRAL WIRES

If the room layout or local codes do not allow for a shared neutral wire, use this layout instead. The GFCIs should be wired for single-location protection (see circuit map 2). Requires two-wire cable.

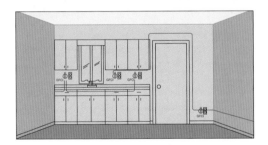

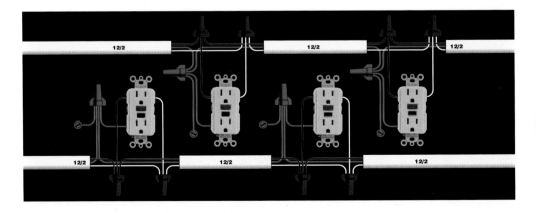

10. 120/240-VOLT RANGE RECEPTACLE

This layout is for a 50- or 60-amp, 120/240-volt dedicated appliance circuit wired with 6/3 cable, as required by code for a large kitchen range. The black and red circuit wires, connected to a double-pole circuit breaker in the circuit breaker panel, each bring 120 volts of power to the setscrew terminals on the receptacle. The white circuit wire attached to the neutral bus bar in the circuit breaker panel is connected to the neutral setscrew terminal on the receptacle.

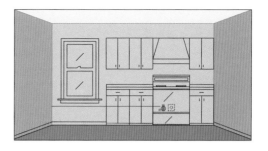

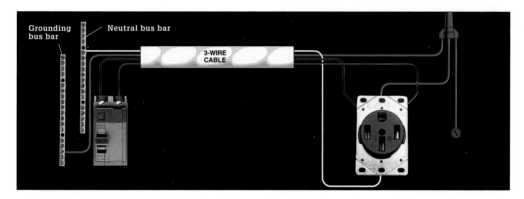

11. 240-VOLT BASEBOARD HEATERS, THERMOSTAT

This layout is typical for a series of 240-volt baseboard heaters controlled by a wall thermostat. Except for the last heater in the circuit, all heaters are wired as shown below. The last heater is connected to only one cable. The size of the circuit and cables are determined by finding the total wattage of all heaters. Requires two-wire cable.

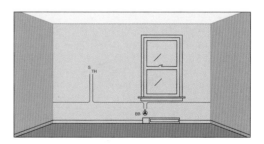

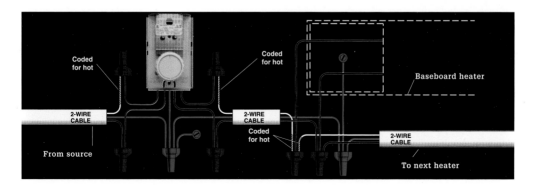

12. THREE-WAY SWITCHES & LIGHT FIXTURE (Fixture Between Switches)

This layout for three-way switches lets you control a light fixture from two locations. Each switch has one common screw terminal and two traveler screws. Circuit wires attached to the traveler screws run between the two switches, and hot wires attached to the common screws bring current from the power source and carry it to the light fixture. Requires two-wire and three-wire cables.

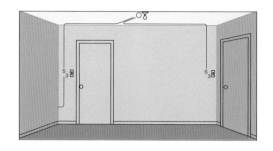

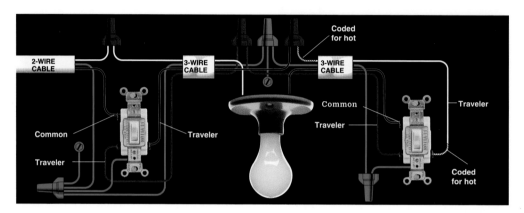

13. THREE-WAY SWITCHES & LIGHT FIXTURE (Fixture at Start of Cable Run)

Use this layout when it is more convenient to locate the fixture ahead of the three-way switches in the cable run. Requires two-wire and three-wire cables.

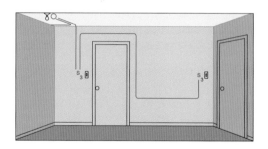

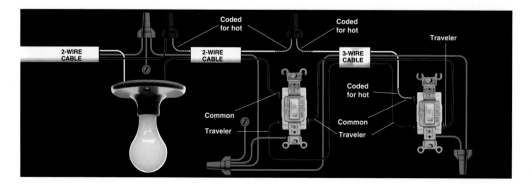

14. FOUR-WAY SWITCH & LIGHT FIXTURE (Fixture at Start of Cable Run)

This layout lets you control a light fixture from three locations. The end switches are three-way and the middle is four-way. A pair of three-wire cables enter the box of the four-way switch. The white and red wires from one cable attach to the top pair of screw terminals (line 1) and the white and red wires from the other cable attaches to the bottom screw terminals (line 2). Requires two three-way switches and one four-way switch and two-wire and three-wire cables.

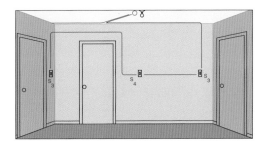

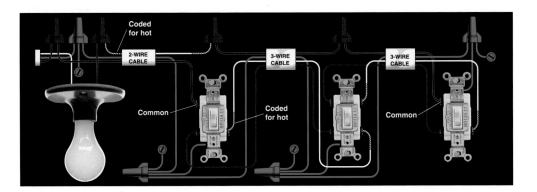

15. FOUR-WAY SWITCH & LIGHT FIXTURE (Fixture at End of Cable Run)

Use this layout when it is more practical to locate the fixture at the end of the cable run. Requires two three-way switches and one four-way switch and two-wire and three-wire cables.

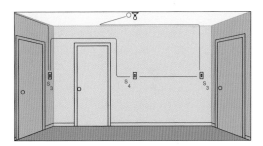

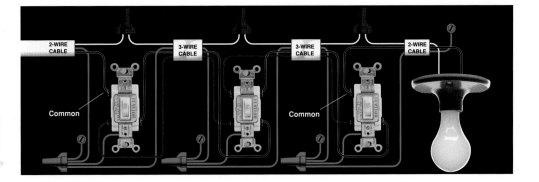

HOME IMPROVEMENT BASICS

Flooring

Like any successful remodeling project, replacing your floor covering requires detailed planning and attention to design. Flooring is not separate from the rest of the room; it should fit into the overall design to create a desired effect. A floor can create excitement and become a focal point or it can serve as a background for the rest of the room.

Through careful planning, you can choose flooring that can be used successfully in multiple rooms, or select a pattern or design that is repeated throughout the room or in adjacent rooms.

Keep in mind that your flooring design will last a long time, especially if you install ceramic tile or wood. In most cases, the only way to change the design of your floor is to install a new floor covering.

In this chapter:

- Installing Underlayment
- Installing Radiant Floor Mats
- Installing Hardwood Strip Flooring
- Installing Laminate Floors
- Installing Parquet Flooring
- Installing Sheet Vinyl
- Evaluating an Existing Floor
- Installing Resilient Tile
- Installing Bamboo Flooring
- Installing Ceramic Tile
- Installing Mosaic Tile
- Installing Carpet Squares
- Refinishing Wood Floors

Installing Underlayment

Underlayment is a layer of sheeting screwed or nailed to the subfloor to provide a smooth, stable surface for the floor covering. The type of underlayment you choose depends in part on the type of floor covering you plan to install. Ceramic and natural stone tile floors usually require an underlayment that stands up to moisture, such as cementboard. For vinyl flooring, use a quality-grade plywood; most warranties are void if the flooring is installed over substandard underlayments. If you want to use your old flooring as underlayment, apply an embossing leveler to prepare it for the new installation. Most wood flooring and carpeting do not require underlayment and are often placed directly on a plywood subfloor.

When you install new underlayment, attach it securely to the subfloor in all areas, including under movable appliances. Notch the underlayment to fit the room's contours. Insert the underlayment beneath door casings and moldings. Once the underlayment is installed, use a latex patching compound to fill gaps, holes, and low spots. This compound is also used to cover screw heads, nail heads, and seams in underlayment. Some compounds include dry and wet ingredients that need to be mixed, while others are premixed. The compound is applied with a trowel or wallboard knife.

Plywood

Fiber/cementboard

Cementboard

Isolation membrane

Tools & Materials ▸

Drill	Floor-patching
Circular saw	compound
Wallboard knife	Latex additive
Power sander	Thin-set mortar
¼" notched trowel	1½" galvanized
Straightedge	deck screws
Utility knife	Fiberglass-mesh
Jigsaw with carbide-	wallboard tape
tipped blade	
⅛" notched trowel	
Flooring roller	
Underlayment	
1" deck screws	

How to Install Plywood Underlayment

Plywood is the most common underlayment for vinyl flooring and some ceramic tile installations. For vinyl, use ¼" exterior-grade, AC plywood. This type has one smooth side for a quality surface. Wood-based floor coverings, like parquet, can be installed over lower-quality exterior-grade plywood. For ceramic tile, use ½" AC plywood. When installing plywood, leave ¼" expansion gaps at the walls and between sheets.

Install a full sheet of plywood along the longest wall, making sure the underlayment seams are not aligned with the subfloor seams. Fasten the plywood to the subfloor using 1" deck screws driven every 6" along the edges and at 8" intervals in the field of the sheet.

Continue fastening sheets of plywood to the subfloor, driving the screw heads slightly below the underlayment surface. Leave ¼" expansion gaps at the walls and between sheets. Offset seams in subsequent rows.

Using a circular saw or jigsaw, notch the plywood to meet the existing flooring in doorways. Fasten the notched sheets to the subfloor.

Mix floor-patching compound and latex or acrylic additive following the manufacturer's directions. Spread it over seams and screw heads, using a wallboard knife.

Let the patching compound dry, then sand the patched areas, using a power sander.

How to Install Cementboard

Ceramic and natural stone tile floors usually require an underlayment that stands up to moisture, such as cementboard. Fiber/cementboard is a thin, high-density underlayment used under ceramic tile and vinyl flooring in situations where floor height is a concern. Cementboard is used only for ceramic tile or stone tile installations. It remains stable even when wet, so it is the best underlayment to use in areas that are likely to get wet, such as bathrooms. Cementboard is more expensive than plywood, but a good investment for a large tile installation.

Mix thin-set mortar according to the manufacturer's directions. Starting at the longest wall, spread the mortar on the subfloor in a figure eight pattern using a ¼" notched trowel. Spread only enough mortar for one sheet at a time. Set the cementboard on the mortar with the rough side up, making sure the edges are offset from the subfloor seams.

Fasten the cementboard to the subfloor using 1¼" cementboard screws driven every 6" along the edges and 8" throughout the sheet. Drive the screw heads flush with the surface. Continue spreading mortar and installing sheets along the wall. *Option: If installing fiber/cementboard underlayment, use a 3/16" notched trowel to spread the mortar, and drill pilot holes for all screws.*

Cut cementboard pieces as necessary, leaving an ⅛" gap at all joints and a ¼" gap along the room perimeter. For straight cuts, use a utility knife to score a line through the fiber-mesh layer just beneath the surface, then snap the board along the scored line.

To cut holes, notches, or irregular shapes, use a jigsaw with a carbide-tipped blade. Continue installing cementboard sheets to cover the entire floor.

Place fiberglass-mesh wallboard tape over the seams. Use a wallboard knife to apply thin-set mortar to the seams, filling the gaps between sheets and spreading a thin layer of mortar over the tape. Allow the mortar to set for two days before starting the tile installation.

How to Install Isolation Membrane

Isolation membrane is used to protect ceramic tile installations from movement that may occur on cracked concrete floors. This product is used primarily for covering individual cracks, but it can be used over an entire floor. Isolation membrane is also available in a liquid form that can be poured over the project area.

Thoroughly clean the subfloor, then apply thin-set mortar with a ⅛" notched trowel. Start spreading the mortar along a wall in a section as wide as the membrane and 8 to 10 ft. long. *Note: For some membranes, you must use a bonding material other than mortar. Read and follow manufacturer's directions.*

Roll out the membrane over the mortar. Cut the membrane to fit tightly against the walls, using a straightedge and utility knife.

Starting in the center of the membrane, use a heavy floor roller to smooth out the surface toward the edges. This frees trapped air and presses out excess bonding material.

Repeat steps 1 through 3, cutting the membrane as necessary at the walls and obstacles, until the floor is completely covered with membrane. Do not overlap the seams, but make sure they're tight. Allow the mortar to set for two days before installing the tile.

Installing Raised Underlayment Panels

Concrete floors are practical and durable—and generally cold and uncomfortable. For a fast and easy makeover, you can now find raised underlayment panels that simply rest on the concrete and provide a surface for other flooring materials. The tongue-and-groove plywood panels have dimpled plastic on the bottom. This allows air to circulate underneath so that the concrete stays dry, and insulates the flooring above. The assembled panels can support laminates and resilient sheets or tiles. And you can install them in a weekend.

How to Install Raised Underlayment Panels

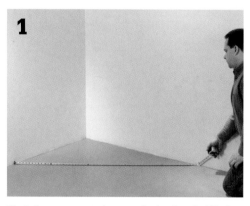

Start at one corner, and measure the length and width of the room from that starting point. Calculate the number of panels you will need to cover the space in both directions. If the starting corner is not square, trim the first row of panels to create a straight starting line.

Create an expansion gap around the edges. Place ¼" spacers at all walls, doors, and other large obstacles. To make your own spacers, cut sheets of ¼" plywood to the thickness of the panels, and hold them in place temporarily with masking tape.

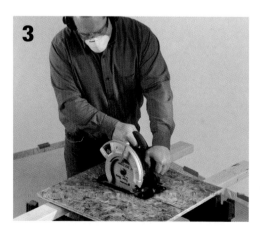

Dry-lay a row of panels across the room. If the last row will be less than 6" wide, balance it by trimming the first panel or the starting row, if necessary, to account for the row end pieces.

Starting in the corner, lay the first panel with the grooved side against the ¼" spacers. Slide the next panel into place and press-fit the groove of the second panel into the tongue of the first. Check the edges against the wall.

5

Repeat these steps to complete the first row. If necessary, tap the panels into place with a scrap piece of lumber and a rubber mallet or hammer—just be careful not to damage the tongue or groove edges. Starting with the second row, stagger the seams so that the panels interlock.

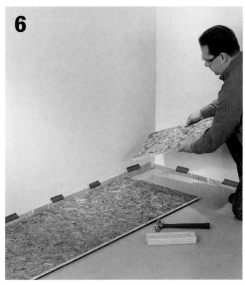

6

Cut the last panel to fit snugly between the next-to-last panel and the ¼" spacer on the far wall. Install the last panel at an angle and tap it down. Continue working from the starting point, checking after each row to be sure the panels are square and level.

7

When you reach the last row and last panel to complete your installation, you may have to cut the panel to fit. Measure for fit, allowing for the ¼" expansion gap from the wall. Cut the panel and fit it into place.

8

When all the panels are in place and the finished floor is installed, remove the spacers from around the perimeter of the room.

Installing Radiant Floor Mats

Floor-warming systems require very little energy to run and are designed to heat floors only; they generally are not used as sole heat sources for rooms.

A typical floor-warming system consists of one or more thin mats containing electric resistance wires that heat up when energized like an electric blanket. The mats are installed beneath the tile and are hardwired to a 120-volt GFCI circuit. A thermostat controls the temperature, and a timer turns the system off automatically.

The system shown in this project includes two plastic mesh mats, each with its own power lead that is wired directly to the thermostat. Radiant mats may be installed over a plywood subfloor, but if you plan to install floor tile you should put down a base of cementboard first, and then install the mats on top of the cementboard.

A crucial part of installing this system is to use a multimeter to perform several resistance checks to make sure the heating wires have not been damaged during shipping or installation.

Electrical service required for a floor-warming system is based on size. A smaller system may connect to an existing GFCI circuit, but a larger one will need a dedicated circuit; follow the manufacturer's requirements.

To order a floor-warming system, contact the manufacturer or dealer (see Resources, page 554). In most cases, you can send them plans and they'll custom-fit a system for your project area.

Tools & Materials ▸

Vacuum cleaner	Electric wire fault
Multimeter	indicator (optional)
Tape measure	Radiant floor mats
Scissors	12/2 NM cable
Router/rotary tool	Conduit
Marker	Wire connectors
Trowel	Thinset mortar
or rubber float	Thermostat with sensor
Notched trowel	Junction box(es)
Staple gun	Tile or stone
Hot glue gun	floorcovering

A radiant floor-warming system employs electric heating mats that are covered with floor tile to create a floor that's cozy under foot.

Installation Tips ▸

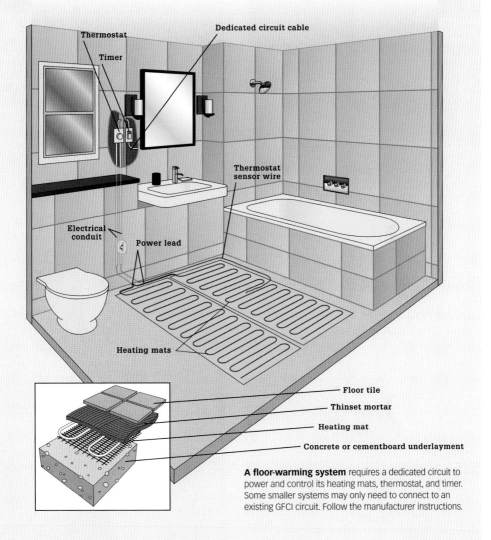

Thermostat

Timer

Dedicated circuit cable

Thermostat
sensor wire

Electrical
conduit

Power lead

Heating mats

Floor tile

Thinset mortar

Heating mat

Concrete or cementboard underlayment

A floor-warming system requires a dedicated circuit to power and control its heating mats, thermostat, and timer. Some smaller systems may only need to connect to an existing GFCI circuit. Follow the manufacturer instructions.

- Each radiant mat must have a direct connection to the power lead from the thermostat, with the connection made in a junction box in the wall cavity. Do not install mats in series.
- Do not install radiant floor mats under shower areas.
- Do not overlap maps or let them touch.
- Do not cut heating wire or damage heating wire insulation.
- The distance between wires in adjoining mats should equal the distance between wire loops measured center to center.

Installing a Radiant Floor-warming System

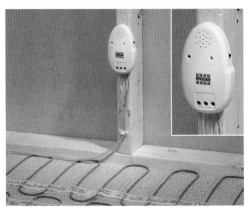

Floor-warming systems must be installed on a circuit with adequate amperage and a GFCI breaker. Smaller systems may tie into an existing circuit, but larger ones need a dedicated circuit. Follow local building and electrical codes that apply to your project.

An electric wire fault indicator monitors each floor mat for continuity during the installation process. If there is a break in continuity (for example, if a wire is cut) an alarm sounds. If you choose not to use an installation tool to monitor the mat, test for continuity frequently using a multimeter.

How To Install a Radiant Floor-warming System

Install electrical boxes to house the thermostat and timer. In most cases, the box should be located 60" above floor level. Use a 4"-deep × 4"-wide double-gang box for the thermostat/timer control if your kit has an integral model. If your timer and thermostat are separate, install a separate single box for the timer.

Drill access holes in the sole plate for the power leads that are preattached to the mats (they should be over 10 ft. long). The leads should be connected to a supply wire from the thermostat in a junction box located in a wall near the floor and below the thermostat box. The access hole for each mat should be located directly beneath the knockout for that cable in the thermostat box. Drill through the sill plate vertically and horizontally so the holes meet in an L-shape.

3

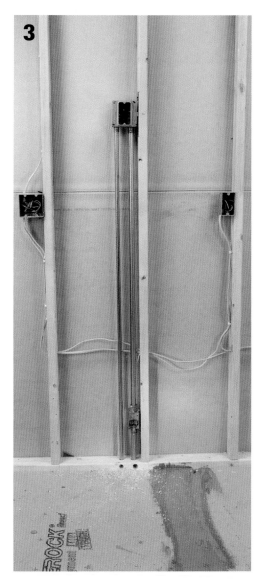

Clean the floor surface thoroughly to get rid of any debris that could potentially damage the wire mats. A vacuum cleaner generally does a more effective job than a broom.

5

Test for resistance using a multimeter set to measure ohms. This is a test you should make frequently during the installation, along with checking for continuity. If the resistance is off by more than 10% from the theoretical resistance listing (see manufacturer's chart in installation instructions), contact a technical support operator for the kit manufacturer. For example, the theoretical resistance for the 1 × 50 ft. mat seen here is 19, so the ohms reading should be between 17 and 21.

6

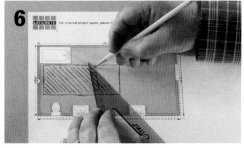

Finalize your mat layout plan. Most radiant floor warming mat manufacturers will provide a layout plan for you at the time of purchase, or they will give you access to an online design tool so you can come up with your own plan. This is an important step to the success of your project, and the assistance is free.

Run conduit from the electrical boxes to the sill plate. The line for the supply cable should be ¾" conduit. If you are installing multiple mats, the supply conduit should feed into a junction box about 6" above the sill plate and then continue into the ¾" hole you drilled for the supply leads. The sensor wire needs only ½" conduit that runs straight from the thermostat box via the thermostat. The mats should be powered by a dedicated 20-amp GFCI circuit of 12/2 NM cable run from your main service panel to the electrical box (this is for 120-volt mats—check your instruction manual for specific circuit recommendations).

(continued)

7

Unroll the radiant mat or mats and allow them to settle. Arrange the mat or mats according to the plan you created. It's okay to cut the plastic mesh so you can make curves or switchbacks, but do not cut the heating wire under any circumstances, not even to shorten it.

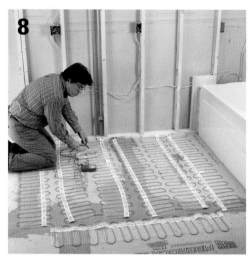

8

Finalize the mat layout and then test the resistance again using a multimeter. Also check for continuity in several different spots. If there is a problem with any of the mats, you should identify it and correct it before proceeding with the mortar installation.

9

Run the thermostat sensor wire from the electrical box down the ½" conduit raceway and out the access hole in the sill plate. Select the best location for the thermostat sensor and mark the location onto the flooring. Also mark the locations of the wires that connect to and lead from the sensor.

Variation: If your local codes require it, roll the mats out of the way and cut a channel for the sensor and the sensor wires into the floor or floor underlayment. For most floor materials, a spiral cutting tool does a quick and neat job of this task. Remove any debris.

Bond the mats to the floor. If the mats in your system have adhesive strips, peel off the adhesive backing and roll out the mats in the correct position, pressing them against the floor to set the adhesive. If your mats have no adhesive, bind them with strips of double-sided carpet tape. The thermostat sensor and the power supply leads should be attached with hot glue (inset photo) and run up into their respective holes in the sill plate if you have not done this already. Test all mats for resistance and continuity.

Cover the floor installation areas with a layer of thinset mortar that is thick enough to fully encapsulate all the wires and mats (usually around ¼" in thickness). Check the wires for continuity and resistance regularly and stop working immediately if there is a drop in resistance or a failure of continuity. Allow the mortar to dry overnight.

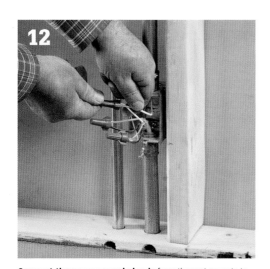

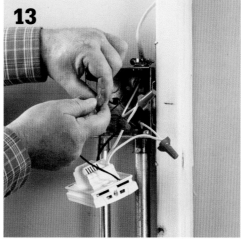

Connect the power supply leads from the mat or mats to the NM cable coming from the thermostat inside the junction box near the sill. Power must be turned off. The power leads should be cut so about 8" of wire feeds into the box. Be sure to use cable clamps to protect the wires.

Connect the sensor wire and the power supply lead (from the junction box) to the thermostat/timer according to the manufacturer's directions. Attach the device to the electrical box, restore power, and test the system to make sure it works. Once you are convinced that it is operating properly, install flooring and repair the wall surfaces.

Installing Hardwood Strip Flooring

Tongue-and-groove hardwood flooring has always been popular with homeowners. It offers an attractive look, is one of the longest lasting floor coverings, and can be stripped and refinished to look like new.

Oak has been the most common type of strip flooring because of its durability and wood graining, and it's the species most people think of when hardwood is mentioned. Other woods, such as maple, cherry, and birch, are also becoming popular.

Exotic species of wood from around the world are now finding their way into American homes as people want a premium strip or plank floor that is unique and stylish, and expresses their personalities. The more than sixty exotic hardwoods include Brazilian cherry, Australian cypress, Honduran mahogany, tobaccowood, teak, zebrawood, and bamboo—which is not really wood but a type of grass.

This section describes how to install nailed-down tongue-and-groove flooring, how to install a decorative medallion, and how to install tongue-and-groove strip flooring over troweled-on adhesive. Customizing your floor with borders, accents, and medallions is easier than you may think. A number of manufacturers produce a variety of decorative options made to match the thickness of your floor.

Tools & Materials ▸

Rosin paper	Nail set
Utility knife	Hammer
Chalk line	Pry bar
8d finish nails	Wood mallet
Drill	Power nailer
Staple	Pull bar

Real hardwood flooring has depth of beauty and warmth underfoot that even the highest quality laminate imitations struggle to match.

How to Install Tongue-and-Groove Hardwood Flooring

Cover the entire subfloor with rosin paper. Staple the paper to the subfloor, overlapping edges by 4". Cut the paper with a utility knife to butt against the walls.

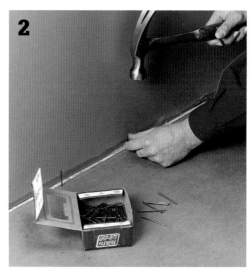

Make a mark on the floor ½" from the starter wall at both ends of the wall. Snap a chalk line between the marks. Nail 8d finish nails every 2" to 3" along the chalk line to mark the location for your first row.

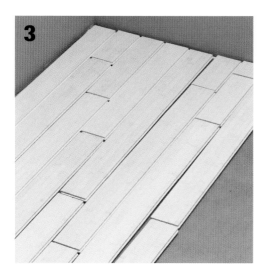

Lay out the first 8 rows of flooring in a dry run with the groove side facing the wall. Make sure the first row of boards is straight. Arrange the boards to get a good color and grain mix. Offset the ends by at least 6".

Place the starter row against the nails on the chalk line. Drill pilot holes in the flooring every 6" to 8", about ½" from the groove edge. Face nail the first row until the nail heads are just above the boards, then sink them using a nail set. (Be careful not to hit the boards with your hammer or you'll mar the surface.)

(continued)

5

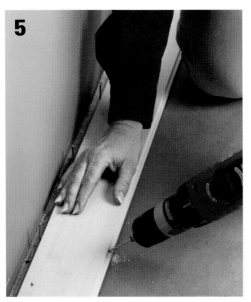

Drill pilot holes every 6" to 8" directly above the tongue, keeping the drill at a 45° angle.

Tip ▶

To install crooked boards, drill pilot holes above the tongue and insert nails. Fasten a scrap board to the subfloor using screws. Force the floor board straight using a pry bar and a scrap board placed in front of the flooring. With pressure on the floor board, blind nail it into place.

6

Blind nail a nail into each pilot hole. Keep the nail heads ½" out, then set them just below the surface, using a nail set.

7

Set the second row of boards in place against the starter row, fitting together the tongue and groove connections. Use a scrap board and wood mallet to tap the floor boards together. Drill pilot holes and blind nail the boards. Do this for the next few rows.

8

To install the last board in a row, place the tongue and groove joints together, then place a flooring pull bar over the end of the board. Hit the end of the pull bar with a hammer until the board slides into place. Stay ½" away from the walls.

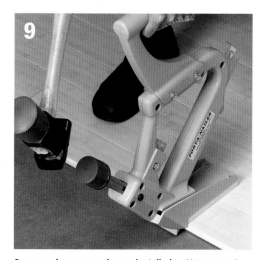

Once you have several rows installed and have enough room, use a power nailer. Place the nailer lip over the edge of the board and strike it with a mallet. Drive a nail 2" from the end of each board and about every 8" in the field. Keep a few rows of flooring laid out ahead of you as you work, and keep the joints staggered.

When you're out of room for the power nailer, drill pilot holes and blind nail the boards. For the last rows, drill pilot holes in the top of the boards, ½" from the tongue, and face nail them. The last row may need to be ripped to size. Pull the last row into place using the flooring pull bar, leaving a ½" gap along the wall. Drill pilot holes and face nail.

Tip ▶

Install a reducer strip or transition strip between the wood floor and an adjoining room. Cut the strip to size. Fit the strip's groove over the floor board's tongue, then drill pilot holes and face nail. Set the nails with a nail set. Fill all visible nail holes with wood putty.

To install around an object, cut a notch in the board. For larger obstacles, cut 45° miters in boards so grooves face away from the object. Rip tongues off the boards. Set the boards against the object and flooring, fitting mitered ends together. Drill pilot holes and face nail in place. Apply silicone caulk between the floor and board edge.

To reverse directions of the tongue and groove for doorways, glue a spline into the groove of the board. Fit the groove of the next board onto the spline, then nail the board in place.

Installing Laminate Floors

Laminate flooring comes in a floating system that is simple to install, even if you have no experience with other home-improvement projects. You may install a floating laminate floor right on top of plywood, concrete slab, sheet vinyl, or hardwood flooring. Just be sure to follow the manufacturer's instructions.

The pieces are available in planks or squares in a variety of different sizes, colors, and faux finishes—including wood and ceramic. The part you see is really a photographic print. Tongue-and-groove edges lock pieces together, and the entire floor floats on the underlayment. At the end of this project there are a few extra steps to take if your flooring manufacturer recommends using glue on the joints.

The rich wood tones of beautiful laminate planks may cause you to imagine hours of long, hard installation work, but this is a DIY project that you can do in a single weekend. Buy the manufactured planks at a home-improvement or flooring store and install laminate flooring with the step-by-step instructions offered in the following pages.

Tools & Materials ▸

Circular saw	Painter's tape
Underlayment	Chisel
½" spacers	Rubber mallet
Tapping block	Drawbar
Scrap foam	Finish nails
Speed square	Nail set strap clamps
Manufacturer glue	Threshold and screws

Laminate strip floors install quickly, wear well and are among the cheapest floor coverings you can find. Overall they have improved in appearance but the lower quality products continue to be fairly unconvincing imitations of natural materials.

How to Install a Floating Floor

To install the underlayment, start in one corner and unroll the underlayment to the opposite wall. Cut the underlayment to fit, using a utility knife or scissors. Overlap the second underlayment sheet according to the manufacturer's recommendations, and secure the pieces in place with adhesive tape.

Working from the left corner of the room to right, set wall spacers and dry lay planks (tongue side facing the wall) against the wall. The spacers allow for expansion. If you are flooring a room more than 26 ft. long or wide, you need to buy appropriate-sized expansion joints. *Note: Some manufacturers suggest facing the groove side to the wall.*

Final uncut plank
ends here

Set a new plank right side up, on top of the previously laid plank, flush with the spacer against the wall at the end run. Line up a speed square with the bottom plank edge and trace a line. That's the cutline for the final plank in the row.

Press painter's tape along the cutline on the top of the plank to prevent chips when cutting. Score the line drawn in Step 3 with a utility knife. Turn the plank over and extend the pencil line to the backside.

(continued)

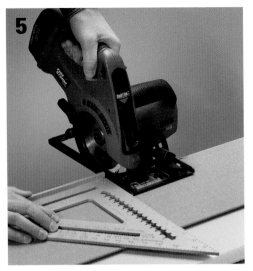

5

Clamp the board (face down) and rigid foam insulation or plywood to a work table. The foam reduces chipping. Clamp a speed square on top of the plank, as though you are going to draw another line parallel to the cutline—use this to make a straight cut. Place the circular saw's blade on the waste side of the actual cutline.

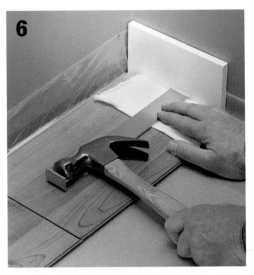

6

To create a tight fit for the last plank in the first row, place a spacer against the wall and wedge one end of a drawbar between it and the last plank. Tap the other end of the drawbar with a rubber mallet or hammer. Protect the laminate surface with a thin cloth.

7

Continue to lay rows of flooring, making sure the joints are staggered. This prevents the entire floor from relying on just a few joints, and keeps the planks from lifting. Staggering also stengthens the floor, because the joints are shorter and more evenly distributed.

8

To fit the final row, place two planks on top of the last course; slide the top plank up against the wall spacer. Use the top plank to draw a cutline lengthwise on the middle plank. Cut the middle plank to size using the same method as in Step 3, just across the grain. The very last board must be cut lengthwise and widthwise to fit.

How to Work Around Obstacles

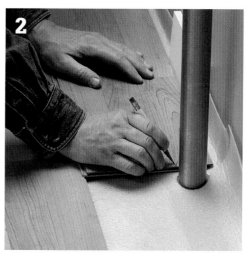

Position a plank and use a pencil to make two marks along the length of the plank, indicating the points where the obstacle begins and ends.

Position the plank end against the obstacle. Make two marks with a pencil, this time on the end of the plank to indicate where the obstacle falls along the width of the board.

Use a speed square to extend the four lines. The space at which they intersect is the part of the plank that needs to be removed to make room for the obstacle to go through it. Use a drill with a Forstner bit, or a hole saw the same diameter as the space within the intersecting lines, and drill through the plank at the X. You'll be left with a hole; extend the cut to the edges with a jigsaw.

Install the plank by locking the tongue-and-groove joints with the preceding board. Fit the end piece in behind the pipe or obstacle. Apply manufacturer-recommended glue to the cut edges, and press the end piece tightly against the adjacent plank. Wipe away excess glue with a damp cloth.

In image 1:
Mark indicates left edge of the pipe

Mark indicates right outside edge of the pipe

Installing Parquet Flooring

For a hardwood floor with great design appeal, consider installing a parquet floor. It offers more visual interest than strip flooring without sacrificing the beauty and elegance of wood. Parquet comes in a variety of patterns and styles to create geometric designs. It can range from elaborate, custom-designed patterns on the high end, to the more common herringbone pattern, to the widely available and less expensive block design.

Parquet has experienced a radical transformation over the years. A few years ago, each individual piece of parquet was hand-cut and painstakingly assembled piece by piece. Today, parquet is prefabricated so the individual pieces making up the design are available as single tiles, which not only has reduced the cost, but has made the flooring easier to install.

Many types and designs of parquet floors are available, from custom-made originals to standard patterns, but they are all installed the same way—set in adhesive on a wood subfloor. The effort can be very rewarding: Parquet can be used to create shapes not possible with other wood flooring.

The finger block pattern is one of the most widely available parquet coverings and also one of the least expensive. The configuration of perpendicular strips of wood emphasizes the different grains and natural color variations.

Tools & Materials ▸

Tape measure	Putty knife
Chalk line	Rubber mallet
Carpenter's square	100- to 150-pound
Parquet flooring	floor roller
Adhesive	Jigsaw
Notched trowel	Solvent

Parquet flooring tiles are made with real hardwood and can be a great vehicle for introducing exotic wood species at a reasonable cost. The custom parquet floor seen here is expensive, but a basic parquet floor with stock tiles is an affordable option and an easy DIY project.

How to Install Parquet Flooring

Mark the centerpoint of each wall. Snap chalk lines between the marks on opposite walls to establish your reference lines. Use the 3-4-5 triangle method to check the lines for squareness (see page 181).

Lay out a dry run of panels from the center point along the reference lines to adjacent walls. Place ¼" spacers along the walls to allow for expansion. If more than half of the last panel needs to be cut off, adjust the lines by half the width of the panel. Snap new working lines, if necessary.

Put enough adhesive on the subfloor for your first panel, using a putty knife. Spread the adhesive into a thin layer with a notched trowel held at a 45° angle. Apply the adhesive right up to the working lines, but do not cover them.

Place the first panel on the adhesive so two sides are flush with the working lines. Take care not to slide or twist the panel when setting it into place. This panel must be positioned correctly to keep the rest of your floor square.

(continued)

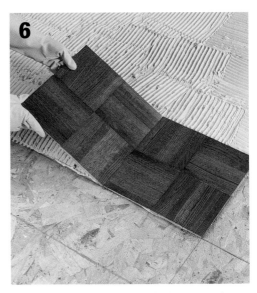

Apply enough adhesive for six to eight panels and spread it with a notched trowel.

Set the next panel in place by holding it at a 45° angle and locking the tongue-and-groove joints with the first panel. Lower the panel onto the adhesive without sliding it. Install remaining panels the same way.

After every six to eight panels are installed, tap them into the adhesive with a rubber mallet.

For the last row, align panels over the top of the last installed row. Place a third row over the top of these, with the sides butted against ½" spacers along the wall. Draw a line along the edge of the third panels onto the second row, cut the panels at the marks, and install.

To work around corners or obstacles, align a panel over the last installed panel, then place another panel on top of it as in step 8. Keep the top panel ½" from the wall or obstacle and trace along the opposite edge onto the second panel (top). Move the top two panels to the adjoining side, making sure not to turn the top panel. Make a second mark on the panel the same way (bottom). Cut the tile with a jigsaw and install.

Within 4 hours of installing the floor, roll the floor with a 100- to 150-pound floor roller. Wait at least 24 hours before walking on the floor again.

How to Install Parquet in a Diagonal Layout

Establish perpendicular working lines following Step 1 on page 171. Measure 5 ft. from the centerpoint along each working line and make a mark. Snap chalk lines between the 5 ft. marks. Mark the centerpoint of these lines, then snap a chalk line through the marks to create a diagonal reference line.

Lay out a dry run of tiles along a diagonal line. Adjust your starting point as necessary. Lay the flooring along the diagonal line using adhesive, following the steps for installing parquet (pages 171 to 173). Make paper templates for tile along walls and in corners. Transfer the template measurements to tiles, and cut to fit.

Installing Sheet Vinyl

Preparing a perfect underlayment is the most important phase of resilient sheet vinyl installation. Cutting the material to fit the contours of the room is a close second. The best way to ensure accurate cuts is to make a cutting template. Some manufacturers offer template kits, or you can make your own. Be sure to use the recommended adhesive for the sheet vinyl you are installing. Many manufacturers require that you use their glue for installation. Use extreme care when handling the sheet vinyl, especially felt-backed products, to avoid creasing and tearing.

Tools & Materials ▸

Linoleum knife	Heat gun
Framing square	¹⁄₁₆" V-notched trowel
Compass	Straightedge
Scissors	Vinyl flooring
Non-permanent	Masking tape
felt-tipped pen	Heavy butcher
Utility knife	or brown
Straightedge	wrapping paper
¼" V-notched trowel	Duct tape
J-roller	Flooring adhesive
Stapler	³⁄₈" staples
Flooring roller	Metal threshold bars
Chalk line	Nails

Sheet vinyl has no seams (or at least very few seams), which makes it a practical choice for wet areas such as bathrooms. Advancing technology has made a host of new patterns and styles available, including the mosaic tile look-alike pattern seen here.

Tools for Resilient Floors

Tools for resilient flooring include: a heat gun (A), J-roller (B), floor roller (C), framing square (D), sponge (E), hammer (F), notched trowel (G), stapler (H), linoleum knife (I), utility knife (J), wallboard knife (K), chalk line (L), straightedge (M).

Buying & Estimating

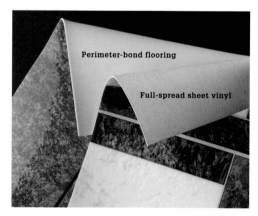

Resilient sheet vinyl comes in full-spread and perimeter-bond styles. Full-spread sheet vinyl has a felt-paper backing and is secured with adhesive that is spread over the floor before installation. Perimeter-bond flooring, identifiable by its smooth, white PVC backing, is laid directly on underlayment and is secured by a special adhesive spread along the edges and seams.

Resilient tile comes in self-adhesive and dry-back styles. Self-adhesive tile has a pre-applied adhesive protected by wax paper backing that is peeled off as the tiles are installed. Dry-back tile is secured with adhesive spread onto the underlayment before installation. Self-adhesive tile is easier to install than dry-back tile, but the bond is less reliable. Don't use additional adhesives with self-adhesive tile.

Evaluating an Existing Floor

The first step in preparing for a new floor covering is evaluating your old floor. A careful examination can help you decide whether to repair damaged areas, or replace the flooring altogether.

Evaluating your floor is a three-step process. Begin by identifying the existing floor material and the installation method used. Is your sheet vinyl attached using the full-spread method or the perimeter-bond method? Is your carpet glued down or stretched? Next, check the condition of the floor. Is it securely attached or is it loose in spots? Is it chipped or cracked? Finally, note the height of the existing floor in relation to adjoining floor surfaces. Is it significantly higher than surrounding floors?

A new floor covering or underlayment can often be installed on top of existing flooring. If the existing flooring is not sound or smooth, however, you will have to do some preparation work. Applying a floor leveler is one way to make your existing floor easier to use. More complex preparations may involve removing and replacing the underlayment or making spot repairs to the subfloor.

Warning ▸

Resilient flooring manufactured before 1986 may contain asbestos, which can cause severe lung problems if inhaled. The recommended method for dealing with asbestos-laden flooring is to cover it with an underlayment. If the flooring must be removed, do not do the work yourself. Instead, consult a certified asbestos-abatement contractor.

Determining the number and type of coverings already on your floor is an important early evaluation step. Too many layers of flooring and underlayment can stress floor joists and ultimately cause a new floor to fail. An easy way to check for old flooring is to remove floor vents.

How to Install Perimeter-bond Sheet Vinyl

Unroll the flooring on any large, flat, clean surface. To prevent wrinkles, sheet vinyl comes from the manufacturer rolled with the pattern-side out. Unroll the sheet and turn it pattern-side up for marking.

For two-piece installations, overlap the edges of the sheets by at least 2". Plan to have the seams fall along the pattern lines or simulated grout joints. Align the sheets so the pattern matches, then tape the sheets together with duct tape.

Position the paper template over the sheet vinyl and tape it in place. Trace the outline of the template onto the flooring using a non-permanent felt-tipped pen.

Remove the template. Cut the sheet vinyl with a sharp linoleum knife or a utility knife with a new blade. Use a straightedge as a guide for making longer cuts.

(continued)

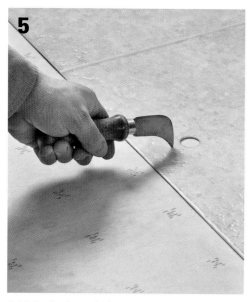

Cut holes for pipes and other permanent obstructions. Cut a slit from each hole to the nearest edge of the flooring. Whenever possible, make slits along pattern lines.

Roll up the flooring loosely and transfer it to the installation area. Do not fold the flooring. Unroll and position the sheet vinyl carefully. Slide the edges beneath door casings.

Cut the seams for two-piece installations using a straightedge as a guide. Hold the straightedge tightly against the flooring, and cut along the pattern lines through both pieces of vinyl flooring.

Remove both pieces of scrap flooring. The pattern should now run continuously across the adjoining sheets of flooring.

9

Fold back the edges of both sheets. Apply a 3" band of multipurpose flooring adhesive to the underlayment or old flooring, using a ¼" V-notched trowel or wallboard knife.

10

Lay the seam edges one at a time onto the adhesive. Make sure the seam is tight, pressing the gaps together with your fingers, if needed. Roll the seam edges with a J-roller or wallpaper seam roller.

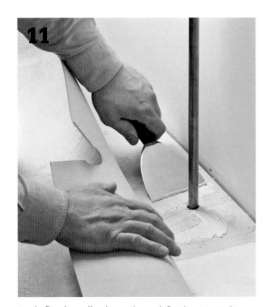

11

Apply flooring adhesive underneath flooring cuts at pipes or posts and around the entire perimeter of the room. Roll the flooring with the roller to ensure good contact with the adhesive.

12

If you're applying flooring over a wood underlayment, fasten the outer edges of the sheet with ⅜" staples driven every 3". Make sure the staples will be covered by the base molding.

Installing Resilient Tile

As with any tile installation, resilient tile requires carefully positioned layout lines. Before committing to any layout and applying tile, conduct a dry run to identify potential problems.

Keep in mind the difference between reference lines (see opposite page) and layout lines. Reference lines mark the center of the room and divide it into quadrants. If the tiles don't lay out symmetrically along these lines, you'll need to adjust them slightly, creating layout lines. Once layout lines are established, installing the tile is a fairly quick process. Be sure to keep joints between the tiles tight and lay the tiles square.

Tiles with an obvious grain pattern can be laid so the grain of each tile is oriented identically throughout the installation. You can also use the quarter-turn method, in which each tile has its pattern grain running perpendicular to that of adjacent tiles. Whichever method you choose, be sure to be consistent throughout the project.

Tools & Materials ›

Tape measure	Heat gun
Chalk line	Resilient tile
Framing square	Flooring adhesive
Utility knife	(for dry-back tile)
1/16" notched trowel	

Resilient tiles have a pattern layer that is bonded to a vinyl base and coated with a transparent wear layer. Some come with adhesive pre-applied and covered by a paper backing, others have dry backs and are designed to be set into flooring adhesive.

Check for noticeable directional features, like the grain of the vinyl particles. You can set the tiles in a running pattern so the directional feature runs in the same direction (top), or in a checkerboard pattern using the quarter-turn method (bottom).

How to Make Reference Lines for Tile Installation

Position a reference line (X) by measuring along opposite sides of the room and marking the center of each side. Snap a chalk line between these marks.

Measure and mark the centerpoint of the chalk line. From this point, use a framing square to establish a second reference line perpendicular to the first one. Snap the second line (Y) across the room.

Check the reference lines for squareness using the 3-4-5 triangle method. Measure along reference line X and make a mark 3 ft. from the centerpoint. Measure from the centerpoint along reference line Y and make a mark at 4 ft.

Measure the distance between the marks. If the reference lines are perpendicular, the distance will measure exactly 5 ft. If not, adjust the reference lines until they're exactly perpendicular to each other.

How to Install Dry-backed Resilient Tile

Snap perpendicular reference lines with a chalk line. Dry-fit tiles along layout line Y so a joint falls along reference line X. If necessary, shift the layout to make the layout symmetrical or to reduce the number of tiles that need to be cut.

If you shift the tile layout, create a new line that is parallel to reference line X and runs through a tile joint near line X. The new line, X1, is the line you'll use when installing the tile. Use a different colored chalk to distinguish between lines.

Dry-fit tiles along the new line, X1. If necessary, adjust the layout line as in steps 1 and 2.

If you adjusted the layout along X1, measure and make a new layout line, Y1, that's parallel to reference line Y and runs through a tile joint. Y1 will form the second layout line you'll use during installation.

5

Apply adhesive around the intersection of the layout lines using a trowel with ¹⁄₁₆" V-shaped notches. Hold the trowel at a 45° angle and spread adhesive evenly over the surface.

6

Spread adhesive over most of the installation area, covering three quadrants. Allow the adhesive to set according to the manufacturer's instructions, then begin to install the tile at the intersection of the layout lines. You can kneel on installed tiles to lay additional tiles.

7

When the first three quadrants are completely tiled, spread adhesive over the remaining quadrant, then finish setting the tile.

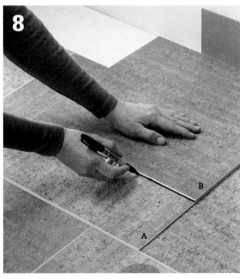

8

To cut tiles to fit along the walls, place the tile to be cut (A) face up on top of the last full tile you installed. Position a ⅛"-thick spacer against the wall, then set a marker tile (B) on top of the tile to be cut. Trace along the edge of the marker tile to draw a cutting line.

(continued)

To mark tiles for cutting around outside corners, make a cardboard template to match the space, keeping a ⅛" gap along the walls. After cutting the template, check to make sure it fits. Place the template on a tile and trace its outline.

9

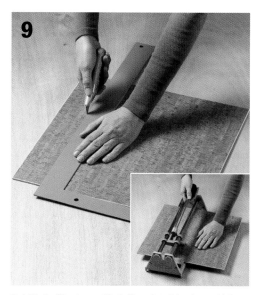

Cut tile to fit using a utility knife and straightedge. Hold the straightedge securely against the cutting line to ensure a straight cut. *Option: You can use a ceramic-tile cutter to make straight cuts in thick vinyl tiles (see inset).*

10

Install cut tiles next to the walls. If you're precutting all tiles before installing them, measure the distance between the wall and install tiles at various points in case the distance changes.

11

Continue installing tile in the remaining quadrants until the room is completely covered. Check the entire floor. If you find loose areas, press down on the tiles to bond them to the underlayment. Install metal threshold bars at room borders where the new floor joins another floor covering.

How to Install Self-adhesive Resilient Tile

Once your reference lines are established, peel off the paper backing and install the first tile in one of the corners formed by the intersecting layout lines. Lay three or more tiles along each layout lines in the quadrant. Rub the entire surface of each tile to bond the adhesive to the floor underlayment.

Begin installing tiles in the interior area of the quadrant. Keep the joints tight between tiles..

Finish setting full tiles in the first quadrant, then set the full tiles in an adjacent quadrant. Set the tiles along the layout lines first, then fill in the interior tiles.

Continue installing the tile in the remaining quadrants until the room is completely covered. Check the entire floor. If you find loose areas, press down on the tiles to bond them to the underlayment. Install metal threshold bars at room border where the new floor joins another floor covering.

Installing Bamboo Flooring

It looks like hardwood and is available in traditional tongue-and-groove form and in laminate planks. But bamboo is not wood. It's really a grass—and one of the most popular flooring materials today.

Bamboo flooring is made by shredding stalks of the raw material, then pressing them together with a resin that holds the shreds in their finished shape. Not only is bamboo a fast-growing and renewable crop, the companies that make bamboo flooring use binders with low emissions of volatile organic compounds (VOCs). The result is tough, economical, and ecologically friendly. In other words, it's just about perfect for flooring.

If you choose tongue-and-groove bamboo, the installation techniques are the same as for hardwoods. Bamboo is also available as a snap-fit laminate for use in floating floors. In this project we show Teragren Synergy Strand in Java (see Resources, page 554): thin, durable planks that are glued to the underlayment.

Tools & Materials ▸

Adhesive	Moisture level meter
Carpenter's level	Notched trowel
Carpenter's square	Rubber mallet
Chalk line	Scrap lumber
Cleaning supplies	Shims
Flat-edged trowel	Straightedge
Marking pen or pencil	Weighted roller
Measuring tape	

Tips for a Successful Installation ▸

60° 70°
RECOMMENDED
TEMPERATURE
RANGE

40% 60%
RECOMMENDED
HUMIDITY
RANGE

Bamboo plank flooring should be one of the last items installed on any new construction or remodeling project. All work involving water or moisture should be completed before floor installation. Room temperature and humidity of installation area should be consistent with normal, year-round living conditions for at least a week before installation. Room temperature of 60 to 70° F and humidity range of 40 to 60% is recommended.

About radiant heat: The subfloor should never exceed 85° F. Check the manufacturer's suggested guidelines for correct water temperature inside heating pipes. Switch on the heating unit three days before flooring installation. Room temperature should not vary more than 15° F year-round. For glue-down installations, leave the heating unit on for three days following installation.

How to Install Bamboo Planks

1

2

Give the bamboo time to adjust to installation conditions. Store it for at least 72 hours in or near the room where it will be installed. Open the packages for inspection, but do not store the planks on concrete or near outside walls.

Even though thin-plank bamboo is an engineered material, it can vary in appearance. Buy all planks from the same lot and batch number. Then visually inspect the planks to make sure they match. Use the same lighting as you will have in the finished room.

3

4

Inspect wood surfaces. The planks and underlayment should have no more than 12% moisture. Bamboo planks can be installed on plywood or oriented strandboard at least ¾" thick. The underlayment must be structurally sound.

Make sure the underlayment is level. It should not change by more than ⅛" over 10 feet. If necessary, apply a floor leveler to fill any low places, and sand down any high spots. Prevent squeaks by driving screws every 6" into the subfloor below.

(continued)

5

Sweep and vacuum the floor surface, then measure all room dimensions.

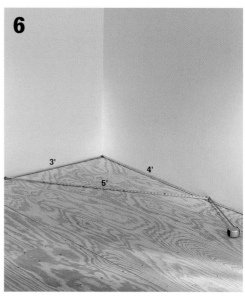

6

3'

4'

5'

Check corners for squareness using the 3-4-5 triangle method.

7

The planks should be perpendicular to the floor joists below. Adjust your starting point if necessary. Snap a chalk line next to the longest wall. The distance from the wall should be the same at both ends, leaving ½" for expansion.

8

Lay the first course of planks with the tongue edge toward the wall. Align the planks with the chalk line. Hold the edge course in place with wedges or by nailing through the tongue edge. This row will anchor the others, so make sure it stays securely in place.

9

Once the starter row is in place, install the planks using a premium wood-flooring adhesive. Be sure to follow the manufacturer's instructions. Begin at the chalk line and apply enough adhesive to lay down one or two rows of planks. Spread the adhesive with a V-notched trowel at a 45° angle. Let the adhesive sit for the specified time.

10

When the adhesive is tacky and ready to use, lay the first section of bamboo planks. Set each plank in the adhesive by placing a clean piece of scrap lumber on top and tapping it down with a rubber mallet. Check the edge of each section to make sure it keeps a straight line.

11

After you finish the first section, cover the next area with adhesive and give it time to become tacky. This slows down the project, but it prevents you from using more adhesive than you can use—and it allows the section you just finished to set up.

12

When the adhesive is ready, lay down the next section of planks. Fit the new planks tightly against the previous section, taking care not to knock the finished section out of alignment. If the planks have tongue-and-groove edges, fit them carefully into place.

(continued)

Continue applying adhesive and installing planks, one section at a time, to cover the entire floor. When adhesive gets on the flooring surface, wipe it off quickly.

At the edges and around any fixed objects, such as doorways or plumbing pipes, leave a ½" gap for expansion. Use shims to maintain the gaps if needed. These spaces can be covered with baseboards, base shoes, and escutcheons.

As you finish each section, walk across it a few times to maximize contact between the planks and the adhesive. When all the planks are in place, clean the surface and use a clean weighted roller. Push the roller in several directions, covering the entire surface many times.

In places that are difficult to reach with a roller, lay down a sheet of protective material, such as butcher paper, and stack weights on the paper. Let the finished floor sit for at least 24 hours, then clean the surface and remove any spacers from the expansion gaps. Finally, install the finishing trim.

Installing Ceramic Tile

Ceramic tile installation starts with the same steps as installing resilient tile. You snap perpendicular reference lines and dry-fit tiles to ensure the best placement.

When setting tiles, work in small sections so the mortar doesn't dry before the tiles are set. Use spacers between tiles to ensure consistent spacing. Plan an installation sequence to avoid kneeling on set tiles. Be careful not to kneel or walk on tiles until the designated drying period is over.

Tools & Materials ▸

¼" square trowel	Thin-set mortar
Rubber mallet	Tile
Tile cutter	Tile spacers
Tile nippers	Grout
Hand-held tile cutter	Latex grout additive
Needlenose pliers	Wall adhesive
Grout float	2 × 4 lumber
Grout sponge	Grout sealer
Soft cloth	Tile caulk
Small paint brush	Sponge brush

Ceramic floor tile continues to be one of the most popular DIY floorcoverings. It is relatively easy to install, is very durable and, depending on the style you choose, can be quite affordable.

How to Install Ceramic Tile

1

Make sure the subfloor is smooth, level, and stable. Spread thin-set mortar on the subfloor for one sheet of cementboard. Place the cementboard on the mortar, keeping a ¼" gap along the walls.

2

Fasten it in place with 1¼" cementboard screws. Place fiberglass-mesh wallboard tape over the seams. Cover the remainder of the floor, following the steps on page 152.

3

Draw reference lines and establish the tile layout (see page 181). Mix a batch of thin-set mortar, then spread the mortar evenly against both reference lines of one quadrant, using a ¼" square-notched trowel. Use the notched edge of the trowel to create furrows in the mortar bed.

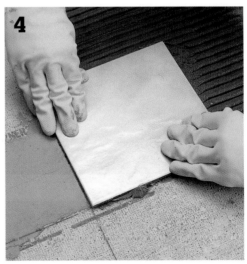

4

Set the first tile in the corner of the quadrant where the reference lines intersect. When setting tiles that are 8" square or larger, twist each tile slightly as you set it into position.

Using a soft rubber mallet, gently tap the central area of each tile a few times to set it evenly into the mortar.

Variation: For large tiles or uneven stone, use a larger trowel with notches that are at least ½" deep.

Variation: For mosaic sheets, use a ³⁄₁₆" V-notched trowel to spread the mortar and a grout float to press the sheets into the mortar. Apply pressure gently to avoid creating an uneven surface.

To ensure consistent spacing between tiles, place plastic tile spacers at the corners of the set tile. With mosaic sheets, use spacers equal to the gaps between tiles.

(continued)

Position and set adjacent tiles into the mortar along the reference lines. Make sure the tiles fit neatly against the spacers.

To make sure the tiles are level with one another, place a straight piece of 2 × 4 across several tiles, then tap the board with a mallet.

Lay tile in the remaining area covered with mortar. Repeat steps 2 to 7, continuing to work in small sections, until you reach walls or fixtures.

Measure and mark tiles to fit against walls and into corners (see pages 183 to 184). Cut the tiles to fit. Apply thin-set mortar directly to the back of the cut tiles, instead of the floor, using the notched edge of the trowel to furrow the mortar

11

Set the cut pieces of tile into position. Press down on the tile until each piece is level with adjacent tiles.

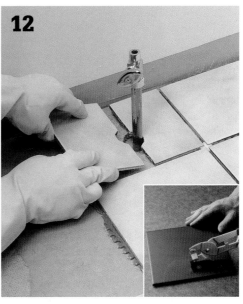

12

Measure, cut, and install tiles that require notches or curves to fit around obstacles (inset), such as exposed pipes or toilet drains.

13

Carefully remove the spacers with needlenose pliers before the mortar hardens.

14

Apply mortar and set tiles in the remaining quadrants, completing one quadrant before starting the next. Inspect all of the tile joints and use a utility knife or grout knife to remove any high spots of mortar that could show through the grout.

(continued)

Install threshold material in doorways. If the threshold is too long for the doorway, cut it to fit with a jigsaw or circular saw and a tungsten-carbide blade. Set the threshold in thin-set mortar so the top is even with the tile. Keep the same space between the threshold as between tiles. Let the mortar set for at least 24 hours.

Prepare a small batch of floor grout to fill the tile joints. When mixing grout for porous tile, such as quarry or natural stone, use an additive with a release agent to prevent grout from bonding to the tile surfaces.

Starting in a corner, pour the grout over the tile. Use a rubber grout float to spread the grout outward from the corner, pressing firmly on the float to completely fill the joints. For best results, tilt the float at a 60° angle to the floor and use a figure eight motion.

Use the grout float to remove excess grout from the surface of the tile. Wipe diagonally across the joints, holding the float in a near-vertical position. Continue applying grout and wiping off excess until about 25 square feet of the floor has been grouted.

19

Wipe a damp grout sponge diagonally over about 2 square feet of the floor at a time. Rinse the sponge in cool water between wipes. Wipe each area only once since repeated wiping can pull grout back out of joints. Repeat steps 17 to 18 to apply grout to remainder of floor.

20

Allow the grout to dry for about 4 hours, then use a soft cloth to buff the tile surface and remove any remaining grout film.

21

Apply grout sealer to the grout lines, using a small sponge brush or sash brush. Avoid brushing sealer on to the tile surfaces. Wipe up any excess sealer immediately.

Variation: Use a tile sealer to seal porous tile, such as quarry tile or unglazed tile. Following the manufacturer's instructions, roll a thin coat of sealer over the tile and grout joints, using a paint roller and extension handle.

Installing Mosaic Tile

Mosaic tile is an excellent choice for smaller areas. It requires the same preparation and handling as larger tiles, with a few differences. Sheets of mosaic tile are held together by a fabric mesh backing. This makes them more difficult to hold, place, and move. They may not be square with your guidelines when you first lay them down. And mosaic tiles require many more temporary spacers and much more grout.

A few cautions: Variations in color and texture are just as likely among mosaic tile as individual tiles, so buy all your tile from the same lot and batch. Mortar or mastic intended for ceramic tile may not work with glass mosaic tile. Finally, in projects where the finished project will be exposed to the elements, make sure you have adhesive and grout suitable for outdoor use.

Tools & Materials ▸

Carpenter's square
Chalk line
Cleaning supplies
Coarse sponge
Craft/utility knife
Grout sealer
Marking pen
    or pencil
Measuring tape

Notched trowel
Recommended
    adhesive
Rubber mallet
Sanded grout
Scrap lumber
Straightedge
Tile nippers
Tile spacers

Mosaic tiles come in sheets (usually 12 × 12") and can be made from ceramic, porcelain, glass or any number of designer materials. Normally installed for their appearance, mosaics are relatively high maintenance and prone to cracks because of all the grout lines.

How to Install Mosaic Tile

Clean and prepare the area and then draw reference lines (see page 181). Beginning at the center intersection, apply the recommended adhesive to one quadrant. Spread it outward evenly with a notched trowel. Lay down only as much adhesive as you can cover in 10 to 15 minutes.

Select a sheet of mosaic tile. Place several plastic spacers within the grid so that the sheet remains square. Pick up the sheet of tiles by diagonally opposite corners. This will help you hold the edges up so that you don't trap empty space in the middle of the sheet.

3

Gently press one corner into place on the adhesive. Slowly lower the opposite corner, making sure the sides remain square with your reference lines. Massage the sheet into the adhesive, being careful not to press too hard or twist the sheet out of position. Insert a few spacers in the outside edges of the sheet you have just placed. This will help keep the grout lines consistent.

4

When you have placed two or three sheets, lay a scrap piece of flat lumber across the tops and tap the wood with a rubber mallet to set the fabric mesh in the adhesive, and to force out any trapped air.

5

At the outer edges of your work area, you will probably need to trim one or more rows from the last sheet. If the space left at the edge is more than the width of a regular grout line, use tile nippers to trim the last row that will fit. Save these leftover tiles for repairs.

6

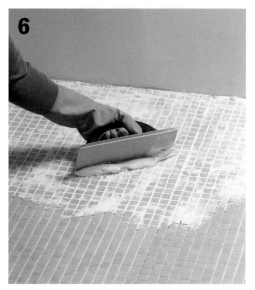

After the adhesive has cured, usually 24 to 48 hours, apply grout (see pages 196 to 197). With many more spaces, mosaic tiles will require more grout. Follow the manufacturer's instructions for spreading and floating the grout. Clean up using the instructions for individual tiles (see page 197).

Installing Carpet Squares

Most carpeting has a single design and is stretched from wall to wall. It covers more square feet of American homes than any other material. But if you want a soft floor covering that gives you more options, carpet squares are an excellent choice.

Manufacturers have found ways to create attractive new carpet using recycled fibers. This not only reuses material that would otherwise become landfill, it reduces waste in manufacturing as well. So, instead of adding to problems of resource consumption and pollution, carpet squares made from recycled materials help reduce them.

The squares are attached to each other and to the floor with adhesive dots. They can be installed on most clean, level, dry underlayment or existing floor. If the surface underneath is waxed or varnished, check with the manufacturer before you use any adhesives on it.

Tools & Materials ▸

Adhesive	Flat-edged trowel
Aviator's snips	Marking pen
Carpenter's square	or pencil
Chalk line	Measuring tape
Cleaning supplies	Notched trowel
Craft/utility knife	Straightedge

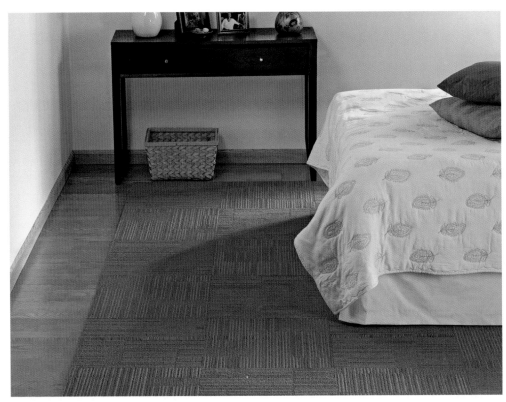

Carpet tiles combine the warmth and comfort of carpet with do-it-yourself installation, custom designs, and easy replacement. They can be laid wall-to-wall or in an area rug style, as shown above.

How to Install Carpet Squares

1

Take the squares out of the package. Be sure the room is well ventilated. Carpet squares should be at room temperature for at least 12 hours before you lay them down.

2

Check the requirements for the recommended adhesive. You can install carpet squares over many other flooring materials, including hardwood, laminates, and resilient sheets or tiles. The carpet squares shown here are fastened with adhesive dots, so almost any existing floor provides a usable surface.

3

Make sure the existing floor is clean, smooth, stable, and dry. Use floor leveler if necessary to eliminate any hills or valleys. If any part of the floor is loose, secure it to the subfloor or underlayment before you install the carpet squares. Vacuum the surface and wipe it with a damp cloth.

4

Snap chalk lines between diagonally opposite corners to find the center point for the room. In rooms with unusual shapes, determine the visual center and mark it. Next, snap chalk lines across the center and perpendicular to the walls. This set of guidelines will show you where to start.

(continued)

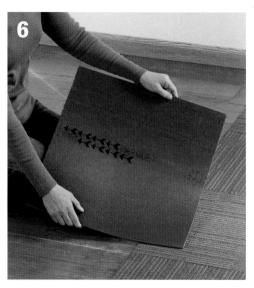

Lay a base row of carpet squares on each side of the two guidelines. When you reach the walls, make note of how much you will need to cut. You should have the same amount to cut on each side. If not, adjust the center point and realign the squares.

Check the backs of the squares before you apply any adhesive. They should indicate a direction, using arrows or other marks, so that the finished pile has a consistent appearance. If you plan to mix colors, this is the time to establish your pattern.

Fasten the base rows in place using the manufacturer's recommended adhesive. This installation calls for two adhesive dots per square. As you place each square, make sure it is aligned with the guidelines and fits tightly against the next square.

When you reach a wall, flip the last square over. Push it against the wall until it is snug. If you are planning a continuous pattern, align the arrows with the existing squares. If you are creating a parquet pattern, turn the new square 90 degrees before marking it.

Mark notches or draw a line across the back where the new square overlaps the next-to-last one. Using a sharp carpet knife, a carpenter's square, and a tough work surface, cut along this line. The cut square should fit neatly in the remaining space.

At a door jamb, place a square face up where it will go. Lean the square against the jamb and mark the point where they meet. Move the square to find the other cutline, and mark that as well. Flip the square over, mark the two lines using a carpenter's square, and cut out the corner.

Finish all four base rows before you fill in the rest of the room. As you work, check the alignment of each row. If you notice a row going out of line, find the point where the direction changed, then remove squares back to that point and start again.

Work outward from the center so that you have a known reference for keeping rows straight. Save the cut pieces from the ends. They may be useful for patching odd spaces around doorways, heat registers, radiator pipes, and when you reach the corners.

Refinishing Wood Floors

Refinishing hardwood floors is one of the first major home improvement projects homeowners attempt. The tools you need are readily available for rent, but perhaps the main reason so many DIYers attempt floor refinishing is that it is a very invasive project that requires a lot of planning and moving of furniture. Doing it yourself allows you to work gradually on your own schedule.

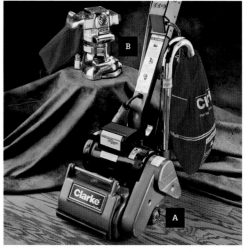

Tools & Materials ▸

Staple gun	Nail set
Zip door	Drum sander
Painter's tape	Sandpaper
Plastic	Power edge sander
Fan	Rotary buffer
Pry bar	Paint scraper
2 × 4 scrap	Sanding block
Wood shims	Tack cloth

A drum sander (A) and an edge sander (B) are rental tools that can tackle just about any floorsanding project.

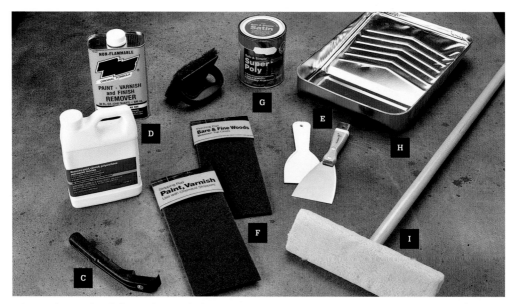

Other products and tools for resurfacing and refinishing floors: Paint scrapers (C) are helpful for removing old finish in corners and other areas that cannot be reached by sanders. When refinishing floors, chemical stripping products (D) are often a more efficient method that yields better results. This is especially true for floors that are uneven, or for parquet and veneered floors, which cannot be sanded. Stripper knives (E) and abrasive pads (F) are used with the stripping products. For the final finish, water-based polyurethane (G) is poured into a paint tray (H) and applied using a wide painting pad with a pole extension (I).

How to Refinish Wood Floors

Staple plastic on all doorways. Place a zip door over the entryway you plan to use for the duration of the project. Use painter's tape and plastic to cover heating and cooling registers, ceiling fans, and light fixtures. Finally, place a fan in a nearby window to blow the circulating dust outside.

Wedge a prybar between the shoe molding and baseboards. Move along the wall as nails loosen. Once removed, place a scrap 2 × 4 board against the wall and, with a pry bar, pry out baseboard at nails. Maintain the gap with wood shims. Drive protruding nails in floor ⅛" below the surface with a nail set.

Practice with the drum sander turned off. Move forward and backward; tilt or raise it off the floor a couple of times. A drum sander is difficult to maneuver. Once it touches the floor it walks forward; if you stop it, it gouges the floor.

For the initial pass with the drum sander, sand with the grain, using 40- or 60-grit sandpaper. For large scratches use 20 or 30. Start two-thirds down the room length on the right side; work your way to the left. Raise drum. Start motor. Slowly lower drum to the floor. Lift the sander off the floor as you approach the wall. Move to the left 2 to 4" and then walk it backwards the same distance you just walked forward. Repeat.

(continued)

5

When you get to the far left side of the room, turn the machine around and repeat the process. Overlap the sanded two-thirds to feather out the ridgeline. Repeat this drum sanding process 3 or 4 times using 120-grit paper. For the final pass or two use finer paper (150-grit).

6

Use a power edge sander along the walls, using the same grit that you last used with the drum sander. Make a succession of overlapping half-circles as you move along the entire perimeter of the room. Next, run a rotary buffer over the floor twice: first with an 80-grit screen and then with a 100-grit screen. Finally, use a random orbital sander to smooth out the floor.

7

Use a paint scraper to get to corners and hard-to-reach nooks. Pull the scraper toward you with a steady downward pressure. Pull with the grain. Next, sand with a sanding block.

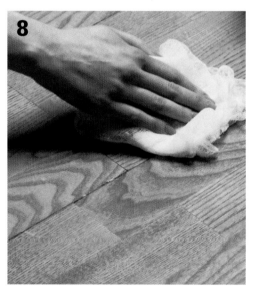

8

Remove all plastic on doors, windows, and fixtures and then sweep and vacuum to prepare the room for finish. Wipe up fine particles with a tack cloth.

9

Seal the sanded wood with a 1:1 mixture of water-based polyurethane and water, using a painting pad and pole.

10

Allow the floor to dry. Buff the surface lightly to remove any raised wood grain, using a medium abrasive pad. Vacuum the surface, using a bristle attachment, then wipe with a tack cloth.

11

Apply at least two coats of undiluted polyurethane finish to get a hard, durable finish. Allow the finish to dry; repeat step 10 and then add a final coat. Do not overbrush.

12

When the final coat is dry, buff the surface with water and fine abrasive pad. Wait at least 72 hours before replacing the shoe molding.

Walls & Ceilings

Walls and ceilings are much more than structural barriers dividing your house into separate areas. They are canvases awaiting an inspired treatment that can set mood, distinguish space, and reflect your personality within each individual room.

Through creative design and a thoughtful selection of colors, textures, and materials, nearly any wall and ceiling design you dream up can become a reality. From basic painted wallboard and traditional wood paneling to elegant glass block and distinct veneer plaster finishes, there is an ever-increasing variety of wall and ceiling finish materials available to you. Most home centers and lumberyards keep an impressive selection in stock and can easily accommodate special orders.

In this chapter:

- Installing Paneling
- Installing Beadboard Wainscoting
- Building Glass Block Walls
- Applying Veneer Plaster
- Paneling Ceilings
- Installing Suspended Ceilings
- Installing Acoustical Ceiling Tiles
- Installing Metal Ceilings
- Installing Base Molding
- Installing Picture Rail
- Installing Chair Rail
- Installing Crown Molding

Installing Paneling

Paneling is a versatile wall-surfacing material that comes in a wide range of styles, colors, and prices. Paneling sheets are made from a variety of materials for numerous applications:

Solid and veneer wood paneling is durable and easy to clean. Available in finished and unfinished sheets, wood paneling brings a warm, rich tone to any room. It is often used as wainscoting (pages 214 to 219) and also can be used as an inexpensive cover-up for damaged plaster.

Laminate panels are sheets of MDF, particleboard, or plywood faced with paper, print or vinyl. Laminates are available in hundreds of colors, styles, and patterns, providing a durable alternative to paint or wallcoverings.

FRP (fiberglass reinforced plastic), extruded plastic, and vinyl panels contain solid material throughout the panel, creating a low-maintenance, water-resistant wall surface for bathrooms, utility rooms, garages and workshops, as well as numerous commercial applications.

Tileboard is moisture-resistant hardboard coated with melamine, providing a durable, easy-to-clean plastic finish. It's designed to replicate the appearance of ceramic tile, for use in bathrooms, laundry rooms, and kitchens.

Bamboo paneling is gaining in popularity due to its unique look and green-friendly specs. Panels are constructed of strips of bamboo laminated to a fabric backing, which allows it to conform to any type of surface, flat or curved.

Most paneling is available in 4×8, 4×9, and 4×10 sheets. Some manufacturers also offer sheets in sixty-inch widths. Paneling that is ¼" or less in thickness requires a solid backer of at least ½" wallboard; paneling ⅜" thick or more is rigid enough to be fastened directly to framing with sixteen-inch O.C. spacing. Installation typically involves a panel adhesive, either applied in beads along the wall or framing, or troweled onto the back surface of the panel. Make sure to check the manufacturer's instructions for the product you purchase.

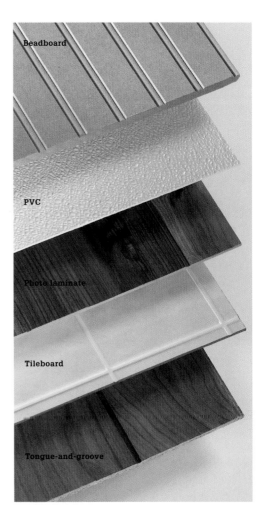

Beadboard

PVC

Photo laminate

Tileboard

Tongue-and-groove

Tools & Materials ▸

Pry bar	Compass
Stud finder	Jigsaw
Tape measure	Caulk gun
Plumb bob	Paneling sheets
Circular saw	4d finish nails
Straightedge	Wood stain
Hammer	Panel adhesive
Carpenter's level	Powdered chalk

How to Install Wood Paneling

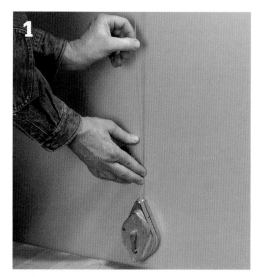

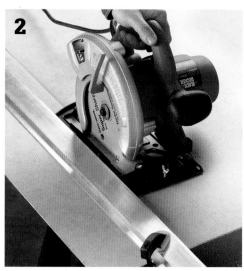

Starting in the corner farthest from the entry, use a stud finder to locate the center of the stud closest to, but less than 48" from, the corner. Find and mark stud centers every 48" from this first stud. Snap a plumb chalk line down the wall at each location. Paneling seams will fall along these lines.

Lay the first paneling sheet face-side down. Measure the distance from corner to the first plumb mark and add 1" to allow for scribing. Use a circular saw and clamped straightedge to cut paneling to this measurement.

Position the first sheet of paneling against the wall so that the cut edge is 1" away from the corner, and the opposite, finished edge is plumb. Temporarily tack the top of the paneling to the wall.

Spread the legs of a compass to 1¼", then run the compass down the full height of the wall to scribe the corner irregularities onto the face of the paneling. Remove paneling from wall.

(continued)

5

Lay the paneling face-side up and cut along the scribe line with a jigsaw. To prevent splintering, use a fine-tooth woodcutting blade. The scribed edge will fit perfectly against the wall corner.

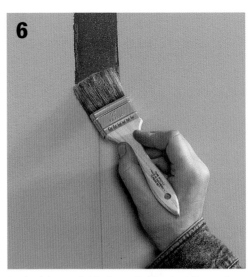

6

Apply stain or paint to the wall at the plumb lines so the backer will not show through the slight gaps at joints. Select a color that matches the color of the paneling edges, which may be darker than the paneling surface.

7

Use a caulk gun to apply 2" long beads of panel adhesive to the wall at 6" intervals and in a continuous, wavy bead about 1" back from plumb lines (to prevent adhesive from seeping out through the joints). For new construction, apply adhesive directly to the studs.

8

Attach the paneling to the top of the wall, using 4d finishing nails driven every 16". Press the paneling against the adhesive, then pull it away from the wall. Press the paneling back against the wall when the adhesive is tacky, about 2 minutes.

9

Hang the remaining paneling so that there is a slight space at the joints. This space allows paneling to expand in damp weather. Use a dime as a spacing gauge.

How to Cut Openings in Paneling

For window, door and other openings, measure the opening and mark the outline on the backside of the paneling. Cut to size using a circular saw and straightedge. Install as you would a full sheet of paneling (page 212).

For receptacles, switches, fixtures, and heating vents, coat the edges of electrical boxes and ductwork with chalk.

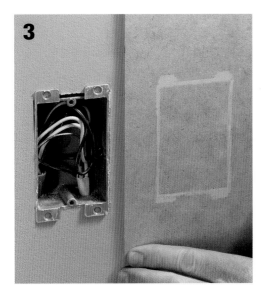

Press the paneling against the wall, so the backside presses against the outlet or vent—the chalk outline will transfer to the paneling.

Lay the paneling face-side down. Drill a hole at one corner of each outline, then use a jigsaw with a fine-tooth woodcutting blade to make the cutouts.

Installing Beadboard Wainscoting

Wainscoting refers to virtually any specialized treatment of the lower three to four feet of interior walls. The form demonstrated here, using tongue-and-groove boards, first gained popularity in the early twentieth century. Recently, it has re-emerged as a stylish way to dress up a room.

Typical tongue-and-groove boards for wainscoting are made of pine, fir, or other softwoods and measure ¼" to ¾" thick. Each board has a tongue on one edge, a groove on the other, and usually a decorative bevel or bead on each edge. Boards are cut to length, then attached with nails, most of which are driven through the tongues of the boards. This technique, known as blindnailing, hides the nails from view.

Once installed, the wainscoting is capped at a height of 30" to 36" with a molding called a *cap rail*. The exact height of the wainscoting is a matter of personal preference. When installed to the height of the furniture in the room, wainscoting provides visual symmetry. It also allows the cap rail to double as a chair rail, protecting the lower portion of the walls from damage.

When installed over finished wallboard, wainscoting usually requires that nailers be fastened to the wall studs to provide a reliable backing for nailing. You can skip this step if you know there is consistent blocking between the studs to substitute for this backing. However, this is usually difficult to confirm unless the walls were framed with tongue-and-groove wainscoting in mind.

Wainscoting can be painted or stained. Oil-based stains can be applied before or after installation, since most of the stain will be absorbed into the wood and won't interfere with the tongue-and-groove joints. If you're painting, choose a latex-based paint; it will resist cracking as the joints expand and contract with changes in the weather.

Tools & Materials ▸

Pencil	Tape measure
Level	Paintbrush
Circular saw	Tongue-and-groove
Miter saw	boards
Miter box	Finish nails
Hammer	1 × 3 furring strips
Nail set	2" 10d finish nails
Plane	Receptacle box
Circuit tester	extenders, as required
Pry bar	Paint or stain

Tongue-and-groove wainscoting boards are milled with smooth faces or contoured to add additional texture to your walls. For staining, choose a wood species with a pronounced grain. For painting, poplar is a good choice, since it has few knots and a consistent, closed grain that accepts paint evenly.

How to Prepare for a Wainscoting Project

Measure to make a plan drawing of each wall in your project. Indicate the locations of fixtures, receptacles, and windows. Use a level to make sure the corners are plumb. If not, mark plumb lines on the walls to use as reference points.

Condition the planking by stacking it in the room where it will be installed. Place spacers between the planks to let air circulate around each board, allowing the wood to adjust to the room's temperature and humidity. Wait 72 hours before staining or sealing the front, back, and edges of each plank.

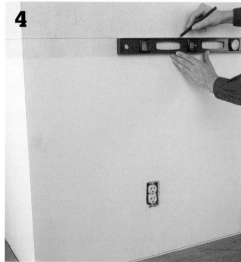

Remove the baseboard moldings, along with any receptacle cover plates, vent covers, or other wall fixtures within the area you plan to cover. Before you begin, turn off the electricity to the circuits in the area.

Mark the walls with level lines to indicate the top of the wainscoting. Mark a line ¼" from the floor to provide a small gap for expansion at the floor.

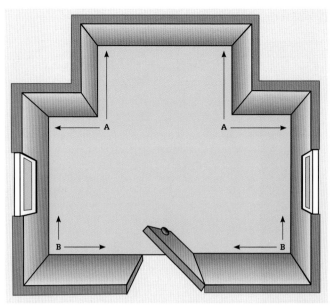

Begin installation at the corners.
Install any outside corners (A) first, working your way toward the inside corners. In sections of a room that have no outside corners, start at the inside corners (B), and work your way toward the door and window casings. Calculate the number of boards required for each wall, using the measurements on the drawing you created earlier (length of wall divided by width of one plank). When making this calculation, remember that the tongues are removed from the corner boards. If the total number of boards for a wall includes a fraction of less than ½ of a board, plan to trim the first and last boards to avoid ending with a board cut to less than half its original width.

How to Install Wainscoting at Outside Corners

Cut a pair of boards to the widths indicated in the calculations you developed during the planning process.

Position the boards at the corner, butting them to create a plumb corner. Facenail the boards in place, then nail the joint, using 6d finish nails. Drive the nails to within ⅛" of the face of the boards, then finish with a nail set.

Position a piece of corner trim and nail it in place, using 6d finish nails. Install the remaining boards (opposite, steps 5 and 6).

How to Install Wainscoting at Inside Corners

1

Hold a level against the first board and hold the board flush with the corner. If the wall is out of plumb, trim the board to compensate: Hold the board plumb, position a compass at the inside corner of the wall, and use it to scribe a line down the board.

2

Cut along the scribed line with a circular saw. Subsequent boards may require minor tapering with a plane to adjust for plumb.

3

Hold the first board in the corner, leaving a ¼" gap for expansion, and facenail into the center of the board at each nailer location, using 6d finish nails. Drive the top nails roughly ½" from the edge so they'll be hidden from view once the cap rail is attached.

4

Install a second board at the corner by butting it against the first one, then facenailing in at least two locations. Nail to within ⅛" of the face of the board, then use a nail set to finish.

5

Position subsequent boards. Leave a ¹⁄₁₆" gap at each joint to allow for seasonal expansion. Use a level to check every third board for plumb. If the wainscoting is out of plumb, adjust the fourth board, as necessary, to compensate.

6

Mark and cut the final board to fit. If you're at a door casing, cut the board to fit flush with the casing (trim off at least the tongue). If you're at an inside corner, make sure it is plumb. If not, scribe and trim the board to fit.

How to Make a Cutout

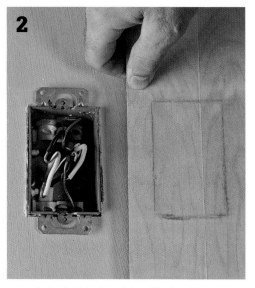

1

Test the receptacle (inset) to make sure the power is off. Then, unscrew and remove the receptacle from the box. Coat the edges of the electrical box with bright colored chalk.

2

Press the back of the board that will be installed over the receptacle, directly against the electrical box, to create a cutting outline.

3

Lay the board face down and drill a large pilot hole near one corner of the outline. Use a jigsaw fitted with a fine-tooth woodcutting blade to make the cutout. Be careful not to cut outside the lines.

4

Facenail the wainscoting to the wall, then reattach the receptacle with the tabs overlapping the wainscoting so the receptacle is flush with the opening. You may need longer screws.

Tip ▸

When paneling around a receptacle with thick stock, you will need to attach a receptacle box extender to the inside of the box, then reconnect the receptacle so it is flush with the opening in the paneling.

How to Install Wainscoting Around a Window

On casement windows, install wainscoting up to the casings on the sides and below the window. Install ½" cove molding, quarter round, or other trim to finish the edges.

On double-hung windows, remove any window trim and install wainscoting up to the jambs on the sides and below the window. Cut the stool to fit over the wainscoting, then reinstall the apron.

How to Finish a Wainscoting Project

Cut baseboard moldings (pages 242 to 245) to fit over the wainscoting and attach them by nailing 6d finishing nails at the stud locations. If you plan to install a base shoe, leave a small gap at the floor.

Cut cap rail to fit as you would contoured chair rail (page 249). At doors and windows, install the cap rail so its edge is flush with the side casings.

Attach the cap rail by nailing 4d finish nails through the flats of the moldings at the stud locations so that nails enter both the studs and the wainscoting. Set the nails with a nail set.

Building Glass Block Walls

With its ability to transmit light, a glass block partition wall defines separate living areas while maintaining a sense of openness. You can find glass block at specialty distributors and home centers in a variety of patterns, shapes, and sizes, along with all the products needed for the installation.

You can build your wall to any height. Top a low wall with a course of bullnose blocks to give it a finished rounded edge, or with flat block to create a shelf. To build a full-height wall, calculate the number of courses of block you'll have, then frame-in a header to fill the remaining space between the finished block and the ceiling.

Because of its weight, a glass block wall requires a sturdy foundation. A four-inch-thick concrete basement floor should be strong enough, but a wood floor may need to be reinforced. Contact the local building department for requirements in your area. Also bear in mind that glass block products and installation techniques vary by manufacturer—ask a glass block retailer or manufacturer for advice about the best products and methods for your project.

Tools & Materials ▸

Chalk line
Circular saw
Jigsaw
Paintbrush
Drill
Mixing box
Trowel
Level
Pliers
Jointing tool
Nylon- or natural-
   bristle brush
Sponge
2 × 6 lumber
16d common nails
Water-based
   asphalt emulsion
Panel anchors
2½" drywall screws
Foam expansion
   strips
Glass block mortar
8" glass blocks
¼" T-spacers
Board
Reinforcement wire
16-gauge wire
Caulk or wall trim
Baseboard

Glass block has many uses in modern up-scale homes and today's installation systems allow homeowners to easily work with it.

How to Build a Glass Block Wall

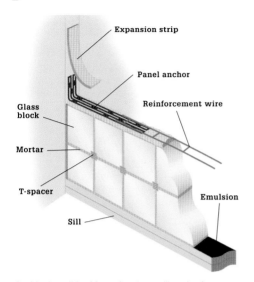

The block wall in this project has a sill made of two 2 × 6s cut to the exact width of the block. This provides a stable base to help resist floor movement and protect the lower courses. The block wall is secured to an anchor stud in an adjoining wall, by means of metal panel anchors. Expansion strips between the two walls allow for movement.

Dry-lay the first course of glass block, using a ⅜" wood spacer between the wall and the first block, and ¼" spacers between the remaining blocks, to set the gaps for the mortar joints. Mark the wall position onto the floor, then remove the blocks. Snap chalk lines along the marks to create the sill outline.

Determine the sill thickness based on the size of your baseboard and thickness of the floorcovering. Rip 2 × 6 lumber to the width of the block. If the end blocks are shaped, trim the sill pieces to match, using a jigsaw. Fasten the sill to the subfloor and framing below with 16d common nails. Apply asphalt emulsion to the sill, using a paintbrush.

Mark plumb lines on the adjoining wall, straight up from sides of the sill. Mark the finished height of each course along the lines. Fasten a panel anchor to the anchor stud at the top of every second course, using 2½" drywall screws. Cut expansion strips to size and adhere them to the wall between the anchors.

(continued)

Mix only as much mortar as you can apply in about 30 minutes. Lay a ⅜"-thick mortar bed on the sill, enough for three or four blocks. Set the first block, using ¼" T-spacers at the mortar joint locations (follow the manufacturer's directions for modifying T-spacers at the bottom and sides of the wall). Do not place mortar between blocks and expansion strips. Butter the trailing edge of each subsequent block with enough mortar to fill the sides of both blocks.

Lay the remainder of the course. If the wall has a corner, work from both ends toward the center, and install the corner piece last. Use ¼" T-spacers between blocks to maintain proper spacing. Plumb and level each block as you work, then check the entire course, using a flat board and a level. Tap blocks into place using a rubber mallet—do not strike them with a metal tool.

At the top of the course, fill the joints with mortar, and then lay a ¼" bed of mortar for the second course. Lay the block for the second course, checking each block for level and plumb as you work.

Apply a ⅛" bed of mortar over the second course, then press the panel anchor into the mortar. Repeat this process at each anchor location.

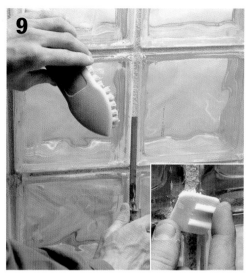

Add reinforcement wire in the same joints as the panel anchors, overlapping the anchors by 6". Also overlap the wire by 6" where multiple pieces are needed. At corners, cut the inner rail of the wire, bend the outer rail to follow the corner, then tie the inner rail ends together with 16-gauge wire. Add another ⅛" mortar bed, then lay the next course of block.

Build the wall in complete courses, checking the mortar after each course. When it is hard enough to resist light finger pressure (usually within 30 minutes), twist off the T-spacer tabs (inset) and pack mortar in the voids. Then, tool all of the joints with a jointing tool. Remove excess mortar from the glass, using a brush or damp sponge.

Clean the glass block thoroughly, using a wet sponge and rinsing it often. Allow the surface to dry, then remove cloudy residue with a clean, dry cloth. After the mortar has cured for two weeks, apply a sealant. Caulk the seam between the glass block and the adjoining wall, or cover the gap with trim.

Reinstall the flooring, if necessary, then cut baseboard to fit around the sill (see pages 242 to 245). If the end of your wall has curved (bullnose) block, wrap the end with three pieces of trim.

Applying Veneer Plaster

While gypsum wallboard all but wiped out traditional plaster and lath in the 1940s, a new generation of plaster products now make plaster easier and cheaper to apply, leading to renewed popularity for this classic material.

Veneer plaster systems provide a solid, uniform wall surface that is highly resistant to nail pops, cracks and surface damage. A skim coat of plaster is troweled onto a gypsum wallboard base that has a distinctive blue color, commonly called blueboard. While blueboard is installed like standard wallboard, it has a highly absorptive face paper to which the wet-mix plaster bonds. Blueboard joints do not need to be taped as precisely as standard wallboard joints, and seams and fastener heads do not show through the finished plaster surface, a common problem with standard wallboard.

Veneer systems are available in one-coat and two-coat systems. One-coat systems have a single layer of finish plaster applied directly to the blueboard base; two-coat systems, a rough basecoat for the finish plaster to mechanically "key" or bond to, providing a more rigid surface. Finish plaster can be troweled smooth or tooled for a texture. Sand and other additives can be used to create coarser textures.

Applying veneer plaster effectively does take some time to master, but no more so than that of any masonry technique that requires troweling. The key is to apply the plaster in quick, short strokes, called "scratching in," and then to immediately trowel it over with a steady, even stroke to smooth the plaster to a consistent thickness, typically 1⁄16" to 1⁄8".

Tools & Materials ▸

Stapler
Hammer
Heavy-duty 1⁄2"
 drill with
 mixing paddle
16-gal. drum
Mortar hawk
12" trowel
Fine-wire rake
 or broom
 (for basecoat)
Spray water bottle

Metal corner bead with
 mesh flanges
11⁄4" wallboard screws
Non-adhesive fiberglass
 mesh tape
1⁄4" staples
Clean potable water
Dry-mix veneer
 basecoat plaster (for
 two-coat application)
Dry-mix veneer
 finish plaster

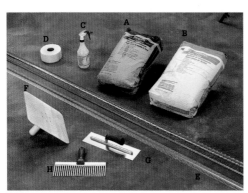

Tools and materials for installing veneer plaster include: dry-mix veneer plaster basecoats (A); finish plaster (B), available for smooth or textured applications; spray bottle for moistening surfaces (C); non-adhesive fiberglass mesh tape for covering blueboard panel seams and inside corners (D); outside corner beads with metal beads and mesh flanges (E); mortar hawk (F); 12" trowel (G); thin-wire rake for roughening the base coat (H).

ONE- AND TWO-COAT VENEER PLASTER SYSTEMS

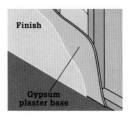

One-coat veneer plaster systems use a single, 1⁄16"- to 3⁄32"-thick coat of finish plaster applied directly to a blueboard base. The coat can be troweled smooth or textured, resulting in a hard, monolithic surface.

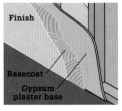

Two-coat veneer plaster systems are composed of a 1⁄16" to 1⁄8" basecoat plaster applied to blueboard, followed by a 1⁄16"- to 3⁄32"-thick coat of finish plaster. The finish coat bonds with the scratched basecoat surface, forming a more uniform and monolithic surface than that of a one-coat system.

How to Apply a One-Coat Veneer Plaster System

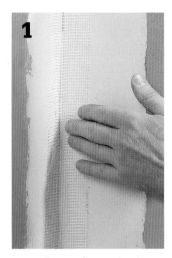

Cover all seams first. Apply a thin layer of plaster along all flat seams and corner bead, feathering out the edges by 6". For inside corners, apply a thin bed of plaster and embed the loose tape, then cover with another thin layer. Allow all taped seams to set.

Variation: Blueboard joints can also be reinforced with paper tape. Embed the tape in a thin plaster bed, then and cover with another thin layer to conceal the tape fully. *Note: Some manufacturers recommend setting-type compound for embedding paper tape; always follow the manufacturer's directions for the products you use.*

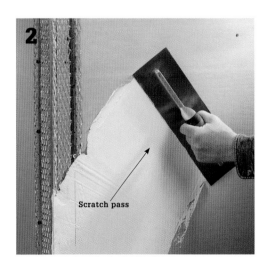

Scratch pass

Smooth pass

After the seams have set, begin plastering the surface, beginning at one corner and moving to the opposite. Start with ceilings and then do the walls, completing one entire surface before moving on to the next. To apply the plaster, tightly scratch in the material up the wall (photo left), then immediately double-back over it, smoothing over the material to a thickness of ⅟₁₆ to ³⁄₃₂", as specified by the manufacturer. Use tight, quick strokes to apply the plaster during the "scratch pass" and long, even strokes to achieve consistency during the "smooth pass."

(continued)

Continue to apply plaster by scratching in and smoothing over the surface. Don't worry about uniformity and trowel ridges at this point. Rather, make sure the entire surface is completely concealed with a relatively even plaster coat, 1/16" to 3/32"-thick.

Once the plaster begins to firm, trowel the surface to fill any voids and remove tooling marks and imperfections, integrating the surface into a uniform smoothness.

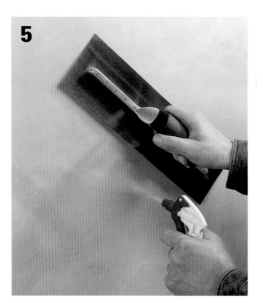

Prior to the plaster setting, make a final pass with the trowel to smooth the surface, using water sparingly. Do not over trowel; stop before the plaster begins to darken and sets.

Variation: For textured surfaces, skip the final troweling and work the surface with a texturing tool to achieve the desired results. *Note: Sand or texture added to the plaster mixture does not require tooling.*

How to Apply Basecoat in a Two-Coat Veneer Plaster System

1

Apply a thin layer of basecoat along all flat seams and corner bead, feathering out the edges by 6". For inside corners, apply a thin bed of basecoat and embed the loose tape, then cover with another thin layer. Allow all taped seams to set.

2

Scratch pass

Smooth pass

After the seams have set, tightly scratch in basecoat, then immediately double-back over it, smoothing over the material to a thickness of ¹⁄₁₆" to ⅛", as specified by the manufacturer. Use tight, quick strokes to apply basecoat for the "scratch pass" and long, even strokes to achieve consistency for the "smooth pass."

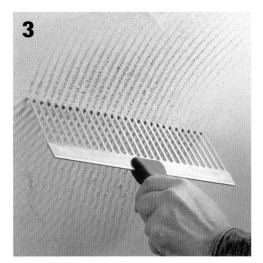

3

Once the plaster begins to firm or "take up," trowel the surface to fill any voids and remove tooling marks and imperfections, integrating the surface into a reasonably uniform surface—do not over-trowel to a smooth surface. Create keys for the final coat, using a thin-wire rake to roughen the basecoat.

4

Approximately two hours after the basecoat has set, the finish coat can be applied using the same techniques as for a one-coat veneer plaster system (see pages 225 to 226).

Paneling Ceilings

Tongue-and-groove paneling is a pleasing alternative to a wallboard ceiling, particularly in a knee-wall attic. Pine paneling is most common, but any tongue-and-groove material can be used. These materials are typically ⅜" to ¾" thick and are attached directly to ceiling joists and rafters (over faced insulation, when required). Most codes require you to install ⅜" wallboard as a fire stop under ceiling material thinner than ¼".

Allow for waste by purchasing 15% more material than the square footage of the ceiling; add more for waste if the ceiling requires many angled cuts. Since the tongue portion on most pieces slips into the groove on an adjacent piece, square footage is based on the exposed face (called the reveal) once the boards are installed. A compound miter saw is the best tool for ensuring clean cuts. This is especially important if the ceiling includes non-90° angles.

Tongue-and-groove boards are attached with flooring nails driven through the shoulder of the tongue into each rafter (called blindnailing because the nail heads are covered by the next board). Nailing through the board face is only necessary on the first and last course and on scarf joints.

Layout is very important to the success of a paneled surface, because the lines clearly reveal flaws such as pattern deviations, misaligned walls, and installation mistakes. Before beginning the installation, measure to see how many boards will be installed (using the reveal measurement). If the final board will be less than 2 inches wide, trim the first, or starter board, by trimming the long edge that abuts the wall.

If the angle of the ceiling peak is not parallel to the wall, you must compensate for the difference by ripping the starter piece at an angle so that the leading edge, and every piece thereafter, is parallel to the peak.

Tools & Materials ▶

Chalk line
Compound miter saw
Circular saw
Drill
Nail set
Tongue-and-groove
    paneling

1¾" spiral
    flooring nails
Trim molding

Tongue-and-groove paneling can be installed directly over rafters or joists or over wallboard. In attic installations, it's important to insulate first, adding a separate vapor barrier if required by building codes. Local code may also require that paper-faced insulation behind a kneewall be covered with drywall or other material.

How to Panel a Ceiling

1

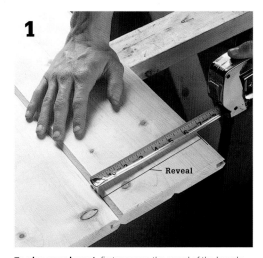

Reveal

To plan your layout, first measure the reveal of the boards. Fit two pieces together and measure from the bottom edge of the upper board to the bottom edge of the lower board. Calculate the number of boards needed to cover one side of the ceiling by dividing the reveal dimension into the overall distance between the top of the wall and the peak.

2

Rafters

Side wall

Use the calculation from step 1 to make a control line for the first row of panels—the starter boards. At both ends of the ceiling, measure down from the peak an equal distance, and make a mark to represent the top (tongue) edges of the starter boards. Snap a chalk line through the marks.

3

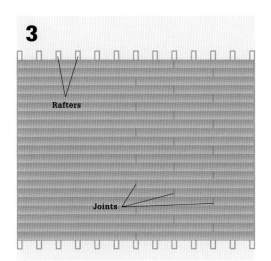

Rafters

Joints

If the boards aren't long enough to span the entire ceiling, plan the locations of the joints. Staggering the joints in a three-step pattern will make them less conspicuous. Note that each joint must fall over the middle of a rafter. For best appearance, select boards of similar coloring and grain for each row.

4

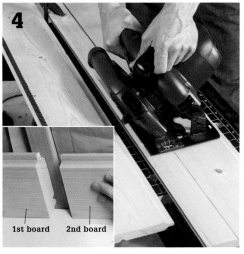

1st board   2nd board

Rip the first starter board to width by bevel-cutting the bottom (grooved) edge. If the starter row will have joints, cut the board to length using a 30° bevel cut on the joint end only. Two beveled ends joined together form a scarf joint (inset), which is less noticeable than a butt joint. If the board spans the ceiling, square-cut both ends.

(continued)

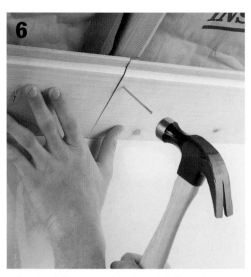

Position the first starter board so the tongue is on the control line. Leave a ⅛" gap between the square board end and the end wall. Fasten the board by nailing through its face about 1" from the grooved edge and into the rafters. Then, blind-nail through the base of the tongue into each rafter, angling the nail backward at 45°. Drive the nail heads beneath the wood surface, using a nail set.

Cut and install any remaining boards in the starter row one at a time, making sure the scarf joints fit together tightly. At each scarf joint, drive two nails through the face of the top board, angling the nail to capture the end of the board behind it. If necessary, predrill the nail holes to prevent splitting.

Cut the first board for the next row, then fit its grooved edge over the tongue of the board in the starter row. Use a hammer and a scrap piece of paneling to drive downward on the tongue edge, seating the grooved edge over the tongue of the starter board. Fasten the second row with blind-nails only.

As you install successive rows, measure down from the peak to make sure the rows remain parallel to the peak. Correct any misalignment by adjusting the tongue-and-groove joint slightly with each row. You can also snap additional control lines to help align the rows.

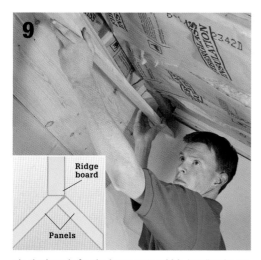

Rip the boards for the last row to width, beveling the top edges so they fit flush against the ridge board. Facenail the boards in place. Install paneling on the other side of the ceiling, then cut and install the final row of panels to form a closed joint under the ridge board (inset).

Install trim molding along walls, at joints around obstacles, and along inside and outside corners, if desired. (Select-grade 1 × 2 works well as trim along walls.) Where necessary, bevel the back edges of the trim or miter-cut the ends to accommodate the slope of the ceiling.

Tips for Paneling an Attic Ceiling ▸

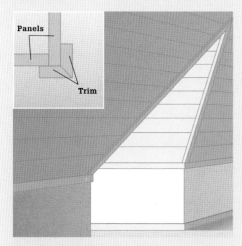

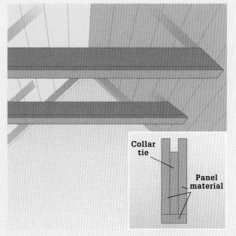

Use mitered trim to cover joints where panels meet at outside corners. Dormers and other roof elements create opposing ceiling angles that can be difficult to panel around. It may be easier to butt the panels together and hide the butt joints with custom-cut trim. The trim also makes a nice transition between angles.

Wrap collar ties or exposed beams with custom-cut panels. Install the paneling on the ceiling first. Then, rip-cut panels to the desired width. You may want to include a tongue-and-groove joint as part of the trim detail. Angle-cut the ends of the trim so it fits tight to the ceiling panels.

Installing Suspended Ceilings

Suspended ceilings are traditionally popular ceiling finishes for basements and utility areas, particularly because they hang below pipes and other mechanicals while providing easy access to them. However, the commercial appearance and grainy texture of basic ceiling tiles make them an unlikely choice for formal areas such as living rooms. Basic tiles are not your only option.

Suspended ceiling tile manufacturers have a wide array of ceiling tiles to choose from that go above and beyond traditional institutional tiles. Popular styles mimic historical tin tiles and add depth to the ceiling while minimizing sound and vibration noise.

A suspended ceiling is a grid framework made of lightweight metal brackets hung on wires attached to ceiling or floor joists. The frame consists of T-shaped main beams (mains), cross-tees (tees), and L-shaped wall angles. The grid supports ceiling panels, which rest on the flanges of the framing pieces. Panels are available in 2 × 2-ft. or 2 × 4-ft. sizes, in a variety of styles. Special options include insulated panels, acoustical panels that absorb sound, and light-diffuser screens for use with fluorescent lights. Generally, metal-frame ceiling systems are more durable than ones made of plastic.

To begin your ceiling project, devise the panel layout based on the size of the room, placing equally sized trimmed panels on opposite sides to create a balanced look. Your ceiling must also be level. For small rooms, a 4-foot or 6-foot level will work, but a water level is more effective for larger jobs. You can make a water level with two water-level ends (available at hardware stores and home centers) attached to flexible plastic tubing.

Tools & Materials ▸

Water level	Utility knife
Chalk line	Suspended ceiling
Drill	kit (frame)
Aviation snips	Screw eyes
String	Hanger wires
Lock-type clamps	Ceiling panels
Screw-eye driver	1½" drywall screws
Pliers	or masonry nails
Straightedge	

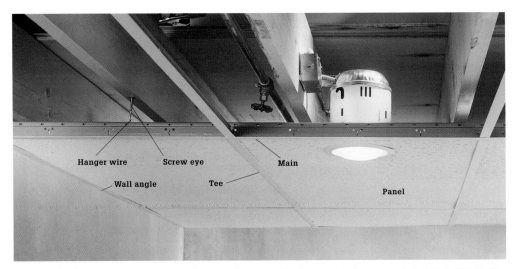

Hanger wire   Screw eye   Main

Wall angle   Tee

Panel

Suspended ceilings are the most common ceiling choice in areas, such as basements, where access to the joist cavities needs to be maintained. They're also installed as a way to conceal problem ceilings.

Installing a Suspended Ceiling

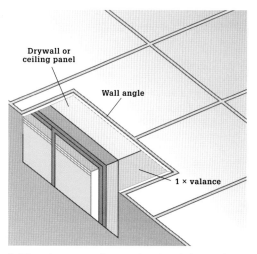

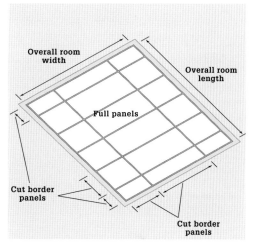

Build a valance around basement awning windows so they can be opened fully. Attach 1 × lumber of an appropriate width to joists or blocking. Install drywall (or a suspended-ceiling panel trimmed to fit) to the joists inside the valance.

Draw your ceiling layout on paper, based on the exact dimensions of the room. Plan so that trimmed border panels on opposite sides of the room are of equal width and length (avoid panels smaller than ½-size). If you include lighting fixtures in your plan, make sure they follow the grid layout.

How to Install a Suspended Ceiling

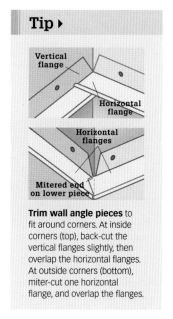

Make a mark on one wall that represents the ceiling height plus the height of the wall angle. Use a water level to transfer that height to both ends of each wall. Snap a chalk line to connect the marks. This line represents the top of the ceiling's wall angle.

Attach wall angle pieces to the studs on all walls, positioning the top of the wall angle flush with the chalk line. Use 1½" drywall screws (or short masonry nails driven into mortar joints on concrete block walls). Cut angle pieces using aviation snips.

Tip ▶

Trim wall angle pieces to fit around corners. At inside corners (top), back-cut the vertical flanges slightly, then overlap the horizontal flanges. At outside corners (bottom), miter-cut one horizontal flange, and overlap the flanges.

(continued)

3

Mark the location of each main on the wall angles at the ends of the room. The mains must be parallel to each other and perpendicular to the ceiling joists. Set up a guide string for each main, using a thin string and lock-type clamps (inset). Clamp the strings to the opposing wall angles, stretching them very taut so there's no sagging.

4

Install screw eyes for hanging the mains, using a drill and screw-eye driver. Drill pilot holes and drive the eyes into the joists every 4 ft., locating them directly above the guide strings. Attach hanger wire to the screw eyes by threading one end through the eye and twisting the wire on itself at least three times. Trim excess wire, leaving a few inches of wire hanging below the level of the guide string.

5

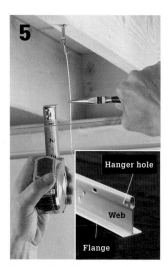

Hanger hole

Web

Flange

Measure the distance from the bottom of a main's flange to the hanger hole in the web (inset). Use this measurement to prebend each hanger wire. Measure up from the guide string and make a 90° bend in the wire, using pliers.

6

Following your ceiling plan, mark the placement of the first tee on opposite wall angles at one end of the room. Set up a guide string for the tee, using a string and clamps, as before. This string must be perpendicular to the guide strings for the mains.

7

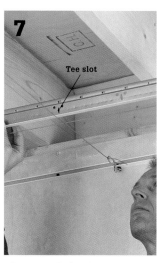

Tee slot

Trim one end of each main so that a tee slot in the main's web is aligned with the tee guide string, and the end of the main bears fully on a wall angle. Set the main in place to check the alignment of the tee slot with the string.

8

Cut the other end of each main to fit, so that it rests on the opposing wall angle. If a single main cannot span the room, splice two mains together, end-to-end (the ends should be fashioned with male-female connectors). Make sure the tee slots remain aligned when splicing.

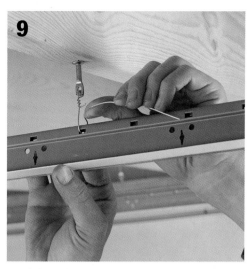

9

Install the mains by setting the ends on the wall angle and threading the hanger wires through the hanger holes in the webs. The wires should be as close to vertical as possible. Wrap each wire around itself three times, making sure the main's flange is level with the main guide string. Also install a hanger near each main splice.

10

Attach tees to the mains, slipping the tabbed ends into the tee slots on the mains. Align the first row of tees with the tee guide string; install the remaining rows at 4-ft. intervals. If you're using 2 × 2-ft. panels, install 2-ft. cross-tees between the midpoints of the 4-ft. tees. Cut and install the border tees, setting the tee ends on the wall angles. Remove all guide strings and clamps.

11

Place full ceiling panels into the grid first, then install the border panels. Lift the panels in at an angle, and position them so they rest on the frame's flanges. Reach through adjacent openings to adjust the panels, if necessary. To trim the border panels to size, cut them face-up, using a straightedge and utility knife (inset).

Installing Acoustical Ceiling Tiles

Easy-to-install ceiling tile can lend character to a plain ceiling or help turn an unfinished basement or attic into beautiful living space. Made of pressed mineral and fiberboard, ceiling tiles are available in a variety of styles. They also provide moderate noise reduction.

Ceiling tiles typically can be attached directly to a drywall or plaster ceiling with adhesive. If your ceiling is damaged or uneven, or if you have an unfinished joist ceiling, install 1 × 2 furring strips as a base for the tiles, as shown in this project. Some systems include metal tracks for clip-on installation.

Unless your ceiling measures in even feet, you won't be able to install the 12-inch tiles without some cutting. To prevent an unattractive installation with small, irregular tiles along two sides, include a course of border tiles along the perimeter of the installation. Plan so that tiles at opposite ends of the room are cut to the same width and are at least half the width of a full tile.

Most ceiling tile comes prefinished, but it can be painted to match any decor. For best results, apply two coats of paint using a roller with a ¼" nap. Wait 24 hours between coats.

Tools & Materials ▸

4-ft. level	Stapler
Stepladder	1 × 2 furring strips
Chalk line	8d nails or 2" screws
Utility knife	String
Straightedge	Ceiling tiles
Hammer or drill	Staples
Handsaw	Trim molding

Acoustic tile improves the sound quality inside a home theater and reduces the transmission of sound to the rooms surrounding it.

How to Install Ceiling Tile

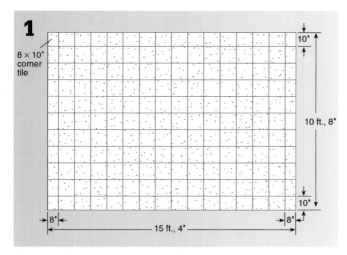

1

8 × 10"
corner
tile

10"

10 ft., 8"

10"

8"

15 ft., 4"

8"

Measure the ceiling and devise a layout. If the length (or width) doesn't measure in even feet, use this formula to determine the width of the border tiles: add 12 to the number of inches remaining and divide by 2. The result is the width of the border tile. (For example, if the room length is 15 ft., 4", add 12 to the 4, then divide 16 by 2, which results in an 8" border tile.)

2

Install the first furring strip flush with the wall and perpendicular to the joists, fastening with two 8d nails or 2" screws at each joist. Measure out from the wall a distance equal to the border tile width minus ¾", and snap a chalk line. Install the second furring strip with its wall-side edge on the chalk line.

3

Install the remaining strips 12" on-center from the second strip. Measure from the second strip and mark the joist nearest the wall every 12". Repeat along the joist on the opposite side of the room, then snap chalk lines between the marks. Install the furring strips along the lines. Install the last furring strip flush against the opposite side wall. Stagger the butted end joints of strips between rows so they aren't all on the same joist.

4

Check the strips with a 4-ft. level. Insert wood shims between the strips and joists as necessary to bring the strips into a level plane.

(continued)

5

Set up taut, perpendicular string lines along two adjacent walls to help guide the tile installation. Inset the strings from the wall by a distance that equals that wall's border tile width plus ½". Use a framing square to make sure the strings are square.

6

Cut the corner border tile to size with a utility knife and straightedge. Cutting the border tiles ¼" short will ease fitting them. The resulting gap between the tile and wall will be covered by trim. Cut only on the edges without the stapling flange.

7

Position the corner tile with the flange edges aligned with the two string lines and fasten it to the furring strips with four ½" staples. Cut and install two border tiles along each wall, making sure the tiles fit snugly together.

8

Fill in between the border tiles with full-size tiles. Continue working diagonally in this manner, toward the opposite corner. For the border tiles along the far wall, trim off the flange edges and staple through the faces of the tiles, close to the wall.

9

Install the final row of tiles, saving the far corner tile and its neighbor for last. Cut the last tile to size, then remove the tongue and nailing flange along the side edges. Finish the job by installing trim along the edges.

Installing Metal Ceilings

Today's metal ceilings offer the distinctive elegance of 19th-century tin tile in a durable, washable ceiling finish. Available at home centers and specialty distributors, metal ceiling systems include field panels (in 2 × 2-, 2 × 4-, and 2 × 8-ft. sizes), border panels that can be cut to fit your layout, and cornice molding for finishing the edges. The panels come in a variety of materials and finishes ready for installation, or they can be painted.

To simplify installation, the panels have round catches, called nailing buttons, that fit into one another to align the panels where they overlap. The buttons are also the nailing points for attaching the panels. Use 1" decorative conehead nails where nail heads will be exposed, and ½" wire nails where heads are hidden.

Install your metal ceiling over a smooth layer of ⅜" or ½" plywood, which can be fastened directly to the ceiling joists with drywall screws, or installed over an existing finish. The plywood provides a flat nailing surface for the panels. As an alternative, some manufacturers offer a track system for clip-on installation.

Begin your installation by carefully measuring the ceiling and snapping chalk lines to establish the panel layout. For most tile patterns, it looks best to cover the center of the space with full tiles only, then fill in along the perimeter with border panels, which are not patterned. Make sure your layout is square.

Tools & Materials ▸

Chalk line	Field panels
Level	Border panels with
Tin snips	molding edge
Drill with ⅛"	Cornice molding
metal bit	Masking tape
Compass	½" wire nails
Metal file	1" conehead nails
⅜" or ½" plywood	Wood block
2" drywall screws	

Real metal ceilings have traditional embossed patterns with an unmistakable luxurious quality. But, they are expensive and a bit unwieldy to install. Acoustic panels with an embossed vinyl pattern layer are much cheaper and easier to install, but are also less authentic.

How to Install a Metal Tile Ceiling

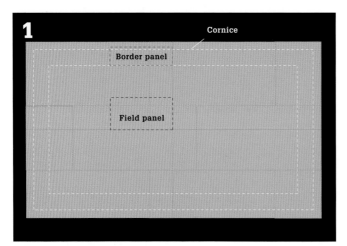

1 Cornice / Border panel / Field panel

2

Measure to find the center of the ceiling, then snap perpendicular chalk lines intersecting the center. On the walls, mark a level reference line representing the bottom edges of the cornice molding. Where possible, plan to install the panels so they overlap toward the room's entrance, to help conceal the seams.

Align the first field panel with the chalk lines at the ceiling's center, and attach it with ½" wire nails along the edges where another panel will overlap it. Drive the nails beside the nailing buttons—saving the buttons for nailing the overlapping panel.

3

4

Continue to install field panels, working along the length of the area first, then overlapping the next row. Make sure the nailing buttons are aligned. Underlap panels by sliding the new panel into position beneath the installed panel, then fasten through both panels at the nailing buttons, using 1" conehead nails. Where field panels meet at corners, drill ⅛" pilot holes for the conehead nails.

Cut the border panels to width so they will underlap the cornice by at least 1". Use sharp tin snips, and cut from the edge without edge molding. Install the panels so the nailing buttons on the molding align with those on the field panels. Fasten through the buttons with conehead nails, and along the cut edge with wire nails. At corners, miter-cut the panels, and drive conehead nails every 6" along the seam.

5

6

Install each cornice piece with its bottom edge on the level line. Drive 1" conehead nails through the nailing buttons and into the wall studs. Don't nail the ends until the succeeding piece is in place. Fasten the top edges to the ceiling.

At inside corners, install one cornice piece tightly into the corner, then scribe the mating piece to fit, using masking tape and a compass. Cut along the scribed line with tin snips, and make minor adjustments with a metal file. You may have to cut the mating piece several times, so start with plenty of length. If you have several corners, use this technique to cut templates for the corner pieces.

7

8

At outside corners, cut the ends of two scrap pieces at a 33° angle. Fit the pieces together at the corner, then trim and mark each piece in turn, making minor adjustments until they fit well. Use the scrap pieces as templates for marking the workpieces. Fasten near the corner only when both mating pieces are in place.

Using a hammer and a piece of wood, carefully tap any loose joints to tighten them. If the cornice will be left unpainted, file the joints for a perfect fit. If you're painting the ceiling, seal the seams with paintable silicone caulk, then apply two coats of paint using a roller with a ¼" nap. Allow the first coat to dry for 24 hours before applying the second coat.

Installing Base Molding

Baseboard trim is installed to conceal the joint between the finished floor and the wallcovering. It also serves to protect the wallboard at the floor. Installing plain, one-piece baseboard such as ranch-style base or cove base is a straightforward project. Outside corner joints are mitered, inside corners are coped, and long runs are joined with scarf cuts.

The biggest challenge to installing base is dealing with out-of-plumb and nonsquare corners. However, a T-bevel makes these obstacles easy to overcome.

Plan the order of your installation prior to cutting any pieces and lay out a specific piece for each length of wall. It may be helpful to mark the type of cut on the back of each piece so you don't have any confusion during the install.

Locate all studs and mark them with painter's tape, 6 inches higher than your molding height. If you need to make a scarf joint along a wall, make sure it falls on the center of a stud. Before you begin nailing trim in place, take the time to pre-finish the moldings. Doing so will minimize the cleanup afterward.

Tools & Materials ▸

Pencil	Pneumatic finish nail
Tape measure	gun & compressor
Power miter saw	Moldings
T-bevel	Pneumatic fasteners
Coping saw	Carpenter's glue
Metal file set	Finishing putty

How to Install One-piece Base Molding

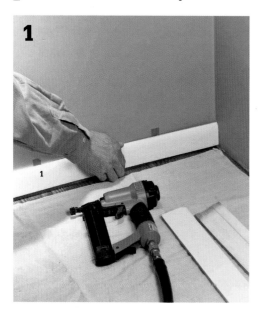

Measure, cut, and install the first piece of baseboard. Butt both ends into the corners tightly. For longer lengths, it is a good idea to cut the piece slightly oversized (up to 1/16" on strips over 10 ft. long) and "spring" it into place. Nail the molding in place with two nails at every stud location.

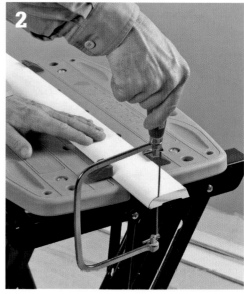

Cut the second piece of molding oversized by 6" to 10" and cope-cut the adjoining end to the first piece. Fine-tune the cope with a metal file and sandpaper. Dry-fit the joint, adjusting it as necessary to produce a tight-fitting joint.

3

Check the corner for square with a framing square. If necessary, adjust the miter cut of your saw. Use a T-bevel to transfer the proper angle. Cut the second piece (coped) to length and install it with two nails at each stud location.

4

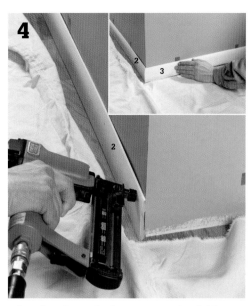

Adjust the miter angle of your saw to cut the adjoining outside corner piece (3). Test-fit the cut to ensure a tight joint (inset photo). Remove the mating piece of trim and fasten the first piece for the outside corner joint.

5

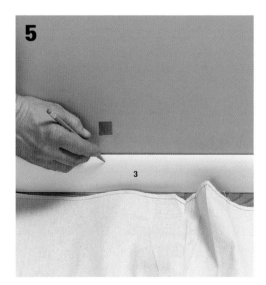

Lay out any scarf joints by placing the piece in position so that the previous joint is tight and then marking the center of a stud location nearest the opposite end. Set the angle of your saw to a 30° angle and cut the molding at the marked location.

6

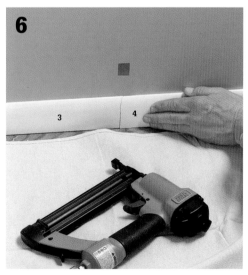

Nail the third piece in place, making sure the outside corner joint is tight. Cut the end of the fourth piece to match the scarf joint angle and nail it in place with two nails at each stud location. Add the remaining pieces of molding, fill the nail holes with putty, and apply a final coat of finish.

How to Install Built-up Base Molding

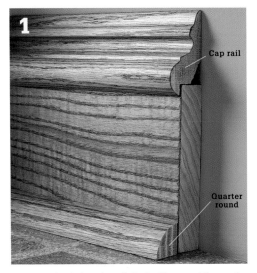

Cap rail

Quarter round

Dress up simple baseboard stock with cap moldings and base shoe or quarter round. The baseboard can be made of solid wood, as shown above, or from strips of veneered plywood, as shown at right.

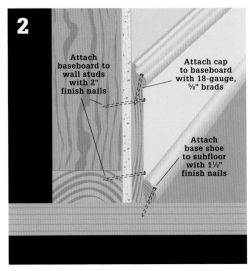

Attach baseboard to wall studs with 2" finish nails

Attach cap to baseboard with 18-gauge, ⁵⁄₈" brads

Attach base shoe to subfloor with 1½" finish nails

Built-up baseboard requires more attention to the nailing schedule than simple one-piece baseboards. The most important consideration (other than making sure your nails are all driven into studs or other solid wood) is that the base shoe must be attached to the floor, while the baseboard is attached to the wall. This way, as the gap between the wall and floor changes, the parts of the built-up molding can change with them.

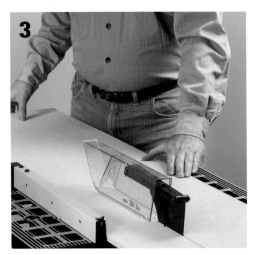

Cut the plywood panel into 6" strips with a table saw or a straightedge guide and a circular saw. Lightly sand the strips, removing any splinters left from the saw. Then, apply the finish of your choice to the moldings and the plywood strips.

Tip ▶

Baseboard can be built up on the back with spacer strips so it will project further out from the wall. This can allow you to match existing casings or to create the impression of a thicker molding. However, the cap rail needs to be thick enough to cover the plywood edge completely, or the core of the panel may be visible.

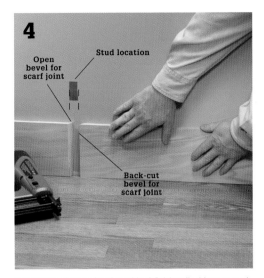

Install the plywood strips with 2" finish nails driven at stud locations. Use scarf joints on continuous runs, driving pairs of fasteners into the joints. Cut and install moldings so that all scarf joints fall at stud locations.

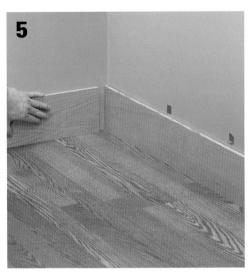

Test-fit inside corner butt joints before cutting a workpiece. If the walls are not square or straight, angle or bevel the end cut a few degrees to fit the profile of the adjoining piece. The cap molding will cover any gaps at the top of the joint.

Miter outside corners squarely at 45°. Use wood glue and 1¼" brad nails to pull the mitered pieces tight, and then nail the base to the wall at stud locations with 2" finish nails. Small gaps at the bottom or top of the base molding will be covered with cap or base shoe.

Use a brad nailer with 18-gauge, ⅝" brads to install the cap and base shoe moldings along the edges of the plywood base. Fit scarf joints on longer lengths, coped joints on inside corners, and miter joints on outside corners. Stagger the seams so that they do not line up with the base molding seams, following the suggested nailing pattern (right). Set any protruding nails with a nail set and fill all nail holes with putty.

Installing Picture Rail

Picture rail molding is a specialty molding that was installed in many older homes so the homeowners could avoid making nail holes in the finished walls. Picture rail molding is a simple but elegant way to add style to any room. Special picture hanging hooks slide over the molding and artwork may be hung with a cord over the hook. Picture rail molding also provides its own decorative touch, breaking up the vertical lines from floor to ceiling. For this reason, it is also installed as a decorative touch by itself.

Picture rail molding is easy to install but should be reinforced with screws, not brads or nails, especially if you are hanging large, heavy items. Depending upon the style of your home, picture rail can be hung anywhere from 1 ft. to a few inches down from the ceiling. In some homes, picture rail is added just below the cornice or crown molding to add an additional layer of depth. When applied this way, it is commonly referred to as a frieze board.

In the example shown, the picture rail is installed using a level line to maintain height. If your ceiling is uneven, you may choose to install picture rail a constant distance from the ceiling to avoid an uneven appearance.

Traditionally, picture rail (see top of photo) is used in conjunction with special hooks to hang artwork in formal rooms without penetrating the wall with fasteners.

Tools & Materials ▸

Ladder	4-ft. level
Pencil	or laser level
Stud finder	Drill with bits
Tape measure	Painter's tape
Power miter saw	Moldings
T-bevel	Pneumatic fasteners
Pneumatic finish nail	1⅝" wallboard screws
gun & compressor	Hole filler

How to Install Picture Rail Molding

1

Measure down the desired distance from the ceiling and draw a level reference line around the room using a pencil and a 4-ft. level (or, take advantage of modern technology and use a laser level). While you are up there, use a stud finder to locate the framing members, and mark the locations on the walls with blue painter's tape.

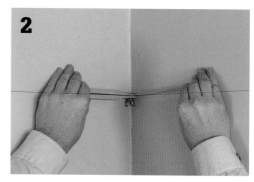

2

Most corners are close to 90°, but to cut a tight inside corner, the actual angle must be divided exactly in half. Use a T-bevel to measure the angle of the corner, tightening the lock nut with the blade and the handle on the reference line.

3

Place the T-bevel on the table of your power miter saw and adjust the miter blade so that it matches the angle. With the T-bevel tight to the fence, read the angle the saw is set to when it aligns with the T-bevel. If the blade is angled to the right of zero degrees the angle is larger than 90; to the left, smaller.

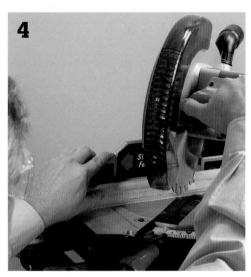

4

Read the angle from the miter saw table, divide the number by two, and add or subtract that number from 45 degrees to find the proper cutting angle for each corner. Cut each molding slightly longer than the measured length.

5

Nail the molding at the stud locations, covering the level line around the room (if you're using a laser level, you simply keep it in position and turned on to cast a reference line you can follow). After each molding is completely nailed in place, go back to each stud location and drive 1⅝" wallboard screws into the molding through counter-bored pilot holes.

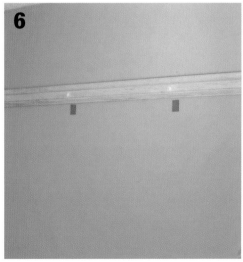

6

Fill nail holes with wood filler. Let the filler dry and sand it smooth. Then apply a final coat of paint over the molding face.

Installing Chair Rail

Chair rail molding typically runs horizontally along walls at a height of around 36" (the rule of thumb is to install it one-third of the way up the wall). Originally installed to protect walls from collisions with chair backs, today chair rail is commonly used to divide a wall visually. Chair rail may cap wainscoting, serve as a border for wallpaper, or divide two different colors on a wall. Interesting chair rail profiles can be effective alone on a one-color wall.

Stock chair rail moldings are available at most lumberyards and home centers. However, more intricate and elaborate chair rails can be created by combining multiple pieces of trim. Keep in mind the height of your existing furnishings when installing a chair rail. It would be disappointing to discover that the new molding has a bad visual effect with your couch or chair backs when the project is completed.

Tools & Materials ▸

Pencil	Metal file set
Stud finder	Moldings
Tape measure	Pneumatic fasteners
Power miter saw	Painter's tape
4-ft. level	Carpenter's glue
Air compressor	Finishing putty
Finish nail gun	Finishing materials

Chair rail once was installed to protect fragile walls from chair backs, but today it is mainly installed as a decorative accent that breaks up dull walls visually.

How to Install Chair Rail

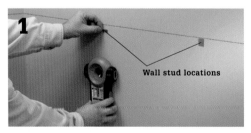

Wall stud locations

On the starting wall of your installation, measure up to the height at which you plan to install the chair rail, minus the width of the molding. Mark a level line at this height around the room. Locate all studs along the walls and mark their locations with painter's tape below the line.

Measure, cut, and install the first piece of chair rail with the ends cut squarely, butting into both walls (in a wall run with two inside corners). Nail the molding in place with two 2" finish nails at each stud location.

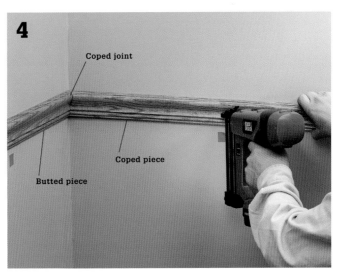

Miter-cut the second piece of molding with a power miter saw and then cope the end with a coping saw. Clean up the edge of the cope cut with a metal file to ensure a tight fit. Dry-fit the piece to check for any gaps in the joint.

When the coped joint fits tightly, measure, mark, and cut the opposing end of the second piece of trim squarely with a miter saw. Nail the second piece in place with two nails at each stud location. Follow the level line with the bottom edge of the molding.

Install the third piece of chair rail with a cope cut at one end. Use a butt joint where the molding runs into door and window casings. Fill all nail holes with putty and apply a final coat of finish to the molding.

Option: Cut a mitered return for the chair rail in areas where it will end without joining into another molding. Cut the return with a miter saw and glue it in place, using painter's tape to hold it until the glue dries.

Installing Crown Molding

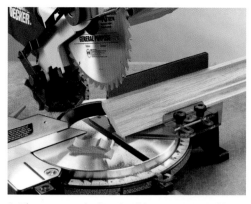

Simply put, crown molding is angled trim that bridges the joint between the ceiling and the wall. In order to cover this joint effectively, crown moldings are "sprung." This means that the top and bottom edges of the molding have been beveled, so when the molding is tilted away from the wall at an angle the tops and bottoms are flush on the wall and ceiling surfaces. Some crown moldings have a 45° angle at both the top and the bottom edges; another common style ("38° crown") has a 38° angle on one edge and a 52° angle on the other edge.

Installing crown molding can be a challenging and sometimes confusing process. Joints may be difficult for you to visualize before cutting, and wall and ceiling irregularities can be hard to overcome. If you have not worked on crown molding joints before, it is recommended that your first attempt be made with paint-grade materials. Stain-grade crown is commonly made of solid hardwood stock, which makes for expensive cutting errors, and difficulty concealing irregularities in joints.

Inside corner joints of crown molding should be cope cut, not mitered, except in the case of very intricate profile crown that is virtually impossible to cope (and must therefore be mitered). While mitering inside corners may appear to save time and produce adequate results, after a few changing seasons the joints will open up and be even more difficult to conceal.

Cutting compound miters is tricky. Here, crown molding is cut with the workpiece held against a fence or fence extension. This hand-held approach is quick and effective, but takes some getting used to. A practically foolproof option is to use an adjustable jig, such as the compound miter jig shown here.

Tools & Materials ▸

Pencil	Nail set
Tape measure	Hammer
Circular saw	Metal files
Straightedge guide	2 × 4 material
Drill with bits	for backing
Coping saw	3" wallboard screws
Power miter saw	Carpenter's glue
Pneumatic finish	Crown molding
nail gun	2", 1½" finish nails
Framing square	Fine-grit sandpaper
or combination	Hole filler
square	Paint and brushes

Basic crown molding softens the transitions between walls and ceilings. If it is made from quality hardwood crown molding can be quite beautiful when installed and finished with a clear topcoat. But historically, it is most often painted—either the same color as the ceiling (your eye tends to see it as a ceiling molding, not a wall molding) or with highly elaborate painted and carved details.

How to Install Basic Crown Molding

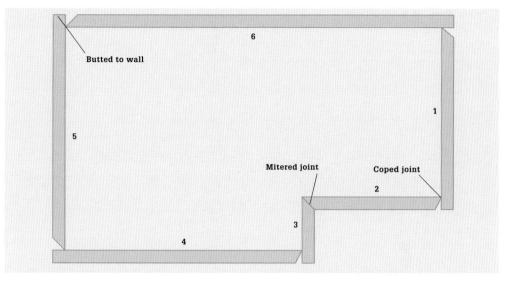

Butted to wall

6

1

5

Mitered joint   **Coped joint**

2

3

4

Plan the order of the installation to minimize the number of difficult joints on each piece and use the longest pieces for the most visible sections of wall. Notice that the left end of first piece is cope-cut rather than butted into the wall. Cope-cutting the first end eliminates the need to cope-cut both ends of the final piece, and places the cuts in the same direction. This simplifies your installation, making the method to cut each piece similar.

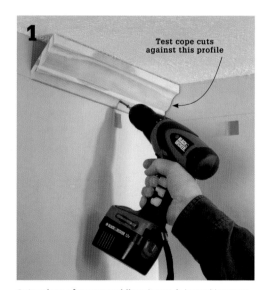

1

Test cope cuts
against this profile

Cut a piece of crown molding about 1-ft. long with square ends. Temporarily install the piece in the corner of the last installation wall with two screws driven into the blocking. This piece serves as a template for the first cope cut on the first piece of molding.

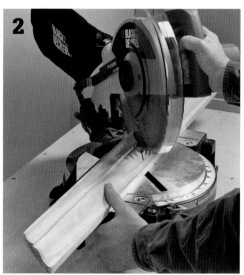

2

Place the first piece of molding upside down and sprung against the fence of the miter saw. Mark a reference line on the fence for placement of future moldings, and cut the first coped end with an inside miter cut to reveal the profile of the piece.

(continued)

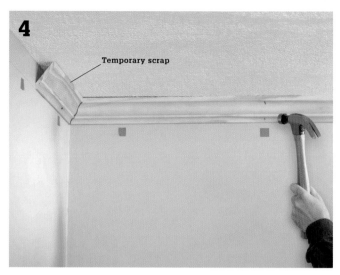

Cope-cut the end of the first piece with a coping saw. Carefully cut along the profile, angling the saw as you cut to back-bevel the cope. Test-fit the coped cut against the temporary scrap from Step 1. Fine-tune the cut with files and fine-grit sandpaper.

Measure, cut to length, and install the first piece of crown molding, leaving the end near the temporary scrap loose for final fitting of the last piece. Nail the molding at the top and bottom of each stud location.

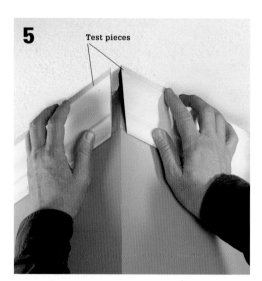

Cut two test pieces to check the fit of outside corners. Start with each molding cut at 45°, adjusting the angles larger or smaller until the joints are tight. Make sure the test moldings are properly aligned and are flush with the ceiling and walls. Make a note of your saw settings once the joint fits tightly.

Position the actual stock so a cut end is flush against the wall at one end and, at the other end, mark the outside corner on the back edge of the molding. Miter-cut the piece at the mark, according to the angles you noted on the test pieces.

7

Measure and cut the third piece with an outside corner miter to match the angle of your test pieces. Cut the other end squarely, butting it into the corner. Install the piece with nails driven at stud locations. Install the subsequent pieces of crown molding, coping the front end and butting the other as you work around the room.

8

To fit the final piece, cope the end and cut it to length. Remove the temporary scrap piece from Step 3, and slide the last molding into position. Nail the last piece at the stud locations when the joints fit well, and finish nailing the first piece.

9

Fill all nail holes (use spackling compound if painting; wait until the finish is applied and fill with tinted putty for clear finishes). Use a putty knife to force spackling compound or tinted wood putty into loose joints and caulk gaps ⅛" or smaller between the molding and the wall or ceiling with flexible, paintable, latex caulk.

10

Lightly sand the filled nail holes and joint gaps using fine sandpaper. Sand the nail holes flush with the surface of the moldings and paint the entire project.

Windows & Doors

Once you've got a feel for the style of windows or doors you'd like to add to your home, the next step involves careful planning. You'll need to consider how a new door or window meets your needs for energy efficiency, durability, ease of maintenance, and security.

There's also the equally important matter of how a new window or door will impact your home's livability. Will it face a direction that takes advantage of sunlight and prevailing breezes or make the room stifling hot in mid July? Adding a window to a living space may also bring matters of egress into consideration. Building codes mandate that your project window must satisfy these requirements.

In this chapter:

- Framing & Installing Windows
- Installing Garden Windows
- Installing Bay Windows
- Installing Skylights
- Installing Tubular Skylights
- Installing Interior Doors
- Installing Entry Doors
- Installing Storm Doors
- Installing Patio Doors
- Installing Door & Window Casing

Framing & Installing Windows

Many windows must be custom-ordered several weeks in advance. To save time, you can complete the interior framing before the window unit arrives, but be sure you have the exact dimensions of the window unit before building the frame. Do not remove the outside wall surface until you have the window and accessories and are ready to install them.

Follow the manufacturer's specifications for rough opening size when framing for a window. The listed opening is usually 1" wider and ½" taller than the actual dimensions of the window unit. The following pages show techniques for wood-frame houses with platform framing.

If your house has balloon framing where wall studs pass continuously from one floor to the next, use the method shown on page 271 to install a header. Consult a professional to install a window on the second story of a balloon-framed house.

If your home's exterior has siding or is stucco, see pages 34 to 35 for tips on removing these surfaces and making the opening.

Tools & Materials ▸

Tape measure	10d common nails,
Pencil	1" galvanized
Combination square	roofing nails
Hammer	Shims
Level	2× lumber
Circular saw	⅛" plywood
Handsaw	Building paper
Pry bar	Drip edge
Nippers	10d galvanized
Drill	casing nails
Reciprocating saw	8d casing nails
Stapler	Fiberglass insulation
Nail set	Paintable
Caulk gun	silicone caulk

Correct framing techniques will ensure ease of installation and keep your windows operating smoothly.

How to Frame a Window Opening

Prepare the project site and remove the interior wall surfaces (pages 30 to 31). Measure and mark the rough opening width on the sole plate. Mark the locations of the jack studs and king studs on the sole plate. Where practical, use the existing studs as king studs.

Measure and cut the king studs, as needed, to fit between the sole plate and the top plate. Position the king studs and toenail them to the sole plate with 10d nails.

Check the king studs with a level to make sure they are plumb, then toenail them to the top plate with 10d nails.

King stud · Old stud · Top of header

Old stud · King stud · Double sill

Measuring from the floor, mark the top of the rough opening on one of the king studs. This line represents the bottom of the window header. For most windows, the recommended rough opening is ½" taller than the height of the window frame.

Measure and mark where the top of the window header will fit against the king studs. The header size depends on the distance between the king studs. Use a carpenter's level to extend the lines across the old studs to the opposite king stud.

Measure down from the header line and mark the double rough sill on the king stud. Use a carpenter's level to extend the lines across the old studs to the opposite king stud. Make temporary supports (page 29) if removing more than one stud.

(continued)

7

Bottom of sill

Set a circular saw to its maximum blade depth, then cut through the old studs along the lines marking the bottom of the rough sill and along the lines marking the top of the header. Do not cut the king studs. On each stud, make an additional cut about 3" above the sill cut. Finish the cuts with a handsaw.

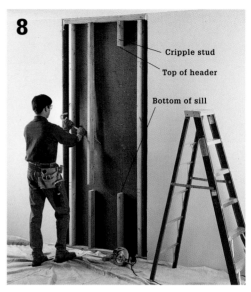

8

Cripple stud

Top of header

Bottom of sill

Knock out the 3" stud sections, then tear out the old studs inside the rough opening, using a pry bar. Clip away any exposed nails, using nippers. The remaining sections of the cut studs will serve as cripple studs for the window.

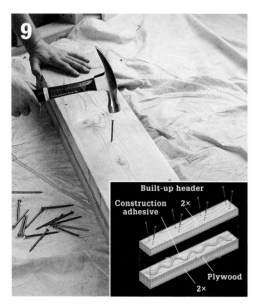

9

Built-up header

Construction adhesive   2×

Plywood 2×

Build a header to fit between the king studs on top of the jack studs, using two pieces of 2× lumber sandwiched around ½" plywood.

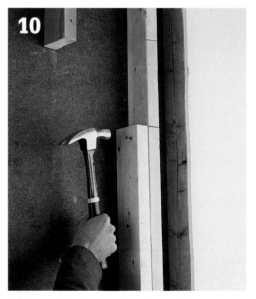

10

Cut two jack studs to reach from the top of the sole plate to the bottom header lines on the king studs. Nail the jack studs to the king studs with 10d nails driven every 12".

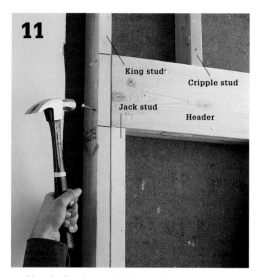

11

King stud

Cripple stud

Jack stud

Header

Position the header on the jack studs, using a hammer if necessary. Attach the header to the king studs, jack studs, and cripple studs, using 10d nails.

12

Rough opening

Build the rough sill to reach between the jack studs by nailing a pair of 2 × 4s together. Position the rough sill on the cripple studs, and nail it to the jack studs and cripple studs with 10d nails.

How to Install a Replacement Window with a Nailing Flange

1

Remove the existing window and set the new window into the rough opening. Center it left to right, and shim beneath the sill to level it. On the exterior side, measure out from the window on all sides, and mark the siding for the width of the brick molding you'll install around the new window. Extend layout lines to mark where you'll cut the siding.

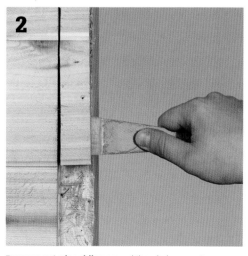

2

Remove exterior siding around the window area to expose the wall sheathing. Use a zip tool to separate vinyl siding for removal or use a pry bar and hammer to remove wood clapboard. For more on removing exterior surfaces, (see pages 32 to 33).

(continued)

Cover the sill and rough opening framing members with self-adhesive, rolled flashing. Apply additional strips of flashing behind the siding and up the sill flashing. Finish flashing with a strip along the header. The flashing should cover the front edges and sides of the opening members.

Apply a bead of silicone caulk around the back face of the window flange, then set it into the rough opening, centering it side-to-side in the opening. Tack the window in place by driving one roofing nail partway through the top flange. On the interior side, level and plumb the window, using shims to make any necessary adjustments.

Tack the window to the header at one end of the nailing flange, using a 1" galvanized roofing nail. Drive a roofing nail through the other top corner of the flange to hold the window in place, then secure the flange all around the window with more roofing nails. Apply strips of rolled, self-adhesive flashing to cover the window flanges. Start with a strip that covers the bottom flange, then cover the side flanges, overlapping the bottom flashing and extending 8 to 10" above the window. Complete the flashing with a strip along the top, overlapping the side flashing.

Install a piece of metal drip edge behind the siding and above the window. Secure it with silicone caulk only.

7

8

Cut and attach brick molding around the window, leaving a slight gap between the brick molding and the window frame. Use 8d galvanized casing nails driven into pilot holes to secure the brick molding to the rough framing. Miter the corner joints. Reinstall the siding in the window installation area, trimming as needed.

Use high-quality caulk to fill the gap between the brick molding and the siding. On the interior side, fill gaps between the window frame and surrounding framing with foam backer rod, low-expansion foam, or fiberglass insulation. Install the interior casing.

Tip Installation Variation: Masonry Clips ▸

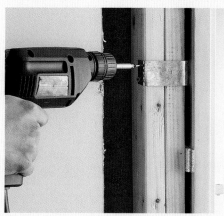

Use metal masonry clips when the brick molding on a window cannot be nailed because it rests against a masonry or brick surface. The masonry clips hook into precut grooves in the window jambs (above, left) and are attached to the jambs with screws. After the window unit is positioned in the rough opening, the masonry clips are bent around the framing members and anchored with screws (above, right). *Note: Masonry clips can also be used in ordinary lap siding installations if you want to avoid making nail holes in the smooth surface of the brick moldings. For example, windows that are precoated with polymer-based paint can be installed with masonry clips so that the brick moldings are not punctured with nails.*

How to Install a Round-Top Window

Remove the exterior wall surface as directed on pages 32 to 33, then test-fit the window, centering it in the rough opening. Support the window with wood blocks and shims placed under the side jambs and mullion post. Check to make sure the window is plumb and level, and adjust the shims, if necessary.

Trace the outline of the brick molding on the wood siding. Remove the window after finishing the outline. *Note: If you have vinyl or metal siding, you should have enlarged the outline to make room for the extra J-channel moldings required by these sidings.*

Tips for Framing a Round-top Window ▸

Create a template to help you mark the rough opening on the sheathing. Scribe the outline of the curved frame on cardboard, allowing an extra ½" for adjustments within the rough opening. A ¼ × 1¼" metal washer makes a good spacer for scribing the outline. Cut out the template along the scribed line.

Tape the template to the sheathing, with the top flush against the header. Use the template as a guide for attaching diagonal framing members across the top corners of the framed opening. The diagonal members should just touch the template. Outline the template on the sheathing as a guide for cutting the exterior wall surface.

3

Cut the siding along the outline just down to the sheathing. For a round-top window, use a reciprocating saw held at a low angle. For straight cuts, use a circular saw adjusted so the blade cuts through only the siding. Use a sharp chisel to complete the cuts at the corners.

4

Cut 8"-wide strips of building paper and slide them between the siding and sheathing around the entire window opening. Bend the paper around the framing members and staple it in place. Work from the bottom up, so each piece overlaps the piece below. *Note: You can also use adhesive-backed, rolled flashing instead of building paper.*

5

Cut a length of drip edge to fit over the top of the window, then slide it between the siding and building paper. For round-top windows, use flexible vinyl drip edge; for rectangular windows, use rigid metal drip edge (inset).

6

Insert the window in the opening, and push the brick molding tight against the sheathing. Nail through the brick molding, as usual, to secure the window in the opening.

Installing Garden Windows

Although often found in kitchens, a garden window is an attractive option for nearly any room in your home. Projecting out from the wall 16 to 24", garden windows add space to a room, making it feel larger. The glass roof and box-like design make them ideal growing environments for plants or display areas for collectibles. Garden windows also typically include front- or side-opening windows. These allow for ventilation and are usually available in either awning or casement style.

Home stores often stock garden windows in several common sizes. However, it may be difficult to locate a stock window that will fit in your existing window rough opening. In cases like this you must rebuild the rough opening to the proper size. It may be worth the added expense to custom-order your garden window to fit into the existing rough opening.

The large amount of glass in a garden window has a direct effect on the window's energy efficiency. When purchasing a garden window, as a minimum, look for double-pane glass with low-emissivity (low-E) coatings. More expensive super-efficient types of glass are available for severely cold climates.

Installation methods for garden windows vary by manufacturer. Some units include a nailing flange that attaches to the framing and holds the window against the house. Other models hang on a separate mounting frame that attaches to the outside of the house. In this project, the garden window has a built-in mounting sleeve that slides into the rough opening and is attached directly to the rough framing.

Tools & Materials ▸

Tape measure	2 × 4s
Hammer	Shims
Level	Exterior trim
Framing square	Building paper
Circular saw	3" screws
Wood chisel	Drip edge
Stapler	Construction adhesive
Drill and bits	4d siding nails
Caulking gun	8d galvanized
Utility knife	casing nails
Garden window kit	Interior trim
Wood strips	Paintable silicone caulk

A garden window's glass roof makes it an ideal sun spot for houseplants. It can also help a room feel larger.

How to Install a Garden Window

Prepare the project site and remove the interior and exterior trim, then remove the existing window.

Check the rough opening measurements to verify the correct window sizing. The rough opening should be about ½" larger than the window height and width. If necessary, attach wood strips to the rough framing as spacers to bring the opening to the required size.

Use a level to check that the sill of the rough opening is level and the side jambs are plumb. Use a framing square to make sure each corner is square. The rough framing must be in good condition in order to support the weight of the garden window. If the framing is severely deteriorated or out of plumb or square, you may need to reframe the rough opening (pages 40 to 43).

Insert the garden window into the opening, pressing it tight against the framing. Support the unit with notched 2 × 4s under the bottom edge of the window until it has been fastened securely to the framing.

(continued)

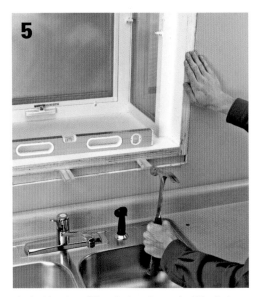

The inside edge of the window sleeve should be flush with the interior wall surface. Check the sill of the garden window for level. Shim beneath the lower side of the sill, if necessary, to make it level.

Once the garden window is in place and level, hold a piece of window trim in place along the exterior of the window and trace the outline onto the siding. Remove the window. Cut the siding down to the sheathing using a circular saw.

Install strips of building paper between siding and sheathing. Wrap them around the framing and staple them in place. On the sides, work from the bottom up so each piece overlaps the piece below. Reposition the window and reshim. Make sure the space between the window and the siding is equal to the width of the trim on all sides.

Drill countersunk pilot holes every 12" to 16" through the window sleeve into the rough header, jack studs, and sill.

Insert shims between the window sleeve and rough frame at each hole location along the top and sides to prevent bowing of the window frame. Fasten the window to the framing using 3" screws. Continue checking for level, plumb, and square as the screws are tightened.

Locate and mark the studs nearest the edges of the window using a stud finder. Cut two pieces of siding to fit behind the brackets, and tack them in place over the marked studs with 4d siding nails. Position the support brackets with the shorter side against the siding and the longer side beneath the window. Fasten the brackets to the window and the studs using the included screws.

Cut a piece of drip edge to length, apply construction adhesive to its top flange, and slide it under the siding above the window. Cut each trim piece to size. Position the trim and attach it using 8d galvanized casing nails driven through pilot holes. Seal the edges of the trim with a bead of paintable silicone caulk, approximately ⅜" wide.

Cut all protruding shims flush with the framing using a utility knife or handsaw. Insulate or caulk gaps between the window sleeve and the wall. Finish the installation by reinstalling the existing interior trim or installing new trim.

Installing Bay Windows

Modern bay windows are preassembled for easy installation, but it will still take several days to complete an installation. Bay windows are large and heavy, and installing them requires special techniques.

Have at least one helper to assist you, and try to schedule the work when there's little chance of rain. Using prebuilt bay window accessories will speed your work (see next page).

A large bay window can weigh several hundred pounds, so it must be anchored securely to framing members in the wall and supported by braces attached to framing members below the window. Some window manufacturers include cable-support hardware that can be used instead of metal support braces.

Before purchasing a bay window unit, check with the local building department regarding the code requirements. Many local codes require large windows and low bay windows with window seats to be glazed with tempered glass for safety.

Cutaway view

Cripple stud
Building paper
Header (double 2 × 8s with ½" plywood)
Preattached head board
Side jamb
Preattached seat board
Rough sill (double 2 × 6s with ½" plywood)

Metal flashing
Roof frame
Sheathing
Shingles
Building paper
Drip edge
Insulation

Skirt board
Plastic vapor barrier
Furring strip
Insulation
Plywood skirt bottom
Wall sheathing
Siding

Tools & Materials ▸

Straightedge
Circular saw
Wood chisel
Pry bar
Drill
Level
Nail set
Stapler
Aviation snips
Roofing knife
Caulk gun
Utility knife
T-bevel
Bay window unit
Prebuilt roof frame kit
Metal support brackets
2× lumber
16d galvanized common nails
16d and 8d galvanized casing nails
3" and 2" galvanized utility screws

16d casing nails
Tapered wood shims
Building paper
Fiberglass insulation
6-mil polyethylene sheeting
Drip edge
1" roofing nails
Step flashing
Shingles
Top flashing
Roofing cement
2 × 2 lumber
5½" skirt boards
¾" exterior-grade plywood
Paintable silicone caulk

Tips for Installing a Bay Window ▸

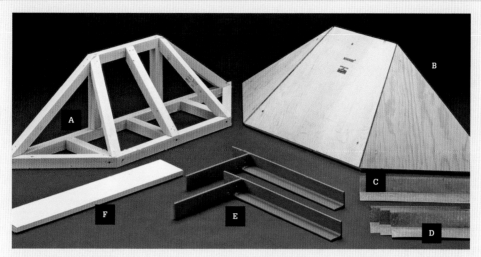

Use prebuilt accessories to ease installation of a bay window. Roof frames (A) come complete with sheathing (B), metal top flashing (C), and step flashing (D) and can be special-ordered at most home centers. You will have to specify the exact size of your window unit and the angle (pitch) you want for the roof. You can cover the roof inexpensively with building paper and shingles or order a copper or aluminum shell. Metal support braces (E) and skirt boards (F) can be ordered at your home center if not included with the window unit. Use two braces for bay windows up to 5 ft. wide and three braces for larger windows. Skirt boards are clad with aluminum or vinyl and can be cut to fit with a circular saw or miter saw.

Construct a bay window frame similar to that for a standard window (see page 257) but use a built-up sill made from two 2 × 6s sandwiched around ½" plywood. Install extra jack studs under the sill ends to help carry the window's weight.

Build an enclosure above the bay window if the roof soffit overhangs the window. Build a 2 × 2 frame (top) to match the angles of the bay window, and attach the frame securely to the wall and overhanging soffit. Install a vapor barrier and insulation, then finish the enclosure so it matches the siding (bottom).

How to Install a Bay Window

Prepare the project site and remove interior wall surfaces (pages 32 to 35), then frame the rough opening. Remove the exterior wall surfaces. Mark for removal a section of siding directly below the rough opening. The width of the marked area should equal that of the window unit and the height should equal that of the skirt board.

Set the blade on a circular saw just deep enough to cut through the siding, then cut along the outline. Stop just short of the corners to avoid damaging the siding outside the outline. Use a sharp chisel to complete the corner cuts. Remove the cut siding inside the outline.

Position the support braces along the rough sill within the widest part of the bay window and above the cripple stud locations. Add cripple studs to match the support brace locations, if necessary. Draw outlines of the braces on the top of the sill. Use a chisel or circular saw to notch the sill to a depth equal to the thickness of the top arm of the support braces.

Slide the support braces down between the siding and the sheathing. Pry the siding material away from the sheathing slightly to make room for the braces, if necessary. *Note: On stucco, you will need to chisel notches in the masonry surface to fit the support braces.*

5

16d nails

Attach the braces to the rough sill with galvanized 16d common nails. Drive 3" utility screws through the front of the braces and into the rough sill to prevent twisting.

6

Lift the bay window onto the support braces and slide it into the rough opening. Center the unit within the opening.

7

Check the window unit to make sure it is level. If necessary, drive shims under the low side to level the window. Temporarily brace the outside bottom edge of the unit with 2 × 4s to keep it from moving on the braces.

8

Sheathing

Set the roof frame on top of the window, with the sheathing loosely tacked in place. Trace the outline of the window and roof unit onto the siding. Leave a gap of about ½" around the roof unit to allow room for flashing and shingles.

9

Jack stud

Side jamb

Mark blocks flush with faces of studs

Shims

If the gap between the side jambs and jack studs is more than 1" wide, mark and cut wood blocks to bridge the gap (smaller gaps require no blocks). Leave a small space for inserting wood shims. Remove the window, then attach blocks every 12" along studs.

(continued)

10

Cut the siding just down to the sheathing along the outline using a circular saw. Stop just short of the corners, then use a wood chisel to complete the corner cuts. Remove the cut siding. Pry the remaining siding slightly away from the sheathing around the roof outline to allow for easy installation of the metal flashing. Cover the exposed sheathing with 8"-wide strips of building paper (step 3, page 260).

11

Shim

Brace

Set the bay window unit back on the braces, and slide it back into the rough opening until the brick moldings are tight against the sheathing. Insert wood shims between the outside end of the metal braces and the seat board (inset). Check the unit to make sure it is level, and adjust the shims, if necessary.

12

Anchor the window by drilling pilot holes and driving 16d casing nails through the brick molding and into the framing members. Space nails every 12", and use a nail set to drive the nail heads below the surface of the wood.

13

Blocking

Shim

Jack stud

Drive wood shims into the spaces between the side jambs and the blocking or jack studs and between the headboard and header, spacing the shims every 12". Fill the spaces around the window with loosely packed fiberglass insulation. At each shim location, drive 16d casing nails through the jambs and shims and into the framing members. Cut off the shims flush with the framing members using a handsaw or utility knife. Use a nail set to drive the nail heads below the surface. If necessary, drill pilot holes to prevent splitting the wood.

14

Staple sheet plastic over the top of the window unit to serve as a vapor barrier. Trim the edges of the plastic around the top of the window using a utility knife.

15

Remove the sheathing pieces from the roof frame, then position the frame on top of the window unit. Attach the roof frame to the window and to the wall at stud locations using 3" utility screws.

16

Fill the empty space inside the roof frame with loosely packed fiberglass insulation. Screw the sheathing back onto the roof frame using 2" utility screws.

17

Staple asphalt building paper over the roof sheathing. Make sure each piece of building paper overlaps the one below by at least 5".

18

Cut drip edges with aviation snips, then attach them around the edge of the roof sheathing using roofing nails.

(continued)

19

Step flashing

Cut and fit a piece of step flashing on each side of the roof frame. Adjust the flashing so it overhangs the drip edge by ¼". Flashings help guard against moisture damage.

20

Trim the end of the flashing to the same angle as the drip edge. Nail the flashing to the sheathing with roofing nails.

21

Cut 6"-wide strips of shingles for the starter row. Use roofing nails to attach the starter row shingles so they overhang the drip edge by about ½". Cut the shingles along the roof hips using a straightedge and a roofing knife.

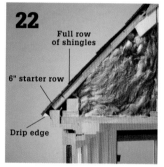

22

Full row of shingles

6" starter row

Drip edge

Nail a full row of shingles over the starter row, aligning the bottom edges with the bottom edge of the starter row. Make sure shingle notches are not aligned.

23

Second step flashing

Install another piece of step flashing on each side of the roof, overlapping the first piece of flashing by about 5".

24

½"

Cut and install another row of full shingles. The bottom edges should overlap the tops of the notches on the previous row by ½". Attach the shingles with roofing nails driven just above the notches.

25

Continue installing alternate rows of step flashing and shingles to the top of the roof. Bend the last pieces of step flashing to fit over the roof hips.

26

When the roof sheathing is covered with shingles, install the top flashing. Cut and bend the ends over the roof hips, and attach it with roofing nails. Attach the remaining rows of shingles over the top flashing.

27

Find the height of the final row of shingles by measuring from the top of the roof to a point ½" below the top of the notches on the last installed shingle. Trim the shingles to fit.

28

Attach the final row of shingles with a thick bead of roofing cement—not nails. Press firmly to ensure a good bond.

29

Make ridge caps by cutting shingles into 1-ft.-long sections. Use a roofing knife to trim off the top corners of each piece, so the ridge caps will be narrower at the top than at the bottom.

30

Install the ridge caps over the roof hips, beginning at the bottom of the roof. Trim the bottom ridge caps to match the edges of the roof. Keep the same amount of overlap with each layer.

(continued)

31

32

At the top of the roof hips, use a roofing knife to cut the shingles to fit flush with the wall. Attach the shingles with roofing cement—do not use any nails.

Staple sheet plastic over the bottom of the window unit to serve as a vapor barrier. Trim the plastic around the bottom of the window.

33

34

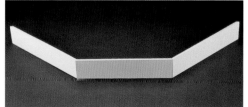

Cut and attach a 2 × 2 skirt frame around the bottom of the bay window using 3" galvanized utility screws. Set the skirt frame back about 1" from the edges of the window.

Cut skirt boards to match the shape of the bay window bottom, mitering the ends to ensure a tight fit. Test-fit the skirt board pieces to make sure they match the bay window bottom.

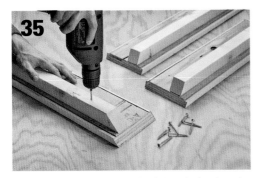

35

Cut a **2 × 2 furring strip** for each skirt board. Miter the ends to the same angles as the skirt boards. Attach the furring strips to the back of the skirt boards, 1" from the bottom edges, using 2" galvanized utility screws.

36

Skirt frame

Furring strip

Skirt board

Attach the skirt board pieces to the skirt frame. Drill ⅛" pilot holes every 6" through the back of the skirt frame and into the skirt boards, then attach the skirt boards with 2" galvanized utility screws.

37

Measure the space inside the skirt boards using a T-bevel to duplicate the angles. Cut a skirt bottom from ¾" exterior-grade plywood to fit this space.

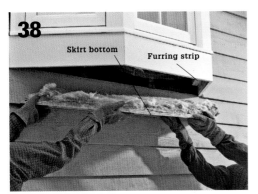

38

Skirt bottom   Furring strip

Lay fiberglass insulation on the skirt bottom. Position the skirt bottom against the furring strips and attach it by driving 2" galvanized utility screws every 6" through the bottom and into the furring strips.

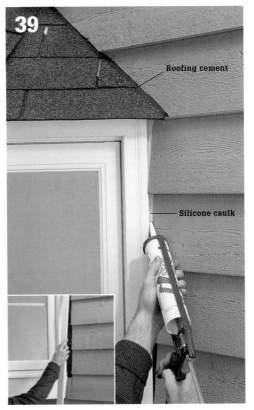

39

Roofing cement

Silicone caulk

Install any additional trim pieces (inset) specified by your window manufacturer using 8d galvanized casing nails. Seal the roof edges with roofing cement, and seal around the rest of the window with paintable silicone caulk.

Installing Skylights

Since skylights let in so much light, their sizing and placement are important considerations. A skylight that's too big can quickly overheat a space, especially in an attic. The same is true of using too many skylights in any one room. For that reason it's often best to position a skylight away from the day's brightest sun. You may want an operable skylight that opens and closes to vent warm air.

When a skylight is installed above an unfinished attic space, a special skylight shaft must be constructed to channel light directly to the room below.

Installing a skylight above finished space involves other considerations. First, the ceiling surface must be removed to expose the rafters. To remove wall and ceiling surfaces, see pages 28 to 31.

A skylight frame is similar to a standard window frame. It has a header and sill, like a window frame, but it has king rafters rather than king studs. Skylight frames also have trimmers that define the sides of the rough opening. Refer to the manufacturer's instructions to determine what size to make the opening for the skylight you select.

With standard rafter-frame roof construction, you can safely cut into one or two rafters as long as you permanently support the cut rafters, as shown in the following steps. If your skylight requires alteration of more than two rafters or if your roofing is made with unusually heavy material, such as clay tile or slate, consult an architect or engineer before starting the project.

Today's good-quality skylight units are unlikely to leak, but a skylight is only as leakproof as its installation. Follow the manufacturer's instructions, and install the flashing meticulously, as it will last a lot longer than any sealant.

Skylights can offer warmth in the winter, cooling ventilation in the summer, and a view of the sky or the treetops around your house during any season. And, of course, skylights provide natural light.

Tools & Materials ▸

4-ft. level	16d and 10d
Circular saw	common nails
Drill	Building paper
Combination square	Roofing cement
Reciprocating saw	Skylight flashing
Pry bar	2", 1¼", and ¾"
Chalk line	roofing nails
Stapler	Finish nails
Caulk gun	Fiberglass insulation
Utility knife	½" wallboard
Aviation snips	Twine
Plumb bob	Wallboard screws
Jigsaw	6-mil polyethylene
Wallboard tools	sheeting
2× lumber	Finishing materials
1 × 4	

How to Install a Skylight

1

Labels: Intermediate rafter; King rafters; Planned rough opening

Use the first rafter on each side of the planned rough opening as a king rafter. Measure and mark where the double header and sill will fit against the king rafters. Then, use a level as a straightedge to extend the marks across the intermediate rafter.

2

Labels: Double header mark; Double sill mark

Brace the intermediate rafter by installing two 2 × 4s between the rafter and the attic floor. Position the braces just above the header marks and just below the sill marks. Secure them temporarily to the rafter and subfloor (or joists) with screws.

3

Label: Sister rafter

Reinforce each king rafter by attaching a full-length "sister" rafter against its outside face. Cut sister rafters from the same size of lumber as existing rafters, matching lengths and end cuts exactly. Work each one into position, flush against the outside face of the king rafters, then nail the sisters to the kings with pairs of 10d common nails spaced 12" apart.

4

Use a combination square to transfer the sill and header marks across the face of the intermediate rafter, then cut along the outermost lines with a reciprocating saw. Do not cut into the roof sheathing. Carefully remove the cutout section with a pry bar. The remaining rafter portions will serve as cripple rafters.

(continued)

Build a double header and double sill to fit snugly between the king rafters, using 2× lumber that is the same size as the rafters. Nail the header pieces together using pairs of 10d nails spaced 6" apart.

Install the header and sill, anchoring them to the king rafters and cripple rafters with 16d common nails. Make sure the ends of the header and sill are aligned with the appropriate marks on the king rafters.

If your skylight unit is narrower than the opening between the king studs, measure and make marks for the trimmers: They should be centered in the opening and spaced according to the manufacturer's specifications. Cut the trimmers from the same 2× lumber used for the rest of the frame, and nail them in place with 10d common nails. Remove the 2 × 4 braces.

Mark the opening for the roof cutout by driving a screw through the sheathing at each corner of the frame. Then, tack a couple of scrap boards across the opening to prevent the roof cutout from falling and causing damage below.

From the roof, measure between the screws to make sure the rough opening dimensions are accurate. Snap chalk lines between the screws to mark the rough opening, then remove the screws.

Tack a straight 1 × 4 to the roof, aligned with the inside edge of one chalk line. Make sure the nail heads are flush with the surface of the board.

Cut through the shingles and sheathing along the chalk line using a circular saw and an old blade or a remodeling blade. Rest the saw foot on the 1 × 4, and use the edge of the board as a guide. Reposition the 1 × 4, and cut along the remaining lines. Remove the cutout roof section.

Remove the shingles around the rough opening with a flat pry bar, exposing at least 9" of building paper on all sides of the opening. Remove whole shingles rather than cutting them.

(continued)

Cut strips of building paper and slide them between the shingles and existing building paper. Wrap the paper so that it covers the faces of the framing members, and staple it in place.

Nailing flange

Spread a 5"-wide layer of roofing cement around the roof opening. Set the skylight into the opening so that the nailing flange rests on the roof. Finally, adjust the unit so it sits squarely in the opening.

Nail through the flange and into the sheathing and framing members with 2" galvanized roofing nails spaced every 6". *Note: If skylight uses L-shaped brackets instead of a nailing flange, follow manufacturer's instructions.*

Adhesive strip

Patch in shingles up to the bottom edge of the skylight unit. Attach the shingles with 1¼" roofing nails driven just below the adhesive strip. If necessary, cut the shingles with a utility knife so they fit against the bottom of the skylight.

Skylight jamb

Side flange

Sill flashing

Spread roofing cement on the bottom edge of the sill flashing, then fit the flashing around the bottom of the unit. Attach flashing by driving ¾" galvanized roofing nails through the vertical side flange (near the top of the flashing) and into the skylight jambs.

Spread roofing cement on the bottom of a piece of step flashing, then slide flashing under the drip edge on one side of the skylight. Step flashing should overlap sill flashing by 5". Press the step flashing down to bond it. Repeat on the opposite side of the skylight.

Patch in the next row of shingles on each side of the skylight, following the existing shingle pattern. Drive a 1¼" roofing nail through each shingle and the step flashing and into the sheathing. Drive additional nails just above the notches in the shingles.

Continue applying alternate rows of step flashing and shingles using roofing cement and roofing nails. Each piece of flashing should overlap the preceding piece by 5".

At the top of the skylight, cut and bend the last piece of step flashing on each side, so the vertical flange wraps around the corner of the skylight. Patch in the next row of shingles.

Spread roofing cement on the bottom of the head flashing to bond it to the roof. Place the flashing against the top of the skylight so the vertical flange fits under the drip edge and the horizontal flange fits under the shingles above the skylight.

Fill in the remaining shingles, cutting them to fit, if necessary. Attach the shingles with roofing nails driven just above the notches.

Apply a continuous bead of roofing cement along the joint between the shingles and the skylight. Finish the interior of the framed opening as desired.

How to Build a Skylight Shaft

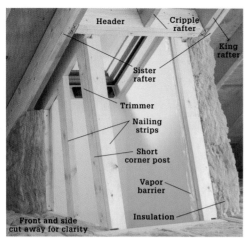

Header — Cripple rafter — King rafter — Sister rafter — Trimmer — Nailing strips — Short corner post — Vapor barrier — Insulation — Front and side cut away for clarity

1

A skylight shaft is made with 2 × 4 lumber and wallboard and includes a vapor barrier and fiberglass insulation. You can build a straight shaft with four vertical sides or an angled shaft that has a longer frame at ceiling level and one or more sides set at an angle. Since the ceiling opening is larger, an angled shaft lets in more direct light than a straight shaft.

Remove any insulation in the area where the skylight will be located; turn off and reroute electrical circuits as necessary. Use a plumb bob as a guide to mark reference points on the ceiling surface, directly below the inside corners of the skylight frame.

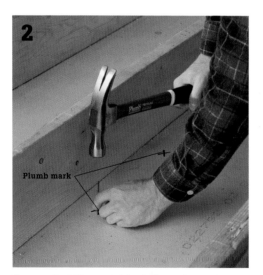

2

Plumb mark

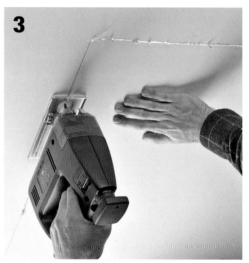

3

If you are installing a straight shaft, use the plumb marks made in step 1 to define the corners of the ceiling opening; drive a finish nail through the ceiling surface at each mark. If you are installing an angled shaft, measure out from the plumb marks and make new marks that define the corners of the ceiling opening; drive finish nails at the new marks.

From the room below, mark cutting lines, then remove the ceiling surface.

Use the nearest joists on either side of the ceiling opening to serve as king joists. Measure and mark where the double header and double sill will fit against the king joists and where the outside edge of the header and sill will cross any intermediate joists.

If you will be removing a section of an intermediate joist, reinforce the king joists by nailing full-length "sister" joists to the outside faces of the king joists using 10d nails.

Install temporary supports below the project area to support the intermediate rafter on both sides of the opening. Use a combination square to extend cutting lines down the sides of the intermediate joist, then cut out the joist section with a reciprocating saw. Pry loose the cutout portion of the joist, being careful not to damage the ceiling surface.

Build a double header and double sill to span the distance between the king joists using 2× dimensional lumber the same size as the joists.

(continued)

8

Cripple joist

9

Trimmers

Install the double header and double sill, anchoring them to the king joists and cripple joists with 10d nails. The inside edges of the header and sill should be aligned with the edge of the ceiling cutout.

Complete the ceiling opening by cutting and attaching trimmers, if required, along the sides of the ceiling cutout between the header and sill. Toenail the trimmers to the header and sill with 10d nails.

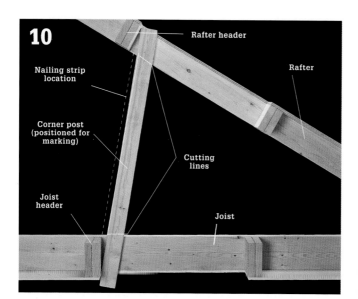

10

Rafter header

Nailing strip location

Rafter

Corner post (positioned for marking)

Cutting lines

Joist header

Joist

Install 2 × 4 corner posts for the skylight shaft. To measure for the posts, begin with a 2 × 4 that is long enough to reach from the top to the bottom of the shaft. Hold the 2 × 4 against the inside of the framed openings, so it is flush with the top of the rafter header and the bottom of the joist header (left photo). Mark cutting lines where the 2 × 4 meets the top of the joist or trimmer and the bottom of the rafter or trimmer (right photo). Cut along the lines, then toenail the posts to the top and bottom of the frame with 10d nails.

11

Attach a 2 × 4 nailing strip to the outside edge of each corner post to provide a nailing surface for attaching the wallboard. Notch the ends of the nailing strips to fit around the trimmers; a perfect fit is not necessary.

Nailing strips

12

Install additional 2 × 4 nailing strips between the corner posts if the distances between posts are more than 24". Miter the top ends of the nailing strips to fit against the rafter trimmers.

Nailing strips

13

Wrap the skylight shaft with fiberglass insulation. Secure the insulation by wrapping twine around the shaft and insulation.

14

From inside the shaft, staple a plastic vapor barrier of 6-mil polyethylene sheeting over the insulation.

Insulation removed for clarity

15

Finish the inside of the shaft with wallboard (pages 48 and 51). *Tip: To reflect light, paint the shaft interior with a light-colored, semigloss paint.*

Wallboard and insulation removed for clarity

Installing Tubular Skylights

Any interior room can be brightened with a tubular skylight. Tubular skylights are quite energy-efficient and are relatively easy to install, with no complicated framing involved.

The design of tubular skylights varies among manufacturers, with some using solid plastic reflecting tubes and others using flexible tubing. Various diameters are also available. Measure the distance between the framing members in your attic before purchasing your skylight to be sure it will fit.

This project shows the installation of a tubular skylight on a sloped, asphalt-shingled roof. Consult the dealer or manufacturer for installation procedures on other roof types.

A tubular skylight is an economical way to introduce more sunlight into a room without embarking on a major framing project.

Tools & Materials ▸

Pencil	Reciprocating saw	Wire cutters	Stiff wire
Drill	Pry bar	Utility knife	2" roofing nails
Tape measure	Screwdriver	Chalk	or flashing screws
Wallboard saw	Hammer	Tubular skylight kit	Roofing cement

How to Install a Tubular Skylight

Drill a pilot hole through the ceiling at the approximate location for your skylight. Push a stiff wire up into the attic to help locate the hole. In the attic, make sure the space around the hole is clear of any insulation. Drill a second hole through the ceiling at the centerpoint between two joists.

Center the ceiling ring frame over the hole and trace around it with a pencil. Carefully cut along the pencil line with a wallboard saw or reciprocating saw. Save the wallboard ceiling cutout to use as your roof-hole pattern. Attach the ceiling frame ring around the hole with the included screws.

In the attic, choose the most direct route for the tubing to reach the roof. Find the center between the appropriate rafters and drive a nail up through the roof sheathing and shingles.

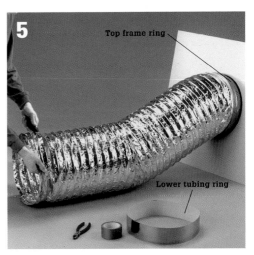

Use the wallboard ceiling cutout, centered over the nail hole, as a template for the roof opening. Trace the cutout onto the roof with chalk. Drill a starter hole to insert the reciprocating saw blade, then cut out the hole in the roof. Pry up the lower portion of the shingles above the hole. Remove any staples or nails around the hole edge.

Pull the tubing over the top frame ring. Bend the frame tabs out through the tubing, keeping two or three rings of the tubing wire above the tabs. Wrap the junction three times around with included PVC tape. Then, in the attic, measure from the roof to the ceiling. Stretch out the tubing and cut it to length with a utility knife and wire cutters. Pull the loose end of tubing over the lower ring and wrap it three times with PVC tape.

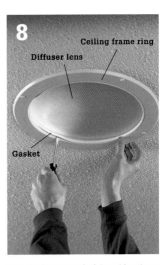

Lower the tubing through the roof hole and slide the flashing into place with the upper portion of the flashing underneath the existing shingles. This is easier with two people, one on the roof and one in the attic.

Secure the flashing to the roof with 2" roofing nails or flashing screws. Seal under the shingles and over all the nail heads with roofing cement. Attach the skylight dome and venting to the frame with the included screws.

Pull the lower end of the tubing down through the ceiling hole. Attach the lower tubing ring to the ceiling frame ring and fasten it with screws. Attach the gasket to the diffuser lens and work the gasket around the perimeter of the ceiling frame. Repack any insulation around the tubing in the attic.

Installing Interior Doors

Creating an opening for a door in a wall involves building a framework about 1" wider and ½" taller than the door's jamb frame. This oversized opening, called a *rough opening*, will enable you to position the door easily and shim it plumb and level. Before framing a door, it's always a good idea to buy the door and refer to the manufacturer's recommendations for rough opening size.

Door frames consist of a pair of full-length king studs and two shorter jack studs that support the header above the door. A header provides an attachment point for wallboard and door casings. On load-bearing walls, it also helps to transfer the building's structural loads down into the wall framework and eventually the foundation.

Door framing requires flat, straight, and dry framing lumber, so choose your king, jack, and header pieces carefully. Sight down the edges and ends to look for warpage, and cut off the ends of pieces with splits.

Tools & Materials ▸

Tape measure
Framing square
Hammer or nail gun
Handsaw or reciprocating saw
Framing lumber
10d or pneumatic framing nails
⅜" plywood (for structural headers)
Construction adhesive

Creating a square, properly sized opening for a door is the most important element of a successful door installation project.

How to Frame a Rough Opening for an Interior Prehung Door

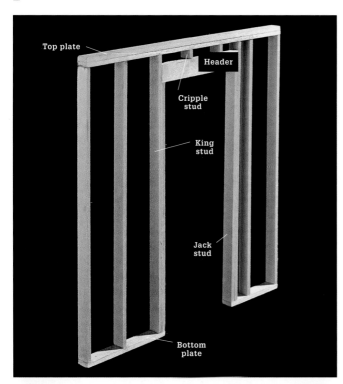

Door frames for prehung doors (left) start with king studs that attach to the top and bottom plates. Inside the king studs, jack studs support the header at the top of the opening. Cripple studs continue the wall-stud layout above the opening. In non-loadbearing walls, the header may be a 2 × 4 laid flat or a built-up header (below). The dimensions of the framed opening are referred to as the rough opening.

Top plate

Header

Cripple stud

King stud

Jack stud

Bottom plate

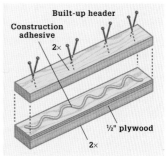

Built-up header

Construction adhesive

2×

½" plywood

2×

To mark the layout for the door frame, measure the width of the door unit along the bottom. Add 1" to this dimension to determine the width of the rough opening (the distance between the jack studs). This gives you a ½" gap on each side for adjusting the door frame during installation. Mark the top and bottom plates for the jack and king studs.

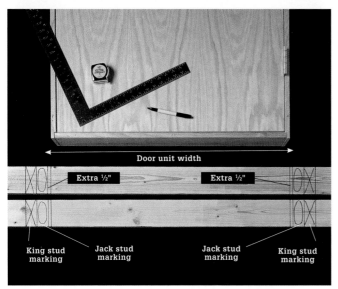

Door unit width

Extra ½"   Extra ½"

King stud marking   Jack stud marking   Jack stud marking   King stud marking

How to Frame a Prehung Door Opening

Mark layout lines for the king and jack studs on the wall's top and sole plates. Cut the king studs slightly longer than the distance between the wall plates, and toenail them in place with 10d nails or 3" pneumatic nails.

Cut the jack studs to length (they should rest on the sole plate). The height of a jack stud for a standard interior door is 83½", or ½" taller than the door. Nail the jack studs to the king studs.

In a partition wall, the header can be a piece of 2× framing lumber that lays flat on top of the jack studs. Cut it to length, and install by endnailing through the king studs or down into the jack studs.

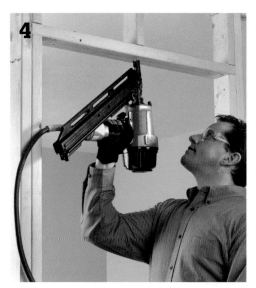

Fasten a cripple stud above the header, halfway between the king studs. It will prevent the header from warping. Toenail it into the top plate, and drive nails into it through the header.

If you haven't cut a sole plate opening for the door yet, do that now with a reciprocating saw or handsaw. Trim the sole plate flush with the jack studs.

How to Frame an Opening for a Load-bearing Wall

Door framing on load-bearing walls will require a structural header that transfers loads above the wall into the jack studs, sole plate, and down into the house foundation. Build it by sandwiching a piece of ³/₈" plywood between two 2 × 4s. Use construction adhesive and nails to fasten the header together.

Install the built-up header by resting it on the jack studs and endnailing through the king studs. Use 10d nails or 3" pneumatic nails.

Toenail a cripple stud between the top plate and header, halfway between the king studs. It transfers structural loads into the header.

Option: Framing Openings for Sliding & Folding Doors

The same basic framing techniques are used, whether you're planning to install a sliding, bifold, pocket, or prehung interior door. The different door styles require different frame openings. You may need to frame an opening 2 to 3 times wider than the opening for a standard prehung door. Purchase the doors and hardware in advance, and consult the hardware manufacturer's instructions for the exact dimensions of the rough opening and header size for the type of door you select.

Most bifold doors are designed to fit in a 80"-high finished opening. Wood bifold doors have the advantage of allowing you to trim the doors, if necessary, to fit openings that are slightly shorter.

Installing a Prehung Interior Door

Install prehung interior doors after the framing work is complete and the wallboard has been installed. If the rough opening for the door has been framed accurately, installing the door takes about an hour.

Standard prehung doors have 4½"-wide jambs and are sized to fit walls with 2 × 4 construction and ½" wallboard. If you have 2 × 6 construction or thicker wall surface material, you can special-order a door to match, or you can add jamb extensions to a standard-sized door (photo, below).

Tools & Materials ▸

Level	Prehung interior door
Hammer	Wood shims
Handsaw	8d casing nails

Tip ▸

1"-thick jamb extension

If your walls are built with 2 × 6 studs, you'll need to extend the jambs by attaching 1"-thick wood strips to the edges of the jamb after the door is installed. Use glue and 4d casing nails when attaching jamb extensions. Make the strips from the same wood as the jamb.

Prehung doors are shipped as single units with the door already hung on hinges attached to pre-installed jambs.

How to Install a Prehung Interior Door

1

Slide the door unit into the framed opening so the edges of the jambs are flush with the wall surface and the hinge-side jamb is plumb.

2

Insert pairs of wood shims driven from opposite directions into the gap between the framing members and the hinge-side jamb, spaced every 12". Check the hinge-side jamb to make sure it is still plumb and does not bow.

3

Anchor the hinge-side jamb with 8d casing nails driven through the jamb and shims and into the jack stud.

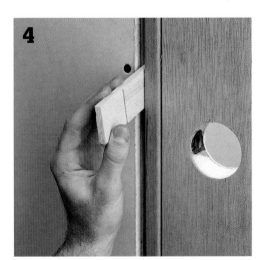

4

Insert pairs of shims in the gap between the framing members and the latch-side jamb and top jamb, spaced every 12". With the door closed, adjust the shims so the gap between door edge and jamb is ⅛" wide. Drive 8d casing nails through the jambs and shims, into the framing members.

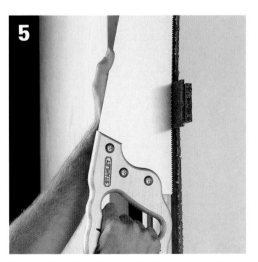

5

Cut the shims flush with the wall surface, using a handsaw. Hold the saw vertically to prevent damage to the door jamb or wall. Finish the door and install the lockset as directed by the manufacturer. See pages 318 to 321 to install trim around the door.

Pocket Doors

Pocket doors are a space-saving alternative to traditional hinged interior doors. Swinging doors can monopolize up to 16 square feet of floor space in a room, which is why pocket doors are a perfect choice for tight spaces, like small bathrooms. Installed in pairs, pocket doors can divide large rooms into more intimate spaces and can still be opened to use the entire area.

Pocket door hardware kits generally are universal and can be adapted for almost any interior door. In this project, the frame kit includes an adjustable track, steel-clad split studs, and all the required hanging hardware. The latch hardware, jambs, and the door itself are all sold separately. Pocket door frames can also be purchased as preassembled units that can be easily installed into a rough opening.

Framing and installing a pocket door is not difficult in new construction or a major remodel. But retrofitting a pocket door in place of a standard door

or installing one in a wall without an existing door, is a major project that involves removing the wall material, framing the new opening, installing and hanging the door, and refinishing the wall. Hidden utilities, such as wiring, plumbing, and heating ducts, must be rerouted if encountered.

The rough opening for a pocket door is at least twice the width of a standard door opening. If you are installing the pocket door in a partition wall, see page 292 to learn how to frame the opening. If the wall is load bearing, you will need to install an appropriately sized header (page 293).

Because pocket doors are easy to open and close and require no threshold, they offer increased accessibility for wheelchair or walker users, provided the handles are easy to use (page 299). If you are installing a pocket door for this purpose, be aware that standard latch hardware may be difficult to use for some individuals.

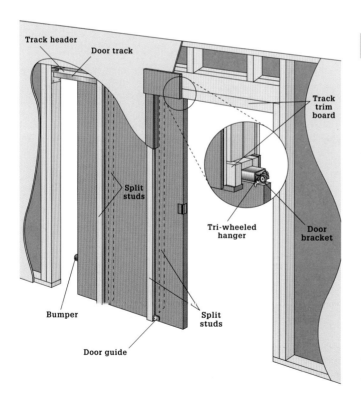

Track header
Door track
Track trim board
Split studs
Tri-wheeled hanger
Door bracket
Bumper
Split studs
Door guide

Tools & Materials ▸

Tape measure
Circular saw
Hammer, nail set
Screwdriver
Level
Drill
Handsaw
Hacksaw
Wallboard tools
2 × 4 lumber
16d, 8d & 6d
 common nails
Pocket door frame kit
Door
1¼" wallboard screws
Wallboard materials
Manufactured pocket door
 jambs (or build jambs
 from 1× material)
8d & 6d finish nails
1½" wood screws
Door casing

How to Install a Pocket Door

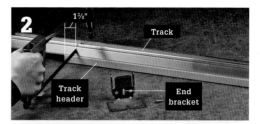

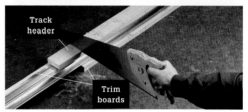

Prepare the project area and frame the rough opening to the manufacturer's recommended dimensions. Measuring from the floor, mark each jack stud at the height of the door plus ¾ to 1½" (depending on the door clearance above the floor) for the overhead door track. Drive a nail into each jack stud, centered on the mark. Leave about ⅛" of the nail protruding.

Remove the adjustable end bracket from the overhead door track. Cut the wooden track header at the mark that matches your door size. Turn the track over and cut the metal track 1⅜" shorter than the wooden track header using a hacksaw (top). Replace the end bracket. Cut the side trim boards along the marks corresponding to your door size, being careful not to cut the metal track (bottom).

Set end brackets of the track on the nails in the jack studs. Adjust the track to level and set the nails. Then drive 8d common nails through the remaining holes in the end brackets.

Snap chalk lines on the floor across the opening, even with the sides of the rough opening. Tap the floor plate spacers into the bottom ends of the pairs of steel-clad split studs. Butt one split stud pair against the door track trim board, check it for plumb, and fasten it to the track header using 6d common nails (left). Center the other split stud pair in the "pocket" and fasten it to the track header. Plumb the split studs again and attach them to the floor with 8d common nails or 2" screws driven through spacer plates (right).

(continued)

5.

6

.7

Tri-wheeled hanger

Lock arm

Cover the open framing with wall-board to the edge of the opening. You may want to leave the wallboard off one side of the wall to allow for door adjustment. Use 1¼" wallboard screws, which will not protrude into the pocket.

Paint or stain the door as desired. When the door has dried, attach two door brackets to the top of the door, using included screws driven through pilot holes. Install the rubber bumper to the rear edge of the door with its included screw.

Slide two tri-wheeled hangers into the overhead door track. Set the door in the frame, aligning the hangers with the door brackets. Then raise the door and press each hanger into the door bracket until it snaps into place. Close the lock arm over the hanger.

8

9

³⁄₁₆"   ³⁄₁₆"

Cut the strike-side jamb to length and width. Fasten it to the jack stud using 8d finish nails, shimming the jamb to plumb as necessary. Close the door and adjust the hanger nuts to fine-tune the door height so the door is parallel with the jamb from top to bottom.

Measure and cut the split jambs to size. Fasten each split jamb to the front edge of the split stud using 8d finish nails. Maintain ³⁄₁₆" clearance on both sides of the door. If necessary, shim between the bumper and door until the door is flush with the jambs when open.

10

11

Measure and cut the split head jambs to size. Use 1½" wood screws driven through countersunk pilot holes to attach the head jamb on the side that has access to the lock arm of the hangers to allow for easy removal of the door. Attach the other head jamb using 6d finish nails. Maintain ³⁄₁₆" clearance on each side of the door.

Install the included door guides on both sides of the door near the floor at the mouth of the pocket. Install the latch hardware according to the manufacturer's directions. Finish the wallboard and install casing around the door. Fill all nail holes, then paint or stain the jambs and casing as desired.

Improving Pocket Door Accessibility ▸

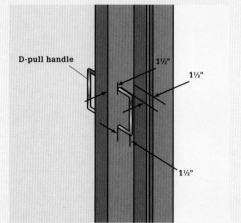

D-pull handle

1½"

1½"

1½"

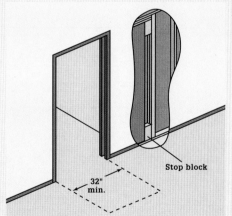

Stop block

32" min.

D-pull handles are easier to use than standard recessed hardware. Choose pulls that project at least 1½" from the door. Mount the pulls 1½" from the edge of the door to provide room for fingers when the door is closed (left). Install a stop block at the back of the frame (right), so the door stops 1½" short of the D-pull to provide room for fingers when the door is open. Because this design reduces the width of the door opening by 3", you must use a 36"-wide door to maintain the recommended doorway width of 32".

Bifold Doors

Bifold doors provide easy access to a closet without requiring much clearance for opening. Most home centers stock kits that include two pairs of prehinged doors, a head track, and all the necessary hardware and fasteners. Typically, the doors in these kits have predrilled holes for the pivot and guide posts. Hardware kits are also sold separately for custom projects. There are many types of bifold door styles, so be sure to read and follow the manufacturer's instructions for the product you use.

Tools & Materials ▶

Tape measure	Screwdriver
Level	Hacksaw
Circular saw	Prehinged bifold doors
Straightedge	Head track
(optional)	Mounting hardware
Drill	Panhead screws
Plane	Flathead screws

A variety of designer bifold doors are available for installation between rooms and closets. They provide the same attractive appearance as French doors but require much less floor space.

How to Install Bifold Doors

1

Cut the head track to the width of the opening using a hacksaw. Insert the roller mounts into the track, then position the track in the opening. Fasten it to the header using panhead screws.

2

Measure and mark each side jamb at the floor for the anchor bracket so the center of the bracket aligns exactly with the center of the head track. Fasten the brackets in place with flathead screws.

3

Check the height of the doors in the opening, and trim if necessary. Insert pivot posts into predrilled holes at the bottoms and tops of the doors. Insert guide posts at the tops of the leading doors. Make sure all posts fit snugly.

4

Fold one pair of doors closed and lift into position, inserting the pivot and guide posts into the head track. Slip the bottom pivot post into the anchor bracket. Repeat for the other pair of doors. Close the doors and check alignment along the side jambs and down the center. If necessary, adjust the top and bottom pivots following the manufacturer's instructions.

French Doors

French doors are made up of two separate doors, hinged on opposing jambs of a doorway. The doors swing out from the center of the doorway and into or out from a room. Like most doors, French doors are typically sold in prehung units, but are also available separately. They are generally available only in wood with a variety of designs and styles to choose from.

Before purchasing a prehung French door unit, determine the size of doors you will need. If you are planning to install the doors in an existing doorway, measure the dimensions of the rough opening from the unfinished framing members, then order the unit to size—the manufacturer or distributor will help you select the proper unit.

You can also pick the prehung unit first, then alter an existing opening to accommodate it (as shown in this project). In this case, build the rough opening a little larger than the actual dimensions of the doors to accommodate the jambs. Prehung units typically require adding 1" to the width and $\frac{1}{2}$" to the height.

If the doorway will be in a load-bearing wall, you will need to make temporary supports (page 29) and install an appropriately sized header. Sizing the header (depth) is critical: it's based on the length of the header, the material it's made from, and the weight of the load it must support. For actual requirements, consult your local building department.

When installing French doors, it is important to have consistent reveals between the two doors and between the top of the doors and the head jamb. This allows the doors to close properly and prevents the hinges from binding.

Tools & Materials ▸

Tape measure	2 × 4 and 2 × 6
Circular saw	lumber
4-ft. level	$\frac{1}{2}$" plywood
Hammer	10d & 16d
Handsaw	common nails
Drill	Wood shims
Utility knife	8d finish nails
Nail set	
Prehung French	
door unit	

Traditionally, French doors open onto the patio or lush garden of a backyard. But you can create stylish entrances inside your home by bringing French doors to formal dining rooms, sitting rooms, dens, and master suites.

How to Install French Doors

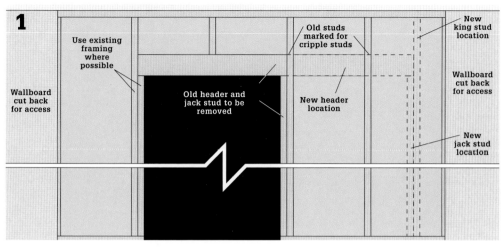

1

Use existing framing where possible

Wallboard cut back for access

Old header and jack stud to be removed

Old studs marked for cripple studs

New header location

New king stud location

Wallboard cut back for access

New jack stud location

Shut off power and water to the area. Remove the wall surfaces from both sides of the wall (pages 276 to 279), leaving one stud bay open on each side of the new rough opening. Also remove or reroute any wiring, plumbing, or ductwork. Lay out the new rough opening, marking the locations of all new jack and king studs on both the top and bottom plates. Where practical, use existing framing members. To install a new king stud, cut a stud to size and align with the layout marks; toenail to the bottom plate with 10d common nails, check for plumb, then toenail to the top plate to secure. Finally, mark both the bottom and top of the new header on one king stud, then use a level to extend the lines across the intermediate studs to the opposite king stud. If using existing framing, measure and mark from the existing jack stud.

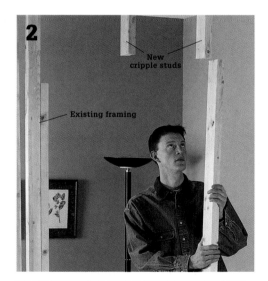

2

New cripple studs

Existing framing

Cut the intermediate studs at the reference marks for the top of the header using a reciprocating saw. Pry the studs away from the sole plates and remove—the remaining top pieces will be used as cripple studs.

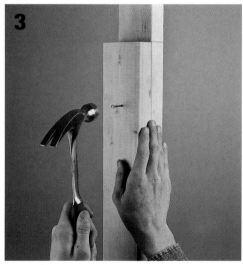

3

To install a jack stud, cut the stud to fit between the sole plate and the bottom of the header, as marked on the king stud. Align it at the mark against the king stud, then fasten it in place with 10d common nails driven every 12".

(continued)

4

Build the header to size (pages 292 to 293) and install, fastening it to the jack studs, king studs, and cripple studs using 16d common nails. Use a handsaw to cut through the bottom plate so it's flush with the inside faces of the jack studs. Remove the cutout portion.

5

Finish the walls (for wallboard installation, see pages 44 to 51) before installing the doors, then set the prehung door unit into the framed opening so the jamb edges are flush with the finished wall surfaces and the unit is centered from side to side.

6

Using a level, adjust the unit to plumb one of the side jambs. Starting near the top of the door, insert pairs of shims driven from opposite directions into the gap between the framing and the jamb, sliding the shims until they are snug. Check the jamb to make sure it remains plumb and does not bow inward.

7

Working down along the jamb, install shims near each hinge and near the floor. Make sure the jamb is plumb, then anchor it with 8d finish nails driven through the jamb and shims and into the framing. Leave the nail heads partially protruding so the jamb can be readjusted later if necessary.

Install shims at the other side jamb, aligning them roughly with the shims of the first jamb. With the doors closed, adjust the shims so the reveal between the doors is even and the tops of the doors are aligned.

Shim the gap between the header and the head jamb to create a consistent reveal along the top when the doors are closed. Insert pairs of shims every 12". Drive 8d finish nails through the jambs and shims and into the framing members.

Drive all the nails fully, then set them below the surface of the wood with a nail set. Cut off the shims flush with the wall surface using a handsaw or utility knife. Hold the saw vertically to prevent damage to the door jamb or wall. Install the door casing.

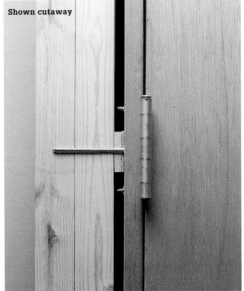

Option: Replace the center mounting screw on each hinge with a 3" wood screw to provide extra support for door hinges and jambs. These long screws extend through the side jambs and deep into the framing members. Be careful not to overtighten screws, which will cause the jambs to bow.

Installing Entry Doors

Few parts of a house have a more dramatic effect on the way your home is perceived than the main entry door. A lovely, well-maintained entryway that is tastefully matched architecturally to the house can utterly transform a home's appearance. In fact, industry studies have suggested that upgrading a plain entry door to a higher-end entry door system can pay back multiple times in the resale of your house. But perhaps more importantly, depending on your priorities, it makes a great improvement in how you feel about your home. Plus, it usually pays benefits in home security and energy efficiency as well.

If you are replacing a single entry door with a double door or a door with a sidelight or sidelights, you will need to enlarge the door opening (see pages 32 to 35). Be sure to file your plans with your local building department and obtain a permit. You'll need to provide temporary support from the time you remove the wall studs in the new opening until you've installed and

secured a new door header that's approved for the new span distance.

The American Craftsman style door with sidelights (see Resources, page 554) installed in this project has the look and texture of a classic wood door, but it is actually created from fiber-glass. Today's fiberglass doors are quite convincing in their ability to replicate wood grain, while still offering the durability and low-maintenance of fiberglass.

Tools & Materials ▸

Tape measure	Shims
Level	Framing nails
Reciprocating saw	Finish nails
Caulk & caulk gun	Nail set
Hammer	Finishing materials

After

Before

Replacing an ordinary entry door with a beautiful new upgrade has an exceptionally high payback in increased curb appeal and in perceived home value, according to industry studies.

How to Replace an Entry Door

1

Remove the old entry door by cutting through the fasteners driven into the jamb with a reciprocating saw (see pages 32 and 35). If the new door or door system is wider, mark the edges of the larger rough opening onto the wall surface. If possible, try to locate the new opening so one edge will be against an existing wall stud. Be sure to include the thickness of the new framing you'll need to add when removing the wall coverings.

2

Frame in the new rough opening for the replacement door (see pages 257 to 261). The instructions that come with the door will recommend a rough opening size, which is usually sized to create a ½" gap between the door and the studs and header. Patch the wall surfaces.

3

Cut metal door dripcap molding to fit the width of the opening and tuck the back edge up behind the wallcovering at the top of the door opening. Attach the dripcap with caulk only–do not use nails or screws.

4

Unpack the door unit and set it in the rough opening to make sure it fits correctly. Remove it. Make sure the subfloor is clean and in good repair, and then apply heavy beads of caulk to the underside of the door sill and to the subfloor in the sill installation area. Use plenty of caulk.

(continued)

5

Set the door sill in the threshold and raise the unit up so it fits cleanly in the opening, with the exterior trim flush against the wall sheathing. Press down on the sill to seat it in the caulk and wipe up any squeeze-out with a damp rag

6

Use a 6-ft. level to make sure the unit is plumb and then tack it to the rough opening stud on the hinge side, using pairs of 10d nails driven partway through the casing on the weatherstripped side of the door (or the sidelight). On single, hinged doors, drive the nails just above the hinge locations. *Note: Many door installers prefer deck screws over nails when attaching the jambs. Screws offer more gripping strength and are easier to adjust, but covering the screw heads is more difficult than filling nail holes.*

7

Drive wood shims between the jamb and the wall studs to create an even gap. Locate the shims directly above the pairs of nails you drove. Doublecheck the door with the level to make sure it is still plumb.

8

Drive shims between the jamb on the latch side of the unit and into the wall stud. Only drive the nails part way. Test for plumb again and then add shims at nail locations (you may need to double-up the shims, as this gap is often wider than the one on the hinge side). Check to make sure the door jamb is not bowed.

9

Drive finish nails at all remaining locations, following the nailing schedule in the manufacturer's installation instructions.

10

Use a nail set to drive the nail heads below the wood surface. Fill the nail holes with wood putty (you'll get the best match if you apply putty that's tinted to match stained wood after the finish is applied). The presence of the wood shims at the nail locations should prevent the jamb from bowing as you nail.

11

Install the lockset, strikeplates, deadbolts or multipoint locks, and any other door hardware. If the door finish has not been applied, you may want to do so first, but generally it makes more sense to install the hardware right away so the door can be operated and locked. Attach the door sill to the threshold and adjust it as needed, normally using the adjustment screws (inset).

12

Apply your door finish if it has not yet been applied. Read the manufacturer's suggestions for finishing very closely and follow the suggested sequences. Some manufacturers offer finish kits that are designed to be perfectly compatible with their doors. Install interior case molding and caulk all the exterior gaps after the finish dries.

Installing Storm Doors

Install a storm door to improve the appearance and weather resistance of an old entry door or to protect a newly installed door against weathering. In all climates, adding a storm door can extend the life of an entry door.

When buying a storm door, look for models that have a solid inner core and seamless outer shell construction. Carefully note the dimensions of your door opening, measuring from the inside edges of the entry door's brick molding. Choose a storm door that opens from the same side as your entry door.

Tools & Materials ▸

Tape measure
Pencil
Plumb bob
Hacksaw
Hammer

Drill and bits
Screwdrivers
Storm door unit
Wood spacer strips
4d casing nails

Adjustable sweeps help make storm doors weathertight. Before installing the door, attach the sweep to the bottom of the door. After the door is mounted, adjust the height of the sweep so it brushes the top of the sill lightly when the door is closed.

How to Cut a Storm Door Frame to Fit a Door Opening

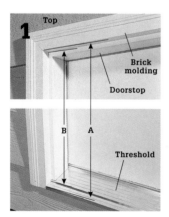

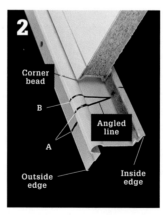

Because entry door thresholds are slanted, the bottom of the storm door frame needs to be cut to match the threshold angle. Measure from the threshold to the top of the door opening along the corner of the brick molding (A), then measure along the front edge of the entry doorstop (B).

Subtract ⅛" from measurements A and B to allow for small adjustments when the door is installed. Measuring from the top of the storm door frame, mark the adjusted points A and B on the corner bead. Draw a line from point A to the outside edge of the frame and from point B to the inside edge. Draw an angled line from point A on the corner bead to point B on the inside edge.

Use a hacksaw to cut down through the bottom of the storm door frame, following the angled line. Make sure to hold the hacksaw at the same slant as the angled line to ensure that the cut will be smooth and straight.

How to Fit & Install a Storm Door

Position the storm door in the opening and push the frame tight against the brick molding on the hinge side of the storm door, then draw a reference line on the brick molding, following the edge of the storm door frame.

Push the storm door frame tight against the brick molding on the latch side, then measure the gap between the reference line and the hinge side of the door frame. If the distance is greater than ⅜", spacer strips must be installed to ensure the door will fit snugly.

To install spacers, remove the door, then nail thin strips of wood to the inside of the brick molding at storm door hinge locations. The thickness of the wood strips should be ⅛" less than the gap measured in step 2.

Replace the storm door and push it tight against the brick molding on the hinge side. Drill pilot holes through the hinge-side frame of the storm door and into the brick molding spaced every 12". Attach the frame with mounting screws.

Remove any spacer clips holding the frame to the storm door. With the storm door closed, drill pilot holes and attach the latch-side frame to the brick molding. Use a coin to keep an even gap between the storm door and the storm door frame.

Center the top piece of the storm door frame on top of the frame sides. Drill pilot holes and screw the top piece to the brick molding. Adjust the bottom sweep, then attach the locks and latch hardware as directed by the manufacturer.

Installing Patio Doors

For easy installation, buy a patio door with the door panels already mounted in a preassembled frame. Try to avoid patio doors sold with frame kits that require complicated assembly.

Because patio doors have very long bottom sills and top jambs, they are susceptible to bowing and warping. To avoid these problems, be very careful to install the patio door so it is level and plumb and to anchor the unit securely to framing members. Yearly caulking and touch-up painting helps prevent moisture from warping the jambs.

Tools & Materials ›

Pencil	Nail set
Hammer	Shims
Circular saw	Drip edge
Handsaw	Building paper
Wood chisel	Silicone and
Stapler	latex caulk
Caulk gun	10d casing nails
Level	3" wood screws
Pry bar	Sill nosing
Cordless screwdriver	Fiberglass insulation
Drill and bits	Patio door kit

Patio doors offer the best qualities of both windows and doors—plenty of natural light, a great view, wide room access, and reasonable security.

If not included with the unit, screen doors can be ordered from most patio door manufacturers. Screen doors have spring-mounted rollers that fit into a narrow track on the outside of the patio door threshold.

Installing Sliding Patio Doors

Bottom rail

Remove heavy glass panels if you must install the door without help. Reinstall the panels after the frame has been placed in the rough opening and nailed at opposite corners. To remove and install the panels, remove the stop rail found on the top jamb of the door unit.

Adjust the bottom rollers after installation is complete. Remove the coverplate on the adjusting screw, found on the inside edge of the bottom rail. Turn the screw in small increments until the door rolls smoothly along the track without binding when it is opened and closed.

Tips for Installing Hinged Patio Doors ▸

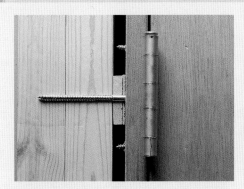

1/8"

Provide extra support for door hinges by replacing the center mounting screw on each hinge with a 3" wood screw. These long screws extend through the side jambs and deep into the framing members.

Keep a uniform 1/8" gap between the door, side jambs, and top jamb to ensure that the door will swing freely without binding. Check this gap frequently as you shim around the door unit.

How to Install a Patio Door

1

Prepare the work area and remove the interior wall surfaces, then frame the rough opening for the patio door. Remove the exterior surfaces inside the framed opening.

2

Test-fit the door unit, centering it in the rough opening. Check to make sure the door is plumb. If necessary, shim under the lower side jamb until the door is plumb and level. Have a helper hold the door in place while you adjust it.

3

Trace the outline of the brick molding onto the siding, then remove the door unit. *Note: If you have vinyl or metal siding, see page 282 for advice on removing the siding.*

4

Cut the siding along the outline, just down to the sheathing using a circular saw. Stop just short of the corners to prevent damage to the remaining siding. Finish the cuts at the corners with a sharp wood chisel.

5

Drip edge

To provide an added moisture barrier, cut a piece of drip edge to fit the width of the rough opening, then slide it between the siding and the existing building paper at the top of the opening. Do not nail the drip edge.

Cut 8"-wide strips of building paper and slide them between the siding and sheathing. Bend the paper around the framing members and staple it in place. Each piece overlaps the piece below it.

Apply several thick beads of silicone caulk to the subfloor at the bottom of the door opening.

Apply silicone caulk around the front edge of the framing members where the siding meets the building paper.

Use a pry bar to center the door in the rough opening so the brick molding is tight against the sheathing. Have a helper hold the door unit from outside.

Check the door threshold to make sure it is level. If necessary, shim under the lower side jamb until the patio door unit is level.

(continued)

If there are gaps between the threshold and subfloor, insert shims coated with caulk into the gaps, spaced every 6". Shims should be snug, but not so tight that they cause the threshold to bow. Clear off excess caulk immediately.

Place pairs of hardwood wedge shims together to form flat shims. Insert the shims every 12" into the gaps between the side jambs and the jack studs. For sliding doors, shim behind the strike plate for the door latch.

Insert shims every 12" into the gap between the top jamb and the header.

From outside, drive 10d casing nails, spaced every 12", through the brick molding and into the framing members. Use a nail set to drive the nail heads below the surface of the wood.

From inside, drive 10d casing nails through the door jambs and into the framing members at each shim location. Use a nail set to drive the nail heads below the surface of the wood.

Remove one of the screws and cut the shims flush with the stop block found in the center of the threshold. Replace the screw with a 3" wood screw driven into the subfloor as an anchor.

Cut off the shims flush with the face of the framing members using a handsaw. Fill gaps around the door jambs and beneath the threshold with loosely packed fiberglass insulation.

Reinforce and seal the edge of the threshold by installing sill nosing under the threshold and against the wall. Drill pilot holes and attach the sill nosing with 10d casing nails.

Make sure the drip edge is tight against the top brick molding, then apply paintable silicone caulk along the top of the drip edge and along the outside edge of the side brick moldings. Fill all exterior nail holes with caulk.

Caulk completely around the sill nosing using your finger to press the caulk into any cracks. As soon as the caulk is dry, paint the sill nosing. Finish the door and install the lockset as directed by the manufacturer.

Installing Door & Window Casing

Door and window casings provide an attractive border around doors and windows. They also cover the gaps between door or window jambs and the surfaces of surrounding walls.

Install door and window casings with a consistent reveal between the inside edges of the jambs and casings, making sure the casings are level and plumb.

In order to fit casings properly, the jambs and wallcoverings must lie in the same plane. If either one protrudes, the casings will not lie flush. To solve this problem, you'll need to remove some material from whichever surface is protruding.

Use a block plane to shave protruding jambs or a surface forming rasp to shave a protruding wallboard edge. Wallboard screws rely on the strength of untorn facing paper to support the wallboard. If the paper around the screws is damaged, drive additional screws nearby where the paper is still intact.

Tools & Materials ▸

Tape measure	Hammer or
Pencil	pneumatic nailer
Combination square	Casing material
Nail set	Plinths and corner
Level	blocks (optional)
Straightedge	4d and 6d finish nails
Power miter saw	Wood putty

Case molding is installed around windows and doors to conceal the gaps between jambs and the wall. Venturing beyond the very common ranch-style casing offers some high design payback.

How to Install Mitered Casing on Doors & Windows

1

On each jamb, mark a reveal line ⅛" from the inside edge. The casings will be installed flush with these lines. *Note: On double-hung windows, the casings are usually installed flush with the edge of the jambs, so no reveal line is needed.*

2

Place a length of casing along one side jamb, flush with the reveal line. At the top and bottom of the molding, mark the points where horizontal and vertical reveal lines meet. (When working with doors, mark the molding at the top only).

3

Make 45° miter cuts on the ends of the moldings. Measure and cut the other vertical molding piece, using the same method.

4

Drill pilot holes spaced every 12" to prevent splitting and attach the vertical casings with 4d finish nails driven through the casings and into the jambs. Drive 6d finish nails into framing members near the outside edge of the casings.

5

Measure the distance between the side casings, and cut top and bottom casings to fit, with ends mitered at 45°. If window or door unit is not perfectly square, make test cuts on scrap pieces to find the correct angle of the joints. Drill pilot holes and attach with 4d and 6d finish nails.

6

Locknail the corner joints by drilling pilot holes and driving 4d finish nails through each corner, as shown. Drive all nail heads below the wood surface, using a nail set, then fill the nail holes with wood putty.

How to Install Butted Door Casings

1

On each jamb, mark a reveal line ⅛" from the inside edge. The casings will be installed flush with these lines.

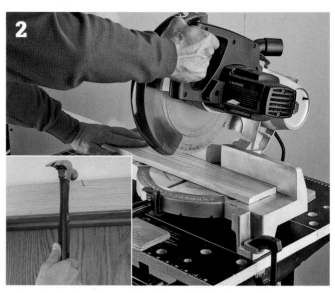

2

Cut the head casing to length. Mark the centerpoint of the head casing and the centerpoint of the head jamb. Align the casing with the head jamb reveal line, matching the centerpoints so that the head casing extends evenly beyond both side jamb casings. Nail the casing to the wall at stud locations and at the jamb (inset).

3

Hold the side casings against the head casing and mark them for cutting, then cut the side casings to fit.

4

Align the side casings with the side jamb reveal lines, then nail the casings to the jambs and framing members. Set the nails, using a nail set. Fill the nail holes with wood putty.

Options for Installing Door & Window Casings

Dress up door casings by adding plinths. Cut the plinths from 1× stock and bevel one edge. Nail the plinths to the jambs with 2" 10d finish nails so the beveled edges are aligned with the reveal lines for the casings. Measure and cut the casings to fit.

Add corner blocks, also known as rosettes, at the ends of the head casing. Attach the corner blocks once the side casings are in place, then cut the head casing to fit. Set the nails, using a nailset, after all pieces are installed.

Backband molding can dress up butted window casings. Install the back band around the perimeter of the window, mitering the joints at the corners. Nail the back band in place with 4d finish nails or pneumatic brads.

Create a decorative door header by nailing a combination of bed and lattice moldings over the top casing. Size the header to overhang the side casings.

Lighting

Artificial lighting is a necessary component of any room, but beyond simply providing illumination, lighting fixtures are an important part of a room's design. From the low-key but modern appearance of recessed canister lights to the elegance of a crystal chandelier, your choice of fixture will go a long way toward defining your remodeled room.

The easiest lighting improvement is to simply make a one-for-one replacement of an old fixture. The electrical connections are simple and, depending on the style you choose, you may not have to do any alterations to the room at all. Just make sure the light the new fixture provides is adequate for your room. In other words, don't replace an old fixture that holds three 60-watt bulbs with a single 25-watt pendant unless you are providing additional new light.

This chapter shows how to hook up the three types of light fixture you're most likely to include in your remodeling plan: an overhead ceiling light, recessed canister lights, and track lighting. If you need to add new wiring to supply the light, see the information on pages 82 through 147. Always shut off power at the main service panel before beginning even the simplest wiring project. Call a professional if you are unsure about your wiring job.

In this chapter:

- Installing Ceiling Lights
- Installing Recessed Ceiling Lights
- Installing Track Lighting

Installing Ceiling Lights

Ceiling fixtures don't have any moving parts and their wiring is very simple, so, other than changing bulbs, you're likely to get decades of trouble-free service from a fixture. This sounds like a good thing, but it also means that the fixture probably won't fail and give you an excuse to update a room's look with a new one. Fortunately, you don't need an excuse. Upgrading a fixture is easy and can make a dramatic impact on a room. You can substantially increase the light in a room by replacing a globe-style fixture by one with separate spot lights, or you can simply install a new fixture that matches the room's décor.

Tools & Materials ▸

Replacement light fixture
Wire stripper
Voltage sensor
Insulated screwdrivers
Wire connectors

Installing a new ceiling fixture can provide more light to a space, not to mention an aesthetic lift. It's one of the easiest upgrades you can do.

How to Replace a Ceiling Light

1

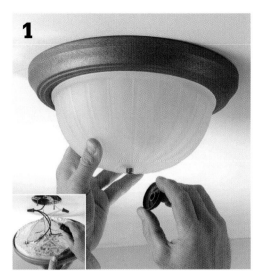

Shut off power to the ceiling light and remove the shade or diffuser. Loosen the mounting screws and carefully lower the fixture, supporting it as you work (do not let light fixtures hang by their electrical wires alone). Test with a voltage sensor to make sure no power is reaching the connections.

2

Remove the twist connectors from the fixture wires or unscrew the screw terminals and remove the white neutral wire and the black lead wire (inset).

3

Before you install the new fixture, check the ends of the wires coming from the ceiling electrical box. They should be clean and free of nicks or scorch marks. If they're dirty or worn, clip off the stripped portion with your combination tool. Then strip away about ¾" of insulation from the end of each wire.

4

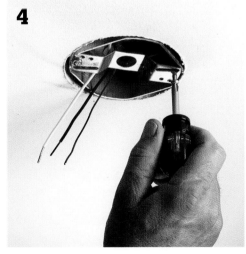

Attach a mounting strap to the ceiling fixture box if there is not one already present. Your new light may come equipped with a strap, otherwise you can find one for purchase at any hardware store.

(continued)

5

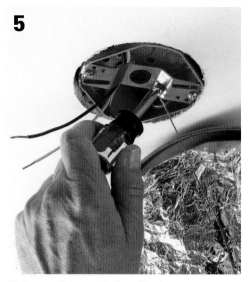

Lift the new fixture up to the ceiling (you may want a helper for this) and attach the bare copper ground wire from the power supply cable to the grounding screw or clip on the mounting strap. Also attach the ground wire from the fixture to the screw or clip.

6

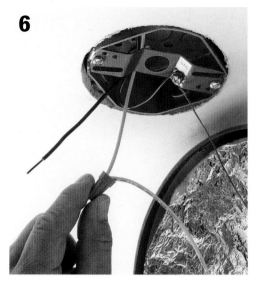

With the fixture supported by a ladder or a helper, join the white wire lead and the white fixture wire with a wire connector (often supplied with the fixture).

7

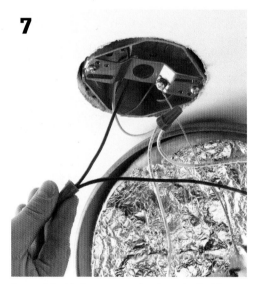

Connect the black power supply wire to the black fixture wire with a wire connector.

8

Position the new fixture mounting plate over the box so the mounting screw holes align. Drive the screws until the fixture is secure against the ceiling. *Note: Some fixtures are supported by a threaded rod or nipple in the center that screws into a female threaded opening in the mounting strap (inset).*

Installing Recessed Ceiling Lights

Recessed lights are versatile fixtures suited for a variety of situations. Fixtures rated for outdoor use can also be installed in roof soffits and overhangs for accent and security lighting. Recessed fixtures can also be installed over showers or tubs. Be sure to use fixture cans and trims rated for bathroom use.

There are recessed lighting cans in all shapes and sizes for almost every type of ceiling or cabinet. Cans are sold for unfinished ceilings (new construction) or for finished ceilings (retrofit installation). Cans are also rated as insulation compatible or for uninsulated ceilings. Be sure to use the correct one for your ceiling to prevent creating a fire hazard.

Choose the proper type of recessed light fixture for your project. There are two types of fixtures: those rated for installation within insulation (left), and those which must be kept at least 3" from insulation (right). Self-contained thermal switches shut off power if the unit gets too hot for its rating. A recessed light fixture must be installed at least ½" from combustible materials.

Tools & Materials ▸

Recessed-lighting can for new construction or remodeling and trim	Circuit tester Cable ripper Combination tool	Pliers Fish tape	Drywall saw NM cable

Recessed ceiling lights often are installed in series to provide exacting control over the amount and direction of light. Spacing the canisters in every other ceiling joist bay is a common practice.

How to Install Recessed Ceiling Lights

Mark the location for the light canister. If you are installing multiple lights, measure out from the wall at the start and end of the run, and connect them with a chalkline snapped parallel to the wall. If the ceiling is finished with a surface (wallboard), see next page.

Install the housing for the recessed fixture. Housings for new construction (or remodeling installations where the installation area is fully accessible from either above or below) have integral hanger bars that you attach to the each joist in the joist bay.

Run electric cable from the switch to each canister location. Multiple lights are generally installed in series so there is no need to make pigtail connections in the individual boxes. Make sure to leave enough extra cable at each location to feed the wire into the housing and make the connection.

Run the feeder cables into the electrical boxes attached to the canister housings. You'll need to remove knockouts first and make sure to secure the cable with a wire staple within 8" of the entry point to the box.

Connect the feeder wires to the fixture wires inside the junction box. Twist the hot lead together with the black fixture wire, as well as the black lead to other fixtures further downline. Also connect the neutral white wires. Join the ground wires and pigtail them to the grounding screw or clip in the box. Finish the ceiling, as desired.

Attach your trim kit of choice. Normally, these are hung with torsion spring clips from notches or hooks inside the canister. This should be done after the ceiling is installed and finished for new construction projects. With certain types of trim kits, such as eyeball trim, you'll need to install the light bulb before the trim kit.

How to Connect a Recessed Fixture Can in a Finished Ceiling

Make the hole for the can. Most fixtures will include a template for sizing the hole. Fish 14/2 cable from the switch location to the hole. Pull about 16" of cable out of the hole for making the connection.

Remove a knockout from the electrical box attached to the can. Thread the cable into the box; secure it with a cable clamp. Remove sheathing insulation. Connect the black fixture wire to the black circuit wire, the white fixture wire to the white circuit wire, and then connect the ground wire to the grounding screw or grounding wire attached to the box.

Retrofit cans secure themselves in the hole with spring-loaded clips. Install the can in the ceiling by depressing the mounting clips so the can will fit into the hole. Insert the can so that its edge is tight to the ceiling. Push the mounting clips back out so they grip the drywall and hold the fixture in place. Install the trim piece.

Installing Track Lighting

Track lighting offers a beautiful and functional way to increase the amount of light in a room or simply to update its look. A variety of fixture and lamp options lets you control the shape, color, and intensity of the light. Installing track lighting in place of an existing ceiling-mounted light fixture involves basic wiring and hand-tool skills, but the connections are even easier to make than with traditional light fixtures. Once installed, the system is very easy to upgrade or expand in the future.

Tools & Materials ▸

Drill/driver and bits
Wire stripper
Screwdriver
Voltage sensor
Toggle bolts

Prewired track
  and fittings
Track light heads
Wire connector
Ceiling box

If you currently have a ceiling-mounted light fixture that is not meeting your lighting needs, it's simple to replace it with a track-lighting fixture. With track lighting you can easily change the type and number of lights, their position on the track, and the direction they aim. These fixtures come in many different styles, including short 3-ft. track systems with just one or two lights up to 12-ft. systems with five or more lights.

How to Install Track Lighting

1

Disconnect the old ceiling light fixture (for remodeling projects) after shutting off power to the circuit at the main service panel. The globe or diffuser and the lamps should be removed before the fixture mounting mechanism is detached.

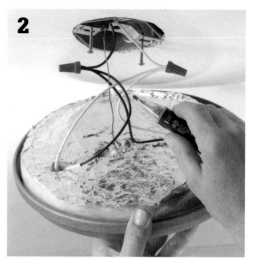

2

Test the fixture wires with a voltage sensor to make sure the circuit is dead. Support the fixture from below while you work—never allow a light fixture to hang by its electrical wires alone. Remove the wire connectors and pull the wires apart. Remove the old light fixture.

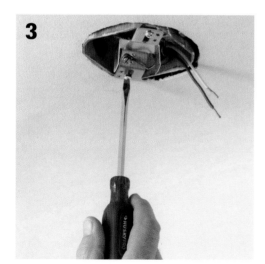

3

Attach the mounting strap for the new track light to the old ceiling box. If the mounting strap has a hole in the center, thread the circuit wires through the hole before screwing the strap to the box. The green or bare copper ground from the circuit should be attached to the grounding screw or clip on the strap or box.

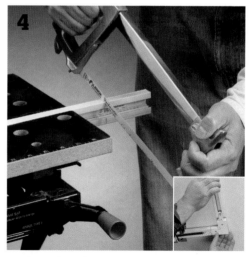

4

Cut the track section to length, if necessary, using a hack saw. Deburr the cut end with a metal file. If you are installing multiple sections of track, assemble the sections with the correct connector fittings (sold separately from your kit). You can also purchase T-fittings or L-fittings (inset photo) if you wish to install tracks in either of these configurations.

(continued)

5

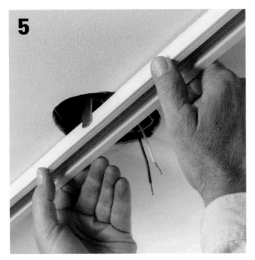

Position the track section in the mounting saddle on the mounting strap and hold it temporarily in place in the location where it will be installed. The track section will have predrilled mounting holes in the back. Draw a marking point on the ceiling at each of these locations. If your track does not have predrilled mounting holes, remove it and drill a ³⁄₁₆" hole in the back every 16".

6

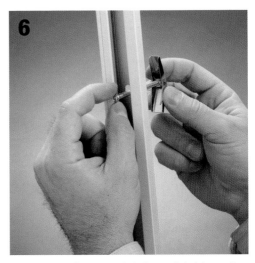

Insert the bolt from a toggle bolt or molly bolt into each predrilled screw location and twist the toggle or molly back onto the free end. These types of hardware have greater holding power than anchor sleeves. Drill a ⅜" dia. access hole in the ceiling at each of the mounting hole locations you marked on the ceiling in step 5.

7

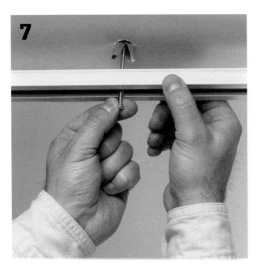

Insert the toggle or molly into the access hole far enough so it clears the top of the hole and the wings snap outward. Then tighten each bolt so the track is snug against the ceiling. If the mounting hole happens to fall over a ceiling joint, simply drive a wallboard screw at that hole location.

8

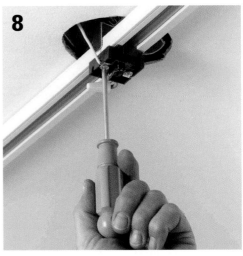

Hook up wires from the track's power supply fitting to the circuit wires. Connect black to black and white to white. The grounding wire from the power supply fitting can either be pigtailed to the circuit ground wire and connected to the grounding screw or clip, or it can be twisted together with the circuit grounding wire at the grounding terminal. Snap the fitting into the track if you have not already done so.

9

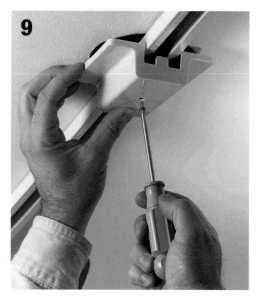

Attach the protective cover that came with your kit to conceal the ceiling box and the electrical connections. Some covers simply snap in place, others require a mounting screw.

10

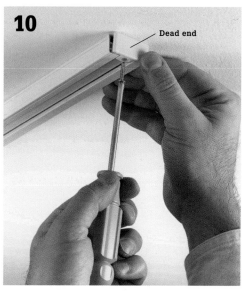

Dead end

Cap the open ends of the track with a dead end cap fitting. These also may require a mounting screw. Leaving track ends open is a safety violation.

11

Insert the light heads into the track by slipping the stem into the track slot and then twisting it so the electrical contact points on the head press against the electrified inner rails of the track slot. Tug lightly on the head to make sure it is secure before releasing it.

12

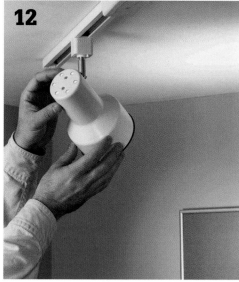

Arrange the track light heads so their light falls in the manner you choose, and then depress the locking tab on each fixture to secure it in position. Restore power and test the lights.

MAJOR
REMODELING

Kitchen Remodeling

Kitchens are remodeled with greater frequency than any other room in the house. This happens often for reasons of style: keeping up with design trends is important to many homeowners. But it also happens for more practical reasons. Kitchens receive a vast amount of wear and tear that results from high usage. Appliances stop working, flooring wears out, cabinets fail, even windows and doors suffer from constant wear. High humidity levels are also an issue in kitchens, where steam is a necessary byproduct of daily life.

The information in this chapter is unique to kitchen remodeling projects. But in practice, you will need to refer to the other chapters in this book to complete all of the design, planning and installation work that go into creating a new kitchen.

In this chapter:

- Planning & Designing Kitchens
- Installing Kitchen Cabinets
- Building Kitchen Islands
- Building Tiled Islands
- Installing Postform Countertops
- Installing Laminate Countertops
- Installing Tile on Countertops
- Installing Tile Backsplashes
- Installing Kitchen Sinks
- Replacing Kitchen Faucets
- Connecting Drains
- Hooking Up Dishwashers
- Installing Food Disposers
- Installing Undercabinet Lights

Planning & Designing Kitchens

Your motives for remodeling your kitchen probably fall into one of two categories: efficiency or appearance. In other words, either your kitchen is inconvenient for your family to use, or you just don't like the way it looks. Or maybe it's both dysfunctional and ugly. A logical place to start, then, is by documenting the elements that need improvement.

Begin by simply taking the time to observe how you now use your kitchen. Keep a notepad handy and jot down any major or minor problems and annoyances that prevent you from being as efficient or as comfortable as you'd like to be when cooking or eating. Also consider how your kitchen is used for special occasions and what issues arise at those times. Don't forget to make note of the positives. If you love having that window over your kitchen sink or the skinny cabinet next to the stove, jot down those observations as well.

Once you have documented the problems with your kitchen, give your imagination permission to roam. Don't worry about money yet. This is your dream kitchen, after all, and there will be plenty of time to bring your fantasies down to earth as you begin the planning stages. Now is the time to consider every possibility. Look at friends' kitchens, at magazine kitchens and at model kitchens. When looking at photographs like the ones included in this book, look at both the overall effect and the individual components. Don't let an odd color scheme scare you away from a faucet that you love. Use a file folder to collect pictures of kitchens or items you like. When it comes down to business, you'll have a refined idea of what you're looking for.

If your kitchen needs remodeling, you will know it. The trick in coming up with a workable design for your space is to get past the "ick" factor and really examine what you have to work with. When you assess your cabinets, you may notice immediately that they are very dark and outdated in appearance. But go past that and ask yourself if they are laid out efficiently. Imagine them as brand new cabinets in the same arrangement, and then try and think of ways you could improve the layout. Whether it's with cabinets or countertops or lighting or appliances, consider the components of your kitchen as generic elements.

Special Considerations

If you're going through the trouble of remodeling your kitchen—and the remodel is not solely for resale value—consider making room for some of your own interests and idiosyncrasies. A pull out recycling center with bins for separating different categories is always a smart idea. A built-in beer refrigerator with a custom tap is great for a home-brew enthusiast. A pull out shelf custom-sized to display a selection of tea is perfectly located next to the kettle. Another, perhaps more practical, investment is the careful measurement of counter heights and seat heights to ergonomically suit your personal needs. Finally, consider how your kitchen will be used over the next five to twenty years. The needs of a family with young children are much different than the needs of empty nesters.

It's okay to hang onto elements you love. Even if your favorite pullout shelf or work table or stool doesn't immediately appear to go with the new elements you hope to introduce, as the owner of the kitchen you're allowed to hang onto the things you're used to working with.

Design Standards

While you may imagine that the answer to every cramped kitchen is to knock down walls and add more space, that's often not the easiest or best solution. One alternative to tearing down the walls, is to add more windows for added light. An extra door, or even a pass-through window from the kitchen to an adjacent room, can also help make the space feel more airy. In short, the cramped feeling may only be one of perception.

Most kitchens fall into one of four categories: Galley, L-shaped, U-shaped and Open Plan. Whether they are small or large, old or new, these floor plans have proven to be popular models for efficient kitchens, though that doesn't mean they'll necessarily be the most efficient for your needs.

Galley: In small homes or city apartments, the galley kitchen is a space-saving choice that is ideal for one or two users. The components may all be lined up along one wall or divided between two parallel walls. For this floor plan to work best, the central galley space should be large enough to allow for all appliances to be open at the same time, with enough space remaining for someone to walk through the middle.

L-shape: This corner kitchen layout can feel roomier than it is in reality, because of the L-shape floor plan. However, the two "arms" might also create an awkward workstation, with little room to set items down mid-way through a meal. Consider taking advantage of the lost central space with a counter-height dining table that can double as a prep station or even a freestanding central island.

U-shape: This layout takes the benefits of a galley kitchen—space-saving solution plus accessibility for one user—and adds a third wall to create the ultimate triangular floor plan. In a compact space, placing the sink at the far end with the refrigerator and range on opposing walls creates a simple workstation. On a larger scale, a sizable island can anchor the center of the room and provide more storage.

Open Plan: Whether the kitchen is located in the middle of a larger great room or off to one side, an open plan layout works best with the addition of a central island or a dividing counter of some type. Perfect for family kitchens or entertaining spaces where the cooks can easily visit with guests, it's important for this floor plan to be well organized so that all necessities are close at hand.

Whatever layout plan you opt for, the most fundamental principle that you don't want to violate is to maintain plenty of free area between appliances, sinks and other elements of the work triangle. In a galley kitchen like the one seen here, the corridor between kitchen walls should be at least 4 ft. wide, and preferably wider.

Common Kitchen Layouts

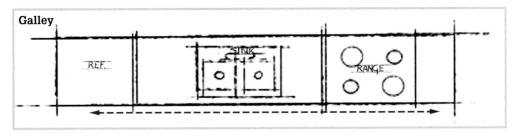

Galley

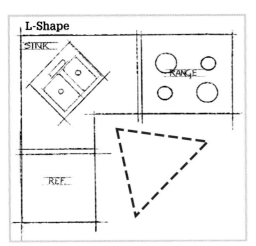

L-Shape

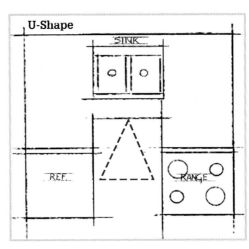

U-Shape

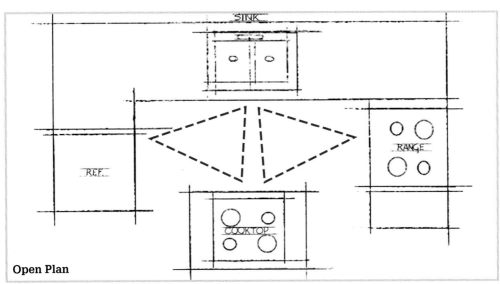

Open Plan

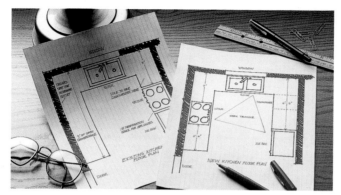

The work triangle is a layout concept that lets you develop a convenient arrangement of the range, sink and refrigerator in the kitchen.

Whether you are doing the work yourself or hiring others, once you have a good idea of the features you want in your new kitchen, it's time to create detailed plan drawings. Good planning drawings will help you in several phases of the planning process:

- Selecting cabinets and appliances to fit your kitchen layout.
- Soliciting accurate work bids when negotiating with plumbers, electricians and other subcontractors.
- Obtaining a building permit at your local Building Inspections office.
- Scheduling the stages of a remodeling project.
- Evaluating the work of contractors. If a carpenter or cabinetmaker fails to meet your expectations, your plan drawings serve as proof that the contractor did not complete the work as agreed.

CODES & STANDARDS

Creating plans for a kitchen can seem like an overwhelming challenge, but fortunately there are guidelines available to help you. Some of these guidelines are legal regulations specified by your local Building Code and must be followed exactly. Most codes have very specific rules for basic construction, as well as for plumbing and electrical installations.

Another set of guidelines, known as standards, are informal recommendations developed over time by kitchen designers, cabinetmakers and appliance manufacturers. These design standards suggest parameters for good kitchen layout, and following them helps ensure that your kitchen is comfortable and convenient to use.

GUIDELINES FOR LAYOUT

The goal of any kitchen layout is to make the cook's work easier and, where possible, to allow other people to enjoy the same space without getting in the way. Understanding the accepted design standards can help you determine whether your present layout is sufficient or if your kitchen needs a more radical layout change or expansion.

Work triangle & traffic patterns. A classic kitchen design concept, the work triangle theory proposes that the sink, range and refrigerator be arranged in a triangular layout according to the following guidelines:

- Position of the triangle should be such that traffic flow will not disrupt the main functions of the kitchen.
- Total distance between the corners of the triangle should be no more than 26 ft. and no less than 12 ft.
- Each side of the triangle should be between 4 and 9 ft. in length.

If two people frequently work in the kitchen simultaneously, the layout should include two work triangles. In a two-triangle kitchen, the triangles may share one side, but they should not cross one another.

Don't fret too much if you can't make the triangle layout work perfectly. Some kitchens, for example, may have four workstations instead of three, and others may not have enough space to accommodate the classic triangle.

For general traffic design, it is recommended to leave 4-ft. "corridors" between all stationary items for walking comfort. Some designers will allow this standard to be reduced to 3 feet in smaller kitchens.

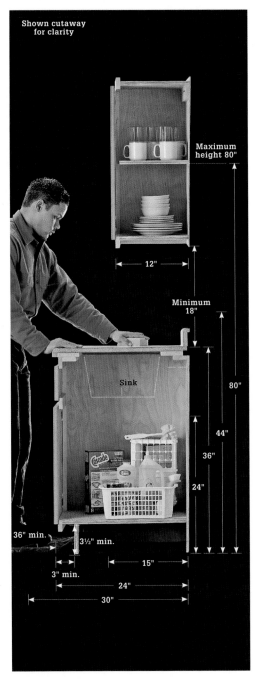

Shown cutaway for clarity

Maximum height 80"

12"

Minimum 18"

Sink

80"

44"

36"

24"

36" min.

3½" min.

15"

3" min.

24"

30"

Dimensions and positions of cabinets follow accepted design standards, as shown here.

The sizes of base cabinets and wall cabinets are fairly uniform among manufacturers, and unless you have them custom-built in unusual sizes, they will conform to the following standards:

- Base cabinets: height—34½"; depth—23" to 24"; width—9" to 48", in 3" increments.
- Wall cabinets: height—12", 15", 18", 24", 30", 33", 42"; depth—12"; width—24", 30", 33", 36", 42", 48".
- Oven cabinets: height—84", 96"; depth—24"; width—27", 30", 33".
- Utility cabinets: height—84"; depth—12", 24"; width—18", 24", 36".

Not every manufacturer will offer all these sizes and styles, so it's a good idea to obtain product catalogs when planning the layout of cabinets. Some other tips:

- Use functional corner cabinets rather than "blind" cabinets that provide no access to the corner area.
- Include at least five storage/organizing units, such as swing-out pantry units, appliance garages and specialized drawers or shelves.

Eating areas. Kitchen tabletops and countertops used for dining are generally positioned 30", 36", or 42" above the floor, and the recommended space for each person varies according to the height of the surface.

Islands. A kitchen island should be positioned so there is at least 36" of clear space between the edges of its countertop and surrounding walls or cabinets

GUIDELINES FOR BASIC CONSTRUCTION

Plans for a major remodeling project that involves moving or adding walls, or building a new room addition must accurately show the locations and dimensions of the new walls and all doors and windows. This will allow the construction carpenter to give you an accurate bid on the work and will allow him to obtain the necessary building permits. If you will be moving walls or adding windows or doors, you must identify load-bearing walls and provide appropriate support during removal and rebuilding.

WINDOWS

Most Building Codes require that kitchens have at least one window, with at least 10 sq. ft. of glass area. Some local Building Codes, however, will allow windowless kitchens, so long as they have proper venting. Kitchen designers recommend that kitchens have windows, doors or skylights that together have a total glass surface area equal to at least 25% of the total floor area.

DOORS

Exterior entry doors should be at least 3 ft. wide and 6½ ft. high. Interior passage doors between rooms must be at least 2½ ft. wide. A kitchen must have at least two points of entry, arranged so traffic patterns don't intrude on work areas.

Examine your circuit breaker panel. It may have an index that identifies circuits serving the kitchen. If your service panel has open slots, an electrician can add additional kitchen circuits relatively easily. If your service panel is full, he may have to install a new service panel at additional cost.

GUIDELINES FOR ELECTRICAL SERVICE & LIGHTING

Nearly any kitchen-remodeling project will require some upgrading of the electrical service. While your old kitchen may be served by a single 120-volt circuit, it's not uncommon for a large modern kitchen to require as many as seven individual circuits. And in a few cases, the extra demands of the new kitchen may require that the main electrical service for your entire house be upgraded by an electrician. By comparing the electrical service in your present kitchen with the requirements described below, you'll get an idea of how extensive your electrical service improvements will need to be. Your plan drawings should indicate the locations of all the outlets, lighting fixtures and electrical appliances in your new kitchen.

The National Electric Code requires the following for kitchens:

- Two small-appliance circuits (120-volt, 20-amp) to supply power for the plug-in countertop appliances.
- Wall outlets spaced no more than 12 ft. apart.
- Countertop outlets spaced no more than 4 ft. apart.
- GFCI (ground-fault circuit interrupter), protected receptacles installed in any general use outlet, whether above counter or at floor level.
- Dedicated circuits for each major appliance. Install a 20-amp, 120-volt circuit for a built-in microwave, a 15-amp circuit for the dishwasher and food disposer. An electrical range, cooktop or wall oven requires a dedicated 50-amp, 240-volt circuit.

The Electric Code only requires that a kitchen have some form of lighting controlled by a wall switch, but kitchen designers have additional recommendations:

- A general lighting circuit (120-volt, 15-amp) that operates independently from plug-in outlets.
- Plentiful task lighting, usually mounted under wall cabinets or soffits, to illuminate each work area.
- Decorative lighting fixtures to highlight attractive cabinets or other features of the kitchen.

GUIDELINES FOR PLUMBING

If your new kitchen layout changes the location of the sink, or if you are planning to add an additional sink or dishwasher, the water supply and drain pipes will need to be upgraded. Your plan drawings should indicate these intended changes.

Extending plumbing lines for a new kitchen is often fairly easy and surprisingly inexpensive, but there are some exceptions you should note:

Old pipes. If your present plumbing is more than 25 years old, there is a good chance the plumber will recommend replacing the pipes before installing the kitchen fixtures. Depending on circumstances, this can be an expensive proposition, but if you're faced with this decision, we strongly urge you to take a deep breath and do what the plumber suggests. Those corroded old pipes will need to be replaced someday, and this work is easier and cheaper if you're already in the process of remodeling the kitchen.

Outdated systems. Older plumbing systems may have drain trap and vent arrangements that violate modern Code requirements. If your plumber needs to run all-new vent pipes, this will increase the costs.

Island sinks. If your new kitchen will include an island sink, your plumber will need to run vent pipes beneath the floor. For this reason, plumbing an island sink is more expensive than plumbing a wall sink.

GUIDELINES FOR HEATING, VENTILATION & AIR-CONDITIONING

Your plan drawings should also show the locations of heating/air-conditioning registers or fixtures in your proposed kitchen. If you're planning a cosmetic make-over or a simple layout change, there is a pretty good chance you can get by with the same registers, radiators or heaters found in your present kitchen.

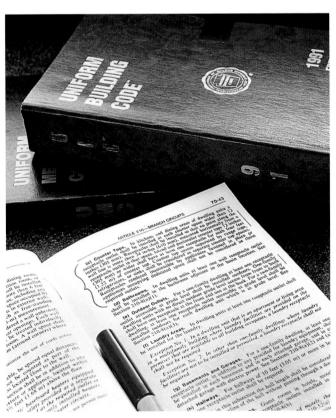

Code books can help you understand the structural, electrical and plumbing requirements for kitchens. In addition to the formal Code books, which are written for professional tradesmen, there are many Code handbooks available that are written for homeowners. Bookstores and libraries carry both the formal Code books and Code handbooks.

But if your new kitchen will be substantially larger than it is now, or if the ratio of wall space filled by glass windows and doors will be greater, it's possible that you'll need to expand its heating and cooling capacity.

Increasing your kitchen's heating and cooling can be as simple as extending ducts by a few feet, or as complicated as installing a new furnace. When installing a large room addition, for instance, you may learn that the present furnace is too small to adequately heat the increased floor space of your home.

How do you determine what your kitchen needs in the way of expanded heating and cooling? Unless you happen to be a mechanical engineer, you'll need to consult a professional to evaluate your heating/ventilation/air-conditioning (HVAC) system. The Code requirements for room heating are quite simple, but the methods used to calculate required energy needs of a room are fairly complex.

The Building Code requires simply that a room must be able to sustain a temperature of 70°F, measured at a point 3 ft. above the floor. HVAC contractors use a complicated formula to calculate the most efficient way to meet this Code requirement. You can make this estimation more accurate by providing the following information:

- The exact dimensions of your kitchen.
- The thickness and amount of insulation in the walls.
- The number of doors and windows, including their size and their energy ratings.
- The total square footage of your house.
- The heating and cooling capacity of your furnace and central air-conditioner, measured in BTUs.

This information, usually printed on the unit's access panel, will help the HVAC contractor determine if the system can adequately serve your new kitchen.

Finally, your cooktop should be equipped with an electric vent hood to exhaust cooking fumes and moisture from the kitchen. The volume of air moved by a vent fan is restricted by Code, so you should always check with a Building Inspector before selecting a vent hood.

Metal ductwork for the vent hood must be run through an exterior wall or through the ceiling. If your cooktop is located in an island cabinet, a special island vent fan is necessary.

Vent hoods are required by some local codes on all ranges and cooktops. The vent fan exhausts cooking fumes and moisture to the outdoors.

Energy Efficiency

For the sake of both environmental resources and your own budget, selecting a kitchen design that incorporates energy- and water-saving appliances is a good idea. Most of the new appliances on the market are more energy efficient than older models, but the relative quality of their performance varies. Do some comparison-shopping when it comes to appliances and you are sure to outfit your kitchen with fixtures that save energy and money.

Lighting is another way to save energy. Consider the aesthetic benefits of adding a skylight or window to your kitchen; now think of the impact that natural lighting will have on your energy budget. Less artificial light will be needed, thus lowering electric bills.

Another way to cut down on energy requirements is to use fluorescent lighting or new innovations like LED lighting in the kitchen. These products not only reduce glare better than incandescent bulbs, they also use a fraction of the energy used by incandescent bulbs and need to be replaced less frequently. Newer versions of fluorescent bulbs produce a more true-to-life light color, rather than the old buzzing overhead tubes that gave everything a greenish hue. Some local building codes require a certain percentage of a kitchen's lighting to be fluorescent, so consider the benefits before lamenting this ordinance.

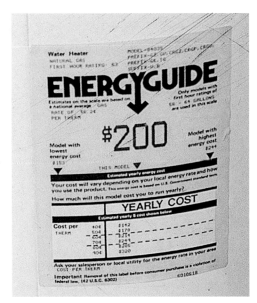

Energy usage labels can be found on most major appliances you'll encounter at the appliance store. More energy efficient models may qualify for a rebate from your local public utility company. Ask the sales staff for information on these programs.

As a general rule, newer appliances are more efficient when it comes to energy and water consumption. For example, this dishwasher has a feature that allows the user to wash only one of the racks, using less water and energy when smaller loads are being cleaned.

Accessible Kitchens ▶

Universal Design and Accessible Design are the terms used by architects, engineers, and product designers to describe making accommodations for the needs of every type of person, regardless of age and physical ability. For example, large handled tools, contrasting typeface, wide doorways, and smooth flooring are all results of Universal Design research. In the kitchen, the consideration of accessibility must be more extensive than almost anywhere else in the home. From safety lighting, to pull out shelves, to the height of counters, planning a kitchen that everyone can easily use requires careful forethought. There are tips on Universal Design throughout this book, offering advice on accessibility for many of the standard kitchen elements.

Universal design for kitchen cabinets puts the majority of items in the comfortable reach zone between 2 and 5 feet above the floor. Using pop-up and pull-down shelves can extend this area. Full-extension hardware on drawers and pull-out shelves eliminates reaching and fumbling for unseen items at the back of drawers and cabinets. Base cabinets installed at various heights serve users of different heights. Hanging some sections of upper cabinets at 12" to 15" above the countertop—rather than 18"—makes it easier to see and access items.

A full-length pantry also increases the amount of storage space in the comfortable reach zone. A pull-out pantry allows for easier viewing of the contents, but make sure the hardware is top quality and operates easily and smoothly. An appliance garage, a cabinet with a tambour door that sits on the countertop, is an excellent way to efficiently use corner space and store heavy or frequently used appliances out of sight. Make sure an electrical outlet or two are inside the garage.

UNIVERSAL TIPS

- Magnetic touch latches or c-shaped handles are the easiest to open.
- Avoid gloss cabinet finishes to reduce glare for the vision impaired.
- Countertops at a variety of heights should be ergonomically correct for a range of different users.

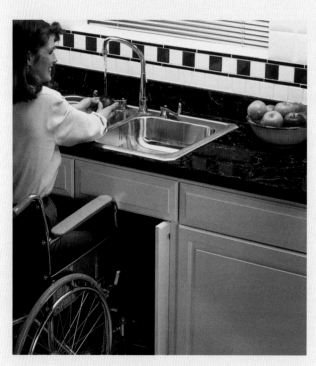

Countertop height and ease of fixture operation are two of the most important aspects of universal design. If your kitchen remodeling project needs to accommodate a person with special needs, most states have agencies that can offer you specific advice for your situation.

Universal Design

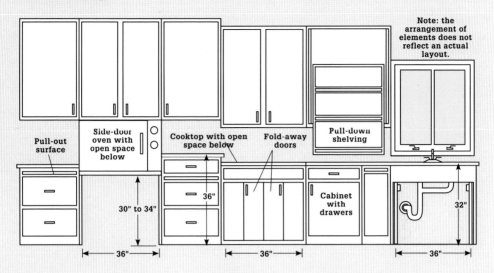

Note: the arrangement of elements does not reflect an actual layout.

Pull-out surface

Side-door oven with open space below

Pull-out surface

Cooktop with open space below

Fold-away doors

Pull-down shelving

30" to 34"

36"

Cabinet with drawers

32"

36"

36"

36"

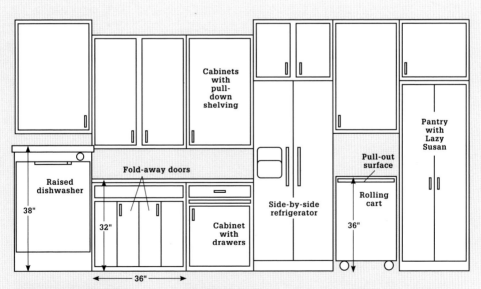

Cabinets with pull-down shelving

Pantry with Lazy Susan

Pull-out surface

Raised dishwasher

Fold-away doors

38"

32"

Cabinet with drawers

Side-by-side refrigerator

Rolling cart

36"

36"

Design your kitchen around a clear, circular space of at least 5 ft. in diameter to provide room for a wheelchair. If your kitchen doesn't have 60" of clear space, allow 48" for pathways. Plan for 30 to 48" of clear approach space in front of all appliances and workstations.

Installing Kitchen Cabinets

Cabinets must be firmly anchored to wall studs, and they must be plumb and level when installed. The best way to ensure this is by attaching a ledger board to the wall to assist in the installation. As a general rule, install the upper cabinets first so your access is not impeded by the base cabinets. (Although some pros prefer to install the base cabinets first so they can be used to support the uppers during installation.) It's also best to begin in a corner and work outward from there.

Tools & Materials ▸

Handscrew clamps
Level
Hammer
Utility knife
Nail set
Stepladder
Drill
Counterbore drill bit
Cordless screwdriver
Jigsaw

Cabinets
Trim molding
Toe-kick molding
Filler strips
Valance
6d finish nails
Finish washers
#10 × 4" wood screws
#8 × 2½" screws
3" drywall screws

Stock cabinets are sold in boxes that are keyed to door and drawer packs (you need to buy these separately). It is important that you realize this when you are estimating your project costs at the building center (often a door pack will cost as much or more than the cabinet). Allow plenty of time for assembling the cabinets out of the box. It can take an hour or more to put some more complex cabinets together.

How to Fit a Corner Cabinet ▸

Before installation, test-fit corner and adjoining cabinets to make sure doors and handles do not interfere with each other. If necessary, increase the clearance by pulling the corner cabinet away from the side wall by no more than 4". To maintain even spacing between the edges of the doors and the cabinet corner, cut a filler strip and attach it to the corner cabinet or the adjoining cabinet. Filler strips should be made from material that matches the cabinet doors and face frames.

How to Prepare Walls

1

Find high and low spots on wall surfaces, using a long, straight 2 × 4. Sand down any high spots.

2

Fill in low spots of wall by applying wallboard compound using a taping knife. Let the compound dry, and then sand it lightly.

3

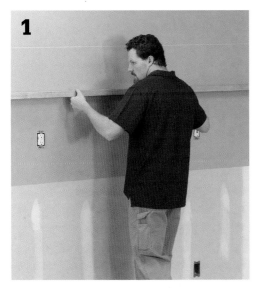

Locate and mark wall studs, using an electronic stud finder. Cabinets normally will be hung by driving screws into the studs through the back of the cabinets.

4

Find the highest point along the floor that will be covered by base cabinets. Place a level on a long, straight 2 × 4, and move the board across the floor to determine if the floor is uneven. Mark the wall at the high point.

(continued)

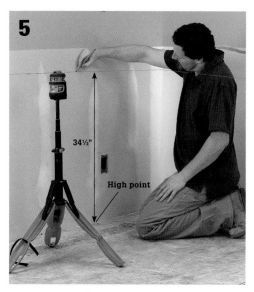

Measure up 34½" from the high-point mark (for standard cabinets). Use a level (a laser level is perfect) to mark a reference line on walls. Base cabinets will be installed with top edges flush against this line.

Measure up 84" from the high-point mark and draw a second reference line. Wall cabinets will be installed with their top edges flush against this line.

Measure down 30" from the wall-cabinet reference line and draw another level line where the bottoms of the cabinets will be. Temporary ledgers will be installed against this line.

Install 1 × 3 temporary ledgers with top edges flush against the reference lines. Attach ledgers with 2½" wallboard screws driven into every other wall stud. Mark stud locations on ledgers. Cabinets will rest temporarily on ledgers during installation (the ledgers alone will not support them, however).

How to Hang Wall Cabinets

1

Position a corner upper cabinet on a ledger (see page 352) and hold it in place, making sure it is resting cleanly on the ledger. Drill ³/₁₆" pilot holes into the wall studs through the hanging strips at the top, rear of cabinet. Attach the cabinet to the wall with 2½" screws. Do not tighten fully until all cabinets are hung.

2

Filler strip

Attach a filler strip to the front edge of the cabinet, if needed (see page 350). Clamp the filler in place, and drill counterbored pilot holes through the cabinet face frame, near hinge locations. Attach filler to cabinet with 2½" cabinet screws or flathead wood screws.

3

Position the adjoining cabinet on the ledger, tight against the corner cabinet or filler strip. Clamp the corner cabinet and the adjoining cabinet together at the top and bottom. Handscrew clamps will not damage wood face frames.

4

Check the front cabinet edges or face frames for plumb. Drill ³/₁₆" pilot holes into wall studs through hanging strips in rear of cabinet. Attach cabinet with 2½" screws. Do not tighten wall screws fully until all cabinets are hung.

(continued)

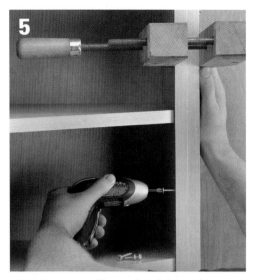

5

Attach the corner cabinet to the adjoining cabinet.
From inside corner cabinet, drill pilot holes through face frame.
Join cabinets with sheet-metal screws.

6

Position and attach each additional cabinet. Clamp
frames together, and drill counterbored pilot holes through
side of face frame. Join cabinets with wood screws. Drill ³⁄₁₆"
pilot holes in hanging strips, and attach cabinet to studs with
wood screws.

7

Join frameless cabinets with #8 × 1¼" panhead wood
screws or wood screws with decorative washers. Each pair of
cabinets should be joined by at least four screws.

8

Fill gaps between the cabinet and wall or neighboring
appliance with a filler strip. Cut the filler strip to fit the space,
then wedge wood shims between the filler and the wall to
create a friction fit that holds it in place temporarily. Drill
counterbored pilot holes through the side of the cabinet (or the
edge of the face frame) and attach filler with screws.

9

Remove the temporary ledger. Check the cabinet run for plumb, and adjust if necessary by placing wood shims behind cabinet, near stud locations. Tighten wall screws completely. Cut off shims with utility knife.

10

Use trim moldings to cover any gaps between cabinets and walls. Stain moldings to match cabinet finish.

11

Attach decorative valance above sink. Clamp valance to edge of cabinet frames, and drill counterbored pilot holes through cabinet frames into end of valance. Attach with sheet-metal screws.

12

Install the cabinet doors. If necessary, adjust the hinges so that the doors are straight and plumb.

How to Install Base Cabinets

1

Begin the installation with a corner cabinet. Draw plumb lines that intersect the 34½" reference line (measured from the high point of the floor—see page 351) at the locations for the cabinet sides.

2

Place cabinet in corner. Make sure the cabinet is plumb and level. If necessary, adjust by driving wood shims under cabinet base. Be careful not to damage flooring. Drill ³⁄₁₆" pilot holes through the hanging strip and into wall studs. Tack the cabinet to the wall with wood screws or wallboard screws.

3

Clamp the adjoining cabinet to the corner cabinet. Make sure the new cabinet is plumb, then drill counterbored pilot holes through the cabinet sides or the face frame and filler strip. Screw the cabinets together. Drill ³⁄₁₆" pilot holes through hanging strips and into wall studs. Tack the cabinets loosely to the wall studs with wood screws or wallboard screws.

4

Use a jigsaw to cut any cabinet openings needed in the cabinet backs (for example, in the sink base seen here) for plumbing, wiring or heating ducts.

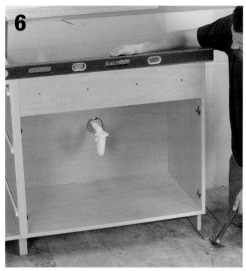

Position and attach additional cabinets, making sure the frames are aligned and the cabinet tops are level. Clamp cabinets together, then attach the face frames or cabinet sides with screws driven into pilot holes. Tack the cabinets to the wall studs, but don't drive screws too tight—you may need to make adjustments once the entire bank is installed.

Make sure all cabinets are level. If necessary, adjust by driving shims underneath cabinets. Place shims behind the cabinets near stud locations to fill any gaps. Tighten wall screws. Cut off shims with utility knife.

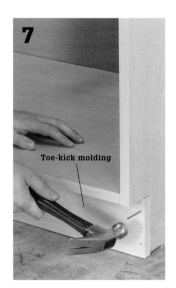

Toe-kick molding

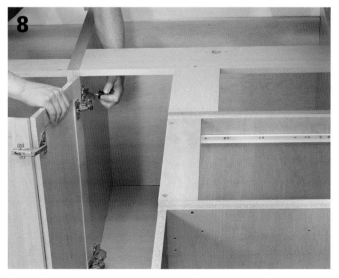

Use trim moldings to cover gaps between the cabinets and the wall or floor. The toe-kick area is often covered with a strip of wood finished to match the cabinets or painted black.

Hang cabinet doors and mount drawer fronts. Test to make sure the drawers close smoothly and the doors fit evenly and flush. Self-closing cabinet hinges (by far the most common type installed today) have adjustment screws that allow you to make minor changes to the hardware to correct any problems.

Building Kitchen Islands

Kitchen islands can be created using a whole range of methods, from repurposing an old table to fine, custom woodworking. But perhaps the easiest (and most failsafe) way to add the conveniences and conviviality of a kitchen island is to make one from stock base cabinets. The cabinets and countertops don't have to match your kitchen cabinetry, but that is certainly an option you should consider. When designing and positioning your new island, be sure to maintain a minimum distance of 3 ft. between the island and other cabinets (4 ft. or more is better).

Tools & Materials ›

Marker
Drill/driver
2 × 4 cleats
Pneumatic nailer
  and 2" finish nails
  or hammer and
  6d finish nails
2 base cabinets
  (approx. 36"
  wide × 24" deep)
Countertop
Wallboard screws

Two base cabinets arranged back-to-back make a sturdy kitchen island base that's easy to install. When made with the same style cabinets and countertops as the rest of the kitchen, the island is a perfect match.

How to Create a Stock-cabinet Island

Set two base cabinets back-to-back in position on the floor and outline the cabinet corners onto the flooring. Remove the cabinets and draw a new outline inside the one you just created to allow for the thickness of the cabinet sides (usually ¾").

Cut 2 × 4 cleats to fit inside the inner outline to provide nailing surfaces for the cabinets. Attach the cleats to the floor with screws or nails. *Tip: Create an L-shape cleat for each inside corner.*

Join the two base cabinets by driving 1¼" wallboard screws through the nailing strips on the backs of the cabinets from each direction. Make sure the cabinet sides are flush and aligned. Lower the base cabinets over the cleats. Check the cabinets for level, and shim underneath the edges of the base if necessary.

Attach the cabinets to the floor cleats using 6d finish nails. Drill pilot holes for nails, and recess nail heads with a nail set. Install a countertop on top of the cabinets (see pages 362 to 385).

Building Tiled Islands

Islands are one of the most requested kitchen features. People love them for many reasons, including their value as bi-level counter space. In most cases, the lower level is used as work space and the upper as casual dining space. The upper level provides a little camouflage for the work space, something that's especially welcome in open-plan kitchens where meal preparation areas can be seen from other areas.

When planning casual dining space, remember that designers suggest at least 24" per person. For the work space, remember that standard design guidelines recommend at least 36" of uninterrupted work space to the side of a sink or cooktop.

On work surfaces, mosaic and other small tile is rarely the best choice. Larger tile requires fewer grout lines, always a good idea when it comes to cleaning and maintenance. But there is no rule that all three elements of a bi-level island have to use the same material. In fact, projects like this offer wonderful opportunities to mix materials or colors or textures. Choose floor tile or tile made especially for counters for the horizontal surfaces, and then branch out when it comes to the backsplash. Wall tile and mosaics work beautifully.

Tools & Materials ▸

Tape measure
Circular saw
Drill
Utility knife
Straightedge
Stapler
Drywall knife
Framing square
Notched trowel
Tile cutter
Carpeted 2 × 4
Mallet
Rubber grout float
Sponge
Foam brush
Caulk gun
Birch plywood
1 × 2 hardwood
2 × 4 lumber
Ceramic tile

Tile spacers
¾" exterior-grade
    (CDX) plywood
4-mil polyethylene
    sheeting
Packing tape
½" cementboard
1¼" deck screws
3" deck screws
Fiberglass mesh tape
Thinset mortar
Grout with latex
    additive
Silicone caulk
Silicone grout sealer
L-brackets
6d finish nails
Drywall screws
Glue

Attractive backsplashes complete tile contertops. Here, individual tiles seamlessly stack side by side to create one cohesive, interwoven pattern. Using the same material and tones as the surrounding countertop allows the pattern to add interest without cluttering the small island, resulting in a sophisticated finished design.

How to Build a Tiled Bi-level Island

Build a 2 × 4 base for the island cabinet by cutting the 2 × 4s to length and joining them in a square frame that lays flat (wide sides down) on the floor. Use metal L-brackets to reinforce the joints. If you don't wish to move the island, fasten the frame to the floor in position with construction adhesive and/or deck screws.

Cut bottom panels the same dimensions as the base frame from ¾" birch plywood. Attach it to the frame with finish nails. Then, cut the side panels to size and shape and fasten them to the edges of the curb with 6d finish nails and adhesive. Slip ¾" shims (scrap plywood works well) beneath the side panels before fastening them.

Cut the 2 × 4 cross supports to length and install them between the side panels at every corner, including the corners created by the L-shape cutout. Use 3" deck screws driven through the side panels and into the ends of the cross supports.

Lightly sand the cabinets and then clean off the dust. Prime and paint the cabinet interior and exterior.

(continued)

Build a face frame from 1 × 2 hardwood to fit the cabinet front. Attach it to the cabinet with 6d finish nails and hang cabinet doors (we installed three 13"-wide overlay doors).

Cut strips of ¾" exterior plywood to make the subbases for the countertops and a backer for the backsplash. The lower counter subbase should over hang by 2" on the front and sides. The upper should overhang 2" on the sides and be centered on the cabinet front to back. Attach the backer and subbases with drywall screws driven down into the 2 × 4 cross supports.

Cut 2" wide strips of plywood for buildup strips and attach to the undersides of the subbases with glue and screws.

Attach tile backerboard to the counter subbases and the backsplash and tape seams and cover screws heads with compound (see page 380).

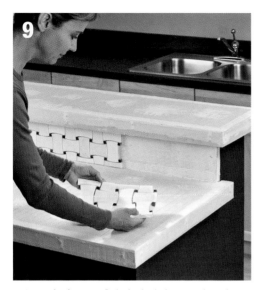

Cut mosaic sheets to fit the backsplash area and attach them with thinset adhesive (see Tiling a Backsplash, page 387).

Cut edge tiles and fasten them around the perimeter of the subbase with thinset adhesive. Hold tiles in place with tape until adhesive sets up. The tiles should be flush or slightly below the bottoms of the buildup strips, and project past the top surfaces so they will be level with the field tiles.

Install the field tiles for the countertops last (see pages 376 to 385).

Choose a suitable grout color and apply it to the tile with a grout float (page 385). Buff off excess once it has dried. Seal the grout with grout sealer.

Installing Postform Countertops

Postform laminate countertops are available in stock and custom colors. Pre-mitered sections are available for two- or three-piece countertops that continue around corners. If the countertop has an exposed end, you will need an endcap kit that contains a preshaped strip of matching laminate. Postform countertops have either a waterfall edge or a no-drip edge. Stock colors are typically available in 4-, 6-, 8-, 10- and 12-foot straight lengths and 6- and 8-foot mitered lengths.

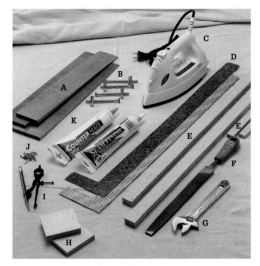

Materials and tools for installing a post-form countertop include: Wood for shimming (A), take-up bolts for drawing miters together (B), household iron (C), endcap laminate to match countertop (D), endcap battens (E), file (F), adjustable wrench (G), buildup blocks (H), compass (I), fasteners (J), silicone caulk and sealer (K).

Post-form countertops are among the easiest and cheapest to install. They are a good choice for beginning DIYers, but the design and color options are fairly limited.

How to Install a Postform Countertop

Tools & Materials ▸

Tape measure
Framing square
Pencil
Straightedge
C-clamps
Hammer
Level
Caulking gun
Jigsaw
Compass
Adjustable wrench

Belt sander
Drill and spade bit
Cordless screwdriver
Postform countertop
Wood shims
Take-up bolts
Drywall screws
Wire brads
Endcap laminate
Silicone caulk
Wood glue

Option: If the saw foot must rest on the good surface of the postform, use a jigsaw fitted with a downstroke blade to cut the postform. If you are unable to locate a downstroke blade, you can try applying tape over the cutting lines, but you are still likely to get tear-out from a normal upstroke jigsaw blade.

1

Use a framing square to mark a cutting line on the bottom surface of the countertop. Cut off the countertop with a jigsaw, using a clamped straight-edge as a guide.

2

Attach the battens from the endcap kit to the edge of the countertop, using carpenter's glue and small brads. Sand out any unevenness with a belt sander.

(continued)

Hold the endcap laminate against the end, slightly overlapping the edges. Activate adhesive by pressing an iron set at medium heat against the endcap. Cool with a wet cloth, then file the endcap laminate flush with the edges of the countertop.

Position the countertop on base cabinets. Make sure the front edge of the countertop is parallel to the cabinet faces. Check the countertop for level. Make sure that drawers and doors open and close freely. If needed, adjust the countertop with shims.

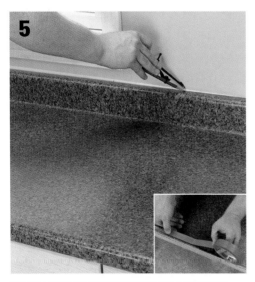

Because walls are usually uneven, use a compass to trace the wall outline onto the backsplash. Set the compass arms to match the widest gap, then move the compass along the length of the wall to transfer the outline to the top of the backsplash. Apply painter's tape to the top edge of the backsplash, following the scribe line (inset).

Remove the countertop. Use a belt sander to grind the backsplash to the scribe line.

Mark cutout for self-rimming sink. Position the sink upside down on the countertop and trace its outline. Remove the sink and draw a cutting line ⅝" inside the sink outline.

Drill a starter hole just inside the cutting line. Make sink cutouts with a jigsaw. Support the cutout area from below so that the falling cutout does not damage the cabinet.

Apply a bead of silicone caulk to the edges of the mitered countertop sections. Force the countertop pieces tightly together.

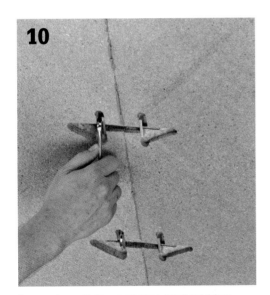

From underneath the countertop, install and tighten miter take-up bolts. Position countertop tightly against the wall and fasten it to the cabinets by driving wallboard screws up through corner brackets and into the countertop. Screws should be long enough to provide maximum holding power, but not long enough to puncture the laminate surface.

Seal the seam between the backsplash and the wall with silicone caulk. Smooth the bead with a wet fingertip. Wipe away excess caulk.

Installing Laminate Countertops

Tools & Materials ▸

Tape measure	Screwdriver
Framing square	Belt sander
Straightedge	File
Scoring tool	Router
Paint roller	¾" particleboard
3-way clamps	Sheet laminate
Caulk gun	Contact cement
J-roller	and thinner
Miter saw	Wood glue
Scribing compass	Drywall screws
Circular saw	

Building your own custom laminate countertop using sheets of plastic laminate and particleboard offers two advantages: the countertop you get will be less expensive than a custom-ordered countertop, and it will allow you more options in terms of colors and edge treatments. A countertop made with laminates also can be tailored to fit any space, unlike premade countertop material that is a standard width (usually 25").

Laminate commonly is sold in 8-ft. or 12-ft. lengths that are about ¹⁄₂₀" thick. In width, they range from 30" strips to 48" sheets. The 30" strips are sized specifically for countertops, allowing for a 25"-wide countertop, a 1½" wide front edge strip and a short backsplash.

The plastic laminate is bonded to the particle-board or MDF substrate with contact cement (although most professional installers use products that are available only to the trades). Water-base contact cement is nonflammable and nontoxic, but solvent-base contact cement (which requires a respirator and is highly flammable) creates a much stronger, more durable bond.

Fabricating your own custom countertop from particleboard and plastic laminate is not exactly an easy DIY project, but it gives you unlimited options and the results can be very satisfying.

Tips for Working with Laminate ▸

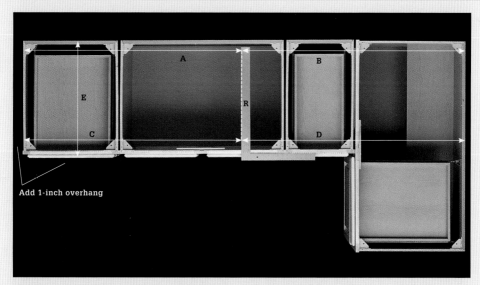

Add 1-inch overhang

Measure along tops of base cabinets to determine the size of the countertop. If wall corners are not square, use a framing square to establish a reference line (R) near the middle of the base cabinets, perpendicular to the front of the cabinets. Take four measurements (A, B, C, D) from the reference line to the cabinet ends. Allow for overhangs by adding 1" to the length for each exposed end, and 1" to the width (E).

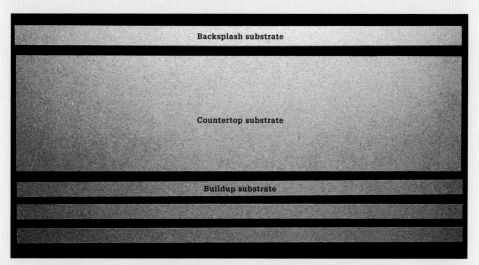

Backsplash substrate

Countertop substrate

Buildup substrate

Lay out cutting lines on the particleboard so you can rip-cut the substrate and build-up strips to size, using a framing square to establish a reference line. Cut core to size using a circular saw with clamped straightedge as a guide. Cut 4" strips of particleboard for backsplash, and for joint support where sections of countertop core are butted together. Cut 3" strips for edge buildups.

How to Create a Laminate Countertop

Join the countertop substrate pieces on the bottom side (see page 369 for sizing and cutting substrate). Attach a 4" particleboard joint support across the seam, using carpenter's glue and 1¼" wallboard screws.

Attach 3"-wide edge buildup strips to the bottom of the countertop, using 1¼" wallboard screws. Fill any gaps on the outside edges with latex wood filler, and then sand the edges with a belt sander.

To determine the size of the laminate top, measure countertop substrate. Laminate seams should not overlap substrate. Add ½" trimming margin to both the length and width of each piece. Measure laminate needed for face and edges of backsplash, and for exposed edges of countertop substrate. Add ½" to each measurement.

4

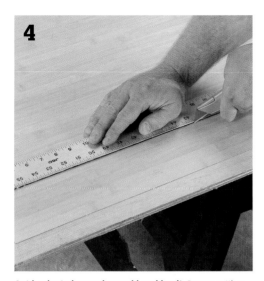

Cut laminate by scoring and breaking it. Draw a cutting line, then etch along the line with a utility knife or other sharp cutting tool. Use a straightedge as a guide. Two passes of scoring tool will help laminate break cleanly.

Option: Some laminate installers prefer to cut laminate with special snips that resemble avaiator snips. Available from laminate suppliers, the snips are faster than scoring and snapping, and less likely to cause cracks or tears in the material. You'll still need to square the cut edges with a trimmer or router.

5

6

Bend laminate toward the scored line until the sheet breaks cleanly. For better control on narrow pieces, clamp a straightedge along scored line before bending laminate. Wear gloves to avoid being cut by sharp edges.

Create tight-piloted seams by using a router and a straight bit to trim edges that will butt together. Measure from cutting edge of the bit to edge of the router baseplate (A). Place laminate on scrap wood and align edges. To guide the router, clamp a straightedge on the laminate at distance A plus ¼", parallel to laminate edge. Trim laminate.

(continued)

Apply laminate to sides of countertop first. Using a paint roller, apply two coats of contact cement to the edge of the countertop and one coat to back of laminate. Let cement dry according to manufacturer's directions. Position laminate carefully, then press against edge of countertop. Bond with J-roller.

Use a router and flush-cutting bit to trim edge strip flush with top and bottom surfaces of countertop substrate. At edges where router cannot reach, trim excess laminate with a file. Apply laminate to remaining edges, and trim with router.

Test-fit laminate top on countertop substrate. Make sure laminate overhangs all edges. At seam locations, draw a reference line on core where laminate edges will butt together. Remove laminate. Make sure all surfaces are free of dust, then apply one coat of contact cement to back of laminate and two coats to substrate. Place spacers made of ¼"-thick scrap wood at 6" intervals across countertop core. Because contact cement bonds instantly, spacers allow laminate to be positioned accurately over core without bonding. Align laminate with seam reference line. Beginning at one end, remove spacers and press laminate to countertop core.

Apply contact cement to remaining substrate and next piece of laminate. Let cement dry, then position laminate on spacers, and carefully align butt seam. Beginning at seam edge, remove spacers and press laminate to the countertop substrate.

Roll the entire surface with a J-roller to bond the laminate to the substrate. Clean off any excess contact cement with a soft cloth and mineral spirits.

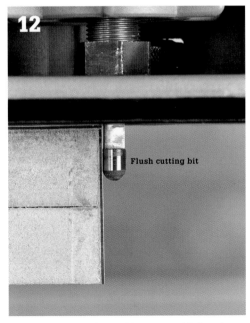

Flush cutting bit

Remove excess laminate with a router and flush-cutting bit. At edges where router cannot reach, trim excess laminate with a file. Countertop is now ready for final trimming with bevel-cutting bit.

(continued)

13

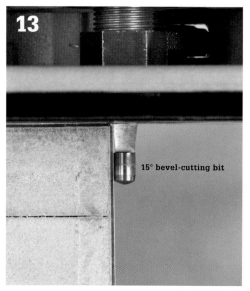

Finish-trim the edges with router and 15° bevel-cutting bit. Set bit depth so that the bevel edge is cut only on top laminate layer. Bit should not cut into vertical edge surface.

Tip ▸

File all edges smooth. Use downward file strokes to avoid chipping the laminate.

14

Cut 1¼"-wide strips of ¼" plywood to form an overhanging scribing strip for the backsplash. Attach to the top and sides of the backsplash substrate with glue and wallboard screws. Cut laminate pieces and apply to exposed sides, top and front of backsplash. Trim each piece as it is applied.

15

Test-fit the countertop and backsplash. Because your walls may be uneven, use a compass to trace the wall outline onto the backsplash scribing strip. Use a belt sander to grind backsplash to scribe line (see page 366).

Apply a bead of silicone caulk to the bottom edge of the backsplash.

Position the backsplash on the countertop, and clamp it into place with bar clamps. Wipe away excess caulk, and let dry completely.

Drive 2" wallboard screws through the countertop and into the backsplash core. Make sure screw heads are countersunk completely for a tight fit against the base cabinet. Install countertops.

Installing Tile on Countertops

Ceramic and porcelain tile remain popular choices for countertops and backsplashes for a number of reasons: It's available in a vast range of sizes, styles and colors; it's durable and repairable; and some tile—not all—is reasonably priced. With careful planning, tile is also easy to install, making a custom countertop a good do-it-yourself project.

The best tile for most countertops is glazed ceramic or porcelain floor tile. Glazed tile is better than unglazed because of its stain resistance, and floor tile is better than wall tile because it's thicker and more durable.

While glazing protects tile from stains, the grout between tiles is still vulnerable because it's so porous. To minimize staining, use a grout that contains a latex additive, or mix the grout with a liquid latex additive. After the grout cures fully, apply a quality grout sealer, and reapply the sealer once a year thereafter. Choosing larger tiles reduces the number of grout lines. Although the selection is a bit limited, if you choose 13" × 13" floor tile, you can span from the front to the back edge of the countertop with a single seam.

The countertop in this project has a substrate of ¾" exterior-grade plywood that's cut to fit and fastened to the cabinets. The plywood is covered with a layer of plastic (for a moisture barrier) and a layer of ½"-thick cementboard. Cementboard is an effective backer for tile because it won't break down if water gets through the tile layer. The tile is adhered to the cementboard with thin-set adhesive. The overall thickness of the finished countertop is about 1½". If you want a thicker countertop, you can fasten an additional layer of plywood (of any thickness) beneath the substrate. Two layers of ¾" exterior-grade plywood without cementboard is also an acceptable substrate.

You can purchase tiles made specifically to serve as backsplashes and front edging. While the color and texture may match, these tiles usually come in only one length, making it difficult to get your grout lines to align with the field tiles. You can solve this problem by cutting your own edging and backsplash tiles from field tiles.

Tools & Materials ▸

Tape measure	Ceramic tile
Circular saw	Tile spacers
Drill	¾" exterior-grade
Utility knife	(CDX) plywood
Straightedge	4-mil polyethylene
Stapler	sheeting
Drywall knife	Packing tape
Framing square	½" cementboard
Notched trowel	1¼" galvanized
Tile cutter	deck screws
Carpeted 2 × 4	Fiberglass mesh tape
Mallet	Thin-set mortar
Rubber grout float	Grout with
Sponge	latex additive
Foam brush	Silicone caulk
Caulk gun	Silicone grout sealer

Ceramic or porcelain makes a durable countertop that is heat-resistant and relatively easy for a DIYer to create. By using larger tiles, you minimize the grout lines (and the cleaning that goes with them).

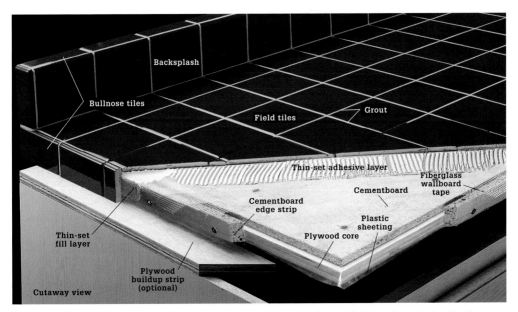

A ceramic tile countertop starts with a core of ¾" exterior-grade plywood that's covered with a moisture barrier of 4-mil polyethylene sheeting. Half-inch cementboard is screwed to the plywood, and the edges are capped with cementboard and finished with fiberglass mesh tape and thin-set mortar. Tiles for edging and backsplashes may be bullnose or trimmed from the factory edges of field tiles.

Options for Backsplashes & Countertop Edges

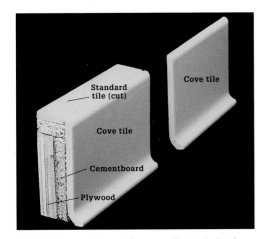

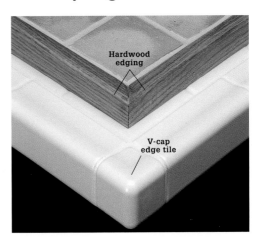

Backsplashes can be made from cove tile attached to the wall at the back of the countertop. You can use the tile alone or build a shelf-type backsplash, using the same construction as for the countertop. Attach the plywood backsplash to the plywood core of the countertop. Wrap the front face and all edges of the plywood backsplash with cementboard before laying tile.

Edge options include V-cap edge tile and hardwood strip edging. V-cap tiles have raised and rounded corners that create a ridge around the countertop perimeter—good for containing spills and water. V-cap tiles must be cut with a tile saw. Hardwood strips should be prefinished with at least three coats of polyurethane finish. Attach the strips to the plywood core so the top of the wood will be flush with the faces of the tiles.

Tips for Laying Out Tile ▸

- You can lay tile over a laminate countertop that's square, level and structurally sound. The laminate cannot have a no-drip edge. Use a belt sander with 60- or 80-grit sandpaper to rough up the surface before setting the tiles. If you're using a new substrate and need to remove your existing countertop, make sure the base cabinets are level front to back, side to side and with adjoining cabinets. If necessary, unscrew a cabinet from the wall and use shims on the floor or against the wall to level it.

- Installing battens along the front edge of the countertop helps ensure the first row of tile is perfectly straight. For V-cap tiles, fasten a 1 × 2 batten along the reference line, using screws. The first row of field tile is placed against this batten. For bullnose tiles, fasten a batten that's the same thickness as the edging tile, plus ⅛" for mortar thickness, to the face of the countertop so the top is flush with the top of the counter. The bullnose tiles are aligned with the outside edge of the batten. For wood edge trim, fasten a 1 × 2 batten to the face of the countertop so the top edge is above the top of the counter. The tiles are installed against the batten.

- Before installing any tile, lay out the tiles in a dry run, using spacers. If your counter is L-shaped, start at the corner and work outward. Otherwise, start the layout at a sink to ensure equal-sized cuts on both sides of the sink. If necessary, shift your starting point so you don't end up cutting very narrow tile segments.

13 × 13" tile   12 × 12" tile   6 × 6" tile   5 × 5" tile   Mosaic tile

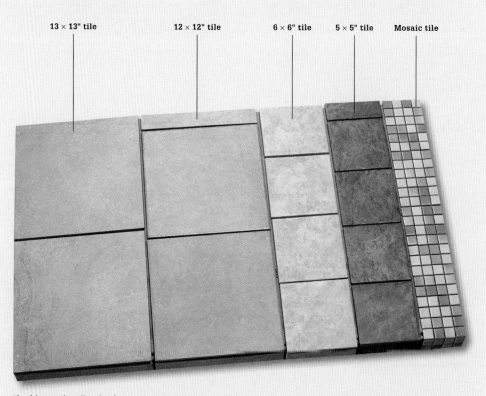

The bigger the tile, the fewer the grout lines. If you want a standard 25"-deep countertop, the only way to get there without cutting tiles is to use mosaic strips or 1" tile. With 13 × 13" tile, you need to trim 1" off the back tile but have only one grout line front to back. As the size of the tile decreases, the number of grout lines increases.

How to Build a Tile Countertop

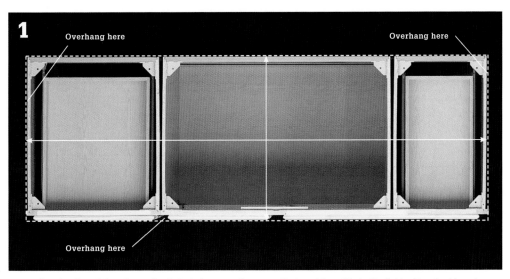

1

Overhang here

Overhang here

Overhang here

Determine the size of the plywood substrate by measuring across the top of the cabinets. The finished top should overhang the drawer fronts by at least ¼". Be sure to account for the thickness of the cementboard, adhesive and tile when deciding how large to make the overhang. Cut the substrate to size from ¾" plywood, using a circular saw. Make cutouts for sinks and other fixtures.

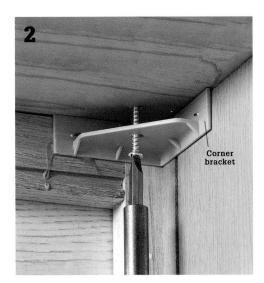

2

Corner bracket

Set the plywood substrate on top of the cabinets, and attach it with screws driven through the cabinet corner brackets. The screws should not be long enough to go through the top of the substrate.

3

Cut cementboard using a straightedge and utility knife or a cementboard cutter with a carbide tip. Hold the straightedge along the cutting line, and score the board several times with the knife. Bend the piece backward to break it along the scored line. Back-cut to finish.

(continued)

Dry-fit cementboard pieces on the plywood core with the rough sides of the panels facing up. Leave a ⅛" gap between the cementboard sheets and a ¼" gap along the perimeter.

Lay the 4-mil plastic moisture barrier over the plywood substrate, draping it over the edges. Tack it in place with a few staples. Overlap seams in the plastic by 6", and seal them with packing tape.

Lay the cementboard pieces rough-side up on the plywood and attach them with cementboard screws driven every 6". Drill pilot holes using a masonry bit, and make sure all screw heads are flush with the surface. Wrap the countertop edges with 1¼"-wide cementboard strips, and attach them to the core with cementboard screws.

Tape all cementboard joints with fiberglass mesh tape. Apply three layers of tape along the front edge where the horizontal cementboard sheets meet the cementboard edging.

8

Fill all gaps and cover all of the tape with a layer of thin-set mortar. Feather out the mortar with a drywall knife to create a smooth, flat surface.

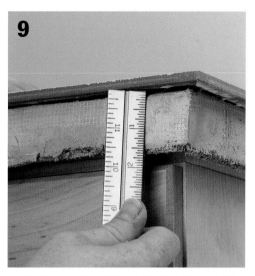

9

Determine the required width of your edge tiles. Lay a field tile onto the tile base so it overhangs the front edge by ½" or so. Then, hold a metal rule up to the underside of the tile and measure the distance from the tile to the bottom of the subbase. Your edge tiles should be cut to this width (the gap for the grout line will cause the edge tile to extend past the subbase, concealing it completely).

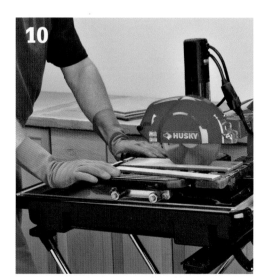

10

Cut your edge tiles to the determined width, using a tile saw. It's worth renting a quality wet saw for tile if you don't own one. Floor tile is thick and difficult to cut with a hand cutter (especially porcelain tiles).

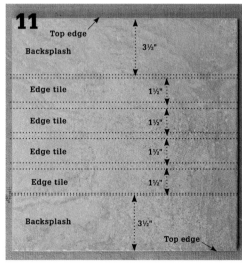

11

Top edge
Backsplash — 3½"
Edge tile — 1½"
Edge tile — 1½"
Edge tile — 1½"
Edge tile — 1½"
Backsplash — 3½"
Top edge

Cut tiles for the backsplash. The backsplash tiles (3½" wide in our project) should be cut with a factory edge on each tile that will be oriented upward when they're installed. You can make efficient use of your tiles by cutting edge tiles from the center area of the tiles you cut to make the backsplash.

(continued)

12

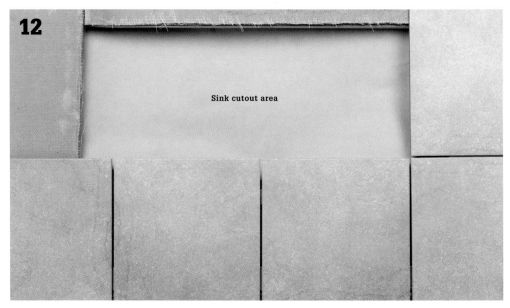

Sink cutout area

Dry-fit tiles on the countertop to find the layout that works best. Once the layout is established, make marks along the vertical and horizontal rows. Draw reference lines through the marks and use a framing square to make sure the lines are perpendicular.

Variation: Laying Out with Small Floor Tiles and Bullnose Edging ▸

Lay out tiles and spacers in a dry run. Adjust starting lines, if necessary. If using battens, lay the field tile flush with the battens, then apply edge tile. Otherwise, install the edging first. If the countertop has an inside corner, start there by installing a ready-made inside corner or cutting a 45° miter in edge tile to make your own inside corner.

Place the first row of field tile against the edge tile, separating the tile with spacers. Lay out the remaining rows of tile. Adjust starting lines if necessary to create a layout using the least number of cut tiles.

13

Use a ⅜" square notched trowel to apply a layer of thinset adhesive to the cementboard. Apply enough for two or three tiles, starting at one end. Hold the trowel at roughly a 30-degree angle and try not to overwork the adhesive or remove too much.

14

Set the first tile into the adhesive. Hold a piece of the edge in tile against the countertop edge as a guide to show you exactly how much the tile should overhang the edge.

15

Cut all the back tiles for the layout to fit (you'll need to remove about 1" of a 13 × 13" tile) before you begin the actual installation. Set the back tiles into the thinset, maintaining the gap for groutlines created by the small spacer nubs cast into the tiles. If your tiles have no spacer nubs, see next step.

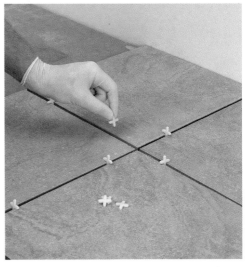

Option: To maintain even grout lines, some beginning tilers insert x-shaped plastic spacers at the joints. This is less likely to be useful with large tiles like those shown here, but it is effective with smaller tile. Many tiles today feature built-in spacing lugs, so the spacers are not necessary. If you use spacers, remove them before the thinset sets. If you leave them in place they will corrupt your grout lines.

(continued)

Variation: To mark border tiles for cutting, allow space for backsplash tiles, grout and mortar by placing a tile against the back wall. Set another tile (A) on top of the last full tile in the field, then place a third tile (B) over tile A and hold it against the upright tile. Mark and cut tile A and install it with the cut edge toward the wall. Finish filling in your field tiles.

To create a support ledge for the edge tiles, prop pieces of 2 × 4 underneath the front edge of the substrate overhang, using wood scraps to prop the ledge tightly up against the substrate.

Apply a thick layer of thinset to the backside of the edge tile with your trowel. This is called "buttering" and it is easier and neater than attempting to trowel adhesive onto the countertop edge. Press the tiles into position so they are flush with the leading edges of the field tiles.

Butter each backsplash tile and press it into place, doing your best to keep all of the grout lines aligned.

19

Mix a batch of grout to complement the tile (keeping in mind that darker grout won't look dirty as quickly as lighter grout). Apply the grout to the grout line areas with a grout float.

20

Let the grout dry until a light film is created on the countertop surface and then wipe off the excess grout using a sponge and warm, clean water.

21

After the grout has dried run a bead of clear silicone caulk along the joint between the backsplash and the wall. Install your sink and faucet.

22

Wait at least one week and then seal the grout lines with a penetrating grout sealer. This is important to do. Sealing the tiles themselves is not a good idea unless you are using unglazed tiles (a poor choice for countertops, however).

Installing Tile Backsplashes

There are few spaces in your home with as much potential for creativity and visual impact as the space between your kitchen countertop and cupboards. A well-designed backsplash can transform the ordinary into the extraordinary.

Tiles for the backsplash can be attached directly to wallboard or plaster and do not require backerboard. When purchasing the tile, order 10 percent extra to cover breakage and cutting. Remove switch and receptacle coverplates and install box extenders to make up for the extra thickness of the tile. Protect the countertop from scratches by covering it with a drop cloth.

Tools & Materials ▸

Level	Straight 1 × 2
Tape measure	Wall tile
Pencil	Tile spacers
Tile cutter	(if needed)
Rod saw	Bullnose trim tile
Notched trowel	Mastic tile adhesive
Rubber grout float	Masking tape
Beating block	Grout
Rubber mallet	Caulk
Sponge	Drop cloth
Bucket	Grout sealer

A tiled backsplash normally extends all the way from countertop to the bottoms of the wall cabinets. The tile pattern also can be extended to the wall underneath your range hood.

Tips for Planning Tile Layouts ▸

Gather planning brochures and design catalogs to help you create decorative patterns and borders for the backsplash.

Break tiles into fragments and make a mosaic backsplash. Always use a sanded grout for joints wider than ⅛".

Add painted mural tiles to create a focal point. Mixing various tile styles adds an appealing contrast.

How to Tile a Backsplash

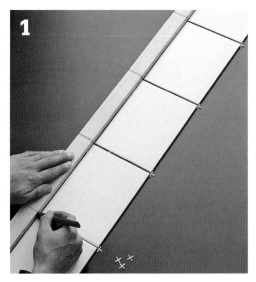

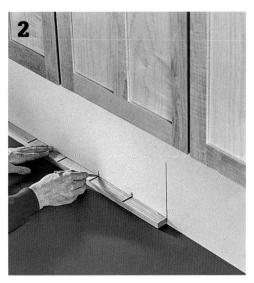

Make a story stick by marking a board at least half as long as the backsplash area to match the tile spacing.

Starting at the midpoint of the installation area, use the story stick to make layout marks along the wall. If an end piece is too small (less than half a tile), adjust the midpoint to give you larger, more attractive end pieces. Use a level to mark this point with a vertical reference line.

While it may appear straight, your countertop may not be level and therefore is not a reliable reference line. Run a level along the counter to find the lowest point on the countertop. Mark a point two tiles up from the low point and extend a level line across the entire work area.

(continued)

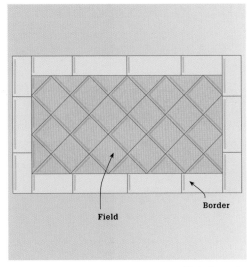

Border

Field

Variation: Diagonal Layout. Mark vertical and horizontal reference lines, making sure the angle is 90°. To establish diagonal layout lines, measure out equal distances from the crosspoint, then connect the points with a line. Additional layout lines can be extended from these as needed. To avoid the numerous, unattractive perimeter cuts common to diagonal layouts, try using a standard border pattern as shown. Diagonally set a field of full tiles, then cut enough half tiles to fill out the perimeter. Finally, border the diagonal field with tiles set square to the field.

4	5	6

Apply mastic adhesive evenly to the area beneath the horizontal reference line, using a notched trowel. Comb the adhesive horizontally with the notched edge.

Starting at the vertical reference line, press tiles into the adhesive using a slight twisting motion. If the tiles are not self-spacing, use plastic spacers to maintain even grout lines. If the tiles do not hang in place, use masking tape to hold them in place until the adhesive sets.

Install a whole row along the reference line, checking occasionally to make sure the tiles are level. Continue installing tiles below the first row, trimming tiles that butt against the countertop as needed.

7

Apply adhesive to an area above the line and continue placing tiles, working from the center to the sides. Install trim tile, such as bullnose tile, to the edges of the rows.

8

When the tiles are in place, make sure they are flat and firmly embedded by laying a beating block against the tile and rapping it lightly with a mallet. Remove the spacers. Allow the mastic to dry for at least 24 hours, or as directed by the manufacturer.

9

Mix the grout and apply it with a rubber grout float. Spread it over the tiles, keeping the float at a low 30° angle, pressing the grout deep into the joints. *Note: For grout joints ⅛" and smaller, be sure to use a non-sanded grout.*

10

Wipe off excess grout, holding the float at a right angle to the tile, working diagonally so as not to remove grout from the joints. Clean any remaining grout from the tiles with a damp sponge, working in a circular motion. Rinse the sponge thoroughly and often.

11

Shape the grout joints by making slow, short passes with the sponge, shaving down any high spots; rinse the sponge frequently. Fill any voids with a fingerful of grout. When the grout has dried to a haze, buff the tile clean with a soft cloth. Apply a bead of caulk between the countertop and tiles. Reinstall any electrical fixtures you removed. After the grout has completely cured, apply grout sealer.

Installing Kitchen Sinks

Most drop-in, self-rimming kitchen sinks are easily installed.

Drop-in sinks for do-it-yourself installation are made from cast iron coated with enamel, stainless steel, enameled steel, acrylic, fiberglass or resin composites. Because cast-iron sinks are heavy, their weight holds them in place and they require no mounting hardware. Except for the heavy lifting, they are easy to install. Stainless steel and enameled-steel sinks weigh less than cast-iron and most require mounting brackets on the underside of the countertop. Some acrylic and resin sinks rely on silicone caulk to hold them in place.

If you are replacing a sink but not the countertop, make sure the new sink is the same size or larger. All old silicone caulk residue must be removed with acetone or denatured alcohol, or the new caulk will not stick.

Shopping Tips ▸

- When purchasing a sink you also need to buy strainer bodies and baskets, sink clips and a drain trap kit.
- Look for basin dividers that are lower than the sink rim—this reduces splashing.
- Drain holes in the back or to the side leave more usable space under the sink.
- When choosing a sink, make sure the predrilled openings will fit your faucet.

Tools & Materials ▸

Caulk gun	Plumber's putty
Spud wrench	or silicone caulk
Screwdriver	Mounting clips
Sink	Jigsaw
Sink frame	Pen or pencil

Drop-in sinks, also known as self-rimming sinks, have a wide sink flange that extends beyond the edges of the sink cutout. They also have a wide back flange to which the faucet is mounted directly.

How to Install a Self-rimming Sink

1

Invert the sink and trace around the edges as a reference for making the sink cutout cutting lines, which should be parallel to the outlines, but about 1" inside of them to create a 1" ledge. If your sink comes with a template for the cutout, use it.

2

Drill a starter hole and cut out the sink opening with a jigsaw. Cut right up to the line. Because the sink flange fits over the edges of the cutout, the opening doesn't need to be perfect, but as always you should try to do a nice, neat job.

3

Attach as much of the plumbing as makes sense to install prior to setting the sink into the opening. Having access to the underside of the flange is a great help when it comes to attaching the faucet body, sprayer and strainer, in particular.

4

Apply a bead of silicone caulk around the edges of the sink opening. The sink flange most likely is not flat, so try and apply the caulk in the area that will make contact with the flange.

5

Place the sink in the opening. Try and get the sink centered right away so you don't need to move it around and disturb the caulk, which can break the seal. If you are installing a heavy cast-iron sink, it's best to leave the strainers off so you can hold the sink at the drain openings.

6

For sinks with mounting clips, tighten the clips from below using a screwdriver or wrench (depending on the type of clip your sink has). There should be at least three clips on every side. Don't overtighten the clips—this can cause the sink flange to flatten or become warped.

Replacing Kitchen Faucets

Most new kitchen faucets feature single-handle control levers and washerless designs that rarely require maintenance. Additional features include brushed metallic finishes, detachable spray nozzles, or even push-button controls.

Connect the faucet to hot and cold water lines with easy-to-install flexible supply tubes made from vinyl or braided steel. If your faucet has a separate sprayer, install the sprayer first. Pull the sprayer hose through the sink opening and attach to the faucet body before installing the faucet.

Tools & Materials ▸

Adjustable wrench
Basin wrench or
  channel-type pliers
Hacksaw
Faucet
Putty knife
Screwdriver
Silicone caulk
Scouring pad
Scouring cleaner
Plumber's putty
Flexible vinyl or
  braided steel
  supply tubes
Drain components
Penetrating oil

Where local codes allow, use plastic tubes for drain hookups. A wide selection of extensions and angle fittings lets you easily plumb any sink configuration. Manufacturers offer kits that contain all the fittings needed for attaching a food disposer or dishwasher to the sink drain system.

Modern kitchen faucets tend to be single-handle models, often with useful features such as a pull-out head that functions as a sprayer. This Price Pfister™ model comes with an optional mounting plate that conceals sink holes when mounted on a predrilled sink flange.

Choosing a New Kitchen Faucet

When choosing a new kitchen faucet, you'll find many options. The best place to start the process is with your sink. In the past, most faucets were mounted directly to the sink deck, which had three or four predrilled holes to accommodate the faucets, spout, sprayer and perhaps a liquid soap dispenser or an air gap for your dishwasher. Modern kitchen faucets don't always conform to this set-up, with many of them designed to be installed in a single hole in the sink deck or in the countertop. If you plan to keep your old sink, look for a faucet that won't leave empty holes in the deck. You can buy snap-in plugs to fill unfilled stainless steel sink holes, or you can add a soap dispenser, but in general you'll have the best luck if you replace like for like.

The two most basic kitchen faucet categories are one-handle and two-handle. One handled models are much more popular now because you can adjust the water temperature easily with just one hand. Another difference is in the faucet body. Some faucets have the taps and the spout mounted onto a faucet body so the spacing between the tailpieces is preset. Others, called widespread faucets, have independent taps and spouts that can be configured however you please, as long as the tubes connecting the taps to the spout reach. This type is best if you are installing the faucet in the countertop (a common way to go about it with new countertops such as solid surface, quartz or granite).

In the past, kitchen faucets almost always had remote pull-out sprayers. The sprayer was attached to the faucet body with a hose directly below the mixing valve. While this type of sprayer is still fairly common, many faucets today have an integral pull-out spout that is very convenient and less prone to failure than the old-style sprayers.

A single-handle, high arc faucet with traditional remote sprayer. The mounting plate is decorative and optional.

Single-handle faucets may require four holes, as does this model with its side sprayer and matching soap/lotion dispenser.

Two-handled faucets are less common, but remain popular choices for traditional kitchens. The gooseneck spout also has a certain elegance, but avoid this type if you have a shallow sink that's less than 8" deep.

A single-handle faucet with pull-out spray head requires only one hole in your sink deck or countertop—a real benefit if your sink is not predrilled or if it is an undermount model.

How to Remove an Old Faucet

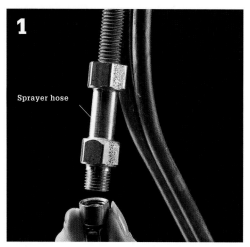

To remove the old faucet, start by clearing out the cabinet under the sink and laying down towels. Turn off the hot and cold stop valves and open the faucet to make sure the water is off. Detach the sprayer hose from the faucet sprayer nipple and unscrew the retaining nut that secures the sprayer base to the sink deck. Pull the sprayer hose out through the sink deck opening.

Spray the mounting nuts that hold the faucet or faucet handles (on the underside of the sink deck) with penetrating oil for easier removal. Let the oil soak in for a few minutes.

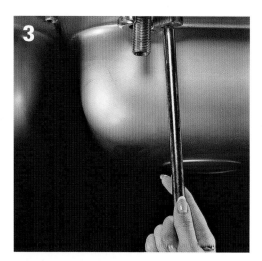

Unhook the supply tubes at the stop valves. Don't reuse old chrome supply tubes. If the stops are missing or unworkable, replace them. Then remove the coupling nuts and the mounting nuts on the tailpieces of the faucet with a basin wrench or channel-type pliers.

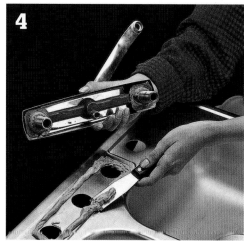

Pull the faucet body from the sink. Remove the sprayer base if you wish to replace it. Scrape off old putty or caulk with a putty knife and clean off the sink with a scouring pad and an acidic scouring cleaner like Bar Keeper's Friend®. *Tip: Scour stainless steel with a back and forth motion to avoid leaving unsightly circular markings.*

How to Install a Kitchen Sink Faucet

Shut off hot and cold water at the faucet stop valves.
Assemble the parts of the deck plate that cover the outer mounting holes in your sink deck (unless you are installing a two-handle faucet, or mounting the faucet directly to the countertop, as in an undermount sink situation). Add a ring of plumber's putty in the groove on the underside of the base plate.

Set the base plate onto the sink flange so it is correctly aligned with the predrilled holes in the flange. From below, tighten the wing nuts that secure the deck plate to the sink deck.

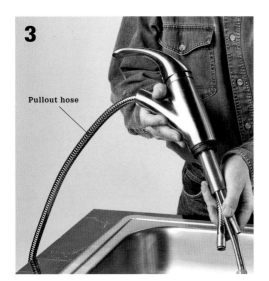

Retract the pullout hose by drawing it out through the faucet body until the fitting at the end of the hose is flush with the bottom of the threaded faucet shank. Insert the shank and the supply tubes down through the top of the deck plate.

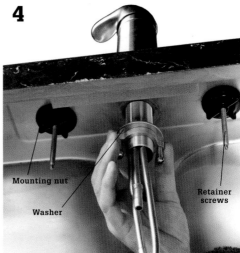

Slip the mounting nut and washer over the free ends of the supply tubes and pullout hose, then thread the nut onto the threaded faucet shank. Hand tighten. Tighten the retainer screws with a screwdriver to secure the faucet.

(continued)

Slide the hose weight onto the pullout hose (the weight helps keep the hose from tangling and makes it easier to retract the hose).

Connect the end of the pullout tube to the outlet port on the faucet body using a quick connector fitting.

Hook up the water supply tubes to the faucet inlets. Make sure the lines are long enough to reach the supply risers without stretching or kinking.

Water supply tube

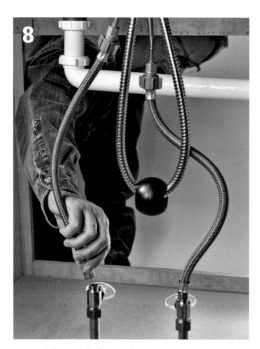

Connect the supply lines to the supply risers at the stop valves. Make sure to get the hot lines and cold lines attached correctly.

Attach the spray head to the end of the pullout hose and turn the fitting to secure the connection. Turn on water supply and test. *Tip: Remove the aerator in the tip of the spray head and run hot and cold water to flush out any debris.*

Variation: One-piece Faucet with Sprayer ▸

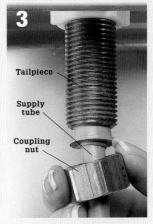

Apply a thick bead of silicone caulk to the underside of the faucet base, then insert the tailpieces of the faucet through the appropriate holes in the sink deck. Press down lightly on the faucet to set it in the caulk.

Slip a friction washer onto each tailpiece and then hand-tighten a mounting nut. Tighten the mounting nut with channel-type pliers or a basin wrench. Wipe up any silicone squeeze-out on the sink deck with a wet rag before it sets up.

Connect supply tubes to the faucet tailpieces—make sure the tubes you buy are long enough to reach the stop valves and that the coupling nuts will fit the tubes and tailpieces.

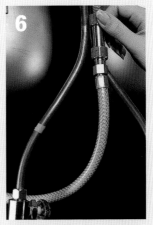

Apply a ¼" bead of plumber's putty or silicone caulk to the underside of the sprayer base. With the base threaded onto the sprayer hose, insert the tailpiece of the sprayer through the opening in the sink deck.

From beneath, slip the friction washer over the sprayer tailpiece and then screw the mounting nut onto the tailpiece. Tighten with channel-type pliers or a basin wrench. Wipe any excess putty or caulk on the sink deck from around the base.

Screw the sprayer hose onto the hose nipple on the bottom of the faucet. Hand-tighten and then give the nut one quarter turn with pliers or a basin wrench. Turn on the water supply at the shutoff, remove the aerator and flush debris from the faucet.

Connecting Drains

Kitchen sink drains don't last forever, but they're very easy and inexpensive to replace. The most common models today are made of PVC plastic pipe and fittings held together with slip fittings. In addition to making the installation fairly forgiving, the slip fitting makes the drain easy to disassemble if it gets clogged. The project shown here is a bit unusual by today's standards, in that it does not include either a dishwasher drain or a garbage disposer. But you will see how to add each of these drain systems to your kitchen sink in the following two sections.

You can buy the parts for the kitchen drain individually (you can usually get better quality materials this way) or in a kit (see photo, next page). Because most kitchen sinks have two bowls, the kits include parts for plumbing both drains into a shared trap, often with a baffle in the T-fitting where the outlet line joins with the tailpiece from the other bowl. If you are installing a disposer, consider installing individual traps to eliminate the baffle, which reduces the flow capacity by half.

Tools & Materials ▸

Flat screwdriver	Teflon tape
Spud wrench	Washers
Trap arm	Waste-T fitting
Mineral spirits	S- or P-trap
Cloth	
Strainer kit	
Plumber's putty	

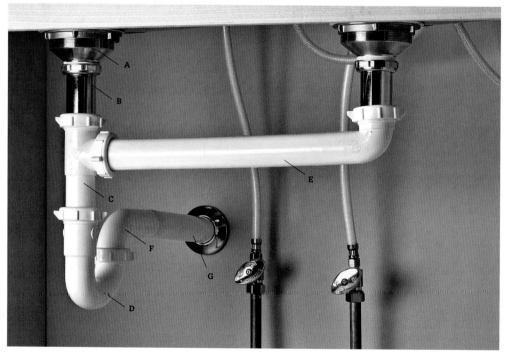

Kitchen sink drains include a strainer basket (A), tailpiece (B), continuous waste T (C), P- or S-trap (D), outlet drain lines (E), trap arm (F), and wall stubout (G).

Drain Kits ▸

Kits for installing a new sink drain include all the pipes, slip fittings, and washers you'll need to get from the sink tailpieces (most kits are equipped for a double bowl kitchen sink) to the trap arm that enters the wall or floor. For wall trap arms, you'll need a kit with a P-trap. For floor drains, you'll need an S-trap. Both drains normally are plumbed to share a trap. Chromed brass or PVC with slip fittings let you adjust the drain more easily and pull it apart and then reassemble if there is a clog. Kitchen sink drains and traps should be 1½" o.d. pipe—the 1¼" pipe is for lavatories and doesn't have enough capacity for a kitchen sink.

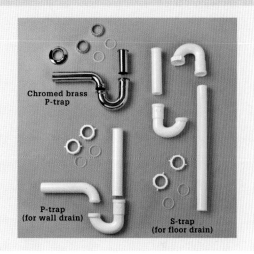

Chromed brass P-trap

P-trap (for wall drain)

S-trap (for floor drain)

Tips for Choosing Drains ▸

Wall thickness varies in sink drain pipes. The thinner plastic material is cheaper and more difficult to obtain a good seal with than the thicker, more expensive tubing. The thin product is best reserved for lavatory drains, which are far less demanding.

Slip joints are formed by tightening a male-threaded slip nut over a female-threaded fitting, trapping and compressing a beveled nylon washer to seal the joint.

Use a spud wrench to tighten the strainer body against the underside of the sink bowl. Normally, the strainer flange has a layer of plumber's putty between it and the sink drain, and a pair of washers (one rubber, one fibrous) below.

How to Hook Up a Kitchen Sink Drain

If you are replacing the sink strainer body, remove the old one and clean the top and bottom of the sink deck around the drain opening with mineral spirits. Attach the drain tailpiece to the threaded outlet of the strainer body, inserting a nonbeveled washer between the parts, if your strainer kits include one. Lubricate the threads or apply Teflon tape so you can get a good, snug fit.

Apply plumber's putty around the perimeter of the drain opening and seat the strainer assembly into it. Add washers below as directed and tighten the strainer locknut using a spud wrench (see photo, previous page) or striking the mounting nubs at the top of the body with a flat screwdriver.

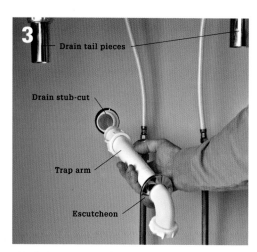

Drain tail pieces

Drain stub-cut

Trap arm

Escutcheon

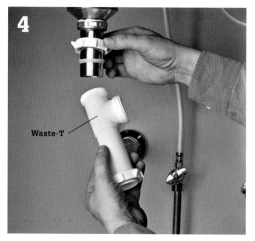

Waste-T

Attach the trap arm to the male-threaded drain stubout in the wall, using a slip nut and beveled compression washer. The outlet for the trap arm should point downward. *Note: The trap arm must be higher on the wall than any of the horizontal lines in the set-up, including lines to dishwasher, disposer, or the outlet line to the second sink bowl.*

Attach a waste-T-fitting to the drain tailpiece, orienting the opening in the fitting side so it will accept the outlet drain line from the other sink bowl. If the waste-T is higher than the top of the trap arm, remove it and trim the drain tailpiece.

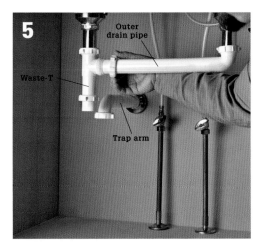

5

Outer drain pipe

Waste-T

Trap arm

Joint the short end of the outlet drain pipe to the tailpiece for the other sink bowl and then attach the end of the long run to the opening in the waste-T. The outlet tube should extend into the T ½" or so—make sure it does not extend far enough to block water flow from above.

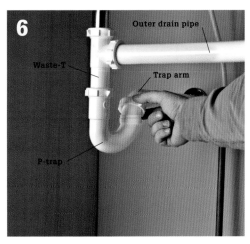

6

Outer drain pipe

Waste-T

Trap arm

P-trap

Attach the long leg of a P-trap to the waste-T and attach the shorter leg to the downward-facing opening of the trap arm. Adjust as necessary and test all joints to make sure they are still tight, and then test the system.

Variation: Drain in Floor ▸

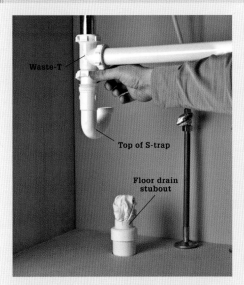

Waste-T

Top of S-trap

Floor drain stubout

If your drain stubout comes up out of the floor instead of the wall, you'll need an S-trap to tie into it instead of a P-trap. Attach one half of the S-trap to the threaded bottom of the waste-T.

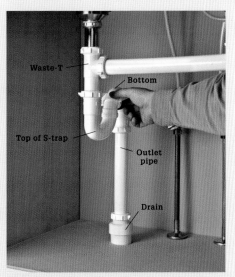

Waste-T

Bottom

Top of S-trap

Outlet pipe

Drain

Attach the other half of the S-trap to the stubout using a slip fitting. This should result in the new fitting facing downward. Join the halves of the S-trap with a slip nut, trimming the unthreaded end if necessary.

Hooking Up Dishwashers

A dishwasher that's past its prime may be inefficient in more ways than one. If it's an old model, it probably wasn't designed to be very efficient to begin with. But more significantly, if it no longer cleans effectively, you're probably spending a lot of time and hot water pre-rinsing the dishes. This alone can consume more energy and water than a complete wash cycle on a newer machine. Even if your old dishwasher still runs, replacing it with an efficient new model can be a good green upgrade.

In terms of sizing and utility hookups, dishwashers are generally quite standard. If your old machine is a built-in and your countertops and cabinets are standard sizes, most full-size dishwashers will fit right in. Of course, you should always measure the dimensions of the old unit before shopping for a new one to avoid an unpleasant surprise at installation time. Also, be sure to review the manufacturer's instructions before starting any work.

Tools & Materials ▸

Screwdrivers	Cable connector
Adjustable wrench	Teflon tape
2-ft. level	Hose clamps
⅝" automotive heater hose	Wire connectors
Automotive heater hose	Carpet scrap
4"-length of ½" copper tubing	Bowl

Replacing an old, inefficient dishwasher is a straightforward project that usually takes just a few hours. The energy savings begin with the first load of dishes and continue with every load thereafter.

How to Replace a Dishwasher

1

Start by shutting off the electrical power to the dishwasher circuit at the service panel. Also, turn off the water supply at the shutoff valve, usually located directly under the floor.

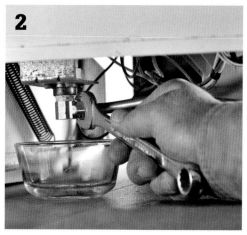

2

Disconnect old plumbing connections. First unscrew the front access panel. Once the access panel is removed, disconnect the water supply line from the L-fitting on the bottom of the unit. This is usually a brass compression fitting, so just turning the compression nut counterclockwise with an adjustable wrench should do the trick. Use a bowl to catch any water that might leak out when the nut is removed.

3

Disconnect old wiring connections. The dishwasher has an integral electrical box at the front of the unit where the power cable is attached to the dishwasher's fixture wires. Take off the box cover and remove the wire connectors that join the wires together.

4

Disconnect the discharge hose, which is usually connected to the dishwasher port on the side of the garbage disposer. To remove it, just loosen the screw on the hose clamp and pull it off. You may need to push this hose back through a hole in the cabinet wall and into the dishwasher compartment so it won't get caught when you pull the dishwasher out.

(continued)

5

Detach the unit from surrounding cabinets before you pull it out. Remove the screws that hold the brackets to the underside of the countertop. Then put a piece of cardboard or old carpet under the front legs to protect the floor from getting scratched, and pull the dishwasher out.

6

Prepare the new dishwasher. Tip it on its back and attach the new L-fitting into the threaded port on the solenoid. Apply some Teflon tape or pipe sealant to the fitting threads before tightening it, to prevent possible leaks.

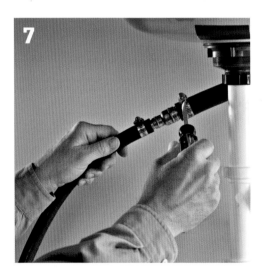

7

Attach a length of new automotive heater hose, usually ⅝" diameter, to the end of the dishwasher's discharge hose nipple with a hose clamp. The new hose you are adding should be long enough to reach from the discharge nipple to the port on the side of the kitchen sink garbage disposer.

8

Prepare for the wiring connections. Like the old dishwasher, the new one will have an integral electrical box for making the wiring connections. To gain access to the box, just remove the box cover. Then install a cable connector on the back of the box and bring the power cable from the service panel through this connector. Power should be shut off at the main service panel at all times.

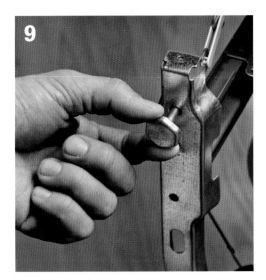

9

10

Install a leveling leg at each of the four corners while the new dishwasher is still on its back. Turn the legs into the threaded holes designed for them. Leave about ½" of each leg projecting from the bottom of the unit. (These will have to be adjusted later to level the appliance.) Tip the appliance up onto the feet and slide it into the opening. Check for level in both directions, and adjust the feet as required.

Once the dishwasher is level, attach the brackets to the underside of the countertop to keep it from moving. Then pull the discharge hose into the sink cabinet and install it so there's a loop that is attached with a bracket to the underside of the countertop. (This loop prevents waste water from flowing from the disposer back into the dishwasher.)

Lengthening a Discharge Hose ▸

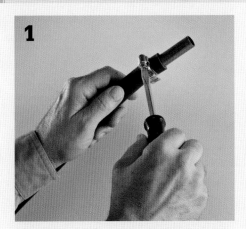

1

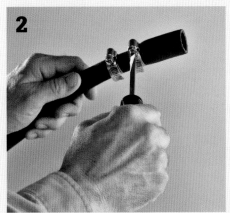

2

If the discharge hose has to be modified to fit onto the disposer port, insert a 4"-long piece of ½" copper tubing into the hose and hold it in place with a hose clamp. This provides a nipple for the rubber adapter that fits onto the disposer.

Clamp the rubber disposer adapter to the end of the copper tubing nipple. Then tighten the hose clamp securely.

(continued)

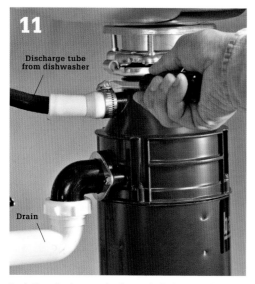

11

Discharge tube
from dishwasher

Drain

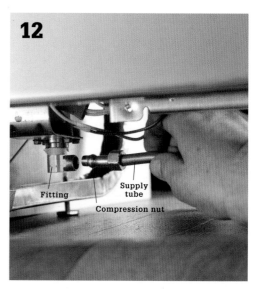

12

Fitting

Supply
tube

Compression nut

Push the adapter over the disposer's discharge nipple and tighten it in place with a hose clamp. If you don't have a disposer, this discharge hose can be clamped directly to a modified sink tailpiece that's installed below a standard sink strainer.

Adjust the L-fitting on the dishwasher's water inlet valve until it points directly toward the water supply tubing. Then lubricate the threads slightly with a drop of dishwashing liquid and tighten the tubing's compression nut onto the fitting. Use an adjustable wrench and turn the nut clockwise.

13

14

Complete the electrical connections by tightening the connector's clamp on the cable. Join the power wires to the fixture wires with wire connectors. Attach the ground wire (or wires) to the grounding screw on the box, and replace the cover.

Install the access panel, usually by hooking it on a couple of prongs just below the dishwasher's door. Install the screws (if any) that hold it in place, and turn on the water and power supplies. Replace the toe-kick panel at the bottom of the dishwasher.

Installing Food Disposers

Food disposers are standard equipment in the modern home, and most of us have come to depend on them to macerate our plate leavings and crumbs so they can exit the house along with waste water from the sink drain. If your existing disposer needs replacing, you'll find that the job is relatively simple, especially if you select a replacement appliance that is the same model as the old one. In that case, you can probably reuse the existing mounting assembly, drain sleeve, and drain plumbing.

Most food disposers are classified as "continuous feed" because they can only operate when an ON/OFF switch on the wall is being actively held down. Let go of the switch, and the disposer stops. Each appliance has a power rating between ⅓ and 1 HP (horsepower). More powerful models bog down less under load and the motors last longer because they don't have to work as hard. They are also costlier.

A disposer is hardwired to a switch mounted in an electrical box in the wall above the countertop. If your kitchen is not equipped for this, consult a wiring guide or hire an electrician. The actual electrical hookup of the appliance is quite simple (you only have to join two wires) but you can hire an electrician if you are not comfortable with the job.

Tools & Materials ▸

Screwdriver
Channel-type pliers
Spud wrench (optional)
Hammer
Hacksaw or tubing cutter
Kitchen drain supplies
Drain auger

Putty knife
Mineral spirits
Plumber's putty
Wire caps
Hose clamps
Threaded Y-fitting
Electrical tape

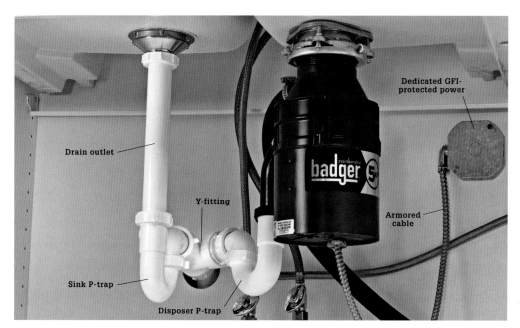

A properly functioning food disposer that's used correctly can actually help reduce clogs by ensuring that large bits of organic matter don't clog the drain system. Many plumbers suggest using separate P-traps for the disposer and the drain outlet tube as shown here.

How to Install a Food Disposer

1

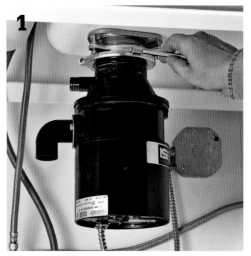

Remove the old disposer if you have one. You'll need to disconnect the drain pipes and traps first. If your old disposer has a special wrench for the mounting lugs, use it to loosen the lugs. Otherwise, use a screwdriver. If you do not have a helper, place a solid object directly beneath the disposer to support it before you begin removal. *Important: Shut off electrical power at the main service panel before you begin removal. Disconnect the wire leads, cap them, and stuff them into the electrical box.*

Tip ▸

Alternate: If you are installing a disposer in a sink that did not previously have one, remove the old sink strainer and drain tailpiece. Scrape up any old plumbers putty and clean the sink thoroughly around the drain opening with mineral spirits.

2

Clear the drain lines all the way to the branch drain before you begin the new installation. Remove the trap and trap arm first.

3

Upper mounting ring

Lower mounting ring

Snap ring

Disassemble the mounting assembly and then separate the upper and lower mounting rings and the backup ring. Also remove the snap ring from the sink sleeve.

4

Sink sleeve

Press the flange of the sink sleeve for your new disposer into a thin coil of plumber's putty that you have laid around the perimeter of the drain opening. The sleeve should be well-seated in the putty.

5

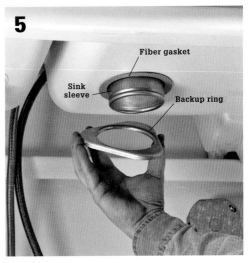

Fiber gasket

Sink sleeve

Backup ring

Slip the fiber gasket and then the backup ring onto the sink sleeve, working from inside the sink base cabinet. Make sure the backup ring is oriented the same way it was before you disassembled the mounting assembly.

6

Insert the upper mounting ring onto the sleeve with the slotted ends of the screws facing away from the backup ring so you can access them. Then, holding all three parts at the top of the sleeve, slide the snap ring onto the sleeve until it snaps into the groove. Tighten the three mounting screws on the upper mounting ring until the tips press firmly against the backup ring (inset photo). It is the tension created by these screws that keeps the disposer steady and minimizes vibrating.

7

Make electrical connections before you mount the disposer unit on the mounting assembly. Make sure the power is still turned off at the service panel. Remove the access plate from the disposer. Attach the white and black feeder wires from the electrical box to the white and black wires (respectively) inside the disposer. Twist a small wire cap onto each connection and wrap it with electrical tape for good measure. Also attach the green ground wire from the box to the grounding terminal on your disposer.

(continued)

8

Knock out the plug in the disposer port if you will be connecting your dishwasher to the disposer. If you have no dishwasher, leave the plug in. Insert a large flathead screwdriver into the port opening and rap it with a mallet. Retrieve the knock plug from inside the disposer canister.

9

Hang the disposer from the mounting ring attached to the sink sleeve. To hang it, simply lift it up and position the unit so the three mounting ears are underneath the three mounting screws and then spin the unit so all three ears fit into the mounting assembly. Wait until after the plumbing hookups have been made to lock the unit in place.

10

Attach the discharge tube to the disposer according to the manufacturer's instructions. It is important to get a very good seal here, or the disposer will leak. Go ahead and spin the disposer if it helps you access the discharge port.

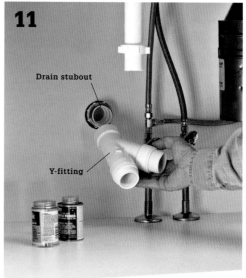

11

Drain stubout

Y-fitting

Attach a Y-fitting at the drain stubout. The Y-fitting should be sized to accept a drain line from the disposer and another from the sink. Adjust the sink drain plumbing as needed to get from the sink P-trap to one opening of the Y.

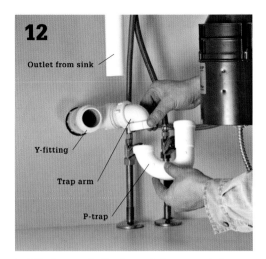

12

Outlet from sink

Y-fitting

Trap arm

P-trap

Install a trap arm for the disposer in the open port of the Y-fitting at the wall stubout. Then, attach a P-trap or a combination of a tube extension and a P-trap so the low end of the trap will align with the bottom of the disposer discharge tube.

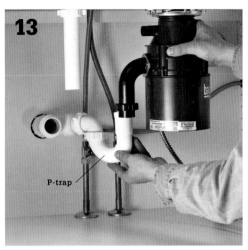

13

P-trap

Spin the disposer so the end of the discharge tube is lined up over the open end of the P-trap and confirm that they will fit together correctly. If the discharge tube extends down too far, mark a line on it at the top of the P-trap and cut through the line with a hacksaw. If the tube is too short, attach an extension with a slip joint. You may need to further shorten the discharge tube first to create enough room for the slip joint on the extension. Slide a slip nut and beveled compression washer onto the discharge tube and attach the tube to the P-trap.

14 Dishwasher discharge tube

Connect the dishwasher discharge tube to the inlet port located at the top of the disposer unit. This may require a dishwasher hookup kit.

15

Lock the disposer into position on the mounting ring assembly once you have tested to make sure it is functioning correctly and without leaks. Lock it by turning one of the mounting lugs with a screwdriver until it makes contact with the locking notch.

Installing Undercabinet Lights

Hardwired undercabinet lights illuminate the kitchen countertop and sink areas that fall in the shadow of ceiling lights. Most of these light fixtures, which are often called *strip lights*, utilize fluorescent, halogen, or xenon bulbs that emit very low levels of heat and are therefore very efficient.

If you are doing a kitchen remodel with all-new cabinets, run the new light circuit wiring before the cabinets are installed. For a retrofit, you'll need to find an available power source to tie into. Options for this do not include the dedicated 20-amp small-appliance circuits that are required in kitchens. The best bet is to run new circuit wire from a convenient ceiling light switch box, but this will mean cutting into the walls to run cable. Another option is to locate a receptacle that's on the opposite side of a shared wall, preferably next to a location where a base cabinet is installed in the kitchen. By cutting an access hole in the cabinet back you can tie into the receptacle box and run cable through the wall behind the cabinets, up to the upper cabinet location, and out the wall to supply the fixture that's mounted to the underside of the upper cabinet.

You can purchase undercabinet lights that are controlled by a wall switch, but most products have an integral on/off button so you can control lights individually.

Tools & Materials ▸

Circuit tester	Wire stripper
Utility knife	Undercabinet
Wallboard saw	lighting kit
Hammer	14/2 NM cable
Screwdriver	Wire connectors
Drill and hole saw	Switch box
Jigsaw	Switch

Undercabinet lights provide directed task lighting that bring sinks and countertop work surfaces out from the shadows. Hardwired lights may be controlled either by a wall switch or an onboard on/off switch located on the fixture. *Note: Do not supply power for lights from a small-appliance circuit.*

How to Install a Hardwired Undercabinet Light

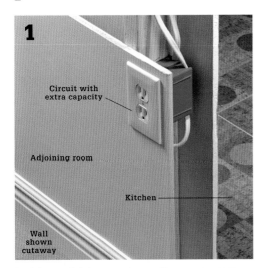

1

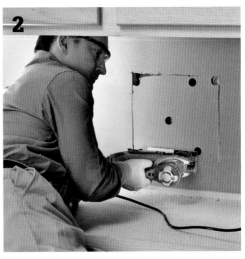

2

Look in an adjoining room for a usable power source in the form of a receptacle that has a box located in the wall behind your base cabinets. Unlike the small-appliance circuit with outlets in your backsplash area, these typically are not dedicated circuits (which can't be expanded). Make sure that the receptacle's circuit has enough capacity to support another load. Shut the power to the receptacle off at the main service panel and test for power.

Cut a hole in the base cabinet back panel, roughly the area where you know the usable receptacle to be. Use a keyhole saw or drywall saw and make very shallow cuts until you have positively identified the locations of the electrical box and cables. Then finish the cuts with a jigsaw.

3

4

Drill an access hole through the cabinet frame and wall for the cable that will feed the undercabinet light. A ½" dia. hole should be about the right size if you are using 12-ga. or 14-ga. sheathed NM cable.

Cut a small access hole (4 × 4" or so) in the back panel of the base cabinet directly below the undercabinet light location.

(continued)

5

Feed cable into the access hole at the light location until the end reaches the access hole below. Don't cut the cable yet. Reach into the access hole and feel around for the free cable end and then pull it out through the access hole once you've found it. Cut the cable, making sure to leave plenty of extra on both ends.

6

String the cable into a piece of flexible conduit that's long enough to reach between the two access holes in the base cabinets. To make patching the cabinet back easier, drill a new access hole for the cable near the square access hole. Attach a connector to each end of the conduit to protect the cable sheathing from the sharp edges of the cut metal.

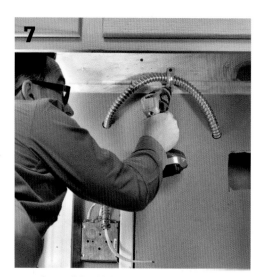

7

Hang the conduit with hanger straps attached to the base cabinet frame or back panel, drilling holes in the side walls of the cabinet where necessary to thread the conduit through. On back panels, use small screws to hang the straps instead of brads or nails. Support the conduit near both the entrance and the exit holes (the conduit should extend past the back panels by a couple of inches).

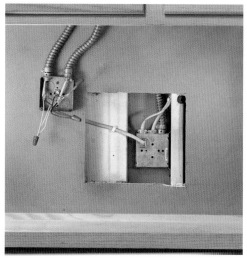

Variation: If you are installing more than one undercabinet light, run cable down from each installation point as you did for the first light. Mount an electrical junction box to the cabinet back near the receptacle providing the power. Run the power cables from each light through flexible conduit and make connections inside the junction box. Be sure to attach the junction box cover once the connections are made.

8

Remove the receptacle from the box you are tying into and insert the new circuit cable into one of the knockouts using a cable clamp. Check a wire capacity chart (see page 90) to make sure the box is big enough for the new conductors. Replace it with a larger box if necessary. Reinstall the receptacle once the connections are made.

9

Install the undercabinet light. Some models have a removable diffuser that allows access to the fixture wires, and these should be screwed to the upper cabinet prior to making your wiring hookups. Other models need to be connected to the circuit wires before installation. Check your manufacturer's installations.

10

Connect wires inside the light fixture according to the light manufacturer's directions. Make sure the incoming cable is stapled just before it enters the light box and that a cable clamp is used at the knockout in the box to protect the cable. Restore power and test the light.

11

Cut patches of hardboard and fit them over the access holes, overlapping the edges of the cutouts. Adhere them to the cabinet backs with panel adhesive.

Green Kitchens ▶

In many ways, a green kitchen is just like any well-designed kitchen. There are windows for natural lighting and air circulation. Surfaces are durable, hygienic, and low-maintenance. The room is well lighted, with overhead fixtures and plenty of task lighting. And the overall plan is designed for maximum work efficiency and tailored to the way the homeowners use the kitchen on a daily basis. In terms of aesthetics, a green kitchen can be just as beautiful, if not more so, than a conventional kitchen.

So what's different about a green kitchen? For starters, it has highly efficient appliances, particularly the refrigerator. It contains sustainable and non-toxic materials, like formaldehyde-free cabinet cases and linoleum flooring. It's also ready to deal with the variety of waste products surrounding food preparation, including organic garbage, recyclable materials, and gray water.

Many green kitchens are further defined by what they don't have: trendy upgrades and extras that do little to improve anyone's daily experience in the kitchen. Depending on the type of cooking you do, you might get a lot of use out of special features, like a pot filler faucet, an extra prep sink, warming drawers, or a commercial-style range. But in reality, most cooks don't get full value from these pricey additions, which take up space and are often over-engineered and energy-inefficient (not to mention the environmental impact of producing them).

Whether you're planning a major kitchen remodel or simply replacing an item or two, here are some of the main elements you should consider for making the space more useful, healthful, and resource-efficient.

Efficiency and common sense are two of the hallmarks of any green room, but this is especially true in the kitchen. Keep the appliances as small as you can and look for natural materials, like this butcherblock countertop made from maple cutoffs.

PORTRAIT OF A GREEN KITCHEN

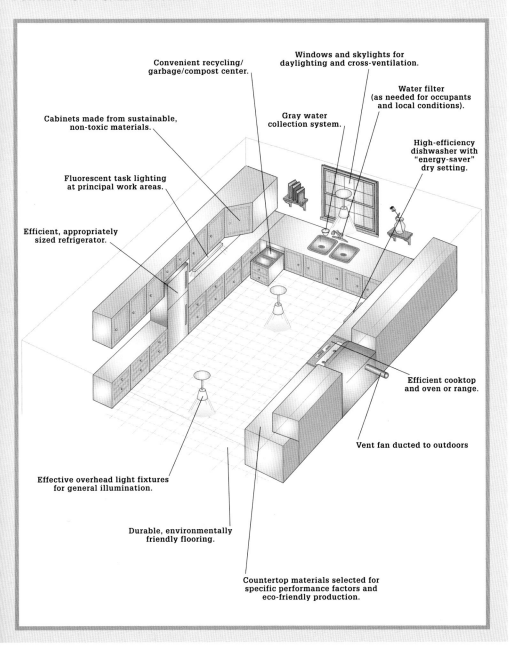

Convenient recycling/garbage/compost center.

Windows and skylights for daylighting and cross-ventilation.

Water filter (as needed for occupants and local conditions).

Cabinets made from sustainable, non-toxic materials.

Gray water collection system.

High-efficiency dishwasher with "energy-saver" dry setting.

Fluorescent task lighting at principal work areas.

Efficient, appropriately sized refrigerator.

Efficient cooktop and oven or range.

Vent fan ducted to outdoors

Effective overhead light fixtures for general illumination.

Durable, environmentally friendly flooring.

Countertop materials selected for specific performance factors and eco-friendly production.

Green Kitchen Appliances ▶

Because it's full of hardworking appliances, the kitchen uses more energy than any other room in the house. Upgrading your old machines with more efficient models is one of the simplest ways to help make your kitchen green. Refrigerators are the big consumers, accounting for up to 15% of the average home's total electricity usage. Fortunately, you don't have to sacrifice quality or style to save energy. Highly efficient appliances, like many other machines, are simply better designed and better built than their hoggish counterparts. And you can't tell a miserly model by its looks.

Lots of do-it-yourselfers install their own appliances; see pages 402 to 407 for steps on installing a high-efficiency dishwasher. A refrigerator is the easiest to install: Just plug it in, slide it in place, and level it. If yours has an icemaker, you'll have to connect a small water line in the back of the unit (and check it for leaks in the beginning).

If you're replacing an existing appliance, find out where you can recycle the old unit. Appliances are a major source of recyclable steel and other materials, and besides, dumping an operable machine in the land-fill just to make room for a new one isn't a very green move. Appliances that still work can find a great home through a local charity organization (this means an old, inefficient appliance is still in circulation, but it postpones the production of a new product, and it helps out those in need). To scrap an ailing or dead appliance, contact your local recycling authority or Earth 911, online at www.earth911.org.

Whatever you do, don't keep your old refrigerator and move it into the garage for backup storage. Keeping a second fridge plugged in will undo all energy-saving efforts from your kitchen upgrades many times over.

European sized refrigerators are becoming increasingly popular as a way to control energy usage. A typical model like the one above has a refrigerator compartment of 7-to-8 cubic feet in capacity, with a freezer that's 3 to 4 cu. ft.

Scale is important and many kitchen appliance manufacturers have begun marketing to this. Narrow dishwashers with smaller compartments offer ample space for some users, and they do their job with much less water and energy.

ENERGY STAR & ENERGYGUIDE LABELS

If you're in the market for a new appliance, it's time to start paying attention to those yellow-and-black ENERGYGUIDE labels you see pasted to the front of many new products. The labels, required by the Federal Trade Commission, help consumers quickly compare models for their energy efficiency. The box in the middle of each label provides the "energy use" of all models in a given class, with an arrow showing where that particular model falls within the range. The label also gives you an estimated annual operating cost for the appliance.

Energy Star is the Department of Energy's wide-reaching program that awards Energy Star status to the most efficient products in a given class. The program applies to major appliances, windows, doors, HVAC systems, and other household items. In general, Energy Star products exceed the federal government's energy-efficiency standards and perform within the top 25% of their category.

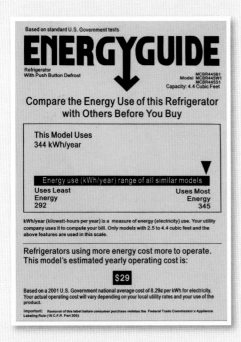

ADDITIONAL RESOURCES FOR CHOOSING & USING KITCHEN APPLIANCES

- U.S. Department of Energy (DOE): www.eere.energy.gov
- Energy Star: www.energystar.gov
- Consumer Reports, for unbiased analysis of appliance performance and other shopping considerations, online at www.consumerreports.org
- American Council for an Energy-Efficient Economy: www.aceee.org

- Your local utility provider
- Your state's energy authority; some states offer rebates on high-efficiency appliances
- Association of Home Appliance Manufacturers: www.aham.org
- The Green Guide: www.thegreenguide.com

Bathroom Remodeling

Bathroom fixtures and materials have changed dramatically in recent years. Tubs can rival healthclub spas, toilets and showerheads are more water efficient, and sinks run the gamut from stainless steel to wood basins.

Before you jump into a bathroom remodeling project, decide what's most important to you. Budget determines how luxurious you can get, but maybe it's worthwhile to splurge on that one item that would make you feel most pampered.

Home centers and kitchen and bath showrooms have a variety of bathroom setups you can browse through to see how the products look and feel. It's always a good idea to see a product in person before doling out the cash.

In this chapter:

- Planning & Designing Bathrooms
- Installing Shower Kits
- Installing Alcove Bathtubs
- Installing 3-piece Tub Surrounds
- Installing Sliding Tub Doors
- Tiling Bathroom Walls
- Installing Toilets
- Installing Wall-hung Vanities
- Installing Vessel Sinks
- Installing Pedestal Sinks
- Installing Vanity Cabinets
- Installing Bathroom Sink Faucets & Drains
- Installing Tub Spouts
- Installing Vanity Lights
- Installing Grab Bars
- Installing Glass Shelving
- Installing Towel Warmers

Planning & Designing Bathrooms

Once you've drawn up your plans and created a materials list, you'll need to have them reviewed by your local building department. Getting approval early in the process can save you time and expense later. To help ensure success, here are some design standards for you to follow:

The National Kitchen and Bath (NKBA) publishes a list of bathroom design standards to help people plan rooms that are safe and accessible to all users (see Resources, page 554).

Your bathroom probably won't conform to all of the recommended standards, but they can help guide your overall plan. What your plan must include is everything prescribed by the local building codes, including plumbing and wiring codes.

Bathroom Design Standards ▶

Codes and permits are necessary to ensure safety in any remodel. They're not the most fun to focus on—not like choosing just the right floor covering or deciding between granite or marble countertops—but they are important.

- Plan doorways with a clear floor space equal to the door's width on the push side and greater than the door's width on the pull side. *Note: Clear floor spaces within the bathroom can overlap.*
- Design toilet enclosures with at least 36" × 66" of space; include a pocket door or a door that swings out toward the rest of the bathroom.
- Install toiletpaper holders approximately 26" above the floor, toward the front of the toilet bowl.
- Place fixtures so faucets are accessible from outside the tub or shower. Add antiscald devices to tub and sink faucets (they are required for shower faucets).
- Avoid steps around showers and tubs, if possible.
- Fit showers and tubs with safety rails and grab bars.
- Install shower doors so they swing open into the bathroom, not the shower.
- Use tempered glass or another type of safety glass for all glass doors and partitions.
- Include storage for soap, towels, and other items near the shower, located within 15" to 48" above the floor. These should be accessible to a person in the shower or tub.
- Provide natural light equal to at least 10% of the floor area in the room.
- Illuminate all activity centers in the bathroom with task and ambient lighting.
- Provide a minimum clearance of 15" from the centerline of sinks to any sidewalls. Double-bowl sinks should have 30" clearance between bowls from centerline to centerline.
- Provide access panels for all electrical, plumbing, and HVAC systems connections.
- Include a ventilation fan that exchanges air at a rate of 8 air changes per hour.
- Choose countertops and other surfaces with edges that are smoothed, clipped, or radiused.

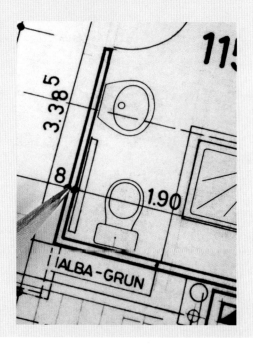

Building Codes for Bathrooms ▸

The following are some of the most common building codes for bathrooms. Contact your local building department for a list of all codes enforced in your area.

- The minimum ceiling height in bathrooms is 7 ft. Minimum floor area is determined by clearances around fixtures.
- Sinks must be at least 4" from side walls and have 21" of clearance in front.
- Sinks must be spaced 4" away from neighboring sinks and toilets, and 2" away from bathtubs.
- Toilets must be centered 15" from side walls and tubs, with 21" clearance in front.
- New and replacement toilets must be low-flow models (1.6 gal./flush).
- Shower stalls must be at least 30" × 30", with 24" of clearance in front of shower openings.
- Steps must be at least 10" deep and no higher than 7¼".
- Faucets for showers and combination tub/showers must be equipped with antiscald devices.
- Supply lines that are ½" in diameter can supply a single fixture, or one sink and one toilet.

- A ¾"-diameter supply line must be used to supply two or more fixtures.
- Waste and drain lines must slope ¼" per foot toward the main DWV stack to aid flow and prevent blockage.
- Each bathroom must be wired with at least one 20-amp circuit for GFCI-protected receptacles, and one 15-amp (minimum) circuit for light fixtures and vent fans without heating elements.
- All receptacles must be GFCI-protected.
- There must be at least one permanent light fixture controlled by a wall switch.
- Wall switches must be at least 60" away from bathtubs and showers.
- Toilet, shower, vanity, or other bathroom compartments must have adequate lighting.
- Light fixtures over bathtubs and showers must be vaporproof, with a UL rating for wet areas.
- Vanity light fixtures with built-in electrical receptacles are prohibited.
- Whirlpool motors must be powered by dedicated GFCI-protected circuits.
- Bathroom vent ducts must terminate no less than 10 ft. horizontally or 3 ft. vertically above skylights.

Note: Codes for accessible bathrooms may differ (see page 429).

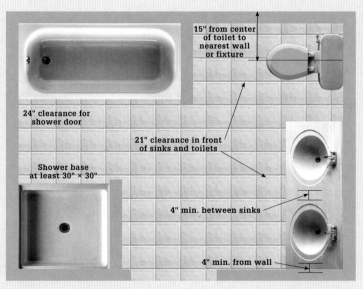

15" from center of toilet to nearest wall or fixture

24" clearance for shower door

21" clearance in front of sinks and toilets

Shower base at least 30" × 30"

4" min. between sinks

4" min. from wall

Follow minimum clearance and size guidelines when planning locations of bathroom fixtures. Easy access to fixtures is fundamental to creating a bathroom that is comfortable, safe, and easy to use.

Accessible Bathrooms (Universal Design)

The safety and accessibility of nearly all aspects of a bathroom can be improved by following universal design guidelines.

For safer floors, add a slip-resistant glaze to ceramic tile, and add nonslip adhesive strips or decals to shower floors. If you're replacing your floor, look for mosaic tiles, vinyl, and cork materials. Matte finishes tend to be less slippery than polished surfaces, and they reduce glare.

Toilets, faucets, sinks, cabinets, tubs, and showers can all be adapted or changed for increased usability by people who have experienced inflexibility or loss of strength.

Toilet height can be adjusted with the installation of a height adapter that raises a standard toilet seat 2 to 5". You can also consider an adjustable-height toilet or a model with a power-lift seat.

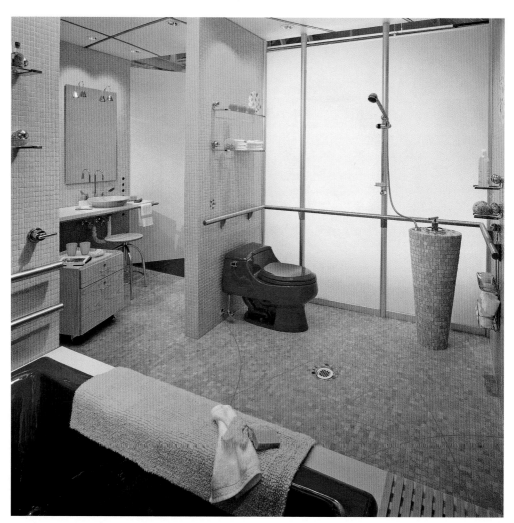

A bathroom designed for accessibility is an increasingly important element found in today's homes.

An integral personal hygiene system can be installed to help people with physical disabilities maintain independence.

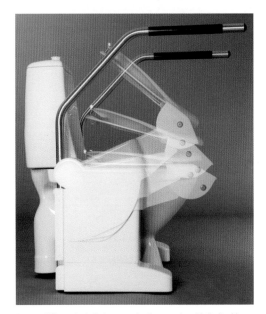

Power-lifts make toilet use easier for people with limited leg or joint strength.

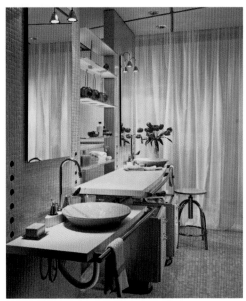

Roll-out base cabinets provide the option of seating space at the countertop.

(continued)

Consider replacing your toilet with a wall-hung style that can be installed at any height, providing additional clear space for maneuvering a wheelchair or walker. To help people with physical disabilities maintain independent personal hygiene, install either a bidet or a toilet with an integral personal hygiene system. Grab bars are a must on walls around the toilet.

Install antiscald guard and volume-control devices on faucets and showerheads. Replace double-handle faucets with single-lever models, which are easier to use. A faucet with motion-sensor operation for hands-free use is a plus.

Change a standard showerhead to an adjustable showerhead mounted on a vertical slide-bar to accommodate people of all heights. Look for handheld models for best control.

Vanities and cabinets with C-shaped pulls or magnetic touch latches are easy to use. Add pull-down hardware to cabinets to bring items within reach for seated people or those with limited mobility.

Install your countertops at varied heights to serve both seated and standing users. Also consider mounting the faucet controls at the side of the sink, rather than the back, for easier access.

If you are replacing your sink, choose a style that is shallower at the front and deeper at the drain. Or install a wall-mounted sink positioned at 30 to 32". Providing a clear space under sinks and low sections of countertop allows seated users to comfortably reach the vanity. Use fold-away doors, remove face frames on base cabinets, or install roll-out base cabinets to gain clear space. Always finish the floor under fold-away or roll-out cabinets. Then insulate hot-water supply pipes or install a protective panel to prevent burns to seated users.

Side-mounted faucet and drain pulls in combination with a wall-mounted sink are easily accessible.

A tilted mirror allows seated or short users to easily see themselves.

Install grab bars in and around the shower and tub. Adding a shower seat or installing a pull-down or permanent seat in the shower allows elderly or disabled family members to sit while bathing. Install a permanently mounted shower seat at 18" high, and be sure the seat is at least 15" deep.

Water controls and faucets on tubs repositioned toward the outside edge at a height of 38 to 48" allows the water to be turned on and adjusted before getting in to bathe. If you're buying a new bathtub, consider one with a side-access door.

Consider replacing a combination tub and shower with a stand-alone shower with a floor that slopes gently toward the drain, rather than a curb to contain water. When fitted with a pull-down seat and an adjustable handheld showerhead, roll-in showers can accommodate people with a wide range of abilities.

Reverse door hinges so the doors open out. That way, the door swing won't be blocked if someone falls.

If needed, widen doorways to 32 to 36" so wheelchair and walker users can enter the bathroom easily. Or, replace a swing door with a pocket door to gain clear space.

Roll-in shower designs, roll-under sinks, grab bars, adjustable slide-bar showers, and open floor space make bathing easier for people with disabilities.

(continued)

A swing-in door makes bathtubs accessible to practically anyone. The door creates a tight seal when closed and cannot be opened if the tub is full.

Install a pocket door in your bathroom to gain more clearance room for wheelchairs and walkers. Pocket doors do not require door stop molding, allowing for some additional clearance.

Recommended Clearances ▸

A bathroom should be planned with enough approach space and clearance room to allow a wheelchair or walker user to enter and turn around easily. The guidelines for approach spaces (patterned areas) and clearances shown here include some ADA guidelines and recommendations from universal design specialists.

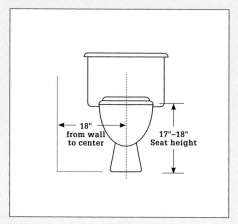

Toilet

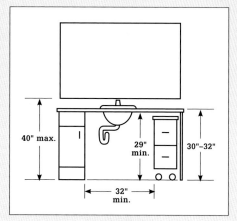

Sink & Vanity

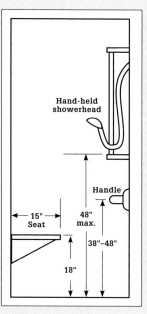

Shower

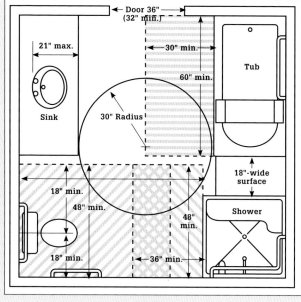

Floor Plan

Installing Shower Kits

The fastest and easiest way to create a new shower in your bathroom is to frame in the stall area with lumber and wallboard and then install a shower enclosure kit. Typically consisting of three fiberglass or plastic walls, these enclosure kits snap together at the corners and nestle inside the flanges of the shower pan to create nearly foolproof mechanical seals. Often, the walls are formed with shelves, soap holders, and other conveniences.

If you are on a tight budget, you can find extremely inexpensive enclosure kits to keep costs down. You can even create your own custom enclosure using waterproof beadboard panels and snap-together connectors. Or, you can invest in a higher grade kit made from thicker material that will last much longer. Some kits are sold with the receptor (and perhaps even the door) included. The kit shown here is designed to be attached directly to wall studs, but others require a backer wall for support. The panels are attached to the backer with high-tack panel adhesive.

A paneled shower surround is inexpensive and easy to install. Designed for alcove installations, they often are sold with matching shower pans (called *receptors*).

Tools & Materials ▸

Tape measure	Masking tape
Pencil	Silicone caulk
Hammer	and caulk gun
Carpenter's square	Shower enclosure kit
Screwdrivers	Shower door
Pipe wrench	Showerhead
Level	Faucet
Strap wrench	Plumbing supplies
Adjustable wrench	Panel adhesive
Pliers	Spud wrench
Drill/driver	Large-head roofing nails
Center punch	Jigsaw
File	Duct tape
Utility knife	Miter box
Hacksaw	

How to Install a Shower Enclosure

1

Remove the wallcovering and floor covering in the installation area. Dispose of the materials immediately and thoroughly clean the area. *Note: Most kits can be installed over wallboard, but more professional-looking results can be achieved if it is removed.*

2

Sill plate

If you are adding a wall to create the alcove, lay out the locations for the studs and plumbing on the new wood sill plate. Also lay out the stud locations on the cap plate that will be attached to the ceiling. Refer to the enclosure kit instructions for exact locations and dimensions of studs. Attach the sill plate to the floor with deck screws and panel adhesive, making sure it is square to the back wall and the correct distance from the side wall.

3

Align a straight 2 × 4 right next to the sill plate and make a mark on the ceiling. Use a level to extend that line directly above the sill plate. Attach the cap plate at that point.

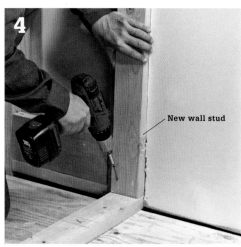

4

New wall stud

Install the 2 × 4 studs at the outlined locations. Check with a level to make sure each stud is plumb, and then attach them by driving deck screws toenail style into the sill plate and cap plate.

(continued)

Cut an access hole in the floor for the drain, according to the installation manual instructions. Drill openings in the sill plate of the wet wall (the new wall in this project) for the supply pipes, also according to the instructions.

Install a drain pipe and branch line and then trim the drain pipe flush with the floor. If you are not experienced with plumbing, hire a plumber to install the new drain line.

Install new supply risers as directed in the instruction manual (again, have a plumber do this if necessary). Also install cross braces between the studs in the wet wall for mounting the faucet body and shower arm.

If the supply plumbing is located in a wall (old or new) that is accessible from the non-shower side, install framing for a removable access panel.

9

Attach the drain tailpiece that came with your receptor to the underside of the unit, following the manufacturer's instructions precisely. Here, an adjustable spud wrench is being used to tighten the tailpiece.

Option: To stabilize the receptor, especially if the floor is uneven, pour or trowel a layer of thinset mortar into the installation area, taking care to keep the mortar out of the drain access hole. Do not apply mortar in areas where the receptor has feet that are intended to make full contact with the floor.

10

Set the receptor in place, check to make sure it is level, and shim it if necessary. Secure the receptor with large-head roofing nails driven into the wall stud so the nailheads pin the flange against the stud. Do not overdrive the nails.

11

Lay out the locations for the valve hole or holes in the end wall panel that will be installed on the wet wall. Check your installation instructions. Some kits come with a template marked on the packaging carton. Cut the access hole with a hole saw and drill or with a jigsaw and fine-tooth blade. If using a jigsaw, orient the panel so the finish surface is facing down.

(continued)

Position the back wall so there is a slight gap (about ½₂") between the bottom of the panel and the rim of the receptor—set a few small spacers on the rim if need be. Tack a pair of roofing nails above the top of the back panel to hold it in place (or, use duct tape). Position both end walls and test the fits. Make clip connections between panels (inset) if your kit uses them.

Remove the end walls so you can prepare the installation area for them. If your kit recommends panel adhesive, apply it to the wall or studs. In the kit shown here, only a small bead of silicone sealant on the receptor flange is required.

Reinstall the end panels, permanently clipping them to the back panel according to the kit manufacturer's instructions. Make sure the front edges of the end panels are flush with the front of the receptor.

Once the panels are positioned correctly and snapped together, fasten them to the wall studs. If the panels have predrilled nail holes, drive roofing nails through them at each stud at the panel tops and every 4" to 6" along vertical surfaces.

16

Install wallcovering material above the enclosure panels and anywhere else it is needed. Use moisture-resistant materials, and maintain a gap of ¼" between the shoulders of the top panel flanges and the wallcovering.

17

Finish the walls and then caulk between the enclosure panels and the wallcoverings with silicone caulk.

18

Install the faucet handles and escutcheon and caulk around the escutcheon plate. Install the shower arm escutcheon and showerhead.

19

Access panel

Make an access panel and attach it at the framed opening created in step 8. A piece of ¼" plywood framed with mitered case molding and painted to match the wall is one idea for access panel covers.

How to Install a Hinged Shower Door

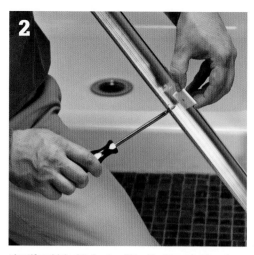

Measure the width of the shower opening. If the walls of the shower slope inward slightly before meeting the base, take your measurement from a higher point at the full width of the opening so you don't cut the door base too short. Cut the base piece to fit using a hacksaw and a miter box. File the cut ends if necessary to deburr them.

Identify which side jamb will be the hinge jamb and which will be the strike jamb according to the direction you want your hinged door to swing—an outward swing is preferred. Prepare the jambs for installation as directed in your instructions.

Place the base jamb on the curb of the shower base. If the joint where the wall meets the curb is sloped, you'll need to trim the corners of the base piece to follow the profile. Place a jamb carefully onto the base and plumb it with a level. Then, mark a drilling point by tapping a centerpunch in the middle of each nail hole in each jamb. Remove the jambs, drill pilot holes, and then attach the jambs with the provided screws.

Remove the bottom track and prepare the shower base curb for installation of the base track, following the manufacturer's directions. Permanently install the bottom track. Bottom tracks (not all doors have them) are usually attached to the side jambs or held in place with adhesive. Never use fasteners to secure them to curb.

Working on the floor or another flat surface, attach the door hinge to the hinge jamb, if required. In most systems, the hinge is fitted over the hinge jamb after you attach it to the wall.

Attach the hinge to the door panel, according to the manufacturer's instructions. Attach any cap fitting that keeps water out of the jamb.

Fit the hinge jamb over the side jamb and adjust it as directed in your instruction manual. Once the clearances are correct, fasten the jambs to hang the door.

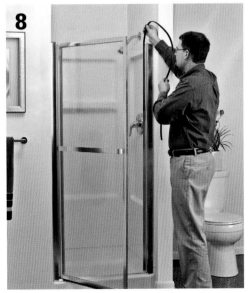

Install the magnetic strike plate and any remaining caps or accessories such as towel rods. Also attach the sweep that seals the passage, if provided.

Installing Alcove Bathtubs

Many of our homes are equipped with an alcove tub that includes a tub surround and shower feature. By combining the tub and the shower in one fixture, you conserve precious bathroom floorspace and simplify the initial installation. Plus, you only have one bathing fixture that needs cleaning.

But because tub/showers are so efficient, they do get a lot of use and tend to have fairly limited lifespans. The fact that the most inexpensive tubs on the market are designed for alcove use also reduces the average tub/shower lifespan. Pressed steel tubs have enamel finishes that crack and craze; plastic and fiberglass tubs get grimy and stained; even acrylic and composite tubs show wear eventually (and as with other fixtures, styles, and colors change too).

Plumbing an alcove tub is a relatively difficult job because getting access to the drain lines attached to the tub and into the floor is often very awkward. Although an access panel is required by most codes, the truth is that many tubs were installed without them or with panels that are too small or hard to reach to be of much use. If you are contemplating replacing your tub, the first step in the decision process should be to find the access panel and determine if it is

sufficient. If it is not (or there is no panel at all), consider how you might enlarge it. Often, this means cutting a hole in the wall on the adjoining room and also in the ceiling below. This creates more work, of course, but compared to the damage caused by a leaky drain from a subpar installation, making an access opening is a small inconvenience.

Tools & Materials ▸

Channel-type pliers	Drain-waste-
Hacksaw	overflow kit
Carpenter's level	1 × 3, 1 × 4,
Pencil	2 × 4 lumber
Tape measure	Galvanized
Saw	roofing nails
Screwdriver	Galvanized
Drill	roof flashing
Adjustable wrench	Thinset mortar
Trowel	Tub & tile caulk
Shims	Propane torch
Galvanized deck screws	

By replacing a dingy old alcove tub with a fresh new one, you can make the tub and shower area as pleasant to use as it is efficient.

Tips for Installing Bathtubs ▸

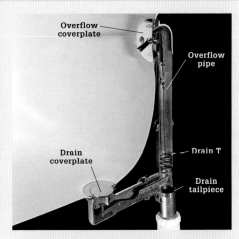

Choose the correct tub for your plumbing setup.
Alcove-installed tubs with only one-sided aprons are sold as either "left-hand" or "right-hand" models, depending on the location of the predrilled drain and overflow holes in the tub. To determine which type you need, face into the alcove and check whether the tub drain is on your right or your left.

A Drain-waste-overflow kit with stopper mechanism must be purchased separately and attached after the tub is set. Available in both brass and plastic types, most kits include an overflow coverplate, an overflow pipe that can be adjusted to different heights, a drain T-fitting, an adjustable drain tailpiece, and a drain coverplate that screws into the tailpiece.

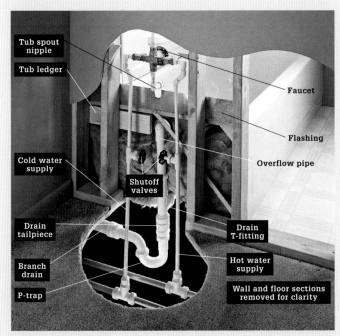

The supply system for a bathtub includes hot and cold supply pipes, shutoff valves, a faucet and handle(s), and a spout. Supply connections can be made before or after the tub is installed.

The drain-waste-overflow system for a bathtub includes the overflow pipe, drain T, P-trap, and branch drain. The overflow pipe assembly is attached to the tub before installation.

How To Remove an Alcove Bathtub

Cut the old supply tubes, if you have access to them, with a reciprocating saw and metal cutting blade or with a hacksaw. Be sure to shut off the water supply at the stop valves first. Cut the shower pipe just above the faucet body and cut the supply tubes just above the stop valves.

Remove the faucet handles, tub spout, shower head and escutcheon, and arm. For the spout, check the underside for a set screw and loosen it if you find one. Then, insert a long screwdriver into the spout and turn the spout counterclockwise.

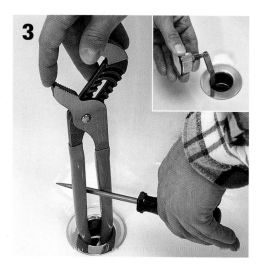

Remove the drain plug, working from the tub side. If the tub has a pop-up drain with linkage, twist the plug to disengage the linkage and remove the plug (inset). Then, insert the handles of a channel-type pliers into the drain opening and past the drain crosspiece. Twist the pliers counterclockwise to remove the plug.

Remove the overflow coverplate (top photo) and then withdraw the pop-up drain linkage through the overflow opening (lower photo).

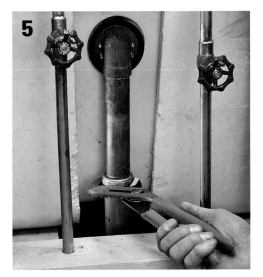

Disconnect the overflow pipe from the drain assembly and remove both parts (your access may not be as unrestricted as seen here). If you need to cut the pipes, go ahead and do it. In most cases, it is difficult to maneuver the tub out with the DWO assembly still attached.

Cut the wall to a line about 6" above the tub rim. Alcove tubs are fastened to the wall studs with nails driven through or above a flange that extends up from the rim. You'll need to remove a bit of the wall covering so you can remove the fasteners.

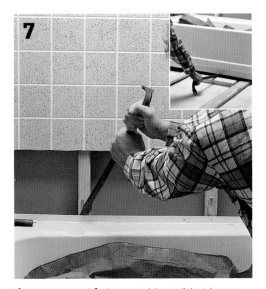

If you can, pry out fasteners and then pull the tub away from the walls by levering between the back rim of the tub and the back wall of the alcove. If it resists, check for adhesive caulk or even flooring blocking the bottom of the apron. If needed, raise the tub and slide a pair of 1 × 4 runners under the skirt edge (inset photo) to make it easier to slide out.

Option: Cut stubborn tubs in half to wrangle them out of the alcove. This has the added benefit of making the tubs easier to get out the door, down the stairs, and into the dumpster.

How to Install a New Alcove Tub

Prepare for the new tub. Inspect and remove old or deteriorated wall surfaces or framing members in the tub area. With today's mold-resistant wallboard products, it makes extra sense to go ahead and strip off the old alcove wallboard down to the studs so you can replace them. This also allows you to inspect for hidden damage in the wall and ceiling cavities.

Check the subfloor for level—if it is not level, use pour-on floor leveler compound to correct it (ask at your local flooring store). Make sure the supply and drain pipes and the shutoff valves are in good repair and correct any problems you encounter. If you have no bath fan in the alcove, now is the perfect time to add one.

Check the height of the crossbraces for the faucet body and the showerhead. If your family members needed to stoop to use the old shower, consider raising the brace for the showerhead. Read the instructions for your new faucet/diverter and check to see that the brace for the faucet body will conform to the requirements (this includes distance from the surround wall as well as height). Adjust the brace locations as needed.

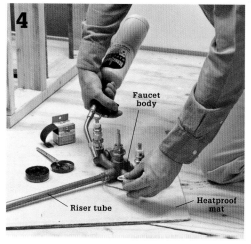

Begin by installing the new water supply plumbing. Measure to determine the required height of your shower riser tube and cut it to length. Solder the bottom of the riser to the faucet body and the top to the shower elbow.

Attach the faucet body to the cross brace with pipe hanger straps. Then, attach supply tubing from the stop valves to the faucet body, making sure to attach the hot water to the left port and cold to the right port. Also secure the shower elbow to its cross brace with a pipe strap. Do not attach the shower arm yet.

Slide the bathtub into the alcove. Make sure tub is flat on the floor and pressed flush against the back wall. If your tub did not come with a tub protector, cut a piece of cardboard to line the tub bottom, and tape pieces of cardboard around the rim to protect the finish from shoes and dropped tools.

Mark locations for ledger boards. To do this, trace the height of the top of the tub's nailing flange onto the wall studs in the alcove. Then remove the tub and measure the height of the nailing flange. Measure down this same amount from your flange lines and mark new ledger board location.

Install 1 × 4 ledger boards. Drive two or three 3"-galvanized deck screws through the ledger board at each stud. All three walls should receive a ledger. Leave an open space in the wet wall to allow clearance for the DWO kit.

(continued)

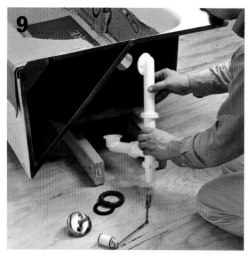

Install the drain-waste-overflow (DWO) pipes before you install the tub. Make sure to get a good seal on the slip nuts at the pipe joints. Follow the manufacturer's instructions to make sure the pop-up drain linkage is connected properly. Make sure rubber gaskets are positioned correctly at the openings on the outside of the tub.

Thread the male-threaded drain strainer into the female-threaded drain waste elbow. Wrap a coil of plumber's putty around the drain outlet underneath the plug rim first. Hand tighten only.

Drain strainer

Attach the overflow coverplate, making sure the pop-up drain controls are in the correct position. Tighten the mounting screws that connect to the mounting plate to sandwich the rubber gasket snugly between the overflow pipe flange and the tub wall. Then, finish tightening the drain strainer against the waste elbow by inserting the handle of a pair of pliers into the strainer body and turning.

Place the tub back into the alcove, taking care not to bump the DWO assembly and disturb the connections. You definitely will want a helper for this job. If the drain outlet of the DWO assembly is not directly over the drain pipe when the tub is in position, you'll need to remove it and adjust the drain line location.

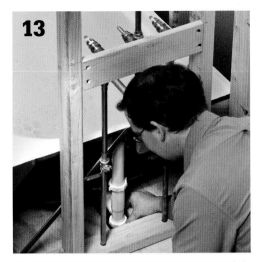

13

Attach the drain outlet from the DWO assembly to the drain P-trap. This is the part of the job where you will appreciate the time you spent creating a roomy access panel for the tub plumbing. Test the drain and overflow to make sure they don't leak. Also test the water supply plumbing, temporarily attaching the handles, spout, and shower arm so you can operate the faucet and the diverter.

14

Drive a 1½" galvanized roofing nail at each stud location, just over the top of the tub's nailing flange. The nail head should pin the flange to the stud. Be careful here—an errant blow or overdriving can cause the enameled finish to crack or craze. *Option: You may choose to drill guide holes and nail through the flange instead.*

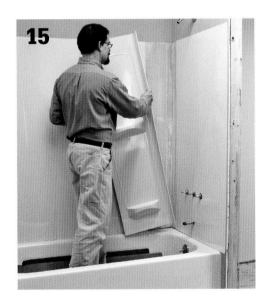

15

Install the wallcoverings and tub surround (see pages 446 to 449 for a 3-piece surround installation). You can also make a custom surround from tileboard or cementboard and tile.

16

Install fittings. First, thread the shower arm into the shower elbow and attach the spout nipple to the valve assembly. Also attach the shower head and escutcheon, the faucet handle/diverter with escutcheon, and the tub spout. Use thread lubricant on all parts.

Installing 3-piece Tub Surrounds

No one wants bathroom fixtures that are aging or yellowed from years of use. A shiny new tub surround can add sparkle and freshness to your dream bath.

Tub surrounds come in many different styles, materials, and price ranges. Choose the features you want and measure your existing bathtub surround for sizing. Surrounds typically come in three or five pieces. A three-panel surround is being installed here, but the process is similar for five-panel systems.

Surface preparation is important for good glue adhesion. Plastic tiles and wallpaper must be removed and textured plaster must be sanded smooth. Surrounds can be installed over ceramic tile that is well attached and in good condition, but it must be sanded and primed. All surfaces must be primed with a water-based primer.

Tools & Materials ▸

Jigsaw	Adhesive
Hole saw	Screwdriver
Drill	Adjustable wrench
Measuring tape	Pry bar
Level	Hammer
Caulking gun	3-piece tub surround
Primer	

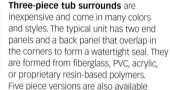

Three-piece tub surrounds are inexpensive and come in many colors and styles. The typical unit has two end panels and a back panel that overlap in the corners to form a watertight seal. They are formed from fiberglass, PVC, acrylic, or proprietary resin-based polymers. Five piece versions are also available and typically have more features such as integral soap shelves and even cabinets.

How to Install a 3-piece Tub Surround

1

Remove the old plumbing fixtures and wallcoverings in the tub area. In some cases you can attach surround panels to old tileboard or even tile, but it is generally best to remove the wallcoverings down to the studs if you can, so you may inspect for leaks or damage.

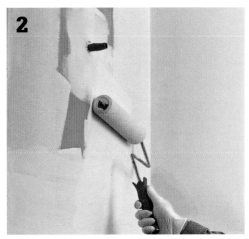

2

Replace the wallcoverings with appropriate materials, such as water and mold-resistant wallboard or cementboard (for ceramic tile installations). Make sure the new wall surfaces are smooth and flat. Some surround kit manufacturers recommend that you apply a coat of primer to sheet goods such as greenboard to create a better bonding surface for the panel adhesive.

3

Test-fit the panels before you start; the tub may have settled unevenly or the walls may be out of plumb. Check the manufacturer's directions for distinguishing right and left panels. Place a panel in position on the tub ledge. Use a level across the top of the panel to determine if it is level. Create a vertical reference line to mark the edge of the panel on the plumbing end.

Test-fitting Tip ▶

Ensure a perfect fit by taping the surround panels to the walls in the tub area. Make sure the tops are level when the overlap seams are aligned and that you have a consistent ⅛" gap between the panel bottoms and the tub flange. Mark the panels for cutting if necessary and, once the panels have been removed, make necessary adjustments to the walls.

(continued)

Some kits are created to fit a range of bathtub dimensions. After performing the test fit, check the fitting instructions to see if you need to trim any of the pieces. Follow the manufacturer's instructions for cutting. Here, we had to cut the corner panels because the instructions advise not to overlap the back or side panel over the corner panels by more than 3". Cut panels using a jigsaw and a fine-tooth blade that is appropriate for cutting fiberglass or acrylic tileboard. The cut panels should be overlapped by panels with factory edges.

Measure and mark the location of the faucets, spout, and shower outlets. Measure in from the vertical reference line (made in step 3) and up from the top of the tub ledge. Re-measure for accuracy, as any cuts to the surround are final. Place the panel face-up on a sheet of plywood. Mark the location of the holes. Cut the holes ½" larger than the pipe diameter. If your faucet has a recessed trim plate (escutcheon), cut the hole to fit the recess. Using a hole saw or a jigsaw, cut out the plumbing outlets.

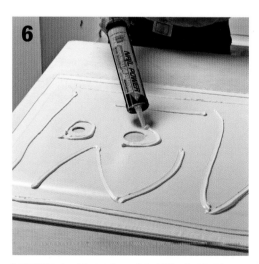

Install the plumbing end panel, test-fitting first. In this surround, the end panels are installed first. Apply adhesive to the back of the plumbing panel. Circle the plumbing outlet holes 1" from the edge. Do not apply adhesive closer than 1" to the double-sided tape (if your kit has tape) or to the bottom edge of the panel.

Remove the protective backing from the tape. Carefully lift the panel by the edges and place against the corner and top of the tub ledge. Press firmly from top to bottom in the corner, then throughout the panel.

8

Test-fit the opposite end panel and make any necessary adjustments. Apply the adhesive, remove the protective backing from the tape, and put in place. Apply pressure to the corner first from top to bottom, and then apply pressure throughout.

9

Apply adhesive to the back panel following the manufacturer's instructions. Remove protective backing from the tape. Lift the panel by the edges and carefully center between the two end panels. When positioned, firmly press in place from top to bottom.

10

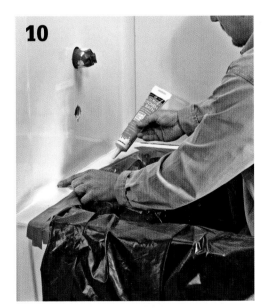

Apply caulk to the bottom and top edges of the panels and at panel joints. Dip your fingertip in water and use it to smooth the caulk to a uniform bead.

11

Apply silicone caulk to escutcheons or trim plates and reinstall them. Allow a minimum of 24 hours for caulk and adhesive to dry thoroughly before using the shower or tub.

Installing Sliding Tub Doors

Curtains on your bathtub shower are a hassle. If you forget to tuck them inside the tub, water flows freely onto your bathroom floor. If you forget to slide them closed, mildew sets up shop in the folds. And every time you brush against them, they stick to your skin. Shower curtains certainly don't add much elegance or charm to a dream bath. Neither does a deteriorated door. Clean up the look of your bathroom, and even give it an extra touch of elegance, with a new sliding tub door.

When shopping for a sliding tub door, you have a choice of framed or frameless. A framed door is edged in metal. The metal framing is typically aluminum but is available in many finishes, including those that resemble gold, brass, or chrome. Glass options are also plentiful. You can choose between frosted or pebbled glass, clear, mirrored, tinted, or patterned glass. Doors can be installed on ceramic tile walls or through a fiberglass tub surround.

Tools & Materials ▸

Measuring tape	Masonry bit
Pencil	for tile wall
Hacksaw	Phillips screwdriver
Miter box	Caulk gun
Level	Masking tape
Drill	Silicone sealant
Center punch	& remover
Razor blade	Tub door kit
Marker	Masking tape

A sliding tub door framed in aluminum gives the room a sleek, clean look and is just one of the available options.

How to Install Sliding Tub Doors

Remove the existing door and inspect the walls. Use a razor blade to cut sealant from tile and metal surfaces. Do not use a razor blade on fiberglass surfaces. Remove remaining sealant by scraping or pulling. Use a silicone sealant remover to remove all residue. Remove shower curtain rods, if present. Check the walls and tub ledge for plumb and level.

Measure the distance between the finished walls along the top of the tub ledge. Refer to the manufacturer's instructions for figuring the track dimensions. For the product seen here, ³⁄₁₆" is subtracted from the measurement to calculate the track dimensions.

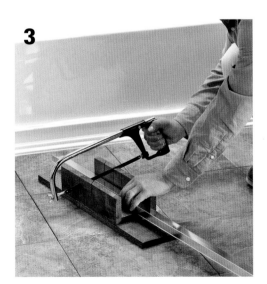

Using a hacksaw and a miter box, carefully cut the track to the proper dimension. Center the track on the bathtub ledge with the taller side out and so the gaps are even at each end. Tape into position with masking tape.

Place a wall channel against the wall with the longer side out and slide it into place over the track so they overlap. Use a level to check the channel for plumb, and then mark the locations of the mounting holes on the wall with a marker. Repeat for the other wall channel. Remove the track.

(continued)

5

Drill mounting holes for the wall channel at the marked locations. In ceramic tile, nick the surface of the tile with a center punch, use a ¼" masonry bit to drill the hole, and then insert the included wall anchors. For fiberglass surrounds, use a ⅛" drill bit; wall anchors are not necessary.

6

Apply a bead of silicone sealant along the joint between the tub and the wall at the ends of the track. Apply a minimum ¼" bead of sealant along the outside leg of the track underside.

7

Position the track on the tub ledge and against the wall. Attach the wall channels using the provided screws. Do not use caulk on the wall channels at this time.

8

Header

Wall channel

Cut and install the header. At a location above the tops of the wall channels, measure the distance between the walls. Refer to the manufacturer's instructions for calculating the header length. For the door seen here, the length is the distance between the walls minus ¹⁄₁₆". Measure the header and carefully cut it to length using a hacksaw and a miter box. Slide the header down on top of the wall channels until seated.

9

Mount the rollers in the roller mounting holes. To begin, use the second-from-the-top roller mounting holes. Follow the manufacturer's instructions for spacer or washer placement and orientation.

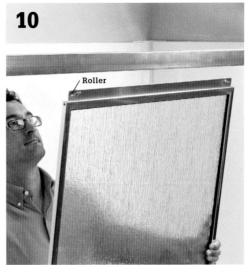

10

Roller

Carefully lift the inner panel by the sides and place the rollers on the inner roller track. Roll the door toward the shower end of the tub. The edge of the panel should touch both rubber bumpers. If it doesn't, remove the door and move the rollers to different holes. Drive the screws by hand to prevent overtightening.

11

Lift the outer panel by the sides with the towel bar facing out from the tub. Place the outer rollers over the outer roller track. Slide the door to the end opposite the shower end of the tub. If the door does not contact both bumpers, remove the door and move the rollers to different mounting holes.

12

Apply a bead of clear silicone sealant to the inside seam of the wall and wall channel at both ends and to the U-shaped joint of the track and wall channels. Smooth the sealant with a fingertip dipped in water.

Tiling Bathroom Walls

Tile is an ideal covering for walls in kitchens and bathrooms, but there's no reason to limit its use to those rooms. It's not as common in North American homes, but in Europe tile has been used in rooms throughout the house for generations. And why not? Beautiful, practical, easy to clean and maintain, tile walls are well suited to many spaces. On the preceding pages, you've seen some design ideas for tile walls.

When shopping for tile, keep in mind that tiles that are at least 6" × 6" are easier to install than small tiles, because they require less cutting and cover more surface area. Larger tiles also have fewer grout lines that must be cleaned and maintained. Check out the selection of trim and specialty tiles and ceramic accessories that are available to help you customize your project.

Most wall tile is designed to have narrow grout lines (less than ⅛" wide) filled with unsanded grout. Grout lines wider than ⅛" should be filled with sanded floor-tile grout. Either type will last longer if it contains, or is mixed with, a latex additive. To prevent staining, it's a good idea to seal your grout after it fully cures, then once a year thereafter.

You can use standard drywall or water-resistant drywall (called "greenboard") as a backer for walls in dry areas. In wet areas, install tile over cementboard. Made from cement and fiberglass, cementboard

cannot be damaged by water, though moisture can pass through it. To protect the framing, install a waterproof membrane, such as roofing felt or polyethylene sheeting, between the framing members and the cementboard. Be sure to tape and finish the seams between cementboard panels before laying the tile.

See page 45 for information on planning and laying out tile walls.

Tools & Materials ▶

Tile-cutting tools	Dry-set tile mortar
Marker	with latex additive
Tape measure	Ceramic wall tile
4-ft. level	Ceramic trim tile
Notched trowel	(as needed)
Mallet	2 × 4
Grout float	Carpet scrap
Grout sponge	Tile grout with latex
Soft cloth	additive
Small paintbrush	Tub & tile caulk
or foam brush	Alkaline grout sealer
Caulk gun	Cardboard
Straight 1 × 2	Story stick/pole

Wall tile is very popular and practical in bathrooms, where it can be used on all surfaces or primarily as an accent. Installing custom-tiled tub and shower surrounds is a popular DIY project.

How to Install Wall Tile in a Bathtub Alcove

Beginning with the back wall, measure up and mark a point at a distance equal to the height of one ceramic tile (if the tub edge is not level, measure up from the lowest spot). Draw a level line through this point, along the entire back wall. This line represents a tile grout line and will be used as a reference line for making the entire tile layout.

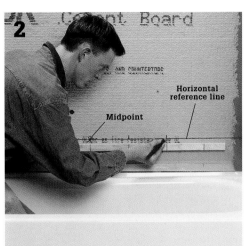

Measure and mark the midpoint on the horizontal reference line. Using a story stick, mark along the reference line where the vertical grout joints will be located. If the story stick shows that the corner tiles will be less than half of a full tile width, move the midpoint half the width of a tile in either direction and mark (shown in next step).

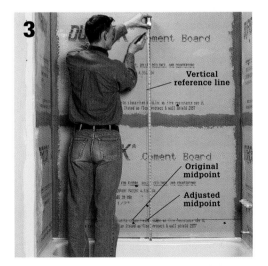

Use a level to draw a vertical reference line through the adjusted midpoint from the tub edge to the ceiling. Measure up from the tub edge along the vertical reference line and mark the rough height of the top row of tiles.

Use the story stick to mark the horizontal grout joints along the vertical reference line, beginning at the mark for the top row of tiles. If the cut tiles at the tub edge will be less than half the height of a full tile, move the top row up half the height of a tile. *Note: If tiling to a ceiling, evenly divide the tiles to be cut at the ceiling and tub edge, as for the corner tiles.*

(continued)

Use a level to draw an adjusted horizontal reference line through the vertical reference line at a grout joint mark close to the center of the layout. This splits the tile area into four workable quadrants.

Use a level to transfer the adjusted horizontal reference line from the back wall to both side walls, then lay out both side walls. Adjust the layout as needed so the final column of tiles ends at the outside edge of the tub. Use only the adjusted horizontal and vertical reference lines for ceramic tile installation.

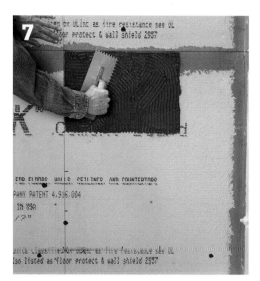

Mix a small batch of thinset mortar containing a latex additive. (Some mortar has additive mixed in by the manufacturer and some must have additive mixed separately.) Spread adhesive on a small section of the wall, along both legs of one quadrant, using a ¼" notched trowel.

Use the edge of the trowel to create furrows in the mortar. Set the first tile in the corner of the quadrant where the lines intersect, using a slight twisting motion. Align the tile exactly with both reference lines. When placing cut tiles, position the cut edges where they will be least visible.

Continue installing tiles, working from the center out into the field of the quadrant. Keep the tiles aligned with the reference lines and tile in one quadrant at a time. If the tiles are not self-spacing, use plastic spacers inserted in the corner joints to maintain even grout lines (inset). The base row against the tub edge should be the last row of tiles installed.

Install remaining tiles, including border areas. Wipe away excess mortar along the top edges of the edge tiles.

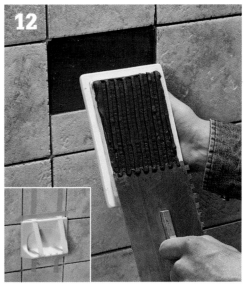

Mark and cut tiles to fit around all plumbing accessories or plumbing fixtures.

Install any ceramic accessories by applying thinset mortar to the back side, then pressing the accessory into place. Use masking tape to support the weight until the mortar dries (inset). Fill the tub with water, then seal expansion joints around the bathtub, floor, and corners with silicone caulk.

Installing Toilets

You can replace a poorly functioning or inefficient toilet with a high-efficiency, high-quality new toilet in just a single afternoon. All toilets made since 1996 have been required to use 1.6 gallons or less per flush, which has been a huge challenge for the industry. Today, the most evolved 1.6-gallon toilets have wide passages behind the bowl and wide (3") flush valve openings—features that facilitate short, powerful flushes. This means fewer second flushes and fewer clogged toilets. These problems were common complaints of the first generation of 1.6-gallon toilets and continue to beleaguer inferior models today. See what toilets are available at your local home center in your price range, then go online and see what other consumers' experiences with those models have been. New toilets often go through a "de-bugging" stage when problems with leaks and malfunctioning parts are more common. Your criteria should include ease of installation, good flush performance, and reliability. With a little research, you should be able to purchase and install a high-functioning economical gravity-flush toilet that will serve you well for years to come.

Tools & Materials ▸

Adjustable wrench
Bucket and sponge
Channel-type pliers
Hacksaw
Penetrating oil
Pliers
Putty knife
Rubber gloves
Screwdriver
Supply tube
Teflon tape
Toilet seat bolts
Toilet seat
Towels
Utility knife
Wax ring with flange

Replacing a toilet is simple, and the latest generation of 1.6-gallon water-saving toilets has overcome the performance problems of earlier models.

How to Install a Toilet

Clean and inspect the old closet flange. Look for breaks or wear. Also inspect the flooring around the flange. If either the flange or floor is worn or damaged, repair the damage. Use a rag and mineral spirits to completely remove residue from the old wax ring. Place a rag into a plastic bag and use it to block toxic sewer gas in the drain opening.

Tip ▸

If you will be replacing your toilet flange or if your existing flange can be unscrewed and moved, orient the new flange so the slots are parallel to the wall. This allows you to insert bolts under the slotted areas, which are much stronger than the areas at the ends of the curved grooves.

Insert new tank bolts (don't reuse old ones) into the openings in the closet flange. Make sure the heads of the bolts are oriented to catch the maximum amount of flange material.

Remove the wax ring and apply it to the underside of the bowl, around the horn. Remove the protective covering. Do not touch the wax ring. It is very sticky. Remove the plastic bag.

(continued)

Lower the bowl onto the flange, taking care not to disturb the wax ring. The holes in the bowl base should align perfectly with the tank bolts. Add a washer and tighten a nut on each bolt. Hand tighten each nut and then use channel-type pliers to further tighten the nuts. Alternate back and forth between nuts until the bowl is secure. *Do not overtighten.*

Attach the toilet tank. Some tanks come with a flush valve and a fill valve preinstalled. For models that do not have this, insert the flush valve through the tank opening and tighten a spud nut over the threaded end of the valve. Place a foam spud washer on top of the spud nut.

Adjust the fill valve as directed by the manufacturer to set the correct tank water level height and install the valve inside the tank. Hand tighten the nylon lock nut that secures the valve to the tank (inset photo) and then tighten it further with channel-type pliers.

With the tank lying on its back, thread a rubber washer onto each tank bolt and insert it into the bolt holes from inside the tank. Then, thread a brass washer and hex nut onto the tank bolts from below and tighten them to a quarter turn past hand tight. Do not overtighten.

Position the tank on the bowl, spud washer on opening, bolts through bolt holes. Put a rubber washer, followed by a brass washer and a wing nut, on each bolt and tighten these up evenly.

You may stabilize the bolts with a large slotted screwdriver from inside the tank, but tighten the nuts, not the bolts. You may press down a little on a side, the front, or the rear of the tank to level it as you tighten the nuts by hand. Do not overtighten and crack the tank. The tank should be level and stable when you're done.

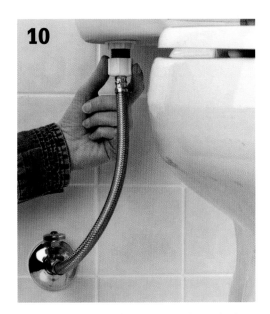

Hook up the water supply by connecting the supply tube to the threaded fill valve with the coupling nut provided. Turn on the water and test for leaks. Do not overtighten.

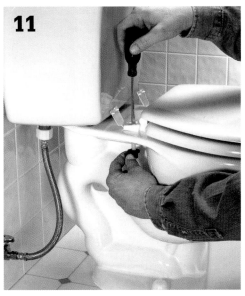

Attach the toilet seat by threading the plastic or brass bolts provided with the seat through the openings on the back of the rim and attaching the nuts.

Installing Wall-hung Vanities

Think of a wall-mounted sink or vanity cabinet and you're likely to conjure up images of public restrooms where these conveniences are installed to improve access for floor cleaning. However, wall-hung sinks and vanities made for home use are very different from the commercial installations.

Often boasting high design, beautiful modern vanities and sinks come in a variety of styles and materials, including wood, metal, and glass. Some attach with decorative wall brackets that are part of the presentation; others look like standard vanities without legs. Install wall-hung sinks and vanities by attaching them securely to studs or wood blocking.

Tools & Materials ▸

Studfinder
Drill
Level
Vanity

Today's wall-hung sinks are stylish and attractive. They must be mounted into studs or added blocking to keep them secure.

How to Install a Wall-hung Vanity Base

1

Remove the existing sink or fixture and inspect the wall framing. Also determine if plumbing supply and waste lines will need to be moved to accommodate the dimensions of the new fixture. Locate the studs in the sink location with a stud finder.

2

Hold the sink or cabinet in the installation area and check to see if the studs align with the sink or sink bracket mounting holes. If they do, skip to step 3. If the studs do not align, remove the wallboard behind the mounting area. Install 2 × 6 blocking between studs at the locations of the mounting screws. Replace and repair wallboard.

3

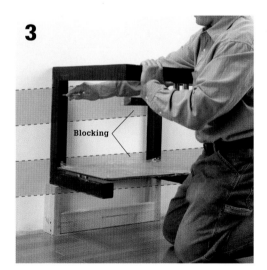

Blocking

Mark the locations of the mounting holes on the wall using a template or by supporting the sink or vanity against the wall with a temporary brace (made here from scrap 2 × 4s) and marking through the mounting holes.

4

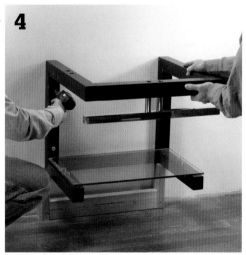

Drill pilot holes at the marks. Have a helper hold the vanity in place while you drive the mounting screws. Hook up the plumbing.

Installing Vessel Sinks

The vessel sink harkens back to the days of washstands and washbowls. Whether it's round, square, or oval, shallow or deep, the vessel sink offers great opportunity for creativity and proudly displays its style. Vessel sinks are a perfect choice for a powder room, where they will have high visibility.

Most vessel sinks can be installed on any flat surface—from a granite countertop to a wall-mounted vanity to an antique dresser. Some sinks are designed to contact the mounting surface only at the drain flange. Others are made to be partially embedded in the surface. Take care to follow the manufacturer's instructions for cutting holes for sinks and faucets.

A beautiful vessel sink demands an equally attractive faucet. Select a tall spout mounted on the countertop or vanity top or a wall-mounted spout to accommodate the height of the vessel. To minimize splashing, spouts should directly flow to the center of the vessel, not down the side. Make sure your faucet is compatible with your vessel choice. Look for a centerset or single-handle model if you'll be custom drilling the countertop—you only need to drill one faucet hole.

Tools & Materials ▸

Jigsaw	Vanity or countertop
Trowel	Vessel sink
Pliers	Pop-up drain
Wrench	P-trap and drain kit
Caulk gun and caulk	Faucet
Sponge	Phillips screwdriver
Drill	

Vessel sinks are available in countless styles and materials, shapes, and sizes. Their one commonality is that they all need to be installed on a flat surface.

Vessel Sink Options

This glass vessel sink embedded in a "floating" glass countertop is a stunning contrast to the strong and attractive frame anchoring it to the wall.

The natural stone vessel sink blends elegantly into the stone countertop and is enhanced by the sleek faucet and round mirror.

The stone vessel sink is complemented by the wall-hung faucet. The rich wood vanity on which it's perched adds warmth to the room.

Vitreous china with a glazed enamel finish is an economical and durable choice for a vessel sink (although it is less durable than stone). Because of the adaptability of both the material and the glaze, the design options are virtually unlimited with vitreous china.

How to Install a Vessel Sink

1

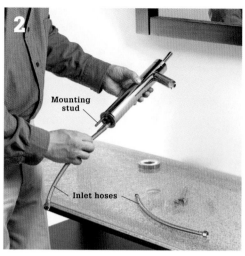

2

Mounting stud

Inlet hoses

Secure the vanity cabinet or other countertop that you'll be using to mount the vessel sink (see pages 464 to 465).

Begin hooking up the faucet. Insert the brass mounting stud into the threaded hole in the faucet base with the slotted end facing out. Hand tighten, and then use a screwdriver to tighten another half turn. Insert the inlet hoses into the faucet body and hand tighten. Use an adjustable wrench to tighten another half turn. Do not overtighten.

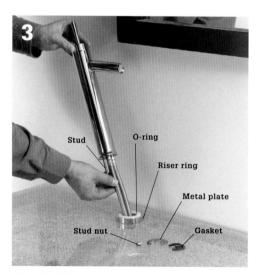

3

Stud

O-ring

Riser ring

Metal plate

Stud nut

Gasket

4

Place the O-ring on top of the riser-ring over the faucet cutout in the countertop. From underneath, slide the rubber gasket and the metal plate over the mounting stud. Thread the mounting stud nut onto the mounting stud and hand tighten. Use an adjustable wrench to tighten another half turn.

To install the sink and pop-up drain, first place the small metal ring between two O-rings and place over the drain cutout.

Place the vessel bowl on top of the O-rings. In this installation, the vessel is not bonded to the countertop.

Put the small rubber gasket over the drain hole in the vessel. From the top, push the pop-up assembly through the drain hole.

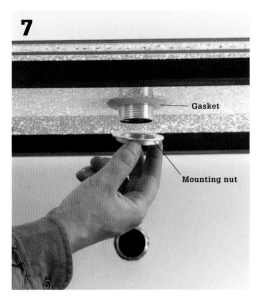

Gasket

Mounting nut

From underneath, push the large rubber gasket onto the threaded portion of the pop-up assembly. Thread the nut onto the pop-up assembly and tighten. Use an adjustable wrench or basin wrench to tighten an additional half turn. Thread the tailpiece onto the pop-up assembly.

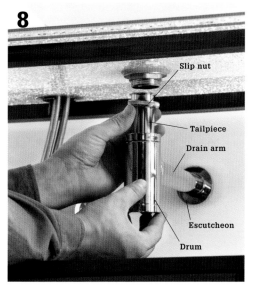

Slip nut

Tailpiece

Drain arm

Escutcheon

Drum

Install the drum trap. Loosen the rings on the top and outlet of the drum trap. Slide the drum trap top hole over the tailpiece. Slide the drain arm into the side outlet, with the flat side of the rubber gasket facing away from the trap. Insert the drain arm into the wall outlet. Hand tighten the rings.

Installing Pedestal Sinks

Pedestal sinks move in and out of popularity more frequently than other sink types, but even during times they aren't particularly trendy, they retain fairly stable demand. You'll find them most frequently in half baths, where their small footprint makes them an efficient choice. Designers are also discovering the appeal of tandem pedestal sinks of late, where the smaller profiles allow for his-and-hers sinks that don't dominate visually.

The primary drawback to pedestal sinks is that they don't offer any storage. Their chief practical benefit is that they conceal plumbing some homeowners would prefer not to see.

Pedestal sinks are mounted in two ways. Most of the more inexpensive ones you'll find at home stores are hung in the manner of wall-hung sinks. The pedestal is actually installed after the sink is hung and its purpose is only decorative. But other pedestal sinks (typically on the higher end of the design scale) have structurally important pedestals that bear most or all of the weight of the sink.

Pedestal sinks are available in a variety of styles and are a perfect fit for small half baths. They keep plumbing hidden, lending a neat, contained look to the bathroom.

How to Install a Pedestal Sink

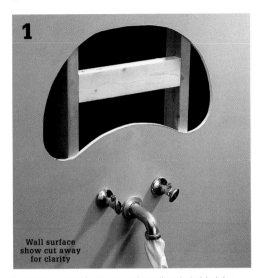

1

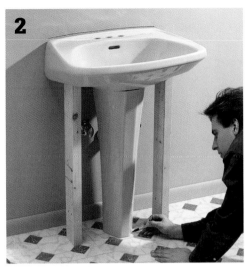

2

Install 2 × 4 blocking between the wall studs, behind the planned sink location. Cover the wall with water-resistant drywall. Waste and supply lines may need to be moved, depending on the sink.

Set the basin and pedestal in position and brace it with 2 × 4s. Outline the top of the basin on the wall, and mark the base of the pedestal on the floor. Mark reference points on the wall and floor through the mounting holes found on the back of the sink and the bottom of the pedestal.

3

4

5

Set aside the basin and pedestal. Drill pilot holes in the wall and floor at the reference points, then reposition the pedestal. Anchor the pedestal to the floor with lag screws.

Attach the faucet, then set the sink on the pedestal. Align the holes in the back of the sink with the pilot holes drilled in the wall, then drive lag screws and washers into the wall brace using a ratchet wrench. Do not overtighten the screws.

Hook up the drain and supply fittings. Caulk between the back of the sink and the wall when installation is finished.

Installing Vanity Cabinets

Most bathroom countertops installed today are integral (one-piece) sink-countertop units made from cultured marble or other solid materials, like solid surfacing. Integral sink-countertops are convenient, and many are inexpensive, but style and color options are limited.

Some remodelers and designers still prefer the distinctive look of a custom-built countertop with a self-rimming sink basin, which gives you a much greater selection of styles and colors. Installing a self-rimming sink is very simple.

Tools & Materials ▸

Pencil	Cardboard
Scissors	Masking tape
Carpenter's level	Plumber's putty
Screwdriver	Lag screws
Channel-type pliers	Tub and tile caulk
Ratchet wrench	Plumber's putty
Basin wrench	

Integral sink-countertops are made in standard sizes to fit common vanity widths. Because the sink and countertop are cast from the same material, integral sink-countertops do not leak, and do not require extensive caulking and sealing.

How to Install a Vanity Cabinet

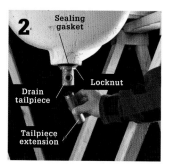

Set the sink-countertop unit onto sawhorses. Attach the faucet and slip the drain lever through the faucet body. Place a ring of plumber's putty around the drain flange, then insert the flange in the drain opening.

Thread the locknut and sealing gasket onto the drain tailpiece, then insert the tailpiece into the drain opening and screw it onto the drain flange. Tighten the locknut securely. Attach the tailpiece extension. Insert the pop-up stopper linkage.

Apply a layer of tub and tile caulk (or adhesive, if specified by the countertop manufacturer) to the top edges of the cabinet vanity, and to any corner braces.

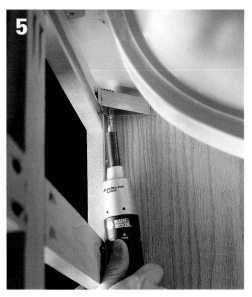

Center the sink-countertop unit over the vanity so the overhang is equal on both sides and the backsplash of the countertop is flush with the wall. Press the countertop evenly into the caulk.

Cabinets with corner braces: Secure the countertop to the cabinet by driving a mounting screw through each corner brace and up into the countertop. *Note: Cultured marble and other hard countertops require predrilling and a plastic screw sleeve.*

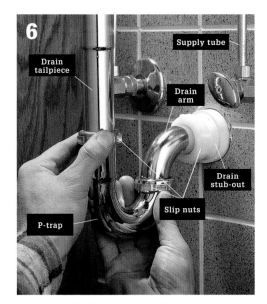

Attach the drain arm to the drain stub-out in the wall, using a slip nut. Attach one end of the P-trap to the drain arm, and the other to the tailpiece of the sink drain, using slip nuts. Connect supply tubes to the faucet tailpieces.

Seal the gap between the backsplash and the wall using tub and tile caulk.

Installing Bathroom Sink Faucets & Drains

One-piece faucets, with either one or two handles, are the most popular fixtures for bathroom installations.

"Widespread" faucets with separate spout and handles are being installed with increasing frequency, however. Because the handles are connected to the spout with flex tubes that can be 18" or longer, widespread faucets can be arranged in many ways.

Tools & Materials ▸

Hacksaw or tin snips	Teflon tape
Channel-type pliers	Faucet kit
Pliers	Pipe joint compound
Basin wrench	Flexible supply tubes
Adjustable wrench	Heat-proof grease
Screwdriver	Loctite (adhesive)
Plumber's putty	

Bathroom sink faucets come in two basic styles: the widespread with independent handles and spout (top); and the single-body, deck-mounted version (bottom).

Bathroom Faucet & Drain Hookups

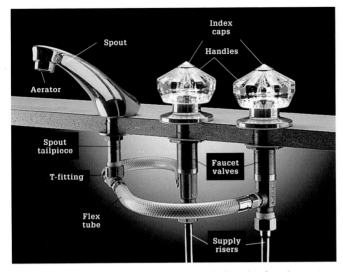

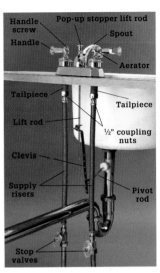

Widespread lavatory faucets have valves that are independent from the spout so they can be configured however you choose, provided that your flex tube connectors are long enough to span the distance.

Single-body lavatory faucets have both valves and the spout permanently affixed to the faucet body. They do not offer flexibility in configurations, but they are very simple to install.

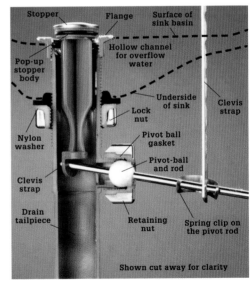

The pop-up stopper fits into the drain opening so the stopper will close tightly against the drain flange when the pop-up handle is lifted up.

The linkage that connects the pop-up stopper to the pop-up handle fits into a male-threaded port in the drain tailpiece. Occasionally the linkage will require adjustment or replacement.

How to Install a Widespread Faucet

Insert the shank of the faucet spout through one of the holes in the sink deck (usually the center hole but you can offset it in one of the end holes if you prefer). If the faucet is not equipped with seals or O-rings for the spout and handles, pack plumber's putty on the undersides before inserting the valves into the deck. *Note: If you are installing the widespread faucet in a new sink deck, drill three holes of the size suggested by the faucet manufacturer.*

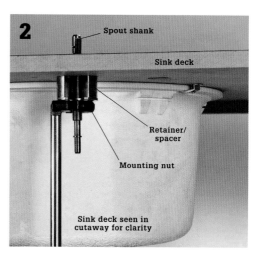

In addition to mounting nuts, many spout valves for widespread faucets have an open-retainer fitting that goes between the underside of the deck and the mounting nut. Others have only a mounting nut. In either case, tighten the mounting nut with pliers or a basin wrench to secure the spout valve. You may need a helper to keep the spout centered and facing forward.

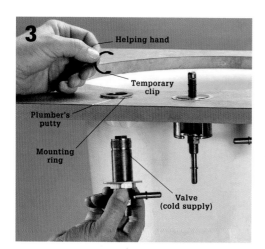

Mount the valves to the deck using whichever method the manufacturer specifies (it varies quite a bit). In the model seen here, a mounting ring is positioned over the deck hole (with plumber's putty seal) and the valve is inserted from below. A clip snaps onto the valve from above to hold it in place temporarily (you'll want a helper for this).

From below, thread the mounting nuts that secure the valves to the sink deck. Make sure the cold water valve (usually has a blue cartridge inside) is in the right-side hole (from the front) and the hot water valve (red cartridge) is in the left hole (from the front). Install both valves.

5

Water outlet (cold)

Water outlet (hot)

Water inlet (spout)

Once you've started the nut on the threaded valve shank, secure the valve with a basin wrench, squeezing the lugs where the valve fits against the deck. Use an adjustable wrench to finish tightening the lock nut onto the valve. The valves should be oriented so the water outlets are aimed at the inlet on the spout shank.

6

T-fitting

Attach the flexible supply tubes (supplied with the faucet) to the water outlets on the valves. Some twist onto the outlets, but others (like the ones above) click into place. The supply hoses meet in a T-fitting that is attached to the water inlet on the spout.

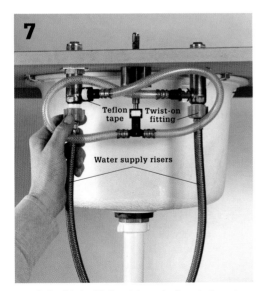

7

Teflon tape

Twist-on fitting

Water supply risers

Attach flexible braided-metal supply risers to the water stop valves and then attach the tubes to the inlet port on each valve (usually with Teflon tape and a twist-on fitting at the valve end of the supply riser).

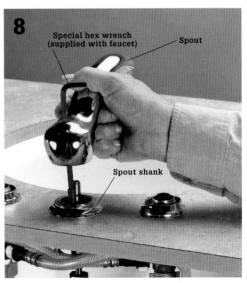

8

Special hex wrench (supplied with faucet)

Spout

Spout shank

Attach the spout. The model shown here comes with a special hex wrench that is threaded through the hole in the spout where the lift rod for the pop-up drain will be located. Once the spout is seated cleanly on the spout shank, tighten the hex wrench to secure the spout. Different faucets will use other methods to secure the spout to the shank.

(continued)

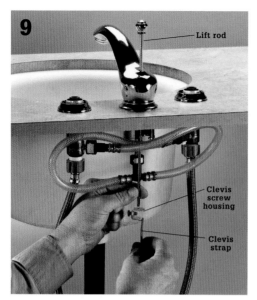

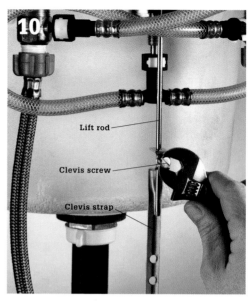

If your sink did not have a pop-up stopper, you'll need to replace the sink drain tailpiece with a pop-up stopper body (often supplied with the faucet). See page 473. Insert the lift rod through the hole in the back of the spout and, from below, thread the pivot rod through the housing for the clevis screw.

Attach the clevis strap to the pivot rod that enters the pop-up drain body, and adjust the position of the strap so it raises and lowers properly when the lift rod is pulled up. Tighten the clevis screw at this point. It's hard to fit a screwdriver in here, so you may need to use a wrench or pliers.

Attach the faucet handles to the valves using whichever method is required by the faucet manufacturer. Most faucets are designed with registration methods to ensure that the handles are symmetrical and oriented in an ergonomic way once you secure them to the valves.

Turn on the water supply and test the faucet. Remove the faucet aerator so any debris in the lines can clear the spout.

Variation: How to Install a Single-body Faucet ▸

Most faucets come with a plastic or foam gasket to seal the bottom of the faucet to the sink deck. These gaskets will not always form a watertight seal. If you want to ensure no water gets below the sink, discard the seal and press a ring of plumber's putty into the sealant groove built into the underside of the faucet body.

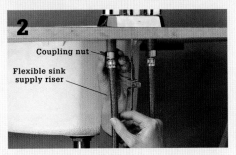

Insert the faucet tailpieces through the holes in the sink. From below, thread washers and mounting nuts over the tailpieces, then tighten the mounting nuts with a basin wrench until snug. Put a dab of pipe joint compound on the threads of the stop valves and thread the metal nuts of the flexible supply risers to these. Wrench tighten about a half-turn past hand tight. Overtightening these nuts will strip the threads. Now tighten the coupling nuts to the faucet tailpieces with a basin wrench.

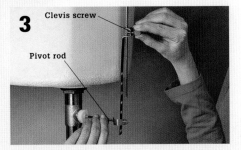

Slide the lift rod of the new faucet into its hole behind the spout. Thread it into the clevis past the clevis screw. Push the pivot rod all the way down so the stopper is open. With the lift rod also all the way down, tighten the clevis to the lift rod.

Grease the fluted valve stems with heatproof grease, then put the handles in place. Put a drop of Loctite on each handle screw before tightening it on. (This will keep your handles from coming loose.) Cover each handle screw with the appropriate index cap—Hot or Cold.

Unscrew the aerator from the end of the spout. Turn the hot and cold water taps on full. Turn the water back on at the stop valves and flush out the faucet for a couple of minutes before turning off the water at the faucet. Check the riser connections for drips. Tighten a compression nut only until the drip stops.

How to Install a Pop-up Drain

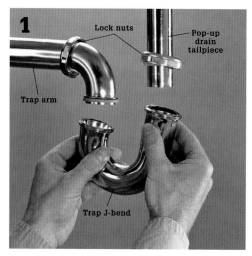

Put a basin under the trap to catch water. Loosen the nuts at the outlet and inlet to the trap J-bend by hand or with channel-type pliers and remove the bend. The trap will slide off the pop-up body tailpiece when the nuts are loose. Keep track of washers and nuts and their up/down orientation by leaving them on the tubes.

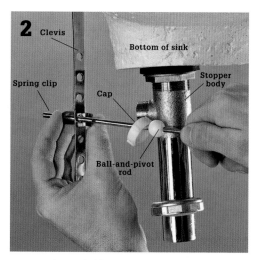

Unscrew the cap holding the ball-and-pivot rod in the pop-up body and withdraw the ball. Compress the spring clip on the clevis and withdraw the pivot rod from the clevis.

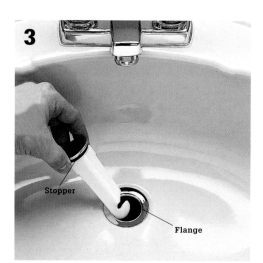

Remove the pop-up stopper. Then, from below, remove the lock nut on the stopper body. If needed, keep the flange from turning by inserting a large screwdriver in the drain from the top. Thrust the stopper body up through the hole to free the flange from the basin, and then remove the flange and the stopper body.

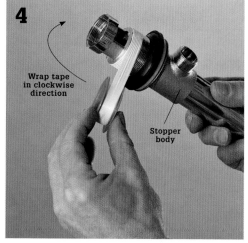

Clean the drain opening above and below, and then thread the locknut all the way down the new pop-up body, followed by the flat washer and the rubber gasket (beveled side up). Wrap three layers of Teflon tape clockwise onto the top of the threaded body. Make a ½"-dia. snake from plumber's putty, form it into a ring, and stick the ring underneath the drain flange.

5

Plumber's putty

From below, face the pivot rod opening directly back toward the middle of the faucet and pull the body straight down to seat the flange. Thread the locknut/washer assembly up under the sink, then fully tighten the locknut with channel-type pliers. Do not twist the flange in the process, as this can break the putty seal. Clean off the excess plumber's putty from around the flange.

6

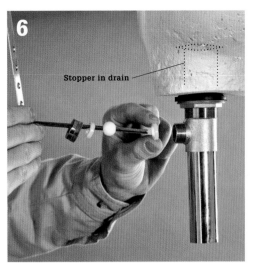

Stopper in drain

Drop the pop-up stopper into the drain hole so the hole at the bottom of its post is closest to the back of the sink. Put the beveled nylon washer into the opening in the back of the pop-up body with the bevel facing back.

7

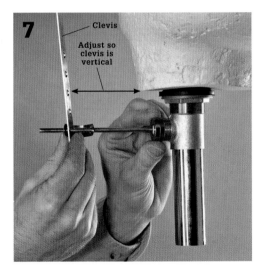

Clevis

Adjust so clevis is vertical

Put the cap behind the ball on the pivot rod as shown. Sandwich a hole in the clevis with the spring clip and thread the long end of the pivot rod through the clip and clevis. Put the ball end of the pivot rod into the pop-up body opening and into the hole in the the stopper stem. Screw the cap on to the pop-up body over the ball.

8

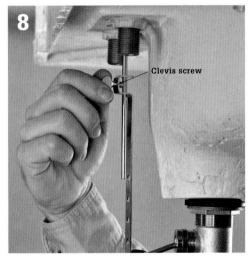

Clevis screw

Loosen the clevis screw holding the clevis to the lift rod. Push the pivot rod all the way down (which fully opens the pop-up stopper). With the lift rod also all the way down, tighten the clevis screw to the rod. If the clevis runs into the top of the trap, cut it short with your hacksaw or tin snips. Reassemble the J-bend trap.

Installing Tub Spouts

In many situations, replacing a bathtub spout can be almost as easy as hooking up a garden hose to an outdoor spigot. There are some situations where it is a bit more difficult, but still pretty simple. The only time it's a real problem is when the spout is attached to a plain copper supply nipple, rather than a threaded nipple. You'll know this is the case if the spout has a setscrew on the underside where it meets the wall. Many bathtub spouts are sold in kits with a matching showerhead and handle or handles. But for a simple one-for-one replacement, spouts are sold separately. You just need to make sure the new spout is compatible with the existing nipple.

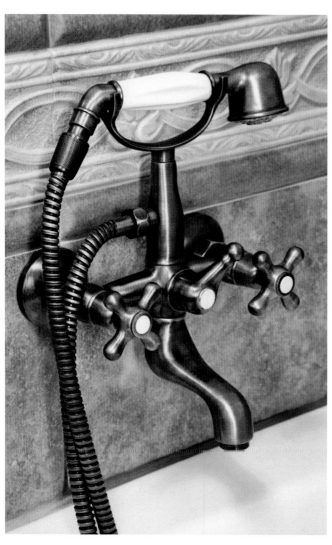

Tub spouts can be relatively complicated plumbing fittings, often performing three or four important functions. The spout itself is simple enough, since its only function is to deliver bathwater to the tub. But the diverter network and pop-up drain contain multiple moving parts that require precise adjustment and occasional repair or replacement (see photo, next page). The diverter is basically a stop valve that's activated by a lever or knob to block flow of water from the spout, forcing it up to a showerhead or out through a handheld showerhead, as seen here.

Diverter lever

Gate diverter

In many bathtub/shower plumbing systems, the spout has the important job of housing the diverter—a gate inside the spout that is operated by a lever with a knob for pulling. An open gate allows water to come out of the spout when the faucet is turned on. When the diverter is pulled shut, the water is redirected up a riser pipe and to the showerhead. Failure of the diverter is one of the most common reasons for replacing a spout.

Tools & Materials ▸

Pliers
Adjustable pliers
Channel-type pliers
Rags
Masking tape
Screwdrivers
Allen wrenches
Replacement spout
Measuring tape

Teflon tape
Utility knife

Installation Tip ▸

If you are installing a brand new tub/shower faucet, it likely contains an antiscald device. Most of these devices work by sensing a decrease in cold water flow and compensating by stemming the hot water flow too. As you install the new plumbing, be aware that faucets with antiscald protection will not function at all if both water supply tubes are not turned on at the stop valve. In other words: you can't test the hot and cold supply independently.

How to Install a Slip-fit Spout

1

Slip fitting: Check underneath the tub spout to look for an access slot or cutout, which indicates the spout is a slip-fit style that is held in place with a setscrew and mounted on a copper supply nipple. Loosen the screw with a hex (Allen) wrench. Pull off the spout.

2

Clean the copper nipple with steel wool. If you find any sharp edges where the nipple was cut, smooth them out with emery paper. Then, insert the O-ring that comes with the spout onto the nipple (see the manufacturer's instructions) and slide the spout body over the nipple in an upside-down position.

3

With the spout upside down for ease of access, tighten the setscrews on the clamp, working through the access slot or cutout, until you feel resistance.

4

Spin the spout so it's right-side up and then tighten the setscrew from below, making sure the wall end of the spout is flush against the wall. Do not overtighten the setscrew.

How to Install a Threaded Spout

If you see no setscrew or slot on the underside of the spout, it is attached to a threaded nipple. Unscrew the tub spout by inserting a heavy-duty flat screwdriver into the spout opening and spinning it counterclockwise.

Tool Tip ▸

Alternatively, grip the spout with a padded pipe wrench or channel-type pliers. Buy a compatible replacement spout at a home center or hardware store.

Copper nipple
with threaded adapter

Wrap several courses of Teflon tape clockwise onto the pipe threads of the nipple. Using extra Teflon tape on the threads creates resistance if the spout tip points past six o'clock when tight.

Twist the new spout onto the nipple until it is flush against the wall and the spout is oriented properly. If the spout falls short of six o'clock, you may protect the finish of the spout with tape and twist it a little beyond hand tight with your channel-type pliers—but don't overdo it; the fitting can crack.

Installing Vanity Lights

Many bathrooms have a single fixture positioned above the vanity, but a light source in this position casts shadows on the face and makes grooming more difficult. Placing light fixtures on either side of the mirror is a better arrangement.

For a remodel, mark the mirror location, run cable, and position boxes before drywall installation. You can also retrofit by installing new boxes and drawing power from the existing fixture.

The light sources should be at eye level; 66" is typical. The size of your mirror and its location on the wall may affect how far apart you can place the sconces, but 36 to 40" apart is a good guideline.

Tools & Materials ▸

Drywall saw
Drill
Combination tool
Circuit tester
Screwdrivers
Hammer
Electrical boxes and braces
Vanity light fixtures
NM cable
Wire connectors

Vanity lights on the sides of the mirror provide even lighting.

How to Replace Vanity Lights in a Finished Bathroom

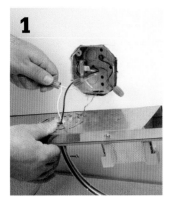

1

2

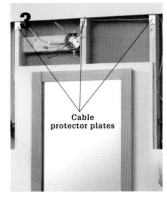

3

Cable
protector plates

Turn off the power at the service panel. Remove the old fixture from the wall and test to make sure that the power is off. Then remove a strip of drywall from around the old fixture to the first studs beyond the approximate location of the new fixtures. Make the opening large enough that you have room to route cable from the existing fixture to the boxes.

Mark the location for the fixtures and install new boxes. Install the boxes about 66" above the floor and 18 to 20" from the centerline of the mirror (the mounting base of some fixtures is above or below the bulb, so adjust the height of the bracing accordingly). If the correct location is on or next to a stud, you can attach the box directly to the stud, otherwise you'll need to install blocking or use boxes with adjustable braces (shown).

Open the side knockouts on the electrical box above the vanity. Then drill ⅝" holes in the centers of any studs between the old fixture and the new ones. Run two NM cables from the new boxes for the fixtures to the box above the vanity. Protect the cable with metal protector plates. Secure the cables with cable clamps, leaving 11" of extra cable for making the connection to the new fixtures. Remove sheathing and strip insulation from the ends of the wires.

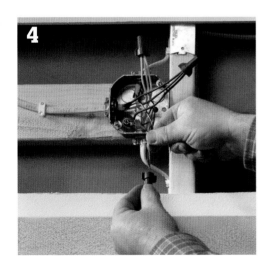

4

5

Connect the white wires from the new cables to the white wire from the old cable, and connect the black wires from the new cables to the black wire from the old cable. Connect the ground wires. Cover all open boxes and then replace the drywall, leaving openings for the fixture and the old box. (Cover the old box with a solid junction box cover plate.)

Install the fixture mounting braces on the boxes. Attach the fixtures by connecting the black circuit wire to the black fixture wire, and connecting the white circuit wire to the white fixture wire. Connect the ground wires. Position each fixture over each box, and attach with the mounting screws. Restore power and test the circuit.

Installing Grab Bars

Bathrooms are beautiful with their shiny ceramic tubs, showers, and floors, but add water and moisture to the mix and you've created the perfect conditions for a fall. The good news is many falls in the bathroom can be avoided by installing grab bars at key locations.

Grab bars help family members steady themselves on slippery shower, tub, and other floor surfaces. Plus, they provide support for people transferring from a wheelchair or walker to the shower, tub, or toilet.

Grab bars come in a variety of colors, shapes, sizes, and textures. Choose a style with a 1¼ to 1½" diameter that fits comfortably between your thumb and fingers. Then properly install it 1½" from the wall with anchors that can support at least 250 pounds.

The easiest way to install grab bars is to screw them into wall studs or into blocking or backing attached to studs. Blocking is a good option if you are framing a new bathroom or have the wall surface removed during a major remodel (see Illustration A). Use 2 × 6 or 2 × 8 lumber to provide room for adjustments, and fasten the blocks to the framing with 16d nails. Note the locations of your blocking for future reference.

As an alternative, cover the entire wall with ¾" plywood backing secured with screws to the wall framing, so you can install grab bars virtually anywhere on the wall (see Illustration B).

Grab bars can be installed in areas without studs. For these installations, use specialized heavy-duty hollow-wall anchors designed to support at least 250 pounds.

Grab bars promote independence in the bathroom, where privacy is especially important. Grab bars not only help prevent slips and falls, they also help people steady themselves in showers and lower themselves into tubs.

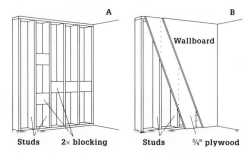

Blocking or backing is required for secure grab bars. If you know where the grab bars will be located, add 2× blocking between studs (Illustration A). You also can cover the entire wall with ¾" plywood backing, which allows you to install grab bars virtually anywhere on the wall.

Tools & Materials ▸

Measuring tape	Masonry bit
Pencil	Grab bar
Stud finder	Hollow-wall anchors
Level	#12 stainless steel screws
Drill	Silicone caulk

How to Install Grab Bars

1

Locate the wall studs in the installation area, using a stud finder. If the area is tiled, the stud finder may not detect studs, so try to locate the studs above the tile, if possible, then use a level to transfer the marks lower on the wall. Otherwise, you can drill small, exploratory holes through grout joints in the tile, then fill the holes with silicone caulk to seal them. Be careful not to drill into pipes.

2

Mark the grab bar height at one stud location, then use a level to transfer the height mark to the stud that will receive the other end of the bar. Position the grab bar on the height marks so at least two of the three mounting holes are aligned with the stud centers. Mark the mounting hole locations onto the wall.

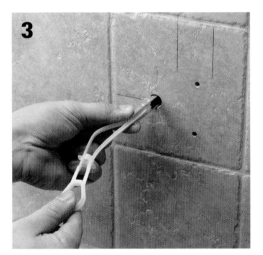

3

Drill pilot holes for the mounting screws. If you are drilling through tile, start with a small bit (about ⅛"), then redrill the hole with the larger bit. For screws that won't hit studs, drill holes for wall anchors, following the manufacturer's directions for sizing. Install anchors, if necessary.

4

Apply a continuous bead of silicone caulk to the back side of each bar end (inset). Secure the bar to the studs using #12 stainless steel screws (the screws should penetrate the stud by at least 1"). Install a stainless steel screw or bolt into the wall anchors. Test the bar to make sure it's secure.

Installing Glass Shelving

Glass shelving is unobtrusive, so it can fit many styles of bathrooms—from sleek modern to Victorian. You can find a wide variety of shelving available in home stores and online.

Most glass shelves are held in place with metal mounts. How the shelves are secured to the mounts and how the mounts are attached to the wall differs. Most shelves have a hidden bracket that is secured to the wall. The mount then slips over the bracket and is secured with a setscrew. The most basic models may have mounts that are screwed directly into the wall with exposed screws. The directions here are for shelving that uses hidden brackets.

If you are installing shelves on a tiled wall, mount the brackets in grout lines if at all possible to minimize the possibility of cracking the tiles. Many glass shelves have some variability in the distance between the mounts.

Tools & Materials ›

Level	Pencil
Drill	Glass shelves

Glass shelves fit any style and size of bathroom. They are held in place with metal mounts attached to the walls.

How to Install Glass Shelves

1

Assemble the shelf and shelf holders (not the brackets). Hold the shelf against the wall in the desired location. On the wall, mark the center point of each holder, where the setscrew is. Remove the shelf from the holders and set aside.

2

Remove the shelves and use the level to extend the mark into a 3" vertical line. Use the level to mark a horizontal line across the centers of these lines.

3

Center the middle round hole of the bracket over the intersection of the vertical and horizontal lines. Mark the center of each of the oblong holes. Put the bracket aside and drill a ¼" hole at each mark. Insert the included wall anchors in the holes. Replace the bracket and insert the screws into the wall anchors and drive the screws. Repeat for the second bracket.

4

Slide a holder over a bracket, check that the shelf mount is level, and tighten the setscrew. Repeat with the other holder. Insert the shelf and fix in place. Check the shelf for level. If it's not level, remove one holder and loosen the bracket screws. Slide the bracket up or down to make the unit level. Replace the holder and shelf.

Installing Towel Warmers

Here's a little bit of luxury that need not be limited to high-end hotel stays. You can have toasty towels in your own bathroom with an easy-to-install towel warmer. In a relatively cold room, this can make stepping out of the shower a much more pleasant experience.

Heated towel racks are available in a wide range of styles and sizes. Freestanding floor models as well as door- and wall-mounted versions can be plugged in for use when desired. Hardwired wall-mounted versions can be switched on when you enter the bathroom so your towels are warm when you step out of the shower. Although installing them requires some electrical skills, the hardwired models do not need to be located near wall receptacles and they do not have exposed cords or extension cords hanging on the wall. However, if you locate the warmer directly above an existing receptacle, you can save a lot of time and mess by running cable up from the receptacle to the new electrical box for the warmer.

Before installing hardwired models, check your local electrical codes for applicable regulations. If you are not experienced with home wiring, have an electrician do this job for you or opt for a plug-in model.

Tools & Materials ▸

Drill	Retrofit electrical
Level	outlet box
Keyhole saw	NM cable
Wiring tools	Towel warmer
Phillips screwdriver	Pencil
Stud finder	Masking tape
Wire connectors	

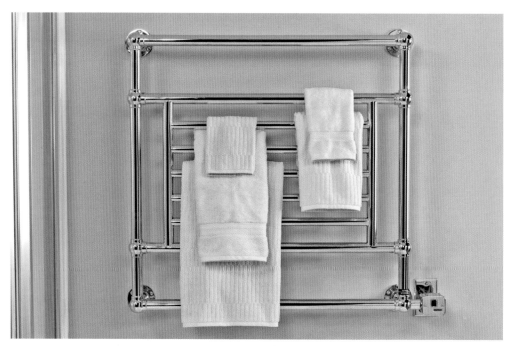

A hard-wired towel warmer offers the luxury of heated towels without the safety concerns of a plug-in device.

How to Install a Hardwired Towel Warmer

Use a stud finder to locate the studs in the area you wish to place the towel warmer. Mark the stud locations with masking tape or pencil lines. Attach the wall brackets to the towel warmer and hold the unit against the wall at least 7" from the floor and 3" from the ceiling or any overhang. Mark the locations of the wall bracket outlet plate (where the electrical connection will be made) and the mounting brackets.

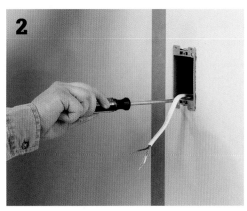

Shut off electrical power at the main service panel. At the mark for the wall bracket outlet, cut a hole in the wallcovering for a retrofit electrical box. Run NM cable from the opening to a GFCI-protected circuit (here, we ran cable down to a receptacle directly beneath it), or install a separate GFCI-protected circuit (you'll need to consult a wiring book or an electrician). Pull the cable through the hole in the retrofit box, and then tighten the cable clamp. Place the box in the hole flush with the wall surface and tighten the mounting screw in the rear of the box. Cut the wires so about 5" extends into the box and strip the insulation off at ⅜" from the end of each wire.

Position the towel warmer over the outlet box and mark the locations of the screw holes for the wall brackets. Make sure the appliance is level. Remove the warmer and drill ¼" pilot holes at the marked locations. If the marks are located over studs, drill ⅛" pilot holes. If not, push wall anchors into the holes. Thread the mounting screws through the brackets. Have a helper hold the towel rack in place and use wire connectors to connect the wires, including the ground wire, according to the instructions.

After the electrical connections are made, fasten the towel rack brackets to the wall. Turn on power and test the towel warmer. Finally, attach the electrical cover plate with integral on/off switch.

Basements
& Attics

Is your house lacking just a little more space but you love it too much to think about moving? Has your life changed since you bought the house and now you find you need a home office for your freelance work or telecommuting, a place for the children in your life to play, or an extra bedroom for a relative? Or maybe now that your obligations have changed, you find yourself fantasizing about a space dedicated to your hobbies?

This chapter can help you determine how best to use your tantalizingly empty attic or basement, inspire you with great design ideas, and give you the practical how-to to tackle the projects on your own.

Over half of houses in North America are more than 30 years old. The attics and basements in these older homes are often significantly underutilized spaces. Even in new construction, attics and basements often are left unfinished so that the new homeowners can determine for themselves how best to incorporate the space.

In this chapter:

- Evaluating Your Attic
- Evaluating Your Basement
- Planning the Framing
- Installing Basement Floors
- Installing Attic Floors
- Installing Basement Walls
- Installing Attic Walls
- Finishing Attic Ceilings
- Adding Basement Egress Windows
- Installing Baseboard Heaters

Evaluating Your Attic

Start your attic evaluation with a quick framing inspection. If the roof is framed with rafters, you can continue to the next test. If it's built with trusses, however, consider remodeling your basement instead. The problem is that the internal supports in trusses leave too little space to work with, and trusses cannot be altered.

The next step is to check for headroom and overall floor space. Most building codes call for 7½ ft. of headroom over 50% of the "usable" floor space, which is defined as any space with a ceiling height of at least 5 ft. Remember that these minimums apply to the finished space—after the flooring and ceiling surfaces are installed. Other things can affect headroom, as well, such as reinforcing the floor frame, and increasing rafter depth for strength or insulation.

You may also find various supports in your attic that are there to strengthen your roof but may limit your space. Collar ties are horizontal boards that join two rafters together in the upper third of the rafter span. They prevent rafter uplift in high winds. Often collar ties can be moved up a few inches but cannot be removed. Rafter ties join rafters in the lower third of their span to prevent spreading. In most attics, the ceiling or floor joists serve as rafter ties. Purlins are horizontal boards that run at right angles to the rafters and are supported by struts. These systems shorten the rafter span, allowing the use of smaller lumber for the rafters. You may be allowed to substitute kneewalls for purlins and struts. If you'll need to have any support system altered or moved, consult an architect or engineer.

The rafters themselves also need careful examination. Inspect them for signs of stress or damage, such as cracks, sagging, and insect infestation. Look for dark areas indicating roof leaks. If you find leaks or you know your roofing is past its useful life, have it repaired or replaced before you start the finishing process. And even if the rafters appear healthy, they may be too small to support the added weight of finish materials. Small rafters can also be a problem if they don't provide enough room for adequate insulation.

At this point, it's a good idea to have a professional check the structural parts of your attic, including the

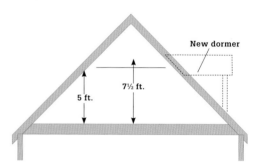

Habitable rooms must be at least 70 sq. ft. total and measure at least 7 ft. in any one direction. To meet headroom requirements, 50% of the usable floor space must have a ceiling height of 7½ ft. You can add to your floor space and headroom by adding protruding windows called dormers. In addition to space, dormers add light and ventilation to your attic.

Rafter framing creates open space in an attic because the rafters carry most of the roof's weight.

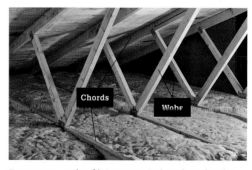

Trusses are made of interconnected cords and webs, which close off most of the attic space.

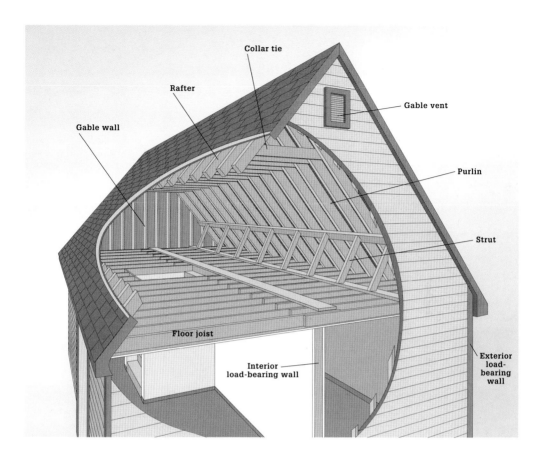

Collar tie

Rafter

Gable wall

Gable vent

Purlin

Strut

Floor joist

Interior load-bearing wall

Exterior load-bearing wall

rafters and everything from the floor down. In some cases, finishing an attic is like adding a story to your home, which means that the structure must have adequate support for the new space. Attic floors are often built as ceiling frames for the level below and are not intended to support living space. Floors can be strengthened with additional joists, known as sister joists or with new joists installed between the existing ones.

Support for the attic floor is provided by the load-bearing walls below and, ultimately, by the foundation. If these elements can't support the finished attic, they'll need to be reinforced. This may be as simple as strengthening the walls with plywood panels or as complicated as adding support posts and beams or reinforcing the foundation.

In addition to these structural matters, there are a few general code requirements you should keep in mind as you inspect your attic. If you plan to add a

bedroom, it will need at least one exit to the outside. This can be a door leading to an outside stairwell or an egress window. Most codes also have minimum requirements for ventilation and natural light, which means you may have to add windows or skylights.

One of the largest expenses of finishing an attic is in providing access: You'll need a permanent stairway at least 36" wide, with room for a 36" landing at the top and bottom. This is an important planning issue because adding a stairway affects the layout and traffic patterns of the attic as well as the floor below.

Finally, take an inventory of existing mechanicals in your attic. While plumbing and wiring runs can be moved relatively easily, other features, such as chimneys, must be incorporated into your plans. This is a good time to have your chimney inspected by a fire official and to obtain the building code specifications for framing around chimneys.

Evaluating Your Basement

The two things that put an end to most basement finishing plans are inadequate headroom and moisture. Begin your evaluation by measuring from the basement floor to the bottom of the floor joists above. Most building codes require habitable rooms to have a finished ceiling height of 7½ ft., measured from the finished floor to the lowest part of the finished ceiling. However, obstructions, such as beams, soffits, and pipes, (spaced at least 4 ft. on center) usually can hang down 6" below that height. Hallways and bathrooms typically need at least 7-ft. ceilings.

While it's impractical to add headroom in a basement, there are some ways of working around the requirements. Ducts and pipes often can be moved, and beams and other obstructions can be incorporated into walls or hidden in closets or other uninhabitable spaces. Also, some codes permit lower ceiling heights in rooms with specific purposes, such as recreation rooms. If headroom is a problem, talk to the local building department before you dash your dreams.

A well-built basement is structurally sound and provides plenty of support for finished space, but before you cover up the walls, floor, and ceiling, check for potential problems. Inspect the masonry carefully. Large cracks may indicate shifting of the soil around the foundation; severely bowed or out-of-plumb walls may be structurally unsound. Small cracks usually cause moisture problems rather than structural woes, but they should be sealed to prevent further cracking. Contact an engineer or foundation contractor for help with foundation problems. If you have an older home, you may find sagging floor joists overhead or rotted wood posts or beams; any defective wood framing will have to be reinforced or replaced.

Your basement's mechanicals are another important consideration. The locations of water heaters, pipes, wiring, circuit boxes, furnaces, and ductwork can have a significant impact on the cost and difficulty of your project. Can you plan around components, or will they have to be moved? Is there enough headroom to install a suspended ceiling so mechanicals can remain accessible? Or, will you have to reroute pipes and ducts to increase headroom? Electricians and HVAC contractors can assess your systems and suggest modifications.

Aside from being dark and scary places, unfinished basements often harbor toxic elements. One of the most common is radon, a naturally occurring radioactive gas that is odorless and colorless. It's believed that prolonged exposure to high levels of radon can cause lung cancer. The Environmental Protection Agency has free publications to help you test for radon and take steps to reduce the levels in your house. For starters, you can perform a "short-term" test using a kit from a hardware store or home center. Look for the phrase "Meets EPA Requirements" to ensure the test kit is accurate. Keep in mind that short-term tests are not as conclusive as professional, long-term tests. If your test reveals high levels of radon, contact a radon specialist.

Another basement hazard is insulation containing asbestos, which was commonly used in older homes for insulating ductwork and heating pipes. In most cases, this insulation can be left alone provided it's in good condition and is protected from damage. If you

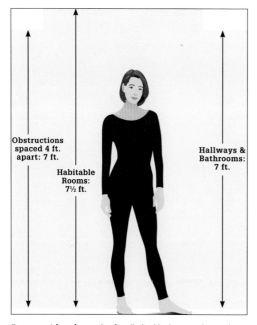

Obstructions spaced 4 ft. apart: 7 ft.

Hallways & Bathrooms: 7 ft.

Habitable Rooms: 7½ ft.

Basement headroom is often limited by beams, ducts, pipes, and other elements. Typical minimums for ceiling height are shown here: 7½ ft. for habitable rooms; 7 ft. for bathrooms and hallways; 7 ft. for obstructions spaced no less than 4 ft. apart.

fear the insulation in your basement poses a hazard, contact an asbestos abatement contractor to have it evaluated or safely removed.

Also check the local codes for exits from finished basements—most codes require two. The stairway commonly serves as one exit, while the other can be a door to the outside, an egress window, or a code-compliant bulkhead (an exterior stairway with cellar doors). Each bedroom will also need an egress window or door for escape.

Stairways must also meet the local code specifications. If yours doesn't, you'll probably have to hire someone to rebuild it.

As a final note, if you're planning to finish the basement in a new house, ask the builder how long you should wait before starting the project. Poured concrete walls and floors need time to dry out before they can be covered. Depending on where you live, you may be advised to wait up to two years, just to be safe.

Rerouting service lines and mechanicals adds quickly to the expense of a project, so consider your options carefully.

Weakened or undersized joists and other framing members must be reinforced or replaced.

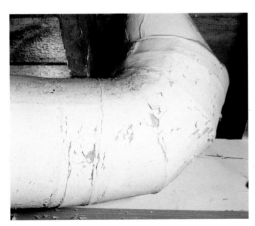

Old insulation containing asbestos poses a serious health risk if it is deteriorating or is disturbed.

Minor cracks such as these in masonry walls and floors usually can be sealed and forgotten, while severe cracking may indicate serious structural problems.

Planning the Framing

Use walls to define your new spaces. Walls can create quiet private retreats or comfortable bathrooms or serve as barriers between formal living areas and dusty, unfinished storage spaces. To determine where your walls should go, start with a thorough investigation of the unfinished space. All obstacles, such as mechanical systems, service lines, floor drains, support columns, chimneys, and roof framing, must be considered. As you work with different layouts, think about which of these elements can be enclosed by walls, which can be hidden within a wall or concealed by a soffit or chase, and which, if any, can be moved.

One technique to help you get started is to draw full-scale "walls" onto your basement floor, using children's sidewalk chalk (on wood attic floors, use wide masking tape instead of chalk). This can help you visualize the planned spaces and give you a better sense of room sizes. Complete the proposed layout in chalk, then walk through the rooms to test the traffic patterns. As you plan your rooms, keep in mind that most building codes require habitable rooms to have at least 70 sq. ft. of floor space and measure a minimum of 7 ft. in any direction.

The next step is to draw floor plans. This doesn't require drafting skills—just a tape measure, a ruler, graph paper, and some pencils. Simply measure your basement or attic floor space, then scale down the dimensions and transfer them to the graph paper. Add all obstacles, windows, doors, and other permanent fixtures. When everything is in place, start experimenting with different layouts. If you have your home's original blueprints, trace the floor plans onto tracing paper and work on new layouts from there.

Creating a successful layout takes time and often requires some creative problemsolving. To help generate ideas for your remodel, study the before-and-after drawings on page 499. While these floor plans may not look like your basement, they include many of the common elements and obstacles involved in a finishing project. They also show how carefully placed walls can transform an unfinished space into several livable areas that still leave room for storage and mechanical elements.

Use graph paper to sketch your wall layouts. Scale your floor plan (aerial view) drawings at ¼" equals 1 ft. For elevation drawings (wall details as viewed from the side), use a scale of ½" equals 1 ft.

Draw layouts onto your basement floor with sidewalk chalk. Use different colors to represent elements other than walls, such as doors, windows, and ceiling soffits. Remove the chalk with a damp rag.

Basement Layouts: Before and After

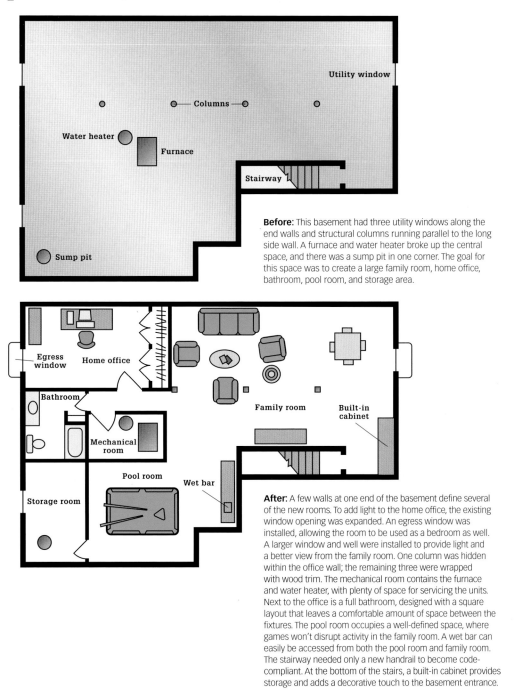

Before: This basement had three utility windows along the end walls and structural columns running parallel to the long side wall. A furnace and water heater broke up the central space, and there was a sump pit in one corner. The goal for this space was to create a large family room, home office, bathroom, pool room, and storage area.

After: A few walls at one end of the basement define several of the new rooms. To add light to the home office, the existing window opening was expanded. An egress window was installed, allowing the room to be used as a bedroom as well. A larger window and well were installed to provide light and a better view from the family room. One column was hidden within the office wall; the remaining three were wrapped with wood trim. The mechanical room contains the furnace and water heater, with plenty of space for servicing the units. Next to the office is a full bathroom, designed with a square layout that leaves a comfortable amount of space between the fixtures. The pool room occupies a well-defined space, where games won't disrupt activity in the family room. A wet bar can easily be accessed from both the pool room and family room. The stairway needed only a new handrail to become code-compliant. At the bottom of the stairs, a built-in cabinet provides storage and adds a decorative touch to the basement entrance.

Installing Basement Floors

Preparing a concrete floor—for carpet, laminate, vinyl, or wood flooring—has changed for the better in dramatic fashion, thanks to new subfloor products that have built-in vapor barriers and cleats that create a slight air gap between the subfloor and the concrete slab. This system allows air to circulate, protecting the finished flooring from any slab moisture. The older method of laying ¾" plywood over a frame of 2 × 4 "sleepers" was difficult, time-consuming, and raised the floor level by 2" or more—a significant drawback in basements where ceiling levels may already be too low. The new dry-floor subfloor systems are less than 1" thick and are very easy to install. There are several types of these dry-floor systems available, but the one most readily available and easiest to use is a product sold in 2 × 2-ft. tongue-and-groove squares.

Although subfloor panels can be adjusted for slight irregularities in the concrete slab, they can't overcome problems with a floor that is badly cracked and heaved. Nor is the built-in air gap beneath the system a solution to a basement that has serious water problems. A badly heaved slab will need to be leveled with a cement-based leveling compound, and serious water problems will need to be rectified before you consider creating finished living space in a basement.

Allow the subfloor panel squares to acclimate in the basement for at least 24 hours with the plastic surfaces facing down before installing them. In humid summer months, the squares—as well as the finished wood flooring product, if that's what you'll be installing—should be allowed to acclimate for a full two weeks before installation.

To estimate the number of 2-ft.-square subfloor panels you'll need, calculate the size of the room in square feet (multiply the width times the length of the room), then divide by 3.3 to determine the number of panels required.

Tools & Materials ›

Long straightedge
Straightedge trowel
Circular saw
  or jigsaw
Hammer
Carpenter's square
Flat pry bar
Dust mask

Eye protection
Portland-cement–
  based leveling
  compound
Dry-floor
  subfloor squares
Leveling shims
Flooring spacers

Shown cutaway for clarity

Wood laminate flooring

Dry-floor subfloor square

Underlayment

Basement slab

Most basement floors need some preparation before flooring can be laid. Patching compound and floor leveler can smooth rough concrete, while a subfloor system creates a new surface that is safe from moisture and feels like a framed wood floor.

Preparing Concrete Floors

Vacuum the floor thoroughly, then use a long straightedge to look for areas of the floor with serious dips or heaves. *Note: Any old floor coverings that may trap moisture should be removed before installing subfloor panels.*

Mix a batch of cement-based mortar and apply the compound to low areas with a straightedge trowel. After the patch dries, scrape the edges to feather the patch into the surrounding floor.

How to Install Subfloor Panels

1

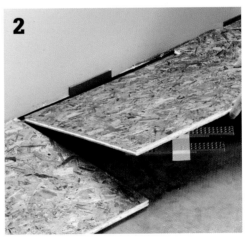

2

Beginning with the longest straight wall in the room, check one corner for square. If necessary, cut the first panel to match the angle of the corner. Position the panel in the corner, using ¼" spacers to create a gap between the panel and the walls, with the grooves of the panel against the spacers. Slide in the next panel, and use a piece of wood and a hammer to tap it firmly against the first panel. Repeat this placement along the entire wall. Cut the last panel to size.

By hand, press along the entire row of panels, looking for low spots. At points where the subfloor flexes, lift the panels and place leveling shims on the floor. In some areas, you may find it necessary to stack two, three, or more shims to create the correct thickness to fill the low spot. Tape the shims to the floor to keep them in place as you reposition the panels.

(continued)

Begin the next row of panels by cutting a half-wide panel, creating offset joints between the rows. Finish the second row, test it for flatness, and shim if necessary. Move on to the third row, this time beginning with a full panel. Work across the entire room in this fashion, testing each row for flatness, shimming where necessary, and making sure joints are offset between rows.

If the room has a floor drain, building code requires that you cut a round patch in the panel that falls directly over the floor drain. This patch can be removed to allow access to the floor drain should it ever be necessary.

For the last row of panels, measure and cut panels to fit, maintaining a ¼" gap between the panels and the wall. Work each panel into place with a flat pry bar. When all panels are in place, you can remove all spacers and continue with the installation of the finished flooring. Laminate flooring can be installed directly over the subfloor panels.

Variation: Where slab moisture is known to be a problem, you can cut vent openings spaced every 8 to 12", sized to match standard metal floor vent covers. Trace the vent opening onto the panel, and cut the opening with a jigsaw.

Variation: If carpeting will be stretched over the dry-floor panels, anchor the panels to the floor around the perimeter of the room and at the center of the room using concrete masonry anchors. Use a powder-actuated nailer to drive 2" nails through the panels and into the concrete slab.

Variation: For vinyl flooring or for engineered wood flooring, install ¼" plywood underlayment over the dry-floor panels, using ½" screws or nails, which won't penetrate the moisture barrier on the underside of the panels. Don't glue the plywood to the subfloor panels, and never glue vinyl flooring directly to the subfloor panels.

Variation: For ceramic tile, install ½" cementboard over the subfloor panels, and attach it using ¾" screws.

6

Where floor heights change, install transition strips or reducers, available in flooring departments of home improvement centers, to bridge the changes in floor heights.

How to Install a Sleeper Floor

Chip away loose or protruding concrete with a masonry chisel and hammer, then vacuum the floor. Roll out strips of 6-mil polyethylene sheeting, extending them 31" up each wall, Overlap strips by 6", then seal the seams with packing tape. Temporarily tape the edges along the walls. Be careful not to damage the sheeting.

Lay out pressure-treated 2 x 4s along the perimeter of the room. Position the boards ½" in from all walls (inset). *Note: Before laying out the sleepers, determine where the partition walls will go. If a wall will fall between parallel sleepers, add an extra sleeper to support the planned wall.*

Using a circular saw, cut the sleepers to fit between the perimeter boards, leaving a ¼" gap at each end. Position the first sleeper so its center is 16" from the outside edge of the perimeter board. Lay out the remaining sleepers, using 16"-on-center spacing.

Where necessary, use tapered cedar shims to compensate for dips and variations in the floor. Place a 4-ft. level across neighboring sleepers. Apply construction adhesive to two wood shims. Slide the shims under the board from opposite sides until the board is level with adjacent sleepers.

5

Fasten the perimeter boards and sleepers to the floor using a powder-actuated nailer or masonry screws. Drive a fastener through the center of each board at 16" intervals. Fastener heads should not protrude above the board's surface. Place a fastener at each shim location, making sure the fastener penetrates both shims.

6

Establish a control line for the first row of plywood sheets by measuring 49" from the wall and marking the outside sleeper at each end of the room. Snap a chalk line across the sleepers at the marks. Run a ¼"-wide bead of adhesive along the first six sleepers, stopping just short of the control line.

7

Position the first sheet of plywood so the end is ½" away from the wall and the grooved edge is flush with the control line. Fasten the sheet to the sleepers using 2" wallboard screws. Drive a screw every 6" along the edges and every 8" in the field. Don't drive screws along the grooved edge until the next row of sheeting is in place.

8

Install the remaining sheets in the first row, maintaining an ⅛" gap between ends. Begin the second row with a half-sheet (4 ft. long) so the end joints between rows are staggered. Fit the tongue of the half sheet into the groove of the adjoining sheet. If necessary, use a sledgehammer and wood block to help close the joint. After completing the second row, begin the third row with a full sheet. Alternate this pattern until the subfloor is complete.

Installing Attic Floors

Before you build the walls that will define the rooms in your attic, you'll need a sturdy floor beneath it all. Existing floors in most unfinished attics are merely ceiling joists for the floor below and are too small to support a living space.

There are several options for strengthening your attic's floor structure. The simplest method is to install an additional, identically sized joist next to each existing joist, connecting the two with nails. This process is known as *sistering*.

Sistering doesn't work when joists are smaller than 2 × 6s, are spaced too far apart, or where there are obstructions, such as plaster keys, from the ceiling below. An alternative is to build a new floor by placing larger joists between the existing ones. By resting the joists on 2 × 4 spacers, you avoid obstructions and minimize damage to the ceiling surface below. However, be aware that the spacers will reduce your headroom by 1½", plus the added joist depth.

To determine the best option for your attic, consult an architect, engineer, or building contractor, as well as a local building inspector. Ask what size of joists you'll need and which options are allowed in your area. Joist sizing is based on the span (the distance between support points), the joist spacing (typically 16" or 24" on-center), and the type of lumber used. In most cases, an attic floor must be able to support 40 pounds per sq. ft. of live load (occupants, furniture) and 10 psf dead load (wallboard, floor covering).

The floor joist cavities offer space for concealing the plumbing, wiring, and ductwork servicing your attic, so consider these systems as you plan. You'll also need to locate partition walls to determine if any additional blocking between joists is necessary.

When the framing is done, the mechanical elements and insulation are in place, and everything has been inspected and approved, complete the floor by installing ¾" tongue-and-groove plywood. If your remodel will include kneewalls, you can omit the subflooring behind the kneewalls, but there are good reasons not to: A complete subfloor will add strength to the floor, and will provide a sturdy surface for storage.

Tools & Materials ▶

Circular saw	16d, 10d, and 8d
Rafter square	common nails
Drill	¾" T&G plywood
Caulk gun	Construction adhesive
2 × joist lumber	2¼" wallboard screws
2 × 4 lumber	

Attic joists typically rest on top of exterior walls and on an interior load-bearing wall, where they overlap from side to side and are nailed together. Always use a sheet of plywood as a platform while working over open joists.

How to Add Sister Joists

1

2

Remove all insulation from the joist cavities and carefully remove any blocking or bridging between the joists. Determine the lengths for the sister joists by measuring the existing joists. Also measure at the outside end of each joist to determine how much of the top corner was cut away to fit the joist beneath the roof sheathing. *Note: Joists that rest on a bearing wall should overlap each other by at least 3".*

Before cutting, sight down both narrow edges of each board to check for crowning—upward arching along the length of the board. Draw an arrow that points in the direction of the arch. Joists must be installed "crown-up;" this arrow designates the top edge. Cut the board to length, then clip the top, outside corner to match the existing joists.

3

4

Set the sister joists in place, flush against the existing joists and with their ends aligned. Toenail each sister joist to the top plates of both supporting walls, using two 16d common nails.

Nail the joists together using 10d common nails. Drive three nails in a row, spacing the rows 12 to 16" apart. To minimize damage to the ceiling surface below caused by the hammering (such as cracking and nail popping), you can use an air-powered nail gun (available at rental stores), or 3" lag screws instead of nails. Install new blocking between the sistered joists, as required by the local building code.

How to Build a New Attic Floor

Remove any blocking or bridging from between the existing joists, being careful not to disturb the ceiling below. Cut 2 × 4 spacers to fit snugly between each pair of joists. Lay the spacers flat against the top plate of all supporting walls, and nail them in place with 16d common nails.

Create a layout for the new joists by measuring across the tops of the existing joists and using a rafter square to transfer the measurements down to the spacers. Following 16"-on center spacing, mark the layout along one exterior wall, then mark an identical layout onto the interior bearing wall. Note that the layout on the opposing exterior wall will be offset 1½", to account for the joist overlap at the interior wall.

To determine joist length, measure from the outer edge of the exterior wall to the far edge of the interior bearing wall. The joists must overlap each other above the interior wall by 3". Before cutting, mark the top edge of each joist. Cut the joists to length, then clip the top outside corners so the ends can fit under the roof sheathing.

Set the joists in place on their layout marks. Toenail the outside end of each joist to the spacer on the exterior wall, using three 8d common nails.

Nail the joists together where they overlap atop the interior bearing wall, using three 10d nails for each. Toenail the joists to the spacers on the interior bearing wall, using 8d nails.

Install blocking or bridging between the joists, as required by the local building code. As a suggested minimum, the new joists should be blocked as close as possible to the outside ends and where they overlap at the interior wall.

How to Install Subflooring

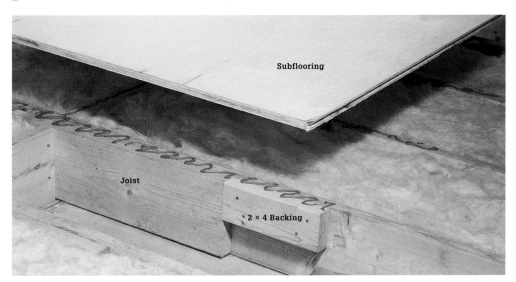

Subflooring

Joist

2 × 4 Backing

Install the subflooring only after all framing, plumbing, wiring, and ductwork is completed and has received the required building inspections. Also install any insulation and complete any caulking necessary for soundproofing. Fasten the sheets with construction adhesive and 2¼" wallboard or deck screws, making sure the sheets are perpendicular to the joists and the end joints are staggered between rows. Where joists overlap at an interior bearing wall, add backing as needed to compensate for the offset in the layout. Nail a 2 × 4 or wider board to the face of each joist to support the edges of the intervening sheets.

Installing Basement Walls

There are two common methods for covering foundation walls. Because it saves space, the more popular method is to attach 2 × 2 furring strips directly to the masonry wall. These strips provide a 1½"-deep cavity between strips for insulation and service lines, as well as a framework for attaching wallboard. The other method is to build a complete 2 × 4 stud wall just in front of the foundation wall. This method offers a full 3½" for insulation and lines, and it provides a flat, plumb wall surface, regardless of the foundation wall's condition.

To determine the best method for your project, examine the foundation walls. If they're fairly plumb and flat, you can consider furring them. If the walls are wavy or out of plumb, however, it may be easier to build stud walls. Also check with the local building department before you decide on a framing method. There may be codes regarding insulation minimums and methods of running service lines along foundation walls.

A local building official can also tell you what's recommended—or required—in your area for sealing foundation walls against moisture. Common types of moisture barriers include masonry waterproofers that

are applied like paint and plastic sheeting installed between masonry walls and wood framing. The local building code will also specify whether you need a vapor barrier between the framing and the wallboard.

Before you shop for materials, decide how you'll fasten the wood framing to your foundation walls and floor. If you're covering a large wall area, it will be worth it to buy or rent a powder-actuated nailer for the job.

Tools & Materials ▸

Caulk gun
Trowel
Paint roller
Circular saw
Drill
Powder-actuated
  nailer
Plumb bob
Silicone caulk

Paper-faced insulation
Hydraulic cement
Masonry waterproofer
2 × 2 and 2 × 4 lumber
2½" wallboard screws
Construction adhesive
Concrete fasteners
Insulation

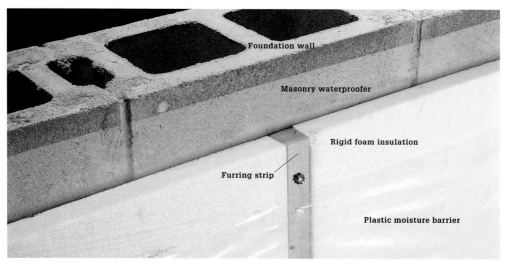

Foundation wall

Masonry waterproofer

Rigid foam insulation

Furring strip

Plastic moisture barrier

Basement walls can be made more livable by installing rigid foam insulation board between wood furring strips and then adding mold-resistant wallcovering. Although codes and practices vary dramatically, the current recommendation is to avoid the use of vapor barriers on the interior side of the wall.

How to Seal and Prepare Masonry Walls

1

Insulate the rim-joist cavities (above the foundation walls) with solid pieces of paper-faced fiberglass insulation. Make sure the paper, which serves as a vapor barrier, faces the room.

2

Sill plate

Apply silicone caulk to the joints between the sill plates and the foundation walls.

3

Fill small cracks with hydraulic cement or masonry caulk, and smooth the excess with a trowel. Ask the building department whether masonry waterproofer or a plastic moisture barrier is required in your area. Apply waterproofer as directed by the manufacturer, or install plastic sheeting following code specifications.

Options for Attaching Wood to Masonry

Masonry nails are the cheapest way to attach wood to concrete block walls. Drive the nails into the mortar joints for maximum holding power and to avoid cracking the blocks. Drill pilot holes through the strips if the nails cause splitting. Masonry nails are difficult to drive into poured concrete.

Self-tapping masonry screws hold well in block or poured concrete, but they must be driven into predrilled holes. Use a hammer drill to drill holes of the same size in both the wood and the concrete after the wood is positioned. Drive the screws into the web portion of the blocks.

(continued)

Webs

Powder-actuated nailers offer the quickest and easiest method for fastening framing to block, poured concrete, and steel. They use individual caps of gunpowder—called loads—to propel a piston that drives a hardened-steel nail (pin) through the wood and into the masonry. The loads are color-coded for the charge they produce, and the pins come in various lengths. *Note: Always drive pins into the solid web portions of concrete blocks, not into the voids. Trigger-type nailers, like the one shown here, are easiest to use, but hammer-activated types are also available. You can buy nailers at home centers and hardware stores, or rent them from rental centers. (Ask for a demonstration at the rental center.) Always wear hearing and eye protection when using these extremely loud tools.*

How to Install Furring Strips on Masonry Walls

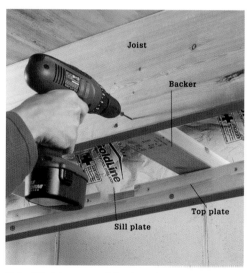

Joist

Backer

Top plate

Sill plate

Cut a 2 × 2 top plate to span the length of the wall. Mark the furring-strip layout onto the bottom edge of the plate, using 16"-on-center spacing. Attach the plate to the bottom of the joists with 2½" wallboard screws. The back edge of the plate should line up with the front of the blocks.

Note: If the joists run parallel to the wall, you'll need to install backers between the outer joist and the sill plate to provide support for ceiling wallboard. Make T-shaped backers from short 2 × 4s and 2 × 2s. Install each so the bottom face of the 2 × 4 is flush with the bottom edge of the joists. Attach the top plate to the foundation wall with its top edge flush with the top of the blocks.

Install a bottom plate cut from pressure-treated 2 × 2 lumber so the plate spans the length of the wall. Apply construction adhesive to the back and bottom of the plate, then attach it to the floor with a nailer. Use a plumb bob to transfer the furring-strip layout marks from the top plate to the bottom plate.

Cut 2 × 2 furring strips to fit between the top and bottom plates. Apply construction adhesive to the back of each furring strip, and position it on the layout marks on the plates. Nail along the length of each strip at 16" intervals.

Option: Leave a channel for the installation of wires or supply pipes by installing pairs of vertically aligned furring strips with a 2" gap between each pair. *Note: Consult local codes to ensure proper installation of electrical or plumbing materials.*

Fill the cavities between furring strips with rigid insulation board. Cut the pieces so they fit snugly within the framing. If necessary, make cutouts in the insulation to fit around mechanical elements, and cover any channels with metal protective plates before attaching the wall surface. Add a vapor barrier if required by local building code.

Installing Attic Walls

Attic kneewalls are short walls that extend from the attic floor to the rafters. They provide a vertical dimension to attic rooms, and without them, attics tend to feel cramped. Kneewalls are typically 5 ft. tall, for a couple of reasons: That's the minimum ceiling height for usable floor space according to most building codes, and it defines a comfortable room without wasting too much floor space. The unfinished space behind kneewalls doesn't have to go to waste: It's great for storage and for concealing service lines. To provide access to this space, create a framed opening in the wall during the framing process.

Kneewalls are similar to partition walls, except they have beveled top plates and angle-cut studs that follow the slope of the rafters. The added stud depth created by the angled cut requires a 2 × 6 top plate. Before starting on your kneewall project, it may help to review the techniques for building a partition wall.

Tools & Materials ▸

Circular saw	2 × 4 and
Level	2 × 6 lumber
Chalk line	16d
T-bevel	8d common nails

Attic kneewalls are just the right height to be backdrops for furniture, and they make a perfect foundation for built-in storage units.

How to Build a Kneewall

Create a storyboard using a straight 2 × 4. Cut the board a few inches longer than the planned height of the wall. Measure from one end and draw a line across the front edge of the board at the exact wall height.

At one end of the room, set the storyboard flat against the outer rafter. Plumb the storyboard with a level while aligning the height mark with the bottom edge of the rafter. Transfer the height mark onto the rafter edge, then make a mark along the front edge of the storyboard onto the subfloor. These marks represent the top and bottom wall plates.

3

Holding the storyboard perfectly plumb, trace along the bottom edge of the rafter to transfer the rafter slope onto the face of the storyboard.

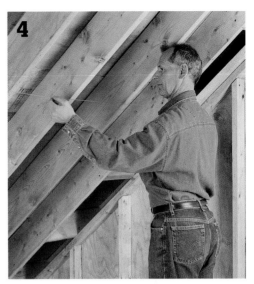

4

Repeat the wall-plate marking process on the other end of the room. Snap a chalk line through the marks—across the rafters and along the subfloor. If necessary, add backing for fastening the top plate to the gable wall.

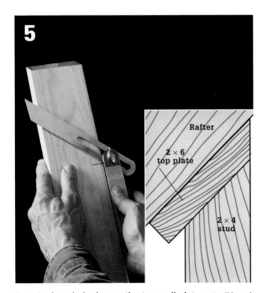

5

Rafter

2 × 6 top plate

2 × 4 stud

To cut a beveled edge on the top wall plate, set a T-bevel to match the rafter-slope line on the storyboard. Use the T-bevel to adjust the blade of a circular saw or table saw to the proper angle. Then, bevel-cut one edge of the 2 × 6 top plate. *Note: When the top plate is laid flat across the rafters, the front edge should be perpendicular to the floor.*

6

Mark the stud locations on the wall plates. Install the plates along the chalk lines, fastening them to the rafters and floor joists, respectively, using 16d nails. Measure and cut each stud to fit, angle-cutting the top end so that it meets flush with the top plate. Toenail each stud in place with three 8d nails.

Finishing Attic Ceilings

By virtue of sloping roofs, most attics naturally have "cathedral" ceilings. It's up to you whether to leave the peaks intact—and apply a finish surface all the way up to the ridge—or to frame-in a horizontal ceiling, creating a flat surface that's more like a standard ceiling. Before deciding, consider the advantages and disadvantages of each treatment.

If your attic has collar ties—horizontal braces installed between opposing rafters—your planning should start with those. Are the ties high enough to meet the code requirements for attic headroom? If not, consult an architect or engineer to see if you can move them up a few inches (do not move or remove them without professional guidance). If the ties are high enough, you can incorporate them into a new ceiling or leave them exposed and wrap them with a finish material, such as wallboard or finish-grade lumber. Do not use collar ties as part of your ceiling frame.

A peaked ceiling is primarily an aesthetic option. Its height expands the visual space of the room, and its rising angles provide a dramatic look that's unique in most homes. Because a peaked ceiling encloses the rafter bays all the way up to the ridge, this treatment may require additional roof vents to maintain proper ventilation.

By contrast, a flat ceiling typically offers a cleaner, more finished appearance closer to that of a conventional room, and flat ceilings offer some practical advantages over peaked styles. First, they provide a concealed space above the ceiling, great for running service lines. If there are vents high on the gable walls, this open space can help ventilate the roof (make sure to insulate above the ceiling). The ceiling itself can hold recessed lighting fixtures or support a ceiling fan. And if your plans call for full-height partition walls, you may want a ceiling frame to enclose the top of the wall.

When determining the height of flat-ceiling framing, be sure to account for the floor and ceiling finishes. And remember that most building codes require a finished ceiling height of at least 90".

Tools & Materials ▸

4-ft. level
Chalk line
Circular saw

2 × 4 and
2 × 6 lumber
10d common nails

Flat attic ceilings provide space for recessed light fixtures, vents, and speakers.

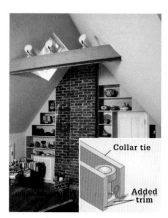

Exposed collar ties can add an interesting architectural element to a peaked ceiling. By adding to the existing ties, you can create a channel for holding small light fixtures.

How to Frame a Flat Ceiling

Make a storyboard for the planned height of the ceiling frame. At one end of the attic, hold the storyboard plumb and align the height mark with the bottom edge of a rafter. Transfer the mark to the rafter. Repeat at the other end of the attic, then snap a chalk line through the marks. This line represents the bottom edge of the ceiling frame.

Using a level and the storyboard, level over from the chalk line and mark two outside rafters on the other side of the attic. Snap a chalk line through the marks. *Note: The storyboard is used merely as a straightedge for this step.*

Cut 2 × 6 joists to span across the rafters, angle-cutting the ends to follow the roof pitch. Check each joist for crowning to make sure you're cutting it so it will be installed with the crowned edge up. Make the overall length about ½" short so the ends of the joists won't touch the roof sheathing.

Nail each joist to the rafters with three 10d common nails at each end. Be sure to maintain 16"- or 24"- on-center spacing between joists to provide support for attaching wallboard or other finish material.

Adding Basement Egress Windows

An egress window brings a pleasant source of natural light and ventilation to a dark, dank basement. More importantly, it can provide a life-saving means of escape in the event of a fire. Before you proceed with this project, read more about building code issues regarding basement egress on page 17. Contact your local building department to apply for the proper permits and to learn more about the code requirements for your area.

As long as the window opens wide enough to meet minimum standards for egress, the particular window style is really up to you. Casement windows are ideal, because they crank open quickly and provide unobstructed escape. A tall, double-hung window or wide sliding window can also work. Select a window with insulated glass and clad with vinyl or aluminum for durability; it will be subject to humidity and temperature fluctuations just like any other above-grade window in your home.

The second fundamental component of a basement egress window project is the subterranean escape well you install outside the foundation. There are several options to choose from: prefabricated well kits made of lightweight plastic that bolt together and are easy to install; corrugated metal wells are a lower-cost option; or, you can build a well from scratch using concrete, stone or landscape timber.

Installing an egress window involves four major steps: digging the well, cutting a new or larger window opening in the foundation, installing the window, and finally, installing the well. You'll save time and effort if you hire a backhoe operator to excavate the well. In most cases, you'll also need a large concrete saw (available at most rental stores) to cut the foundation wall.

Replacing a small basement window with an egress window is a big job, but it is required if you want to convert part of a basement into livable space, especially a bedroom.

Tools & Materials ▸

Tape measure	Caulk and caulk gun
4-ft. level	Gloves
Stakes and string line	Window well
Shovel	and window
Colored masking tape	Pea gravel
Hammer drill with	Plastic sheeting
½". dia. × 12-	Self-tapping
to 16"-long	masonry screws
masonry bit	2× pressure-treated
Concrete saw	lumber
Hand maul	Shims
Wide masonry chisel	Insulation materials
Trowel, miter saw	Concrete sleeve
Drill/driver, hammer	anchors

How to Install an Egress Window & Window Well

Lay out the border of the window well area with stakes and string. Plan the length and width of the excavation to be several feet larger than the window well's overall size to provide extra room for installation and adjustment.

Excavate the well to a depth 6 to 12" deeper than the well's overall height to allow room for drainage gravel. Make sure to have your local public utilities company inspect the well excavation area and okay it for digging before you start.

Measure and mark the foundation wall with brightly colored masking tape to establish the overall size of the window's rough opening (here, we're replacing an existing window). Be sure to take into account the window's rough opening dimensions, the thickness of the rough framing (usually 2x stock) and the width of the structural header you may need to build. Remember also that sill height must be within 44" of the floor. Remove existing wall coverings inside the layout area.

If the floor joists run perpendicular to your project wall, build a temporary support wall parallel to the foundation wall and 6 to 8 ft. from it (for more on building support walls, see page 29). Staple sheet plastic to the wall and floor joists to form a work tent that will help control concrete dust.

(continued)

You'll need to cut through the foundation from both the inside and outside so the blocks will break cleanly. Drill a hole through the wall at each bottom corner with a hammer drill and long masonry bit to give you reference points for marking the outside cuts.

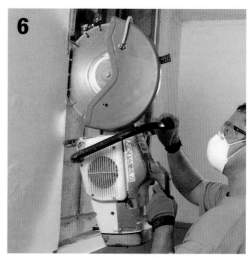

Equip a masonry cutting saw (or large angle grinder) with a diamond blade and set it for a ½" cut to score the blocks first, then reset the saw to full depth and make the final bottom and side cuts through the blocks. Wear a tight-fitting particle mask, ear and eye protection, and gloves for all of this cutting work; the saw will generate a tremendous amount of thick dust. Feed the saw slowly and steadily. Stop and rest periodically so the dust can settle.

Connect the holes you drilled previously with a level and plumb lines to mark the outside foundation wall for cutting. Measure the opening between the holes to make sure it is the correct size and that it is square. Score the cuts first, then make the full-depth cuts.

Strike the blocks with a hand maul to break or loosen the block sections. When all the blocks are removed, carefully chip away remaining debris with a cold chisel to create flat surfaces.

9

In concrete block walls, fill the hollow voids with broken pieces of block, then level and smooth the voids by trowelling on a fresh layer of quick-curing concrete. Flatten the surfaces, and allow the concrete to dry overnight.

10

If your project requires a new header above the new window, build it from pieces of 2× lumber sandwiching some ½" plywood and fastened together with construction adhesive and 10d nails. Slip it into place and tack it temporarily to the mudsill with 3½" deck screws driven toenail style.

11

Cut the sill plate for the window's rough frame from 2× treated lumber that's the same width as the thickness of the foundation wall. Fasten the sill to the foundation with ³⁄₁₆ × 3¼" countersunk masonry screws. Drill pilot holes for the screws first with a hammer drill.

12

Cut two pieces of treated lumber just slightly longer than the opening so they'll fit tightly between the new header and sill. Tap them into place with a maul. Adjust them for plumb and fasten them to the foundation with countersunk masonry screws or powder-actuated fasteners.

(continued)

13

Apply a thick bead of silicone caulk around the outside edges of the rough frame and set the window in its opening, seating the nailing flanges into the caulk. Shim the window so the frame is level and plumb. Test the action of the window to make sure the shims aren't bowing the frame.

14

Attach the window's nailing flanges to the rough frame with screws or nails, as specified by the manufacturer. Check the window action periodically as you fasten it to ensure that it still operates smoothly.

15

Seal gaps between the rough frame and the foundation with a bead of exterior silicone or polyurethane caulk. If the gaps are wider than ¼", insert a piece of backer rod first, then cover it with caulk. On the interior, fill gaps around the window shims with strips of foam backer rod, fiberglass insulation, or a bead of minimally expanding spray foam. Do not distort the window frame.

16

Fill the well excavation with 6 to 12" of pea gravel. This will serve as the window's drain system. Follow the egress well kit instructions to determine the exact depth required; you may need to add more gravel so the top of the well will be above the new window. *Note: We added a drain down to the foundation's perimeter tile for improved drainage as well.*

17

Set the bottom section of the well into the hole, and position it evenly from left to right relative to the window. Adjust the gravel surface to level the well section carefully.

18

Stack the second well section on top of the first, and connect the two with the appropriate fasteners.

19

Fasten the window well sections to the foundation wall with concrete sleeve anchors driven into pre-bored pilot holes. You could also use masonry nails driven with a powder actuated nailer.

20

When all the well sections are assembled and secured, nail pieces of treated lumber trim around the window frame to hide the nailing flange. Complete the well installation by using excavated dirt to backfill around the outside of the well. Pack the soil with a tamper, creating a slope for good drainage. If you are installing a window well cover, set it in place and fasten it according to the manufacturer's instructions. (The cover must be removable.)

Installing Baseboard Heaters

Baseboard heaters are a popular way to provide additional heating for an existing room or primary heat to a converted attic or basement.

Heaters are generally wired on a dedicated 240-volt circuit controlled by a thermostat. Several heaters can be wired in parallel and controlled by a single thermostat (see circuit map 11, page 143).

Baseboard heaters are generally surface-mounted without boxes, so in a remodeling situation, you only need to run cables before installing wallboard. Be sure to mark cable locations on the floor before installing drywall. Retrofit installations are also not difficult. You can remove existing baseboard and run new cable in the space behind.

Tools & Materials ▸

Drill/driver
Wire stripper
Cable ripper
Wallboard saw
Baseboard heater or heaters
240-thermostat (in-heater or in-wall)
12/2 NM cable
Electrical tape
Basic wiring supplies

Baseboard heaters can provide primary or supplemental heat for existing rooms or additions. Install heaters with clear space between the heater and the floor.

Baseboard Thermostats

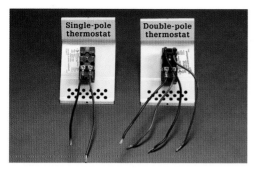

Single-pole and double-pole thermostats work in a similar manner, but double-pole models are safer. The single-pole model will open the circuit (causing shutoff) in only one leg of the power service. Double-pole models have two sets of wires to open both legs, lessening the chance that a person servicing the heater will contact a live wire.

In-heater and wall-mount are the two types of baseboard thermostats you can choose from. If you are installing multiple heaters, a single wall-mount thermostat is more convenient. Individual in-heater thermostats give you more zone control, which can result in energy savings.

How Much Heater Do You Need? ▸

If you don't mind doing a little math, determining how many lineal feet of baseboard heater a room requires is not hard.

1. Measure the area of the room in square feet (length × width): _____
2. Divide the area by 10 to get the baseline minimum wattage: _____
3. Add 5% for each newer window or 10% for each older window: _____
4. Add 10% for each exterior wall in the room: _____
5. Add 10% for each exterior door: _____
6. Add 10% if the space below is not insulated: _____

7. Add 20% if the space above is not well insulated: _____
8. Add 10% if ceiling is more than 8 ft. high: _____
9. Total of the baseline wattage plus all additions: _____
10. Divide this number by 250 (the wattage produced per foot of standard baseboard heater): _____
11. Round up to a whole number. This is the minimum number of feet of heater you need. _____

Note: It is much better to have more feet of heater than is required than fewer. Having more footage of heater does not consume more energy; it does allow the heaters to work more efficiently.

Planning Tips for Baseboard Heaters ▸

- 240-volt heaters are much more energy efficient than 120-volt heaters.
- Baseboard heaters require a dedicated circuit. A 20-amp, 240-volt circuit of 12-gauge copper wire will power up to 16 ft. of heater.
- Do not install a heater beneath a wall receptacle. Cords hanging down from the receptacle are a fire hazard.

- Do not mount heaters directly on the floor. You should maintain at least 1" of clear space between the baseboard heater and the floor covering.
- Installing heaters directly beneath windows is a good practice.
- Locate wall thermostats on interior walls only, and do not install directly above a heat source.

How to Install a 240-volt Baseboard Heater

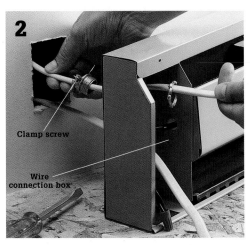

At the heater locations, cut a small hole in the drywall 3 to 4" above the floor. Pull 12/2 NM cables through the first hole: one from the thermostat, the other to the next heater. Pull all the cables for subsequent heaters. Middle-of-run heaters will have two cables, while end-of-run heaters have only one cable.

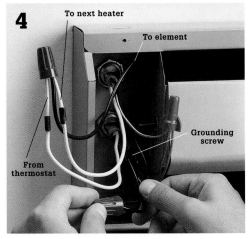

Remove the cover on the wire connection box. Open a knockout for each cable that will enter the box, then feed the cables through the cable clamps and into the wire connection box. Attach the clamps to the wire connection box, and tighten the clamp screws until the cables are gripped firmly.

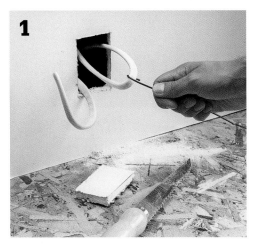

Anchor heater against wall about 1" off floor by driving flathead screws through back of housing and into studs. Strip away cable sheathing so at least ½" of sheathing extends into the heater. Strip ¾" of insulation from each wire using a combination tool.

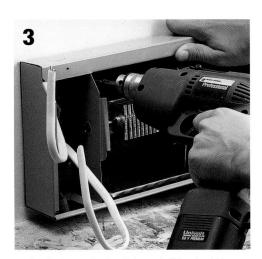

Make connections to the heating element if the power wires are coming from a thermostat or another heater controlled by a thermostat. See next page for other wiring schemes. Connect the white circuit wires to one of the wire leads on the heater. Tag white wires with black tape to indicate they are hot. Connect the black circuit wires to the other wire lead. Connect a grounding pigtail to the green grounding screw in the box, then join all grounding wires with a wire connector. Reattach cover.

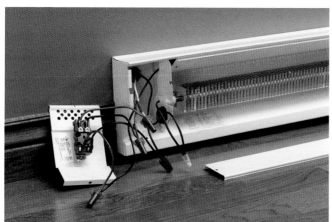

One heater with end-cap thermostat.
Run both power leads (black plus tagged neutral) into the connection box at either end of the heater. If installing a single-pole thermostat, connect one power lead to one thermostat wire and connect the other thermostat wire to one of the heater leads. Connect the other hot LINE wire to the other heater lead. If you are installing a double-pole thermostat, make connections with both legs of the power supply.

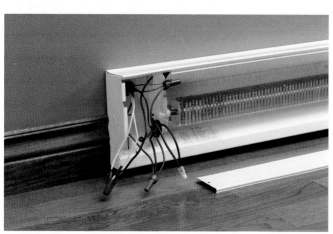

Multiple heaters. At the first heater, join both hot wires from the thermostat to the wires leading to the second heater in line. Be sure to tag all white neutrals hot. Twist copper ground wires together and pigtail them to the grounding screw in the baseboard heater junction box. This parallel wiring configuration ensures that power flow will not be interrupted to the downstream heaters if an upstream heater fails.

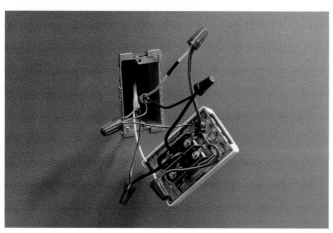

Wall-mounted thermostat. If installing a wall-mounted thermostat, the power leads should enter the thermostat first and then be wired to the individual heaters singly or in series. Hookups at the heater are made as shown in step 4. Be sure to tag the white neutral as hot in the thermostat box as well as in the heater box.

Exterior Improvements

Roofing, siding, and exterior trim details create the outer envelope of your home, safeguarding it from the elements. Aside from their protective purposes, these three systems should also blend together aesthetically to improve your home's appearance. Roofing and siding replacement, in particular, are among the more costly projects you'll face as a homeowner, and generally they're investments you'll make only every few decades or so. For these reasons, it's wise to plan your projects carefully, so you can keep all the relevant factors in mind before you begin.

This chapter will help you get started on the right foot. You'll begin the planning process by evaluating your needs and estimating both price and material quantities required for the job. Then, you'll take a more in-depth look at the wide variety of product options available. New forms and styles of roofing and siding continue to come to market, and there may be some you simply aren't aware of yet. A roofing, siding, or trim project will usually require at least some work at heights. You'll learn important tips for working safely, how to set up scaffolds, and how to prepare your job site to minimize damage, manage debris, and work efficiently.

In this chapter:
- Estimating Roofing, Siding & Trim
- Preparing the Roof for Shingles
- Shingling a Roof
- Installing Vinyl Siding

Estimating Roofing, Siding & Trim

Ordering Roofing Materials

Roofing materials are ordered in squares, with one square equaling 100 square feet. To determine how many squares are needed, first figure out the square footage of your roof. The easiest way to make this calculation is to multiply the length by the width of each section of roof, and then add the numbers together.

For steep roofs and those with complex designs, do your measuring from the ground and multiply by a number based on the slope of your roof. Measure the length and width of your house, include the overhangs, then multiply the numbers together to determine the overall square footage. Using the chart at the lower right, multiply the square footage by a number based on the roof's slope. Add 10 percent for waste, then divide the total square footage by 100 to determine the number of squares you need. Don't spend time calculating and subtracting the areas that won't be covered, such as skylights and chimneys. They're usually small enough that they don't impact the number of squares you need. Besides, it's good to have extra materials for waste, mistakes, and later repairs.

To determine how much flashing you'll need, measure the length of the valley to figure valley flashing, the lengths of the eaves and rakes to figure drip edge, and the number and size of vent pipes to figure vent flashing.

Asphalt shingles come in packaged bundles weighing around 65 pounds each. For typical three-tab shingles, three bundles will cover one square (100 sq. ft.) of roof.

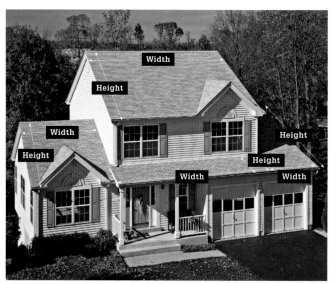

Calculate the roof's surface by multiplying the height of the roof by the width. Do this for each section, then add the totals together. Divide that number by 100, add 10 percent for waste, and that's the number of squares of roofing materials you need.

Conversion Chart

Slope	Multiply by	Slope	Multiply by
2 in 12	1.02	8 in 12	1.20
3 in 12	1.03	9 in 12	1.25
4 in 12	1.06	10 in 12	1.30
5 in 12	1.08	11 in 12	1.36
6 in 12	1.12	12 in 12	1.41
7 in 12	1.16		

Ordering Siding Materials

Siding is sold by the linear foot, square foot, board foot, or square, depending on the type of material. To determine the amount of siding materials you'll need, calculate the square footage of each wall, then add them together to get your total surface area.

To figure the square footage for a wall, multiply the length of the wall by the height. Calculate the area on the gable end of a wall by using the formula for triangles, which is one-half the length of the base multiplied by the height of the triangle. You won't need to subtract for areas covered by windows and doors, and you won't need to add an extra 10 percent for waste. The window and door areas are roughly equal to the amount of waste you'll need.

Use your height and length measurements from the walls to determine how many feet of starter strip, channels, corner posts, and trim you'll need. Keep in mind you'll probably also need to apply trim or channels around all of your doors and windows.

Depending on the siding material you're ordering, you may need extra material to allow for overlap. For example, if you want to install 10" lap siding with an 8" exposure, you'll need to account for a 2" overlap for each board. Likewise, the exposure rate for wood shakes or shingles will determine how many squares you'll need. Depending on the exposure rate, one square of shingles could cover 80 sq. ft, 100 sq. ft, or even 120 sq. ft. Most manufacturers have charts that show how much material is needed to cover a specified number of square feet at various rates of exposure. If you have trouble estimating how much material you need to purchase, ask your supplier for help.

Estimate the amount of siding you'll need by calculating the square footage of each wall, then adding the numbers together. To determine the square footage of a wall, multiply the wall length by its height. Subtract the square footage of all windows and doors, and then add 10 percent for waste to get square footage. Don't forget about corner trim, J-channel and other trim pieces.

Preparing the Roof for Shingles

Working conditions on a roof can be arduous, so make the job as easy as possible by gathering the right tools and equipment before you begin.

Some of these tools, such as a pneumatic nailer and roofer's hatchet, are specific to roofing projects. If you don't have them and don't want to buy them, you can rent them from a rental center.

Specialty roofing tools include roof jacks (A) for use on steep roofs, roofing shovel (B) for tearoff work, pneumatic nailer (C), utility knife with hooked blade (D) for trimming shingles, roofing hammer with alignment guides and hatchet blade (E) for shingle installation, and a release magnet for site cleanup (F).

Use roof jacks on steep roofs. Nail the supports at the fourth or fifth course of shingles, and add the widest board the supports will hold.

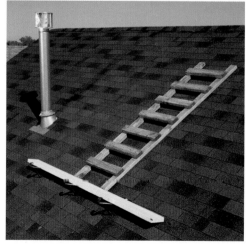

For more secure footing, fashion a roofing ladder by nailing wood strips across a pair of 2 × 4s. Secure the ladder to the roof jacks, and use it to maintain your footing.

Drip edge

Preformed valley flashing

Rolled flashing material

Aviation snips

Vent pipe flashing

Step flashing blanks

Skylight flashing kit (partial)

Roof flashing can be hand cut or purchased in preformed shapes and sizes. Long pieces of valley flashing, base flashing, top saddles, and other nonstandard pieces can be cut from rolled flashing material using aviation snips. Step flashing blanks can be bought in standard sizes and bent to fit. Drip edge and vent pipe flashing are available preformed. Skylight flashing usually comes as a kit with the window. Complicated flashings, such as chimney crickets, can be custom fabricated by a metalworker.

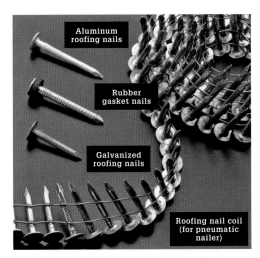

Aluminum roofing nails

Rubber gasket nails

Galvanized roofing nails

Roofing nail coil (for pneumatic nailer)

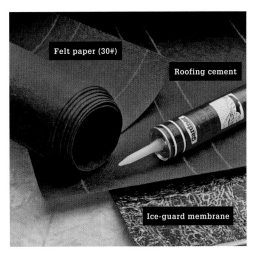

Felt paper (30#)

Roofing cement

Ice-guard membrane

Different fasteners are specially developed for different jobs. Use galvanized roofing nails to hand nail shingles; use aluminum nails for aluminum flashing; use rubber gasket nails for galvanized metal flashing; and use nail coils for pneumatic nailers.

Common roofing materials include 30# felt paper for use as underlayment; ice-guard membrane for use as underlayment in cold climates; and tubes of roofing cement for sealing small holes, cracks, and joints.

How to Tear Off Old Shingles

1

Remove the ridge cap using a flat pry bar. Pry up the cap shingles at the nail locations.

2

Working downward from the peak, tear off the felt paper and old shingles with a roofing shovel or pitchfork.

3

Unless flashing is in exceptional condition, remove it by slicing through the roofing cement that attaches it to the shingles. You may be able to salvage flashing pieces, such as chimney saddles and crickets, and reuse them.

4

After removing the shingles, felt paper, and flashing from the entire tear-off section, pry out any remaining nails and sweep the roof with a broom.

5

If an unexpected delay keeps you from finishing a section before nightfall, cover any unshingled sections, using tarps weighted down with shingle bundles.

How to Replace Damaged Sheathing

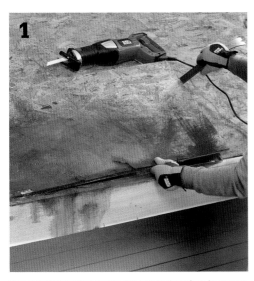

Use a reciprocating saw to cut next to the rafters in an area that extends well beyond the damaged area. Pry out the damaged sections using a pry bar.

Attach 2 × 4 nailing strips to the inside edges of the rafters using 3" deck screws

Use exterior grade plywood to make a patch. Measure the cutout area, allow for a ⅛" gap on all sides for expansion, and cut the patch to size. Attach the patch to the rafters and nailing strips using 2¼" deck screws or 8d ring-shank siding nails.

Option: If your existing roof deck is made of boards (1 × 6 was common before plywood took over the market), it is perfectly acceptable to use plywood when replacing a section of the deck. The plywood should be the same thickness as the boards, generally, ¾".

How to Install Underlayment

Snap a chalk line 35⅝" up from the eaves, so the first course of the 36"-wide membrane will overhang the eaves by ⅜". Install a course of ice and water shield, using the chalk line as a reference, and peeling back the protective backing as you unroll it.

Measuring up from the eaves, make a mark 32" above the top of the last row of underlayment, and snap another chalk line. Roll out the next course of felt paper (or ice guard, if required) along the chalk line, overlapping the first course by 4". *Tip: Drive staples every 6 to 12" along the edges of felt paper, and one staple per sq. ft. in the field area.*

At valleys, roll felt paper across from both sides, overlapping the ends by 36". Install felt paper up to the ridge—ruled side up—snapping horizontal lines every two or three rows to check alignment. Overlap horizontal seams by 4", vertical seams by 12", and hips and ridges by 6". Trim the courses flush with the rake edges.

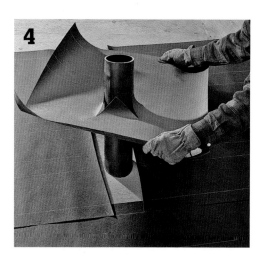

Apply felt paper up to an obstruction, then resume laying the course on the opposite side (make sure to maintain the line). Cut a patch that overlaps the felt paper by 12" on all sides. Make a crosshatch cutout for the obstruction. Position the patch over the obstruction, staple it in place, then caulk the seams with roofing cement.

At the bottom of dormers and sidewalls, tuck the felt paper under the siding where it intersects with the roof. Carefully pry up the siding and tuck at least 2" of paper under it. Also tuck the paper under counter flashing or siding on chimneys and skylights. Leave the siding or counter flashing or siding unfastened until after you install the step flashing.

How to Install Drip Edge

Cut a 45° miter at one end of the drip edge using aviation snips. Place the drip edge along the eaves end of the roof, aligning the mitered end with the rake edge. Nail the drip edge in place every 12".

Overlap pieces of drip edge by 2". Install drip edge across the entire eaves, ending with a mitered cut on the opposite corner.

Apply felt paper, and ice guard if needed, to the roof, overhanging the eaves by ⅜".

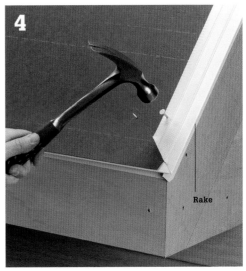

Cut a 45° miter in a piece of drip edge and install it along the rake edge, forming a miter joint with the drip edge along the eaves. Overlap pieces by 2", making sure the higher piece is on top at the overlap. Apply drip edge all the way to the peak. Install drip edge along the other rake edges the same way.

Shingling a Roof

If you want to install asphalt shingles on your roof, then you're in good company. Asphalt shingles, also known as composition shingles, are the roofing of choice for nearly four out of five homeowners in America. They perform well in all types of climate, are available in a multitude of colors, shapes, and textures to complement every housing design, and are less expensive than most other roofing products.

Asphalt shingles are available as either fiberglass shingles or organic shingles. Both types are made with asphalt, the difference being that one uses a fiberglass reinforcing mat, while the other uses a cellulose-fiber mat. Fiberglass shingles are lighter, thinner, and have a better fire rating. Organic shingles have a higher tear strength, are more flexible in cold climates, and are used more often in northern regions.

Although the roofing market has exploded with innovative new asphalt shingle designs, such as the architectural or laminated shingle that offers a three-dimensional look, the standard three-tab asphalt shingle is still the most common, which is the project we're featuring here. The tabs provide an easy reference for aligning shingles for installation.

To help the job get done faster, rent an air compressor and pneumatic roofing gun. This will greatly reduce the time you spend nailing.

Tools & Materials ▸

Aviation snips	Chalk gun
Carpenter's square	Flashing
Chalk line	Shingles
Flat bar	Nailing cartridges
Roofer's hatchet or	Roofing cement
pneumatic nailer	Roofing nails
Utility knife	(⅞", 1¼")
Straightedge	Rubber gasket nails
Tape measure	

Stagger shingles for effective protection against leaks. If the tab slots are aligned in successive rows, water forms channels, increasing erosion of the mineral surface of the shingles. Creating a 6" offset between rows of shingles—with the three-tab shingles shown above—ensures that the tab slots do not align.

How to Install Three-tab Shingles

Cover the roof with felt paper (page 536) and install drip edge (page 537). Snap a chalk line onto the felt paper or ice guard 11½" up from the eaves edge, to mark the alignment of the starter course. This will result in a ½" shingle overhang for standard 12" shingles. *Tip: Use blue chalk rather than red. Red chalk will stain roofing materials.*

Full tab

Half tab

Trim off one-half (6") of an end tab on a shingle. Position the shingle upside down, so the tabs are aligned with the chalk line and the half-tab is flush against the rake edge. Drive ⅞" roofing nails near each end, 1" down from each slot between tabs. Butt a full upside-down shingle next to the trimmed shingle, and nail it. Fill out the row, trimming the last shingle flush with the opposite rake edge.

Apply the first full course of shingles over the starter course with the tabs pointing down. Begin at the rake edge where you began the starter row. Place the first shingle so it overhangs the rake edge by ⅜" and the eaves edge by ½". Make sure the top of each shingle is flush with the top of the starter course, following the chalk line.

Snap a chalk line from the eaves edge to the ridge to create a vertical line to align the shingles. Choose an area with no obstructions, as close as possible to the center of the roof. The chalk line should pass through a slot or a shingle edge on the first full shingle course. Use a carpenter's square to establish a line perpendicular to the eaves edge.

(continued)

Use the vertical reference line to establish a shingle pattern with slots that are offset by 6" in succeeding courses. Tack down a shingle 6" to one side of the vertical line, 5" above the bottom edge of the first-course shingles to start the second row. Tack down shingles for the third and fourth courses, 12" and 18" from the vertical line. Butt the fifth course against the line.

Fill in shingles in the second through fifth courses, working upward from the second course and maintaining a consistent 5" reveal. Slide lower-course shingles under any upper-course shingles left partially nailed, and then nail them down. *Tip: Install roof jacks, if needed, after filling out the fifth course.*

Check the alignment of the shingles after each four-course cycle. In several spots on the last installed course, measure from the bottom edge of a shingle to the nearest felt paper line. If you discover any misalignment, make minor adjustments over the next few rows until it's corrected.

When you reach obstructions, such as dormers, install a full course of shingles above them so you can retain your shingle offset pattern. On the unshingled side of the obstruction, snap another vertical reference line using the shingles above the obstruction as a guide.

Shingle upward from the eaves on the unshingled side of the obstruction using the vertical line as a reference for re-establishing your shingle slot offset pattern. Fill out the shingle courses past the rake edges of the roof, then trim off the excess.

Trim off excess shingle material at the V in the valley flashing using a utility knife and straightedge. Do not cut into the flashing. The edges will be trimmed back farther at a slight taper after both roof decks are completely shingled.

Install shingles on adjoining roof decks, starting at the bottom edge using the same offset alignment pattern shown in steps 1 to 6. Install shingles until courses overlap the center of the valley flashing. Trim shingles at both sides of the valley when finished.

Install shingles up to the vent pipe so the flashing rests on at least one row of shingles. Apply a heavy double bead of roofing cement along the bottom edge of the flange.

(continued)

Place the flashing over the vent pipe. Position the flashing collar so the longer portion of the tapered neck slopes down the roof and the flange lies over the shingles. Nail the perimeter of the flange using rubber gasket nails.

Cut shingles to fit around the neck of the flashing so they lie flat against the flange. Do not drive roofing nails through the flashing. Instead, apply roofing cement to the back of shingles where they lie over the flashing.

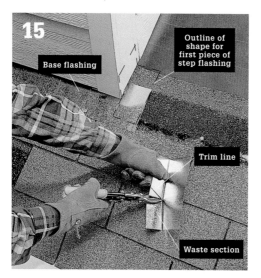

Shingle up to an element that requires flashing so the top of the reveal areas are within 5" of the element. Install base flashing using the old base flashing as a template. Bend a piece of step flashing in half and set it next to the lowest corner of the element. Mark a trim line on the flashing, following the vertical edge of the element. Cut the flashing to fit.

Pry out the lowest courses of siding and any trim at the base of the element. Insert spacers to prop the trim or siding away from the work area. Apply roofing cement to the base flashing in the area where the overlap with the step flashing will be formed. Tuck the trimmed piece of step flashing under the propped area, and secure the flashing. Fasten the flashing with one rubber gasket nail driven near the top and into the roof deck.

Apply roofing cement to the top side of the first piece of step flashing where it will be covered by the next shingle course. Install the shingle by pressing it firmly into the roofing cement. Do not nail through the flashing underneath.

Tuck another piece of flashing under the trim or siding, overlapping the first piece of flashing at least 2". Set the flashing into roofing cement applied on the top of the shingle. Nail the shingle in place without driving nails through the flashing. Install flashing up to the top of the element the same way. Trim the last piece of flashing to fit the top corner of the element. Reattach the siding and trim.

Counterflashing

Base flashing

Shingle up to the chimney base. Use the old base flashing as a template to cut new flashing. Bend up the counter flashing. Apply roofing cement to the base of the chimney and the shingles just below the base. Press the base flashing into the roofing cement and bend the flashing around the edges of the chimney. Drive rubber gasket nails through the flashing flange into the roof deck.

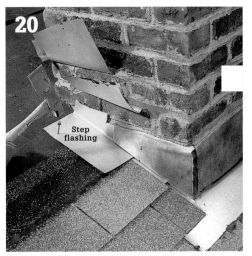

Step flashing

Install step flashing and shingles, working up to the high side of the chimney. Fasten flashing to the chimney with roofing cement. Fold down the counter flashing as you go.

(continued)

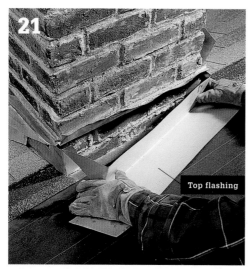

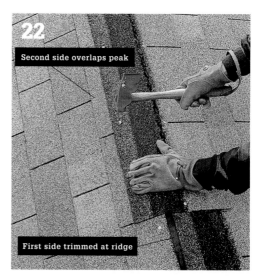

Cut and install top flashing (also called a saddle) around the high side of the chimney. Overlap the final piece of flashing along each side. Attach the flashing with roofing cement applied to the deck and chimney and with rubber gasket nails driven through the flashing base into the roof deck. Shingle past the chimney using roofing cement (not nails) to attach shingles over the flashing.

When you reach a hip or ridge, shingle up the first side until the top of the uppermost reveal area is within 5" of the hip or ridge. Trim the shingles along the peak. Install shingles on the opposite side of the hip or ridge. Overlap the peak no more than 5".

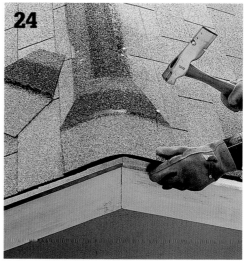

Cut three 12"-sq. cap shingles from each three-tab shingle. With the back surface facing up, cut the shingles at the tab lines. Trim the top corners of each square with an angled cut, starting just below the seal strip to avoid overlaps in the reveal area.

Snap a chalk line 6" down from the ridge, parallel to the peak. Attach cap shingles, starting at one end of the ridge, aligned with the chalk line. Drive two 1¼" roofing nails per cap about 1" from each edge, just below the seal strip.

Following the chalk line, install cap shingles halfway along the ridge, creating a 5" reveal for each cap. Then, starting at the opposite end, install caps over the other half of the ridge to meet the first run in the center. Cut a 5"-wide section from the reveal area of a shingle tab, and use it as a "closure cap" to cover the joint where the caps meet.

Shingle the hips in the same manner using a chalk reference line and cap shingles. Start at the bottom of each hip and work to the peak. Where hips join with roof ridges, install a custom shingle cut from the center of a cap shingle. Set the cap at the end of the ridge and bend the corners so they fit over the hips. Secure each corner with a roofing nail, and cover the nail heads with roofing cement.

After all shingles are installed, trim them at the valleys to create a gap that's 3" wide at the top and widens at a rate of ⅛" per foot as it moves downward. Use a utility knife and straightedge to cut the shingles, making sure not to cut through the valley flashing. At the valleys, seal the undersides and edges of shingles with roofing cement. Also cover exposed nail heads with roofing cement.

Mark and trim the shingles at the rake edges of the roof. Snap a chalk line ⅜" from the edge to make an overhang, then trim the shingles.

Installing Vinyl Siding

Vinyl has become one of the most popular sidings due to its low cost, uniform appearance, and maintenance-free durability. Installation is fairly simple, with each row locking onto the lip of the underlying course, then nailed along the top.

There are a couple of key factors that will make or break your siding project. First, the sheathing must be straight and solid before the siding is applied. The siding will only look as straight and smooth as the wall it's on. Second, determine how the siding should overlap to hide the seams from the main traffic patterns. This usually means starting in the back and working toward the front of the house.

Do not nail the siding tight to the house. The panels need to slide back and forth as they expand and contract with changes in the temperature. If the siding can't move, it will bow and need to be reinstalled. Keep a 1/32" gap between the head of the nail and the siding.

Vinyl siding is available in a wide variety of colors and styles, and with a lot of accessories such as trim, fluted lineals, vertical columns, crown molding, and band boards. The most common vinyl siding is horizontal lap siding, which is shown starting on page 548. This project shows a foam underlayment, which reduces outside noise, protects the siding from dents, and adds an insulation value. Vertical vinyl siding is also available. It's specifically made for vertical applications.

Tools & Materials ▸

Hammer	Zip-lock tool
Circular saw	Snap lock punch
or radial-arm saw	Caulk gun
Clamps	Vinyl siding
Tape measure	J-channel
String	Corner posts
Straightedge	Undersill
Utility knife	Starter strip
Aviation snips	Nails
Level	Cutting table
Chalk line	Safety glasses
Framing square	Silicone caulk
Nail slot punch	

Vinyl siding can look very similar to wood lap siding, but it doesn't require regular upkeep. Vinyl can be installed on any type and style of house.

Cutting Vinyl Siding

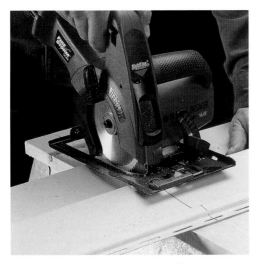

Use a fine-tooth blade installed backward in the saw to cut vinyl siding. Use a radial-arm saw, power miter saw, or a circular saw, and move the blade slowly through the siding. Always wear safety glasses when cutting siding.

Support the siding on a cutting table when cutting. Vinyl siding is too flimsy to be placed across sawhorses without support. You can build a cutting table by fastening a long piece of scrap plywood between two sawhorses.

Using Specialty Tools

A snap lock punch is used to make raised tabs, or dimples, in a cut edge of siding where the nailing hem has been removed. This eliminates the need to facenail the panel.

A nail slot punch is used to make horizontal nail slots in the face of panels. It can also be used to add or elongate the opening of an existing nail slot to match irregular stud spacing.

How to Install Vinyl Siding

Install housewrap following manufacturer instructions. Identify the lowest corner of the house that has sheathing, and partially drive a nail 1½" above the bottom edge of the sheathing. Run a level string to the opposite corner of the wall and partially drive a nail. Do this around the entire house. Snap chalk lines between the nails.

Place the top edge of the starter strip along the chalk line and nail every 10". Nail in the center of the slots and don't nail tight to the house. Keep a ¼" gap between strips, and leave space at the corners for a ½" gap between starter strips and corner posts.

Option: Install foam vinyl siding underlayment on the house using cap nails. Align the bottom of the underlayment with the starting strip. To cut panels to size, score them with a utility knife, then break them over your cutting table. Some panels need to be taped at the seams. Follow manufacturer's recommendations.

Install a corner post, keeping a ¼" gap between the top of the post and the soffit. Extend the bottom of the post ¼" below the bottom of the starter strip. Drive a nail at the top end of the uppermost slot on each side of the post (the post hangs from these nails). Make sure the post is plumb on both sides using a level. Secure the post by driving nails every 8 to 12" in the center of the slots. Do not nail the post tight. Install the other posts the same way.

4

If more than one corner post is needed to span the length of a corner, the upper post overlaps the lower post. For an outside corner post, cut off 1" from the nailing flanges on the bottom edge of the top post. For an inside corner post, cut off 1" from the nailing flange on the upper edge of the bottom post. Overlap the posts by ¾", leaving ¼" for expansion.

5

Measure and cut two J-channels that are the length of a window plus the width of the J-channel. Place one of the J-channels against the side of the window, aligning the bottom edge with the bottom edge of the window. Nail the channel in place. Nail the second J-channel against the opposite side of the window the same way.

6

At the top of the window, measure between the outside edges of the side J-channels and cut a piece of J-channel to fit. Cut a ¾" tab at each end. Bend the tabs down to form a drip edge. Miter cut the face at each end at 45°. Center the J-channel over the window and nail it in place. The top J-channel overlaps the side pieces, and the drip edges fit inside the side pieces. Do this for each window and door.

7

Measure, cut, and install J-channel along the gable ends. Nail the channels every 8 to 12". To overlap J-channels, cut 1" from the nailing hem. Overlap the channels ¾", leaving ¼" for expansion. At the gable peak, cut one channel at an angle to butt against the peak. Miter the channel on the opposite side to overlap the first channel.

(continued)

To install J-channel over a roof line, snap a chalk line along the roof flashing ½" above the roof. Align the bottom edge of the J-channel along the chalk line, and nail the channel in place. Make sure the channel does not make direct contact with the shingles.

Measure, cut, and install undersill beneath each window. The undersill should be flush with the outside lip of the side channels.

Measure, cut, and install undersill along the horizontal eaves on the house. If more than one undersill is needed, cut the nailing hem 1¼" from the end of one undersill. Overlap the undersills by 1".

Snap the locking leg on the bottom of the first panel onto the starter strip, making sure it's securely locked in place. Keep a ¼" gap between the end of the panel and the corner post. Nail the panel a minimum of every 16" on center. Don't drive the nails tight. *Note: This installation shows a vinyl siding underlayment in place.*

12

Overlap panels by 1". Cut panels so the factory cut edge is the one that's visible. Keep nails at least 6" from the end of panels to allow for smooth overlap. Do not overlap panels directly under a window.

13

Place the second row over the first, snapping the locking leg into the lock of the underlying panels. Leave ¼" gap at corners and J-channels. Install subsequent rows, staggering seams at least 24" unless separated by more than three rows. Check every several rows for level. Make adjustments in slight increments, if necessary.

14

For hose spigots, pipes, and other protrusions, create a seam at the obstacle. Begin with a new panel to avoid extra seams. Cut an opening ¼" larger than the obstacle, planning for a 1" overlap of siding. Match the shape and contour as closely as possible. Fit the panels together around the obstruction and nail in place.

15

Place mounting blocks around outlets, lights, and doorbells. Assemble the base around the fixture, making sure it's level, and nail in place. Install siding panels, cutting them to fit around the mounting block with a ¼" gap on each side. Fasten the cover by snapping it over the block.

(continued)

Where panels must be notched to fit below a window, position the panel below the window and mark the edges of the window, allowing for a ¼" gap. Place a scrap piece of siding alongside the window and mark the depth of the notch, keeping a ¼" gap. Transfer the measurement to the panel, mark the notch, and cut it out. Create tabs on the outside face every 6" using a snap lock punch. Install the panel, locking the tabs into the undersill.

Install cut panels between windows and between windows and corners as you would regular panels. Avoid overlapping panels and creating seams in small spaces. The panels need to align with panels on the opposite side of the window.

To fit siding over a window, hold the panel in place over the window and mark it. Use a scrap piece of siding to mark the depth of the cut. Transfer the measurement to the full panel and cut the opening. Fit the cut edge into the J-channel above the window, lock the panel in place, and nail it.

For dormers, measure up from the bottom of the J-channel the height of a panel and make a mark. Measure across to the opposite J-channel. Use this measurement to mark and cut the panel to size. Cut and install panels for the rest of the dormer the same way.

20

Measure the distance between the lock on the last fully installed panel and the top of the undersill under the horizontal eaves. Subtract ¼", then mark and rip a panel to fit. Use a snap lock punch to punch tabs on the outside face every 6". Install the panel, locking the tabs into the undersill.

21

Place a scrap panel in the J-channel along the gable end of the house. Place another scrap over the last row of panels before the gable starts, slide it under the first scrap, and mark the angle where they intersect. Transfer this angle to full panels. Make a similar template for the other side. Cut the panels and set the cut edge into the J-channel, leaving a ¼" gap.

22

Cut the last piece of siding to fit the gable peak. Drive a single aluminum or stainless steel finish nail through the top of the panel to hold it in place. This is the only place where you will facenail the siding.

23

Apply caulk between all windows and J-channel, and between doors and J-channel.

Resources

American Institute of Architects
800-364-9364
www.aiaonline.com

American Lighting Association
800-724-4484
www.americanlightingassoc.com

American Society of Interior Designers
202-546-3480
www.asid.org

Association of Home Appliance
   Manufacturers
202-872-5955
www.aham.org

Certified Forest Products Council
503-224-2205
www.certifiedwood.org

Construction Materials Recycling
   Association
630-548-4510
www.cdrecycling.org

Energy & Environmental Building
   Association
952-881-1098
www.eeba.org

International Residential Code (book)
   International Conference of Building
   Officials
800-284-4406
www.icbo.com

Kohler Co.
800-456-4537
www.kohler.com

Laticrete International
(radiant floor mats)
800-243-4788
www.laticrete.com

Light Gauge Steel Engineers Association
615-279-9251
www.lgsea.com

National Association of the
   Remodeling Industry (NARI)
847-298-9200
www.nari.org

National Fire Protection Agency
617-770-3000
www.nfpa.org

National Kitchen & Bath Association
   (NKBA)
800-843-6522
www.nkba.org

National Wood Flooring Association
800-422-4556
www.woodfloors.org

North American Insulation
   Manufacturers Association
703-684-0084
www.naima.org

Tile Council of America
864-646-8453
www.tileusa.com

U.S. Environmental Protection Agency—
   Indoor Air Quality
www.epa.gov/iaq/

Photo Credits

Alcoa Home Exteriors, Inc.
p. 531, 546

American Standard
p. 438

Armstrong World Industries
p. 174, 180 (left), 236

Brian Greer's Tin-Ceilings
519 570 1447
p. 239

Broan Nutone
p. 327

Ceramic Tiles of Italy
p. 454

CertainTeed, Corp.
p. 530 (lower)

Cherry Tree Design
p. 428 (lower)

Daltile
p. 386

Economic Mobility, Inc.
p. 425 (lower left)

Elkay
p. 348, 426 (left)

The Energy Conservatory
www.energyconservatory.com
p. 218 (right) Energy Star Program

Fotolia / www.fotolia.com
p. 480

General Electric
p. 418 (right)

Ginger
p. 426 (right)

Harrell Remodeling, Inc.
p. 427, 486

IKEA Home Furnishings
p. 416

ISTOCK Photo / www.istock.com,
p. 324 George Peters, 420, 422, 468
   Nicola Gavin, 528

Jacuzzi
p. 428 (top)

Kentucky Wood Floors
p. 170

Kohler
p. 19, 392, 424, 425 (lower right), 446, 484

Kraftmaid
p. 339

Marvin Windows
p. 318

MIRAGE Prefinished Hardwood Floors
p. 162

Oasis Montana
p. 418 (left)

Robert Perron, photographer /
   www.bobperron.com
p. 516 (left & right)

Price Pfister
p. 393 (all), 472 (top & lower)

Seattle Glass Block
p. 220

SieMatic
p. 336

Swanstone
p. 470 (top)

Toto
p. 425 (top)

Urban Homes, NY
p. 340

Brian Vanden Brink, photographer /
   www.brianvandenbrink.com
p. 492

VELUX-America
p. 278

Weather Shield
p. 18 (top)

Western Red Cedar Lumbar Association
p. 228

Conversion Charts

Metric Equivalent

Inches (in.)	1/64	1/32	1/25	1/16	1/8	1/4	3/8	2/5	1/2	5/8	3/4	7/8	1	2	3	4	5	6	7	8	9	10	11	12	36	39.4
Feet (ft.)																								1	3	3 1/12
Yards (yd.)																									1	1 1/12
Millimeters (mm)	0.40	0.79	1	1.59	3.18	6.35	9.53	10	12.7	15.9	19.1	22.2	25.4	50.8	76.2	101.6	127	152	178	203	229	254	279	305	914	1,000
Centimeters (cm)			0.95	1	1.27	1.59	1.91	2.22	2.54	5.08	7.62	10.16	12.7	15.2	17.8	20.3	22.9	25.4	27.9	30.5				91.4		100
Meters (m)																								.30	.91	1.00

Converting Measurements

To Convert:	To:	Multiply by:
Inches	Millimeters	25.4
Inches	Centimeters	2.54
Feet	Meters	0.305
Yards	Meters	0.914
Miles	Kilometers	1.609
Square inches	Square centimeters	6.45
Square feet	Square meters	0.093
Square yards	Square meters	0.836
Cubic inches	Cubic centimeters	16.4
Cubic feet	Cubic meters	0.0283
Cubic yards	Cubic meters	0.765
Pints (U.S.)	Liters	0.473 (Imp. 0.568)
Quarts (U.S.)	Liters	0.946 (Imp. 1.136)
Gallons (U.S.)	Liters	3.785 (Imp. 4.546)
Ounces	Grams	28.4
Pounds	Kilograms	0.454
Tons	Metric tons	0.907

To Convert:	To:	Multiply by:
Millimeters	Inches	0.039
Centimeters	Inches	0.394
Meters	Feet	3.28
Meters	Yards	1.09
Kilometers	Miles	0.621
Square centimeters	Square inches	0.155
Square meters	Square feet	10.8
Square meters	Square yards	1.2
Cubic centimeters	Cubic inches	0.061
Cubic meters	Cubic feet	35.3
Cubic meters	Cubic yards	1.31
Liters	Pints (U.S.)	2.114 (Imp. 1.76)
Liters	Quarts (U.S.)	1.057 (Imp. 0.88)
Liters	Gallons (U.S.)	0.264 (Imp. 0.22)
Grams	Ounces	0.035
Kilograms	Pounds	2.2
Metric tons	Tons	1.1

Converting Temperatures

Convert degrees Fahrenheit (F) to degrees Celsius (C) by following this simple formula: Subtract 32 from the Fahrenheit temperature reading. Then mulitply that number by 5/9. For example, 77°F - 32 = 45. 45 × 5/9 = 25°C.

To convert degrees Celsius to degrees Fahrenheit, multiply the Celsius temperature reading by 9/5, then add 32. For example, 25°C × 9/5 = 45. 45 + 32 = 77°F.

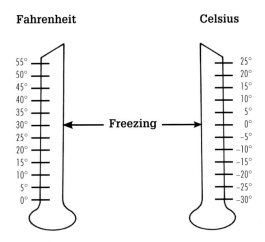

Index